# Fuzzy Reasoning in Decision Making and Optimization

# Studies in Fuzziness and Soft Computing

**Editor-in-chief**
Prof. Janusz Kacprzyk
Systems Research Institute
Polish Academy of Sciences
ul. Newelska 6
01-447 Warsaw, Poland
E-mail: kacprzyk@ibspan.waw.pl
http://www.springer.de/cgi-bin/search_book.pl?series=2941

---

Further volumes of this series can be found at our homepage.

Vol. 60. K.J. Cios (Ed.)
*Medical Data Mining and Knowledge Discovery, 2001*
ISBN 3-7908-1340-0

Vol. 61. D. Driankov and A. Saffiotti (Eds.)
*Fuzzy Logic Techniques for Autonomous Vehicle Navigation, 2001*
ISBN 3-7908-1341-9

Vol. 62. N. Baba and L.C. Jain (Eds.)
*Computational Intelligence in Games, 2001*
ISBN 3-7908-1348-6

Vol. 63. O. Castillo and P. Melin
*Soft Computing for Control of Non-Linear Dynamical Systems, 2001*
ISBN 3-7908-1349-4

Vol. 64. I. Nishizaki and M. Sakawa
*Fuzzy and Multiobjective Games for Conflict Resolution, 2001*
ISBN 3-7908-1341-9

Vol. 65. E. Orłowska and A. Szalas (Eds.)
*Relational Methods for Computer Science Applications, 2001*
ISBN 3-7908-1365-6

Vol. 66. R.J. Howlett and L.C. Jain (Eds.)
*Radial Basis Function Networks 1, 2001*
ISBN 3-7908-1367-2

Vol. 67. R.J. Howlett and L.C. Jain (Eds.)
*Radial Basis Function Networks 2, 2001*
ISBN 3-7908-1368-0

Vol. 68. A. Kandel, M. Last and H. Bunke (Eds.)
*Data Mining and Computational Intelligence, 2001*
ISBN 3-7908-1371-0

Vol. 69. A. Piegat
*Fuzzy Modeling and Control, 2001*
ISBN 3-7908-1385-0

Vol. 70. W. Pedrycz (Ed.)
*Granular Computing, 2001*
ISBN 3-7908-1387-7

Vol. 71. K. Leiviskä (Ed.)
*Industrial Applications of Soft Computing, 2001*
ISBN 3-7908-1388-5

Vol. 72. M. Mareš
*Fuzzy Cooperative Games, 2001*
ISBN 3-7908-1392-3

Vol. 73. Y. Yoshida (Ed.)
*Dynamical Aspects in Fuzzy Decision, 2001*
ISBN 3-7908-1397-4

Vol. 74. H.-N. Teodorescu, L.C. Jain and A. Kandel (Eds.)
*Hardware Implementation of Intelligent Systems, 2001*
ISBN 3-7908-1399-0

Vol. 75. V. Loia and S. Sessa (Eds.)
*Soft Computing Agents, 2001*
ISBN 3-7908-1404-0

Vol. 76. D. Ruan, J. Kacprzyk and M. Fedrizzi (Eds.)
*Soft Computing for Risk Evaluation and Management, 2001*
ISBN 3-7908-1406-7

Vol. 77. W. Liu
*Propositional, Probabilistic and Evidential Reasoning, 2001*
ISBN 3-7908-1414-8

Vol. 78. U. Seiffert and L.C. Jain (Eds.)
*Self-Organizing Neural Network, 2001*
ISBN 3-7908-1417-2

Vol. 79. A. Osyczka
*Evolutionary Algorithms for Single and Multicriteria Design Optimization, 2001*
ISBN 3-7908-1418-0

Vol. 80. P. Wong, F. Aminzadeh and M. Nikravesh (Eds.)
*Soft Computing for Reservoir Characterization and Modeling, 2002*
ISBN 3-7908-1421-0

Vol. 81. V. Dimitrov and V. Korotkich (Eds.)
*Fuzzy Logic, 2002*
ISBN 3-7908-1425-3

Christer Carlsson
Robert Fullér

# Fuzzy Reasoning in Decision Making and Optimization

With 90 Figures
and 5 Tables

Physica-Verlag
A Springer-Verlag Company

Professor Christer Carlsson
Institute for Advanced Management Systems Research
Åbo Akademi University
Lemminkäinengatan 14B
FIN-20520 Åbo
Finland
christer.carlsson@abo.fi

Professor Robert Fullér
Department of Operations Research
Eötvös Loránd University
Kecskeméti ut. 10–12
H-1053 Budapest
Hungary
rfuller@cs.elte.hu

and

Institute for Advanced Management Systems Research
Åbo Akademi University
Lemminkäinengatan 14B
FIN-20520 Åbo
Finland
rfuller@ra.abo.fi

ISSN 1434-9922
ISBN 978-3-7908-2497-1 e-ISBN 978-3-7908-1805-5

Cataloging-in-Publication Data applied for
Die Deutsche Bibliothek – CIP-Einheitsaufnahme
Carlsson, Christer: Fuzzy reasoning in decision making and optimization: with 5 tables/Christer Carlsson; Robert Fullér. – Heidelberg; New York: Physica-Verl., 2002
(Studies in fuzziness and soft computing; Vol. 82)



Physica-Verlag Heidelberg New York
a member of BertelsmannSpringer Science+Business Media GmbH


Printed in Germany



Hardcover Design: Erich Kirchner, Heidelberg

# Preface

Many decision-making tasks are too complex to be understood quantitatively, however, humans succeed by using knowledge that is imprecise rather than precise.

*Fuzzy logic* resembles human reasoning in its use of imprecise information to generate decisions. Unlike classical logic which requires a deep understanding of a system, exact equations, and precise numeric values, fuzzy logic incorporates an *alternative way of thinking*, which allows modeling complex systems using a higher level of abstraction originating from our knowledge and experience.

*Fuzzy logic* allows expressing this knowledge with subjective concepts such as *very big* and a *long time* which are mapped into exact numeric ranges. Since knowledge can be expressed in a more natural by using fuzzy sets, many decision (and engineering) problems can be greatly simplified.

*Fuzzy logic* provides an inference morphology that enables approximate human reasoning capabilities to be applied to knowledge-based systems. The theory of fuzzy logic provides a mathematical strength to capture the uncertainties associated with human cognitive processes, such as thinking and reasoning. The conventional approaches to knowledge representation lack the means for representating the meaning of fuzzy concepts. As a consequence, the approaches based on first order logic do not provide an appropriate conceptual framework for dealing with the representation of commonsense knowledge, since such knowledge is by its nature both lexically imprecise and noncategorical. The developement of fuzzy logic was motivated in large measure by the need for a conceptual framework which can address the issue of lexical imprecision. Some of the essential characteristics of fuzzy logic relate to the following [341]: (i) In fuzzy logic, exact reasoning is viewed as a limiting case of approximate reasoning; (ii) In fuzzy logic, everything is a matter of degree; (iii) In fuzzy logic, knowledge is interpreted a collection of elastic or, equivalently, fuzzy constraint on a collection of variables; (iv) Inference is viewed as a process of propagation of elastic constraints; and (v) Any logical system can be fuzzified.

There are two main characteristics of fuzzy systems that give them better performance for specific applications: (i) Fuzzy systems are suitable for uncertain or approximate reasoning, especially for systems with mathematical models that are difficult to derive; and (ii) Fuzzy logic allows decision making with estimated values under incomplete or uncertain information.

This monograph summarizes the authors' works in the nineties on fuzzy optimization and fuzzy reasoning.

The book is organized as follows. It begins, in Chapter 1 'Fuzzy Sets and Fuzzy Logic', with a short historical survey of development of fuzzy thinking and progresses through an analysis of the extension principle, in which we derive exact formulas for t-norm-based operations on fuzy numbers of $LR$-type, show a generalization of Nguyen's theorem [262] on $\alpha$-level sets of sup-min-extended functions to sup-t-norm-extended ones and provide a fuzzy analogue of Chebyshev's theorem [63].

Fuzzy set theory provides a host of attractive aggregation connectives for integrating membership values representing uncertain information. These connectives can be categorized into the following three classes *union, intersection* and *compensation* connectives. Union produces a high output whenever any one of the input values representing degrees of satisfaction of different features or criteria is high. Intersection connectives produce a high output only when all of the inputs have high values. Compensative connectives have the property that a higher degree of satisfaction of one of the criteria can compensate for a lower degree of satisfaction of another criteria to a certain extent. In the sense, union connectives provide full compensation and intersection connectives provide no compensation. In a decision process the idea of *trade-offs* corresponds to viewing the global evaluation of an action as lying between the *worst* and the *best* local ratings. This occurs in the presence of conflicting goals, when a compensation between the corresponding compabilities is allowed. Averaging operators realize trade-offs between objectives, by allowing a positive compensation between ratings.
In Chapter 2 'Fuzzy Multicriteria Decision Making', we illustrate the applicability of Ordered Weighted Averaging [317] operators to a doctoral student selection problem. In many applications of fuzzy sets such as multi-criteria decision making, pattern recognition, diagnosis and fuzzy logic control one faces the problem of weighted aggregation. In 1994 Yager [321] discussed the issue of weighted min and max aggregations and provided for a formalization of the process of importance weighted transformation. We introduce fuzzy implication operators for importance weighted transformation containing as a subset those ones introduced by Yager.
Then we discuss the issue of weighted aggregations and provide a possibilistic approach to the process of importance weighted transformation when both the importances (interpreted as *benchmarks*) and the ratings are given by symmetric triangular fuzzy numbers. Furthermore, we show that using the possibilistic approach (i) small changes in the membership function of the importances can cause only small variations in the weighted aggregate; (ii) the weighted aggregate of fuzzy ratings remains stable under small changes in the *nonfuzzy* importances; (iii) the weighted aggregate of crisp ratings still re-

mains stable under small changes in the crisp importances whenever we use a continuous implication operator for the importance weighted transformation.

In 1973 Zadeh [333] introduced the compositional rule of inference and six years later [337] the theory of approximate reasoning. This theory provides a powerful framework for reasoning in the face of imprecise and uncertain information. Central to this theory is the representation of propositions as statements assigning fuzzy sets as values to variables. In Chapter 3 'Fuzzy Reasoning', we show two very important features of the compositional rule of inference under triangular norms. Namely, we prove that (i) if the t-norm defining the composition and the membership function of the observation are continuous, then the conclusion depends continuously on the observation; (ii) if the t-norm and the membership function of the relation are continuous, then the observation has a continuous membership function. The stability property of the conclusion under small changes of the membership function of the observation and rules guarantees that small rounding errors of digital computation and small errors of measurement of the input data can cause only a small deviation in the conclusion, i.e. every successive approximation method can be applied to the computation of the linguistic approximation of the exact conclusion.

Possibilisitic linear equality systems (PLES) are linear equality systems with fuzzy coefficients, defined by the Zadeh's extension principle. Kovács [224] showed that the fuzzy solution to PLES with symmetric triangular fuzzy numbers is stable with respect to small changes of centres of fuzzy parameters. First, in Chapter 4 'Fuzzy Optimization', we generalize Kovács's results to PLES with (Lipschitzian) fuzzy numbers and flexible linear programs, and illustrate the sensitivity of the fuzzy solution by several one- and two-dimensional PLES. Then we consider linear (and quadratic) possibilistic programs and show that the possibility distribution of their objective function remains stable under small changes in the membership functions of the fuzzy number coefficients. Furthermore, we present similar results for multiobjective possibilistic linear programs with noninteractive and weakly-noninteractive fuzzy numbers.

In Chapter 5 'Fuzzy Reasoning for Fuzzy Optimization', we interpret fuzzy linear programming (FLP) problems with fuzzy coefficients and fuzzy inequality relations as multiple fuzzy reasoning schemes (MFR), where the antecedents of the scheme correspond to the constraints of the FLP problem and the fact of the scheme is the objective of the FLP problem. Then the solution process consists of two steps: first, for every decision variable, we compute the (fuzzy) value of the objective function, via sup-min convolution of the antecedents/constraints and the fact/objective, then an (optimal) solution to FLP problem is any point which produces a maximal element of the set of fuzzy values of the objective function (in the sense of the given inequality relation). We show that this solution process for a classical (crisp) LP problem results in a solution in the classical sense, and (under well-chosen

inequality relations and objective function) coincides with those suggested by Buckley [15], Delgado et al. [77, 78], Negoita [258], Ramik and Rimanek [275], Verdegay [302, 303] and Zimmermann [344].
Typically, in complex, real-life problems, there are some unidentified factors which effect the values of the objective functions. We do not know them or can not control them; i.e. they have an impact we can not control. The only thing we can observe is the values of the objective functions at certain points. And from this information and from our knowledge about the problem we may be able to formulate the impacts of unknown factors (through the observed values of the objectives). First we state the multiobjective decision problem with independent objectives and then adjust our model to reality by introducing interdependences among the objectives. Interdependences among the objectives exist whenever the computed value of an objective function is not equal to its observed value. We claim that the real values of an objective function can be identified by the help of feed-backs from the values of other objective functions, and show the effect of various kinds (linear, nonlinear and compound) of additve feed-backs on the compromise solution.

Even if the objective functions of a multiobjective decision problem are exactly known, we can still measure the *complexity* of the problem, which is derived from the *grades of conflict* between the objectives. Then we introduce concave utility functions for those objectives that support the majority of the objectives, and convex utility functions for those ones that are in conflict with the majority of the objectives. Finally, to find a good compromise solution we employ the following heuristic: increase the value of those objectives that support the majority of the objectives, because the gains on their (concave) utility functions surpass the losses on the (convex) utility functions of those objectives that are in conflict with the majority of the objectives.

In Chapter 6 'Applications in Management' we present four management applications. In the first case, *Nordic Paper Inc.*, we outline an algorithm for strategic decisions for the planning period 1996-2000 based on the interdependencies between the criteria.

*Strategic Management* is defined as a system of action programs which form sustainable competitive advantages for a corporation, its divisions and its business units in a strategic planning period. A research team of the IAMSR institute has developed a support system for strategic management, called the *Woodstrat*, in two major Finnish forest industry corporations in 1992-96. The system is modular and is built around the actual business logic of strategic management in the two corporations, i.e. the main modules cover the *market position*, the *competitive position*, the *productivity position* and the *profitability* and *financing positions*. The innovation in *Woodstrat* is that these modules are linked together in a hyperknowledge fashion, i.e. when a strong market position is built in some market segment it will have an immediate impact on profitability through links running from key assumptions on expected developments to the projected income statement. There are similar links making the competitive position interact with the market position, and the productivity position interact with both the market and the competitive positions, and with the profitability and financing positions. In the second case, *The Woodstrat projec* we briefly decsribe a support system for strategy formation and show that the effectiveness and usefulness of hyperknowledge support systems for strategy formation can be further advanced using adaptive fuzzy cognitive maps.

*Real options* in option thinking are based on the same principals as financial options. In real options, the options involve *real* assets as opposed to financial ones. To have a *real option* means to have the possibility for a certain period to either choose for or against something, without binding oneself up front. Real options are valued (as financial options), which is quite different with from discounted cashflow investment approaches. The *real option rule* is that one should invest today only if the net present value is high enough to compensate for giving up the value of the option to wait. Because the option to invest loses its value when the investment is irreversibly made, this loss is an opportunity cost of investing. However, the pure (probabilistic) *real option rule* characterizes the present value of expected cash flows and the expected costs by a single number, which is not realistic in many cases. In the third case, *A fuzzy approach to real option valuation*, we consider the *real option rule* in a more realistic setting, namely, when the present values of expected cash flows and expected costs are estimated by trapezoidal fuzzy numbers.

In the fourth case, *Soft computing methods for reducing the bullwhip effect*, we consider a series of companies in a supply chain, each of which orders from its immediate upstream collaborators. Usually, the retailer's order do not coincide with the actual retail sales. The *bullwhip effect* refers to the phenomenon where orders to the supplier tend to have larger variance than sales to the buyer (i.e. demand distortion), and the distortion propagates upstream in an amplified form (i.e. variance amplification). We show that if the members of the supply chain share information with intelligent support technology, and agree on better and better fuzzy estimates (as time advances) on future sales for the upcoming period, then the bullwhip effect can be significantly reduced.

In the quest to develop faster and more advanced, intelligent support systems the introduction of software agents a few years ago has opened new possibilities to build and implement useful support systems. The reason for wanting more advanced and intelligent systems is simple: we want to be able to cope with complex and fast changing business contexts.

In Chapter 7 'Future Trends in Fuzzy Reasoning and Decision Making' we will introduce some software agents we have built and implemented and then show how fuzzy reasoning schemes can be included in the agent constructs in order to enhance their functionality.

# Contents

# 1. Fuzzy Sets and Fuzzy Logic

## 1.1 Fuzzy sets

Fuzzy sets were introduced by Zadeh [332] in 1965 to represent/manipulate data and information possessing nonstatistical uncertainties. It was specifically designed to mathematically represent uncertainty and vagueness and to provide formalized tools for dealing with the imprecision intrinsic to many problems.

*Fuzzy sets* serve as a means of representing and manipulating data that was not precise, but rather fuzzy. There is a strong relationship between *Boolean* logic and the concept of a subset, there is a similar strong relationship between fuzzy logic and fuzzy subset theory. In classical set theory, a subset $A$ of a set $X$ can be defined by its characteristic function $\chi_A$ as a mapping from the elements of $X$ to the elements of the set $\{0,1\}$,

$$\chi_A\colon X \to \{0,1\}.$$

This mapping may be represented as a set of ordered pairs, with exactly one ordered pair present for each element of $X$. The first element of the ordered pair is an element of the set $X$, and the second element is an element of the set $\{0,1\}$. The value zero is used to represent non-membership, and the value one is used to represent membership. The truth or falsity of the statement "$x$ is in $A$" is determined by the ordered pair $(x, \chi_A(x))$. The statement is true if the second element of the ordered pair is 1, and the statement is false if it is 0.

Similarly, a *fuzzy subset* $A$ of a set $X$ can be defined as a set of ordered pairs, each with the first element from $X$, and the second element from the interval $[0,1]$, with exactly one ordered pair present for each element of $X$. This defines a mapping,

$$\mu_A\colon X \to [0,1],$$

between elements of the set $X$ and values in the interval $[0,1]$. The value zero is used to represent complete non-membership, the value one is used to represent complete membership, and values in between are used to represent intermediate degrees of membership. The set $X$ is referred to as the universe of discourse for the fuzzy subset $A$. Frequently, the mapping $\mu_A$ is described as a function, the membership function of $A$. The degree to which the statement

"$x$ is in $A$" is true is determined by finding the ordered pair $(x, \mu_A(x))$. The degree of truth of the statement is the second element of the ordered pair.

**Definition 1.1.1** *[332] Let $X$ be a nonempty set. A fuzzy set $A$ in $X$ is characterized by its membership function*

$$\mu_A \colon X \to [0,1],$$

*and $\mu_A(x)$ is interpreted as the degree of membership of element $x$ in fuzzy set $A$ for each $x \in X$.*

It is clear that $A$ is completely determined by the set of tuples

$$A = \{(x, \mu_A(x)) | x \in X\}.$$

It should be noted that the terms *membership function* and *fuzzy subset* get used interchangeably and frequently we will write simply $A(x)$ instead of $\mu_A(x)$. The family of all fuzzy (sub)sets in $X$ is denoted by $\mathcal{F}(X)$. Fuzzy subsets of the real line are called *fuzzy quantities.*

If $X = \{x_1, \dots, x_n\}$ is a finite set and $A$ is a fuzzy set in $X$ then we often use the notation

$$A = \mu_1/x_1 + \cdots + \mu_n/x_n,$$

where the term $\mu_i/x_i$, $i = 1, \dots, n$, signifies that $\mu_i$ is the grade of membership of $x_i$ in $A$ and the plus sign represents the union.

**Example 1.1.1** *The membership function of the fuzzy set of* real *numbers "close to 1", is can be defined as*

$$A(t) = \exp(-\beta(t-1)^2),$$

*where $\beta$ is a positive real number.*

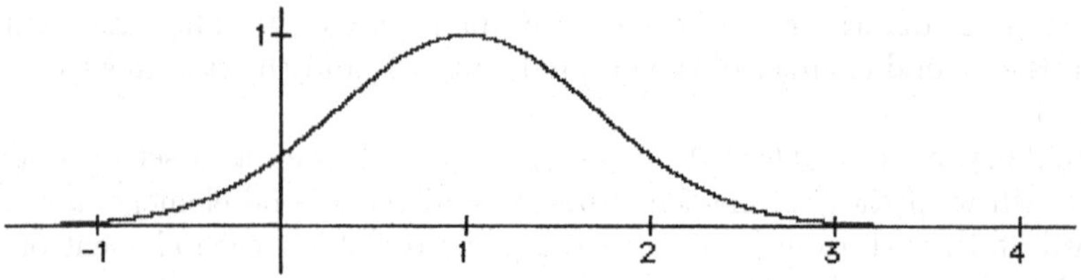


**Fig. 1.1.** A membership function for "x is close to 1".

Let $A$ be a fuzzy subset of $X$; the *support* of $A$, denoted supp$(A)$, is the crisp subset of $X$ whose elements all have nonzero membership grades in $A$.

$$\text{supp}(A) = \{x \in X | A(x) > 0\}.$$

A fuzzy subset $A$ of a classical set $X$ is called *normal* if there exists an $x \in X$ such that $A(x) = 1$. Otherwise $A$ is subnormal. An $\alpha$-level set (or $\alpha$-cut) of a fuzzy set $A$ of $X$ is a non-fuzzy set denoted by $[A]^\alpha$ and defined by

$$[A]^\alpha = \begin{cases} \{t \in X | A(t) \geq \alpha\} & \text{if } \alpha > 0 \\ \text{cl}(\text{supp}A) & \text{if } \alpha = 0 \end{cases}$$

where cl(supp$A$) denotes the closure of the support of $A$. A fuzzy set $A$ of $X$ is called *convex* if $[A]^\alpha$ is a convex subset of $X$ for all $\alpha \in [0, 1]$.

In many situations people are only able to characterize numeric information imprecisely. For example, people use terms such as, about \$3,000, near zero, or essentially bigger than \$5,000. These are examples of what are called *fuzzy numbers.* Using the theory of fuzzy subsets we can represent these fuzzy numbers as fuzzy subsets of the set of real numbers. More exactly,

**Definition 1.1.2** *A fuzzy number A is a fuzzy set of the real line with a normal, (fuzzy) convex and continuous membership function of bounded support. The family of fuzzy numbers will be denoted by $\mathcal{F}$.*

To distinguish a fuzzy number from a crisp (non-fuzzy) one, the former will sometimes be denoted with a tilde $\tilde{}$.

**Definition 1.1.3** *A quasi fuzzy number A is a fuzzy set of the real line with a normal, fuzzy convex and continuous membership function satisfying the limit conditions*

$$\lim_{t \to \infty} A(t) = 0, \quad \lim_{t \to -\infty} A(t) = 0.$$

In the literature the terms *fuzzy number* and *quasi fuzzy number* are often used interchangeably. It is easy to see that the membership function of a fuzzy number $A$ has the following properties:

(i) $\mu_A(t) = 0$, outside of some interval $[c, d]$;
(ii) there are real numbers $a$ and $b$, $c \leq a \leq b \leq d$ such that $\mu_A(t)$ is monotone increasing on the interval $[c, a]$ and monotone decreasing on $[b, d]$;
(iii ) $\mu_A(t) = 1$ for each $x \in [a, b]$.

Let $A$ be a fuzzy number. Then $[A]^\gamma$ is a closed convex (compact) subset of $\mathbb{R}$ for all $\gamma \in [0, 1]$. Let us introduce the notations

$$a_1(\gamma) = \min[A]^\gamma \text{ and } a_2(\gamma) = \max[A]^\gamma.$$

In other words, $a_1(\gamma)$ denotes the left-hand side and $a_2(\gamma)$ denotes the right-hand side of the $\gamma$-cut. It is easy to see that if $\alpha \leq \beta$ then $[A]^\alpha \supset [A]^\beta$. Furthermore, the left-hand side function $a_1\colon [0, 1] \to \mathbb{R}$ is monoton increasing and lower semicontinuous, and the right-hand side function $a_2\colon [0, 1] \to \mathbb{R}$ is monoton decreasing and upper semicontinuous. We shall use the notation

$$[A]^\gamma = [a_1(\gamma), a_2(\gamma)].$$

The support of $A$ is the open interval $(a_1(0), a_2(0))$.

If $A$ is not a fuzzy number then there exists an $\gamma \in [0,1]$ such that $[A]^\gamma$ is not a convex subset of $\mathbb{R}$.

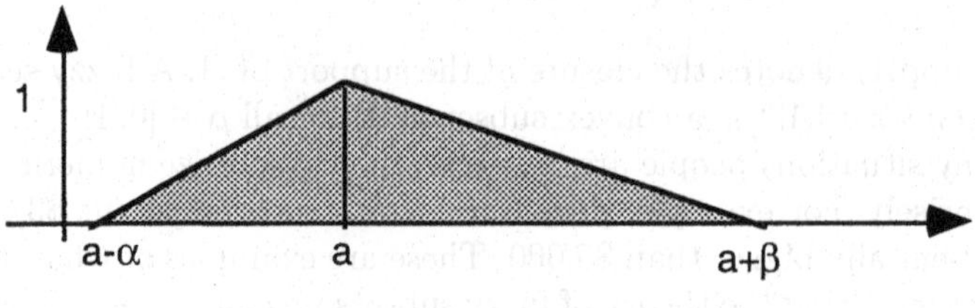


**Fig. 1.2.** Triangular fuzzy number.

**Definition 1.1.4** *A fuzzy set A is called triangular fuzzy number with peak (or center) a, left width $\alpha > 0$ and right width $\beta > 0$ if its membership function has the following form*

$$A(t) = \begin{cases} 1 - \dfrac{a-t}{\alpha} & \text{if } a - \alpha \le t \le a \\ 1 - \dfrac{t-a}{\beta} & \text{if } a \le t \le a + \beta \\ 0 & \text{otherwise} \end{cases}$$

*and we use the notation $A = (a, \alpha, \beta)$. It can easily be verified that*

$$[A]^\gamma = [a - (1-\gamma)\alpha, a + (1-\gamma)\beta], \ \forall \gamma \in [0,1].$$

*The support of A is $(a - \alpha, b + \beta)$. A triangular fuzzy number with center a may be seen as a fuzzy quantity*

*"x is approximately equal to a".*

**Definition 1.1.5** *A fuzzy set A is called trapezoidal fuzzy number with tolerance interval $[a, b]$, left width $\alpha$ and right width $\beta$ if its membership function has the following form*

$$A(t) = \begin{cases} 1 - \dfrac{a-t}{\alpha} & \text{if } a - \alpha \le t \le a \\ 1 & \text{if } a \le t \le b \\ 1 - \dfrac{t-b}{\beta} & \text{if } a \le t \le b + \beta \\ 0 & \text{otherwise} \end{cases}$$

*and we use the notation*

$$A = (a, b, \alpha, \beta). \tag{1.1}$$

*It can easily be shown that*

$$[A]^\gamma = [a - (1-\gamma)\alpha, b + (1-\gamma)\beta], \ \forall \gamma \in [0,1].$$

*The support of $A$ is $(a - \alpha, b + \beta)$.*

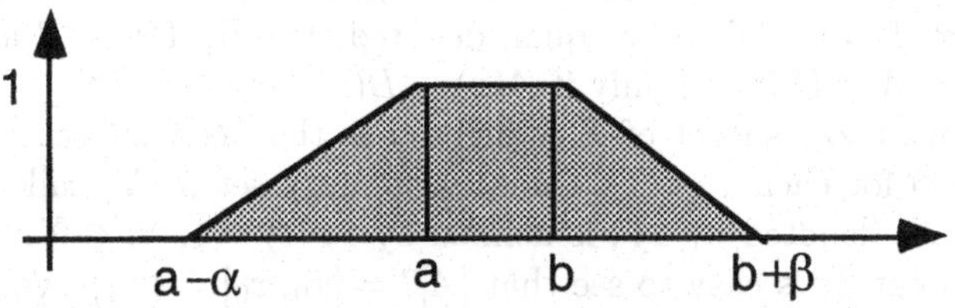


**Fig. 1.3.** Trapezoidal fuzzy number.

A trapezoidal fuzzy number may be seen as a fuzzy quantity

"$x$ is approximately in the interval $[a, b]$".

**Definition 1.1.6** *Any fuzzy number $A \in \mathcal{F}$ can be described as*

$$A(t) = \begin{cases} L\left(\dfrac{a-t}{\alpha}\right) & \textit{if } t \in [a-\alpha, a] \\ 1 & \textit{if } t \in [a, b] \\ R\left(\dfrac{t-b)}{\beta}\right) & \textit{if } t \in [b, b+\beta] \\ 0 & \textit{otherwise} \end{cases}$$

*where $[a, b]$ is the* peak *or* core *of $A$,*

$$L\colon [0,1] \to [0,1], \quad R\colon [0,1] \to [0,1]$$

*are continuous and non-increasing shape functions with $L(0) = R(0) = 1$ and $R(1) = L(1) = 0$. We call this fuzzy interval of $LR$-type and refer to it by*

$$A = (a, b, \alpha, \beta)_{LR}$$

*The support of $A$ is $(a - \alpha, b + \beta)$.*

**Definition 1.1.7** *Let $A = (a, b, \alpha, \beta)_{LR}$ be a fuzzy number of type LR. If $a = b$ then we use the notation*

$$A = (a, \alpha, \beta)_{LR} \tag{1.2}$$

*and say that A is a quasi-triangular fuzzy number. Furthermore if $L(x) = R(x) = 1 - x$, then instead of $A = (a, b, \alpha, \beta)_{LR}$ we simply write*

$$A = (a, b, \alpha, \beta).$$

Let $A$ and $B$ are fuzzy subsets of a classical set $X$. We say that $A$ is a subset of $B$ if $A(t) \leq B(t)$ for all $t \in X$. Let $A$ and $B$ are fuzzy subsets of a classical set $X$. $A$ and $B$ are said to be equal, denoted $A = B$, if $A \subset B$ and $B \subset A$. We note that $A = B$ if and only if $A(x) = B(x)$ for all $x \in X$.

The empty fuzzy subset of $X$ is defined as the fuzzy subset $\emptyset$ of $X$ such that $\emptyset(x) = 0$ for each $x \in X$. The largest fuzzy set in $X$, called universal fuzzy set in $X$, denoted by $1_X$, is defined by $1_X(t) = 1$, $\forall t \in X$. Let $A = \bar{x}_0$ be a fuzzy point. It is easy to see that $[A]^\gamma = [x_0, x_0] = \{x_0\}$, $\forall \gamma \in [0, 1]$.

Following Zadeh [333] we can define the sup-min composition of a fuzzy set and fuzzy relation as follows

**Definition 1.1.8** *Let $C \in \mathcal{F}(X)$ and $R \in \mathcal{F}(X \times Y)$. The membership function of the composition of a fuzzy set C and a fuzzy relation R is defined by*

$$(C \circ R)(y) = \sup_{x \in X} \min\{C(x), R(x, y)\}, \ \forall y \in Y.$$

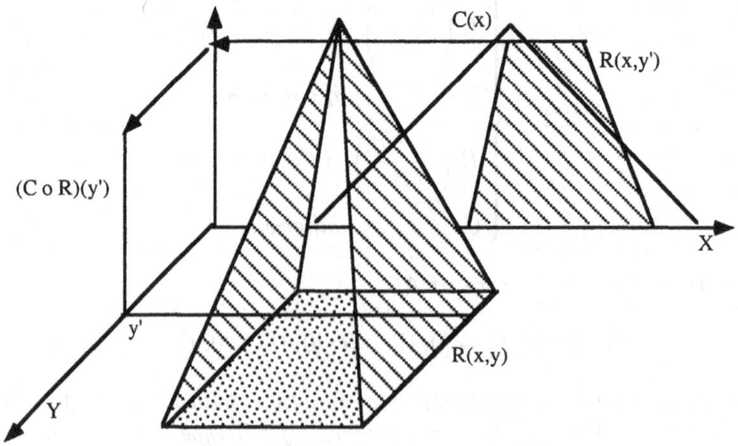


**Fig. 1.4.** Composition of a fuzzy number and a fuzzy relation.

The composition of a fuzzy set $C$ and a fuzzy relation $R$ can be considered as the shadow of the relation $R$ on the fuzzy set $C$. In the above definition we can use any t-norm for modeling the compositional operator.

**Definition 1.1.9** *Let $T$ be a t-norm $C \in \mathcal{F}(X)$ and $R \in \mathcal{F}(X \times Y)$. The membership function of the composition of a fuzzy set $C$ and a fuzzy relation $R$ is defined by*

$$(C \circ R)(y) = \sup_{x \in X} T(C(x), R(x, y)),$$

*for all $y \in Y$.*

For example, if $T(x, y) = T_P(x, y) = xy$ is the product t-norm then the sup-$T$ compositiopn of a fuzzy set $C$ and a fuzzy relation $R$ is defined by

$$(C \circ R)(y) = \sup_{x \in X} T_P(C(x), R(x, y)) = \sup_{x \in X} C(x)R(x, y),$$

and if $T(x, y) = T_L(x, y) = \max\{0, x + y - 1\}$ is the Łukasiewicz t-norm then we get

$$(C \circ R)(y) = \sup_{x \in X} T_L(C(x), R(x, y)) = \sup_{x \in X} \max\{0, C(x) + R(x, y) - 1\}$$

for all $y \in Y$.

**Example 1.1.2** *Let $A$ and $B$ be fuzzy numbers and let $R = A \times B$ a fuzzy relation. Observe the following property of composition*

$$A \circ R = A \circ (A \times B) = B \text{ and } B \circ R = B \circ (A \times B) = A.$$

*This fact can be interpreted as: if $A$ and $B$ have relation $A \times B$ and then the composition of $A$ and $A \times B$ is exactly equal to $B$, and then the composition of $B$ and $A \times B$ is exactly equal to $A$.*

## 1.2 Operations on fuzzy sets

In this section we extend classical set theoretic operations from ordinary set theory to fuzzy sets. We note that all those operations which are extensions of crisp concepts reduce to their usual meaning when the fuzzy subsets have membership degrees that are drawn from $\{0, 1\}$. For this reason, when extending operations to fuzzy sets we use the same symbol as in set theory. Let $A$ and $B$ are fuzzy subsets of a crisp set $X \neq \emptyset$.

**Definition 1.2.1** *The intersection of $A$ and $B$ is defined as*

$$(A \cap B)(t) = \min\{A(t), B(t)\} = A(t) \wedge B(t), \ \forall t \in X.$$

**Definition 1.2.2** *The union of $A$ and $B$ is defined as*

$$(A \cup B)(t) = \max\{A(t), B(t)\} = A(t) \vee B(t), \ \forall t \in X.$$

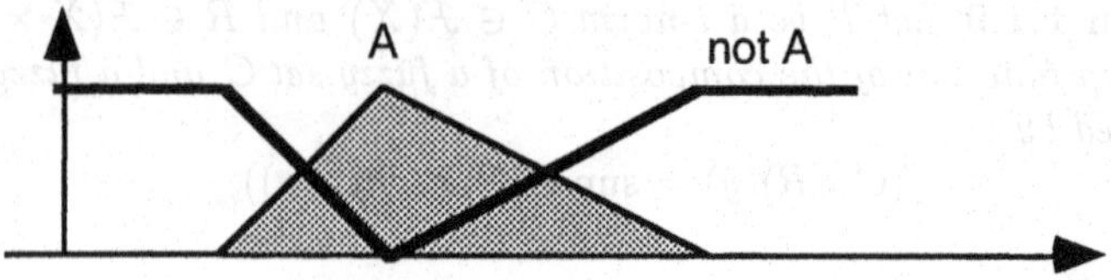


**Fig. 1.5.** *A* and its complement.

**Definition 1.2.3** *The complement of a fuzzy set A is defined as*

$$(\neg A)(t) = 1 - A(t), \ \forall t \in X.$$

Triangular norms were introduced by Schweizer and Sklar [289] to model distances in probabilistic metric spaces. In fuzzy sets theory triangular norms are extensively used to model logical connective *and*.

**Definition 1.2.4** *(Triangular norm.) A mapping*

$$T\colon [0,1] \times [0,1] \to [0,1]$$

*is a triangular norm (t-norm for short) iff it is symmetric, associative, non-decreasing in each argument and $T(a,1) = a$, for all $a \in [0,1]$. In other words, any t-norm $T$ satisfies the properties:*

*Symmetricity:*

$$T(x,y) = T(y,x), \ \forall x, y \in [0,1].$$

*Associativity:*

$$T(x, T(y,z)) = T(T(x,y),z), \ \forall x,y,z \in [0,1].$$

*Monotonicity:*

$$T(x,y) \leq T(x',y') \text{ if } x \leq x' \text{ and } y \leq y'.$$

*One identy:*

$$T(x,1) = x, \ \forall x \in [0,1].$$

These axioms attempt to capture the basic properties of set intersection. The basic t-norms are:

- minimum: $\min(a,b) = \min\{a,b\}$,
- Łukasiewicz: $T_L(a,b) = \max\{a+b-1, 0\}$
- product: $T_P(a,b) = ab$
- weak:

$$T_W(a,b) = \begin{cases} \min\{a,b\} \text{ if } \max\{a,b\} = 1 \\ 0 \qquad\qquad \text{otherwise} \end{cases}$$

- Hamacher [157]:

$$H_\gamma(a,b) = \frac{ab}{\gamma + (1-\gamma)(a+b-ab)}, \ \gamma \geq 0 \tag{1.3}$$

- Dubois and Prade:

$$D_\alpha(a,b) = \frac{ab}{\max\{a,b,\alpha\}}, \ \alpha \in (0,1)$$

- Yager:

$$Y_p(a,b) = 1 - \min\{1, \sqrt[p]{[(1-a)^p + (1-b)^p]}\}, \ p > 0$$

- Frank [113]:

$$F_\lambda(a,b) = \begin{cases} \min\{a,b\} & \text{if } \lambda = 0 \\ T_P(a,b) & \text{if } \lambda = 1 \\ T_L(a,b) & \text{if } \lambda = \infty \\ 1 - \log_\lambda \left[1 + \dfrac{(\lambda^a - 1)(\lambda^b - 1)}{\lambda - 1}\right] & \text{otherwise} \end{cases}$$

All t-norms may be extended, through associativity, to $n > 2$ arguments. The minimum t-norm is automatically extended and

$$T_P(a_1, \dots, a_n) = a_1 \times a_2 \times \cdots \times a_n,$$

$$T_L(a_1, \dots a_n) = \max\left\{ \sum_{i=1}^{n} a_i - n + 1, 0 \right\}.$$

A t-norm $T$ is called strict if $T$ is strictly increasing in each argument. A t-norm $T$ is said to be Archimedean iff $T$ is continuous and $T(x,x) < x$ for all $x \in (0,1)$. Every Archimedean t-norm $T$ is representable by a continuous and decreasing function $f\colon [0,1] \to [0,\infty]$ with $f(1) = 0$ and

$$T(x,y) = f^{-1}(\min\{f(x) + f(y), f(0)\}).$$

The function $f$ is the additive generator of $T$. A t-norm $T$ is said to be nilpotent if $T(x,y) = 0$ holds for some $x, y \in (0,1)$. Let $T_1$, $T_2$ be t-norms. We say that $T_1$ is weaker than $T_2$ (and write $T_1 \leq T_2$) if $T_1(x,y) \leq T_2(x,y)$ for each $x, y \in [0,1]$.

Triangular conorms are extensively used to model logical connective *or*.

**Definition 1.2.5** *(Triangular conorm.) A mapping*

$$S\colon [0,1] \times [0,1] \to [0,1],$$

*is a triangular co-norm (t-conorm) if it is symmetric, associative, non-decreasing in each argument and* $S(a,0) = a$, *for all* $a \in [0,1]$. *In other words, any t-conorm* $S$ *satisfies the properties:*

$S(x, y) = S(y, x)$ *(symmetricity)*
$S(x, S(y, z)) = S(S(x, y), z)$ *(associativity)*
$S(x, y) \leq S(x', y')$ *if* $x \leq x'$ *and* $y \leq y'$ *(monotonicity)*
$S(x, 0) = x, \ \forall x \in [0, 1]$ *(zero identy)*

If $T$ is a t-norm then the equality

$$S(a, b) := 1 - T(1 - a, 1 - b),$$

defines a t-conorm and we say that $S$ is derived from $T$. The basic t-conorms are:

- maximum: $\max(a, b) = \max\{a, b\}$
- Łukasiewicz: $S_L(a, b) = \min\{a + b, 1\}$
- probabilistic: $S_P(a, b) = a + b - ab$
- strong:

$$STRONG(a, b) = \begin{cases} \max\{a, b\} & \text{if } \min\{a, b\} = 0 \\ 1 & \text{otherwise} \end{cases}$$

- Hamacher:

$$HOR_\gamma(a, b) = \frac{a + b - (2 - \gamma)ab}{1 - (1 - \gamma)ab}, \ \gamma \geq 0$$

- Yager:

$$YOR_p(a, b) = \min\{1, \sqrt[p]{a^p + b^p}\}, \ p > 0.$$

**Lemma 1.2.1** *Let $T$ be a t-norm. Then the following statement holds*

$$T_W(x, y) \leq T(x, y) \leq \min\{x, y\}, \ \forall x, y \in [0, 1].$$

*Proof.* From monotonicity, symmetricity and the extremal condition we get

$$T(x, y) \leq T(x, 1) \leq x, \ T(x, y) = T(y, x) \leq T(y, 1) \leq y.$$

This means that $T(x, y) \leq \min\{x, y\}$.

**Lemma 1.2.2** *Let $S$ be a t-conorm. Then the following statement holds*

$$\max\{a, b\} \leq S(a, b) \leq STRONG(a, b), \ \forall a, b \in [0, 1]$$

*Proof.* From monotonicity, symmetricity and the extremal condition we get

$$S(x, y) \geq S(x, 0) \geq x, \ S(x, y) = S(y, x) \geq S(y, 0) \geq y$$

This means that $S(x, y) \geq \max\{x, y\}$.

**Lemma 1.2.3** $T(a, a) = a$ *holds for any* $a \in [0, 1]$ *if and only if $T$ is the minimum norm.*

*Proof.* If $T(a,b) = \min(a,b)$ then $T(a,a) = a$ holds obviously. Suppose $T(a,a) = a$ for any $a \in [0,1]$, and $a \leq b \leq 1$. We can obtain the following expression using monotonicity of $T$

$$a = T(a,a) \leq T(a,b) \leq \min\{a,b\}.$$

From commutativity of $T$ it follows that

$$a = T(a,a) \leq T(b,a) \leq \min\{b,a\}.$$

These equations show that $T(a,b) = \min\{a,b\}$ for any $a, b \in [0,1]$.

**Lemma 1.2.4** *The distributive law of t-norm $T$ on the* max *operator holds for any $a$, $b$, $c \in [0,1]$.*

$$T(\max\{a,b\},c) = \max\{T(a,c),T(b,c)\}.$$

The operation *intersection* can be defined by the help of triangular norms.

**Definition 1.2.6** *(t-norm-based intersection) Let $T$ be a t-norm. The $T$-intersection of $A$ and $B$ is defined as*

$$(A \cap B)(t) = T(A(t),B(t)), \ \forall t \in X.$$

**Example 1.2.1** *Let $T(x,y) = T_L(x,y) = \max\{x+y-1,0\}$ be the Łukasiewicz t-norm. Then we have*

$$(A \cap B)(t) = \max\{A(t)+B(t)-1,0\}, \ \forall t \in X.$$

The operation *union* can be defined by the help of triangular conorms.

**Definition 1.2.7** *(t-conorm-based union) Let $S$ be a t-conorm. The $S$-union of $A$ and $B$ is defined as*

$$(A \cup B)(t) = S(A(t),B(t)), \ \forall t \in X.$$

**Example 1.2.2** *Let $S(x,y) = \min\{x+y,1\}$ be the Łukasiewicz t-conorm. Then we have*

$$(A \cup B)(t) = \min\{A(t)+B(t),1\}, \ \forall t \in X.$$

In general, *the law of the excluded middle* and the *noncontradiction principle* properties are not satisfied by t-norms and t-conorms defining the intersection and union operations. However, the Łukasiewicz t-norm and t-conorm do satisfy these properties.

**Lemma 1.2.5** *If $T(x,y) = T_L(x,y) = \max\{x+y-1,0\}$ then the law of noncontradiction is valid.*

*Proof.* Let $A$ be a fuzzy set in $X$. Then from the definition of t-norm-based intersection we get

$$(A \cap \neg A)(t) = T_L(A(t), 1 - A(t)) = (A(t) + 1 - A(t) - 1) \vee 0 = 0, \ \forall t \in X.$$

**Lemma 1.2.6** *If* $S(x, y) = S_L(x, y) = \min\{1, x + y\}$, *then* the law of excluded middle *is valid.*

*Proof.* Let $A$ be a fuzzy set in $X$. Then from the definition of t-conorm-based union we get

$$(A \cup \neg A)(t) = S_L(A(t), 1 - A(t)) = (A(t) + 1 - A(t)) \wedge 1 = 1,$$

for all $t \in X$.

## 1.3 The extension principle

In order to use fuzzy numbers and relations in any intellgent system we must be able to perform arithmetic operations with these fuzzy quantities. In particular, we must be able to to *add*, *subtract*, *multiply* and *divide* with fuzzy quantities. The process of doing these operations is called *fuzzy arithmetic*. We shall first introduce an important concept from fuzzy set theory called the *extension principle*. We then use it to provide for these arithmetic operations on fuzzy numbers. In general the extension principle pays a fundamental role in enabling us to extend any point operations to operations involving fuzzy sets. In the following we define this principle.

**Definition 1.3.1** *(Zadeh's extension principle) Assume $X$ and $Y$ are crisp sets and let $f$ be a mapping from $X$ to $Y$,*

$$f \colon X \to Y$$

*such that for each $x \in X, f(x) = y \in Y$. Assume $A$ is a fuzzy subset of $X$, using the extension principle, we can define $f(A)$ as a fuzzy subset of $Y$ such that*

$$f(A)(y) = \begin{cases} \sup_{x \in f^{-1}(y)} A(x) & \text{if } f^{-1}(y) \neq \emptyset \\ 0 & \text{otherwise} \end{cases} \tag{1.4}$$

*where $f^{-1}(y) = \{x \in X \mid f(x) = y\}$.*

It should be noted that if $f$ is strictly increasing (or strictly decreasing) then (1.4) turns into

$$f(A)(y) = \begin{cases} A(f^{-1}(y)) & \text{if } y \in Range(f) \\ 0 & \text{otherwise} \end{cases}$$

where $Range(f) = \{y \in Y \mid \exists x \in X \text{ such that } f(x) = y\}$.

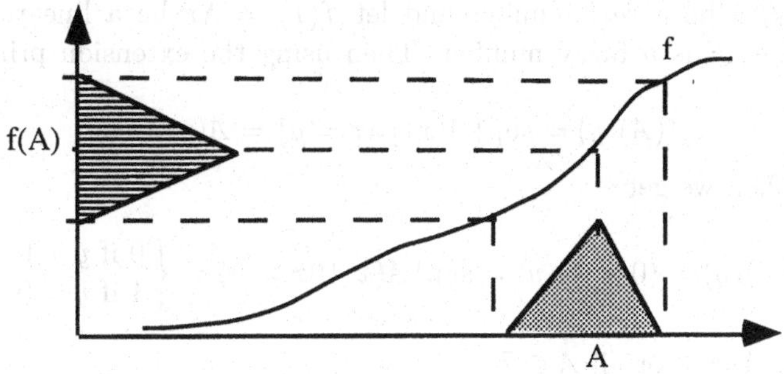


**Fig. 1.6.** Extension of a monotone increasing function.

**Example 1.3.1** *Let $f(x) = x^2$ and let $A \in \mathcal{F}$ be a symmetric triangular fuzzy number with membership function*

$$A(x) = \begin{cases} 1 - \dfrac{|a-x|}{\alpha} & \text{if } |a-x| \le \alpha \\ 0 & \text{otherwise} \end{cases}$$

*Then using the extension principle we get*

$$f(A)(y) = \begin{cases} A(\sqrt{y}) & \text{if } y \ge 0 \\ 0 & \text{otherwise} \end{cases}$$

*that is*

$$f(A)(y) = \begin{cases} 1 - \dfrac{|a-\sqrt{y}|}{\alpha} & \text{if } |a-\sqrt{y}| \le \alpha \text{ and } y \ge 0 \\ 0 & \text{otherwise} \end{cases}$$

**Example 1.3.2** *Let*

$$f(x) = \frac{1}{1+e^{-x}}$$

*be a sigmoidal function and let $A$ be a fuzzy number. Then from*

$$f^{-1}(y) = \begin{cases} \ln\left(\dfrac{y}{1-y}\right) & \text{if } 0 \le y \le 1 \\ 0 & \text{otherwise} \end{cases}$$

*it follows that*

$$f(A)(y) = \begin{cases} A\left(\ln\left(\dfrac{y}{1-y}\right)\right) & \text{if } 0 \le y \le 1 \\ 0 & \text{otherwise.} \end{cases}$$

Let $\lambda \neq 0$ be a real number and let $f(x) = \lambda x$ be a linear function. Suppose $A \in \mathcal{F}$ is a fuzzy number. Then using the extension principle we obtain

$$f(A)(y) = \sup\{A(x) \mid \lambda x = y\} = A(y/\lambda).$$

For $\lambda = 0$ then we get

$$f(A)(y) = (0 \times A)(y) = \sup\{A(x) \mid 0x = y\} = \begin{cases} 0 \text{ if } y \neq 0 \\ 1 \text{ if } y = 0. \end{cases}$$

That is $0 \times A = \bar{0}$ for all $A \in \mathcal{F}$.

If $f(x) = \lambda x$ and $A \in \mathcal{F}$ then we will write $f(A) = \lambda A$. Especially, if $\lambda = -1$ then we have

$$(-1A)(x) = (-A)(x) = A(-x), \; x \in \mathbb{R}.$$

It should be noted that Zadeh's extension principle is nothing else but a straightforward generalization of set-valued functions (see [235] for details). Namely, let $f\colon X \to Y$ be a function. Then the image of a (crisp) subset $A \subset X$ by $f$ is defined by

$$f(A) = \{f(x) \mid x \in A\}$$

and the characteristic function of $f(A)$ is

$$\chi_{f(A)}(y) = \sup\{\chi_A(x) \mid x \in f^{-1}(y)\}$$

Then replacing $\chi_A$ by a fuzzy set $\mu_A$ we get Zadeh's extension principle (1.4).

The extension principle can be generalized to $n$-place functions:

**Definition 1.3.2** *Let $X_1, X_2, \dots, X_n$ and $Y$ be a family of sets. Assume $f$ is a mapping*

$$f\colon X_1 \times X_2 \times \cdots \times X_n \to Y,$$

*that is, for each $n$-tuple $(x_1, \dots, x_n)$ such that $x_i \in X_i$, we have*

$$f(x_1, x_2, \dots, x_n) = y \in Y.$$

*Let $A_1, \dots, A_n$ be fuzzy subsets of $X_1, \dots, X_n$, respectively; then the extension principle allows for the evaluation of $f(A_1, \dots, A_n)$. In particular, $f(A_1, \dots, A_n) = B$, where $B$ is a fuzzy subset of $Y$ such that*

$$f(A_1, \dots, A_n)(y) = \begin{cases} \sup\{\min\{A_1(x_1), \dots, A_n(x_n)\} \mid x \in f^{-1}(y)\} & \text{if } f^{-1}(y) \neq \emptyset \\ 0 & \text{otherwise.} \end{cases} \tag{1.5}$$

For $n = 2$ then the extension principle reads

$$f(A_1, A_2)(y) = \sup\{A_1(x_1) \wedge A_2(x_2) \mid f(x_1, x_2) = y\}.$$

**Example 1.3.3** *(extended addition) Let $f\colon X \times X \to X$ be defined as*

$$f(x_1, x_2) = x_1 + x_2,$$

*i.e. $f$ is the addition operator. Suppose $A_1$ and $A_2$ are fuzzy subsets of $X$. Then using the extension principle we get*

$$f(A_1, A_2)(y) = \sup_{x_1+x_2=y} \min\{A_1(x_1), A_2(x_2)\}$$

*and we use the notation $f(A_1, A_2) = A_1 + A_2$.*

**Example 1.3.4** *(extended subtraction) Let $f\colon X \times X \to X$ be defined as*

$$f(x_1, x_2) = x_1 - x_2,$$

*i.e. $f$ is the subtraction operator. Suppose $A_1$ and $A_2$ are fuzzy subsets of $X$. Then using the extension principle we get*

$$f(A_1, A_2)(y) = \sup_{x_1-x_2=y} \min\{A_1(x_1), A_2(x_2)\},$$

*and we use the notation $f(A_1, A_2) = A_1 - A_2$.*

We note that from the equality

$$\sup_{x_1-x_2=y} \min\{A_1(x_1), A_2(x_2)\} = \sup_{x_1+x_2=y} \min\{A_1(x_1), A_2(-x_2)\},$$

it follows that $A_1 - A_2 = A_1 + (-A_2)$ holds. However, if $A \in \mathcal{F}$ is a fuzzy number then

$$(A - A)(y) = \sup_{x_1-x_2=y} \min\{A(x_1), A(x_2)\},\ y \in \mathbb{R}$$

is not equal to the fuzzy number $\bar{0}$, where $\bar{0}(t) = 1$ if $t = 0$ and $\bar{0}(t) = 0$ otherwise.

**Example 1.3.5** *Let $f\colon X \times X \to X$ be defined as*

$$f(x_1, x_2) = \lambda_1 x_1 + \lambda_2 x_2,$$

*Suppose $A_1$ and $A_2$ are fuzzy subsets of $X$. Then using the extension principle we get*

$$f(A_1, A_2)(y) = \sup_{\lambda_1 x_1+\lambda_2 x_2=y} \min\{A_1(x_1), A_2(x_2)\}$$

*and we use the notation $f(A_1, A_2) = \lambda_1 A_1 + \lambda_2 A_2$.*

**Example 1.3.6** *(extended multiplication) Let $f\colon X \times X \to X$ be defined as*

$$f(x_1, x_2) = x_1 x_2,$$

*i.e. $f$ is the multiplication operator. Suppose $A_1$ and $A_2$ are fuzzy subsets of $X$. Then using the extension principle we get*

$$f(A_1, A_2)(y) = \sup_{x_1 x_2 = y} \min\{A_1(x_1), A_2(x_2)\}$$

*and we use the notation $f(A_1, A_2) = A_1 A_2$.*

**Example 1.3.7** *(extended division) Let $f\colon X \times X \to X$ be defined as*

$$f(x_1, x_2) = x_1 / x_2,$$

*i.e. $f$ is the division operator. Suppose $A_1$ and $A_2$ are fuzzy subsets of $X$. Then using the extension principle we get*

$$f(A_1, A_2)(y) = \sup_{x_1/x_2 = y,\, x_2 \neq 0} \min\{A_1(x_1), A_2(x_2)\}$$

*and we use the notation $f(A_1, A_2) = A_1 / A_2$.*

The extension principle for $n$-place functions is also a straightforward generalization of set-valued functions. Namely, let $f\colon X_1 \times X_2 \to Y$ be a function. Then the image of a (crisp) subset $(A_1, A_2) \subset X_1 \times X_2$ by $f$ is defined by

$$f(A_1, A_2) = \{f(x_1, x_2) \mid x_1 \in A \text{ and } x_2 \in A_2\}$$

and the characteristic function of $f(A_1, A_2)$ is

$$\chi_{f(A_1, A_2)}(y) = \sup\{\min\{\chi_{A_1}(x), \chi_{A_2}(x)\} \mid x \in f^{-1}(y)\}.$$

Then replacing the characteristic functions by fuzzy sets we get Zadeh's extension principle for $n$-place functions (1.5).

Let $A = (a_1, a_2, \alpha_1, \alpha_2)_{LR}$, and $B = (b_1, b_2, \beta_1, \beta_2)_{LR}$, be fuzzy numbers of LR-type. Using the (sup-min) extension principle we can verify the following rules for addition and subtraction of fuzzy numbers of LR-type.

$$A + B = (a_1 + b_1, a_2 + b_2, \alpha_1 + \beta_1, \alpha_2 + \beta_2)_{LR}$$

$$A - B = (a_1 - b_2, a_2 - b_1, \alpha_1 + \beta_2, \alpha_2 + \beta_1)_{LR}$$

furthermore, if $\lambda \in \mathbb{R}$ is a real number then $\lambda A$ can be represented as

$$\lambda A = \begin{cases} (\lambda a_1, \lambda a_2, \alpha_1, \alpha_2)_{LR} & \text{if } \lambda \geq 0 \\ (\lambda a_2, \lambda a_1, |\lambda|\alpha_2, |\lambda|\alpha_1)_{LR} & \text{if } \lambda < 0 \end{cases}$$

In particular if $A = (a_1, a_2, \alpha_1, \alpha_2)$ and $B = (b_1, b_2, \beta_1, \beta_2)$ are fuzzy numbers of trapezoidal form then

$$A + B = (a_1 + b_1, a_2 + b_2, \alpha_1 + \beta_1, \alpha_2 + \beta_2) \tag{1.6}$$

$$A - B = (a_1 - b_2, a_2 - b_1, \alpha_1 + \beta_2, \alpha_2 + \beta_1). \tag{1.7}$$

If $A = (a, \alpha_1, \alpha_2)$ and $B = (b, \beta_1, \beta_2)$ are fuzzy numbers of triangular form then

$$A + B = (a + b, \alpha_1 + \beta_1, \alpha_2 + \beta_2),$$
$$A - B = (a - b, \alpha_1 + \beta_2, \alpha_2 + \beta_1)$$

and if $A = (a, \alpha)$ and $B = (b, \beta)$ are fuzzy numbers of symmetric triangular form then

$$A + B = (a + b,\ \alpha + \beta), \quad A - B = (a - b,\ \alpha + \beta), \quad \lambda A = (\lambda a,\ |\lambda|\alpha).$$

The above results can be generalized to linear combinations of fuzzy numbers.

**Lemma 1.3.1** *Let $A_i = (a_i, \alpha_i)$ be a fuzzy number of symmetric triangular form and let $\lambda_i$ be a real number, $i = 1, \dots, n$. Then their linear combination*

$$A := \lambda_1 A_1 + \cdots + \lambda_n A_n,$$

*can be represented as*

$$A = (\lambda_1 a_1 + \cdots + \lambda_n a_n,\ |\lambda_1|\alpha_1 + \cdots + |\lambda_n|\alpha_n).$$

Assume $A_i = (a_i, \alpha)$, $i = 1, \dots, n$ are fuzzy numbers of symmetric triangular form and $\lambda_i \in [0, 1]$, such that $\lambda_1 + \ldots + \lambda_n = 1$. Then their *convex linear combination* can be represented as

$$A = (\lambda_1 a_1 + \cdots + \lambda_n a_n,\ \lambda_1 \alpha + \cdots + \lambda_n \alpha) = (\lambda_1 a_1 + \cdots + \lambda_n a_n,\ \alpha).$$

Let $A$ and $B$ be fuzzy numbers with $[A]^\alpha = [a_1(\alpha), a_2(\alpha)]$ and $[B]^\alpha = [b_1(\alpha), b_2(\alpha)]$. Then it can easily be shown that

$$[A + B]^\alpha = [a_1(\alpha) + b_1(\alpha), a_2(\alpha) + b_2(\alpha)],$$
$$[A - B]^\alpha = [a_1(\alpha) - b_2(\alpha), a_2(\alpha) - b_1(\alpha)],$$
$$[\lambda A]^\alpha = \lambda[A]^\alpha,$$

where $[\lambda A]^\alpha = [\lambda a_1(\alpha), \lambda a_2(\alpha)]$ if $\lambda \geq 0$ and $[\lambda A]^\alpha = [\lambda a_2(\alpha), \lambda a_1(\alpha)]$ if $\lambda < 0$ for all $\alpha \in [0, 1]$, i.e. any $\alpha$-level set of the extended sum of two fuzzy numbers is equal to the sum of their $\alpha$-level sets. The following two theorems (Nguyen, 1978) show that similar representatins are valid for any extended continuous function.

**Theorem 1.3.1** [262] *Let $f\colon X \to X$ be a continuous function and let $A$ be fuzzy numbers. Then*

$$[f(A)]^\alpha = f([A]^\alpha)$$

*where $f(A)$ is defined by the extension principle (1.4) and*

$$f([A]^\alpha) = \{f(x) \mid x \in [A]^\alpha\}.$$

If $[A]^\alpha = [a_1(\alpha), a_2(\alpha)]$ and $f$ is monoton increasing then from the above theorem we get

$$[f(A)]^\alpha = f([A]^\alpha) = f([a_1(\alpha), a_2(\alpha)]) = [f(a_1(\alpha)), f(a_2(\alpha))].$$

**Theorem 1.3.2** [262] *Let $f\colon X \times X \to X$ be a continuous function and let $A$ and $B$ be fuzzy numbers. Then*

$$[f(A, B)]^\alpha = f([A]^\alpha, [B]^\alpha)$$

*where*

$$f([A]^\alpha, [B]^\alpha) = \{f(x_1, x_2) \mid x_1 \in [A]^\alpha, x_2 \in [B]^\alpha\}.$$

Let $f(x, y) = xy$ and let $[A]^\alpha = [a_1(\alpha), a_2(\alpha)]$ and $[B]^\alpha = [b_1(\alpha), b_2(\alpha)]$ be two fuzzy numbers. Applying Theorem 1.3.2 we get

$$[f(A, B)]^\alpha = f([A]^\alpha, [B]^\alpha) = [A]^\alpha [B]^\alpha.$$

However the equation

$$[AB]^\alpha = [A]^\alpha [B]^\alpha = [a_1(\alpha)b_1(\alpha), a_2(\alpha)b_2(\alpha)]$$

holds if and only if $A$ and $B$ are both nonnegative, i.e. $A(x) = B(x) = 0$ for $x \le 0$.

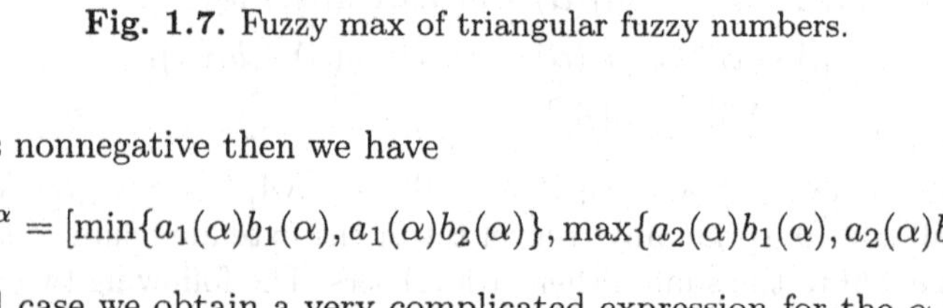

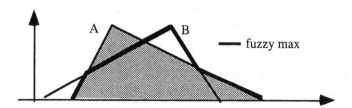


**Fig. 1.7.** Fuzzy max of triangular fuzzy numbers.

If $B$ is nonnegative then we have

$$[A]^\alpha [B]^\alpha = [\min\{a_1(\alpha)b_1(\alpha), a_1(\alpha)b_2(\alpha)\}, \max\{a_2(\alpha)b_1(\alpha), a_2(\alpha)b_2(\alpha)\}].$$

In general case we obtain a very complicated expression for the $\alpha$ level sets of the product $AB$

$$[A]^\alpha [B]^\alpha = [\min\{a_1(\alpha)b_1(\alpha), a_1(\alpha)b_2(\alpha), a_2(\alpha)b_1(\alpha), a_2(\alpha)b_2(\alpha)\},$$

$$\max\{a_1(\alpha)b_1(\alpha), a_1(\alpha)b_2(\alpha), a_2(\alpha)b_1(\alpha), a_2(\alpha)b_2(\alpha)\}].$$

The above properties of extended operations *addition, subtraction* and *multiplication by scalar* of fuzzy fuzzy numbers of type LR are often used in *fuzzy neural networks.*

**Definition 1.3.3** *(fuzzy max) Let* $f(x,y) = \max\{x,y\}$ *and let* $[A]^\alpha = [a_1(\alpha), a_2(\alpha)]$ *and* $[B]^\alpha = [b_1(\alpha), b_2(\alpha)]$ *be two fuzzy numbers. Applying Theorem 1.3.2 we get*

$$[f(A,B)]^\alpha = f([A]^\alpha, [B]^\alpha)$$
$$= \max\{[A]^\alpha, [B]^\alpha\} = [a_1(\alpha) \vee b_1(\alpha), a_2(\alpha) \vee b_2(\alpha)]$$

*and we use the notation* $\max\{A, B\}$.

**Definition 1.3.4** *(fuzzy min) Let* $f(x,y) = \min\{x,y\}$ *and let* $[A]^\alpha = [a_1(\alpha), a_2(\alpha)]$ *and* $[B]^\alpha = [b_1(\alpha), b_2(\alpha)]$ *be two fuzzy numbers. Applying Theorem 1.3.2 we get*

$$[f(A,B)]^\alpha = f([A]^\alpha, [B]^\alpha)$$
$$= \min\{[A]^\alpha, [B]^\alpha\} = [a_1(\alpha) \wedge b_1(\alpha), a_2(\alpha) \wedge b_2(\alpha)]$$

*and we use the notation* $\min\{A, B\}$.

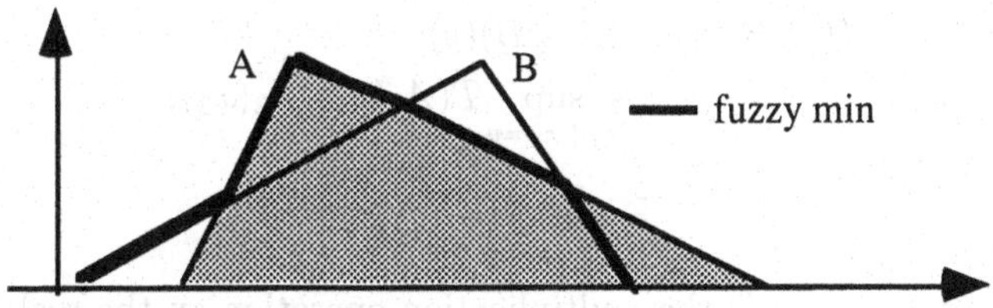


**Fig. 1.8.** Fuzzy min of triangular fuzzy numbers.

The fuzzy max and min are commutative and associative operations. Furthermore, if $A$, $B$ and $C$ are fuzzy numbers then

$$\max\{A, \min\{B, C\}\} = \min\{\max\{A, B\}, \max\{A, C\}\},$$

$$\min\{A, \max\{B, C\}\} = \max\{\min\{A, B\}, \min\{A, C\}\},$$

i.e. min and max are distributive.

## 1.4 t-norm-based operations on fuzzy numbers

In the definition of the extension principle one can use any t-norm for modeling the conjunction operator.

**Definition 1.4.1** *Let* $T$ *be a t-norm and let* $f$ *be a mapping from* $X_1 \times X_2 \times \cdots \times X_n$ *to* $Y$*, Assume* $(A_1, \dots, A_n)$ *is a fuzzy subset of* $X_1 \times X_2 \times \cdots \times X_n$*,* *using the extension principle, we can define* $f(A_1, A_2, \ldots, A_n)$ *as a fuzzy subset of* $Y$ *such that*

$$f(A_1, A_2, \ldots, A_n)(y) = \begin{cases} \sup\{T(A_1(x), \ldots, A_n(x)) \,|\, x \in f^{-1}(y)\} & \textit{if } f^{-1}(y) \neq \emptyset \\ 0 & \textit{otherwise} \end{cases}$$

*This is called the sup-*$T$ *extension principle.*

Specially, if $T$ is a t-norm and $*$ is a binary operation on $\mathbb{R}$ then $*$ can be extended to fuzzy quantities in the sense of the sup-$T$ extension principle as

$$(A_1 * A_2)(z) = \sup_{x_1 * x_2 = z} T(A_1(x_1), A_2(x_2)), \; z \in \mathbb{R}.$$

For example, if $A$ and $B$ are fuzzy numbers, $T_P(u, v) = uv$ is the product t-norm and $f(x_1, x_2) = x_1 + x_2$ is the addition operation on the real line then the sup-product extended sum of $A$ and $B$, called product-sum and denoted by $A + B$, is defined by

$$\begin{aligned} f(A, B)(y) &= (A + B)(y) \\ &= \sup_{x_1 + x_2 = y} T(A_1(x_1), A_2(x_2)) \\ &= \sup_{x_1 + x_2 = y} A_1(x_1) A_2(x_2), \end{aligned}$$

and if $f(x_1, x_2) = x_1 x_2$ is the multiplication operation on the real line then the sup-Łukasiewicz extended product of $A$ and $B$, denoted by $A \times B$, is defined by

$$\begin{aligned} (A \times B)(y) &= \sup_{x_1 x_2 = y} T_L(A_1(x_1), A_2(x_2)) \\ &= \sup_{x_1 x_2 = y} \max\{A_1(x_1) + A_2(x_2) - 1, 0\}. \end{aligned}$$

and if $f(x_1, x_2) = x_1 / x_2$ is the division operation on the real line then the sup-$H_\gamma$ extended division of $A$ and $B$, denoted by $A/B$, is defined by

$$(A/B)(y) = \sup_{x_1/x_2 = y} H_\gamma(A_1(x_1), A_2(x_2)) =$$

$$\sup_{x_1/x_2 = y} \frac{A_1(x_1) A_2(x_2)}{\gamma + (1 - \gamma)(A_1(x_1) + A_2(x_2) - A_1(x_1) A_2(x_2))},$$

where $H_\gamma$ is the Hamacher t-norm (1.3) with parameter $\gamma \geq 0$.

The sup-$T$ extension principle is a very important in fuzzy arithmetic. For example, we have a sequence of symmetric triangular fuzzy numbers $\tilde{a}_i$, $i \in \mathbb{N}$ then their sup-min extended sum $\tilde{a}_1 + \tilde{a}_2 + \cdots + \tilde{a}_n + \cdots$ is always the universal fuzzy set in $\mathbb{R}$ independently of $\alpha$. This means that the minimum norm, because it is too big, might be inappropriate in situations where we have to manipulate with many fuzzy quantities (for example, fuzzy time series analysis, fuzzy linear programming problems, fuzzy control with a large number of rules, etc.).

## 1.5 Product-sum of triangular fuzzy numbers

In this section we will calculate the membership function of the product-sum $\tilde{a}_1 + \tilde{a}_2 + \cdots + \tilde{a}_n + \cdots$ where $\tilde{a}_i$, $i \in \mathbb{N}$ are fuzzy numbers of triangular form. The next theorem can be interpreted as a central limit theorem for mutually product-related identically distributed fuzzy variables of symmetric triangular form (see [274]).

**Theorem 1.5.1** *[121] Let* $\tilde{a}_i = (a_i, \alpha)$, $i \in \mathbb{N}$. *If*

$$A := a_1 + a_2 + \cdots + a_n + \cdots = \sum_{i=1}^{\infty} a_i,$$

*exists and is finite, then with the notations*

$$\tilde{A}_n := \tilde{a}_1 + \cdots + \tilde{a}_n, \; A_n := a_1 + \cdots + a_n, \; n \in \mathbb{N},$$

*we have*

$$\left(\lim_{n\to\infty} \tilde{A}_n\right)(z) = \exp\left(-\frac{|A - z|}{\alpha}\right), \quad z \in \mathbb{R}.$$

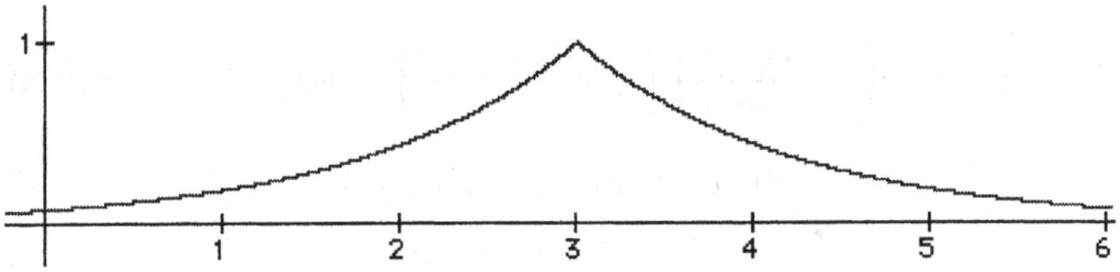


**Fig. 1.9.** The limit distribution of the product-sum of $\tilde{a}_i$'s.

*Proof.* It will be sufficient to show that

$$\tilde{A}_n(z) = \begin{cases} \left(1 - \dfrac{|A_n - z|}{n\alpha}\right)^n & \text{if } |A_n - z| \le n\alpha \\ 0 & \text{otherwise} \end{cases} \tag{1.8}$$

for each $n \geq 2$, because from (1.8) it follows that

$$\left(\lim_{n\to\infty} \tilde{A}_n\right)(z) = \lim_{n\to\infty}\left(1 - \frac{|A_n - z|}{n\alpha}\right)^n$$

$$= \exp\left(-\frac{|\lim_{n\to\infty} A_n - z|}{\alpha}\right)$$

$$= \exp\left(-\frac{|A - z|}{\alpha}\right), \quad z \in \mathbb{R}.$$

From the definition of product-sum of fuzzy numbers it follows that

$$\text{supp}\tilde{A}_n = \text{supp}(\tilde{a}_1 + \cdots + \tilde{a}_n) = \text{supp}\tilde{a}_1 + \cdots + \text{supp}\tilde{a}_n =$$

$$[a_1 - \alpha, a_1 + \alpha] + \cdots + [a_n - \alpha, a_n + \alpha] = [A_n - n\alpha, A_n + n\alpha], \ n \in \mathbb{N}.$$

We prove (1.8) by making an induction argument on $n$. Let $n = 2$. In order to determine $\tilde{A}_2(z)$, $z \in [A_2 - 2\alpha, A_2 + 2\alpha]$ we need to solve the following mathematical programming problem:

$$\left(1 - \frac{|a_1 - x|}{\alpha}\right)\left(1 - \frac{|a_2 - y|}{\alpha}\right) \to \max$$

$$\text{subject to } |a_1 - x| \leq \alpha,$$

$$|a_2 - y| \leq \alpha, \quad x + y = z.$$

By using Lagrange's multipliers method and decomposition rule of fuzzy numbers into two separate parts (see [86]) it is easy to see that $\tilde{A}_2(z)$, $z \in [A_2 - 2\alpha, A_2 + 2\alpha]$ is equal to the optimal value of the following mathematical programming problem:

$$\left(1 - \frac{a_1 - x}{\alpha}\right)\left(1 - \frac{a_2 - z + x}{\alpha}\right) \to \max \tag{1.9}$$

$$\text{subject to } a_1 - \alpha \leq x \leq a_1,$$

$$a_2 - \alpha \leq z - x \leq a_2, \ x + y = z.$$

Using Lagrange's multipliers method for the solution of (1.9) we get that its optimal value is

$$\left(1 - \frac{|A_2 - z|}{2\alpha}\right)^2$$

and its unique solution is

$$x = \frac{a_1 - a_2 + z}{2},$$

where the derivative vanishes. Indeed, it can be easily checked that the inequality

$$\left(1 - \frac{|A_2 - z|}{2\alpha}\right)^2 \geq 1 - \frac{A_2 - z}{\alpha}$$

holds for each $z \in [A_2 - 2\alpha, A_2]$.

In order to determine $\tilde{A}_2(z)$, $z \in [A_2, A_2 + 2\alpha]$ we need to solve the following mathematical programming problem:

$$\left(1 + \frac{a_1 - x}{\alpha}\right)\left(1 + \frac{a_2 - z + x}{\alpha}\right) \to \max \tag{1.10}$$

$$\text{subject to } a_1 \leq x \leq a_1 + \alpha,$$
$$a_2 \leq z - x \leq a_2 + \alpha.$$

In a similar manner we get that the optimal value of (1.10) is

$$\left(1 - \frac{|z - A_2|}{2\alpha}\right)^2.$$

Let us assume that (1.8) holds for some $n \in \mathbb{N}$. By similar arguments we obtain

$$\begin{aligned}\tilde{A}_{n+1}(z) = (\tilde{A}_n + \tilde{a}_{n+1})(z) &= \sup_{x+y=z} \tilde{A}_n(x) \cdot \tilde{a}_{n+1}(y) \\ &= \sup_{x+y=z} \left(1 - \frac{|A_n - x|}{n\alpha}\right)\left(1 - \frac{|a_{n+1} - y|}{\alpha}\right) \\ &= \left(1 - \frac{|A_{n+1} - z|}{(n+1)\alpha}\right)^{n+1},\end{aligned}$$

for $z \in [A_{n+1} - (n+1)\alpha, A_{n+1} + (n+1)\alpha]$, and

$$\tilde{A}_{n+1}(z) = 0,$$

for $z \notin [A_{n+1} - (n+1)\alpha, A_{n+1} + (n+1)\alpha]$. This ends the proof.

**Theorem 1.5.2** *[119] Let $T(x, y) = xy$ and $\tilde{a}_i = (a_i, \alpha_i)$, $i = 1, 2$. Then*

$$(\tilde{a}_1 + \tilde{a}_2)(z) = \begin{cases} c_1(z) & \text{if } |a_1 + a_2 - z| \leq |\alpha_1 - \alpha_2| \\ c_2(z) & \text{otherwise} \\ 0 & \text{if } |a_1 + a_2 - z| > \alpha_1 + \alpha_2 \end{cases}$$

*where*

$$c_1(z) = 1 - \frac{|\, a_1 + a_2 - z \,|}{\alpha_1 \vee \alpha_2},$$

$$c_2(z) = \frac{(\alpha_1+\alpha_2)^2}{4\alpha_1\alpha_2}\left(1 - \frac{|a_1+a_2-z|}{\alpha_1+\alpha_2}\right)^2,$$

*and* $\alpha_1 \vee \alpha_2 = \max\{\alpha_1, \alpha_2\}$.

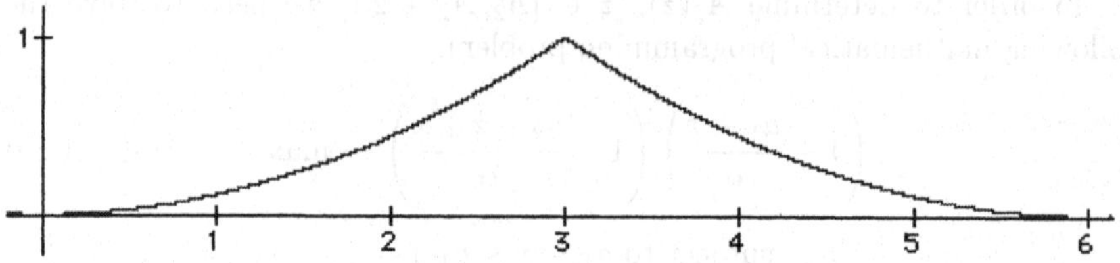


**Fig. 1.10.** Product-sum of fuzzy numbers $\tilde{a}_1 = (1, 3/2)$ and $\tilde{a}_2 = (2, 3/2)$.

Let $\tilde{a}_i = (a_i, \alpha, \beta)_{LR}$, $1 \le i \le n$ be fuzzy numbers of LR-type. In [121] Fullér asked the following question: On what condition will the membership function of the product-sum $\tilde{A}_n$ have the following form

$$\tilde{A}_n(z) = \begin{cases} L^n\left(\dfrac{A_n - z}{n\alpha}\right) & \text{if } A_n - n\alpha \le z \le A_n, \\[2ex] R^n\left(\dfrac{z - A_n}{n\beta}\right) & \text{if } A_n \le z \le A_n + n\beta \end{cases} \tag{1.11}$$

Triesch [298] provided a partial answer to this question that $\tilde{A}_n$ is given by (1.11) if $\log R$ and $\log L$ are concave functions. However, Hong [170] pointed out that the condition given by Triesch is not only sufficient but necessary, too.

## 1.6 Hamacher-sum of triangular fuzzy numbers

If $\tilde{a}$ and $\tilde{b}$ are fuzzy numbers and $\gamma \ge 0$ a real number, then their Hamacher-sum ($H_\gamma$-sum for short) is defined as

$$\begin{aligned}(\tilde{a} + \tilde{b})(z) &= \sup_{x+y=z} H_\gamma(\tilde{a}(x), \tilde{b}(y)) \\ &= \sup_{x+y=z} \frac{\tilde{a}(x)\tilde{b}(y)}{\gamma + (1-\gamma)(\tilde{a}(x) + \tilde{b}(y) - \tilde{a}(x)\tilde{b}(y))},\end{aligned}$$

for $x, y, z \in \mathbb{R}$, where $H_\gamma$ the Hamacher t-norm (1.3) with parameter $\gamma$.

In the next two lemmas we shall calculate the exact membership function of $H_\gamma$-sum of two symmetric triangular fuzzy numbers having common width $\alpha > 0$ for each permissible value of parameter $\gamma$.

**Lemma 1.6.1** *[123] Let $0 \leq \gamma \leq 2$ and $\tilde{a}_i = (a_i, \alpha)$, $i = 1, 2$. Then their $H_\gamma$-sum, $\tilde{A}_2 = \tilde{a}_1 + \tilde{a}_2$, has the following membership function:*

$$\tilde{A}_2(z) = \frac{\left(1 - \dfrac{|A_2 - z|}{2\alpha}\right)^2}{1 + (\gamma - 1)\left(\dfrac{|A_2 - z|}{2\alpha}\right)^2}$$

*if $|A_2 - z| < 2\alpha$ and $\tilde{A}_2(z) = 0$, otherwise, where $A_2 = a_1 + a_2$.*

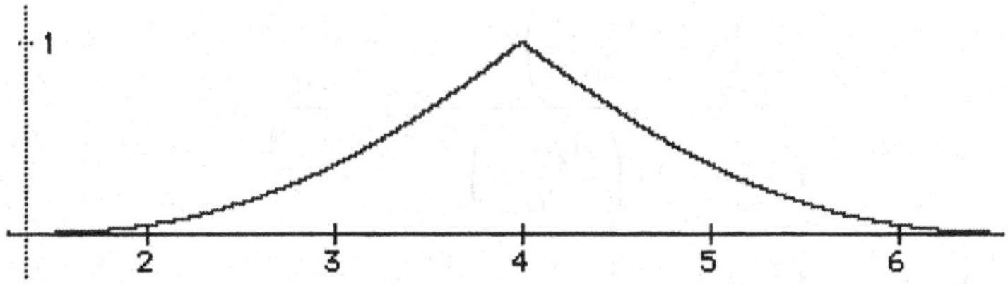


**Fig. 1.11.** $H_{1.5}$-sum of fuzzy numbers $\tilde{a}_1 = (1, 1.3)$ and $\tilde{a}_2 = (3, 1.3)$.

*Proof.* We need to determine the value of $\tilde{a}_2(z)$ from the following relationships:

$$\tilde{A}_2(z) = (\tilde{a}_1 + \tilde{a}_2)(z) =$$

$$\sup_{x+y=z} \frac{\tilde{a}_1(x)\tilde{a}_2(y)}{\gamma + (1-\gamma)(\tilde{a}_1(x) + \tilde{a}_2(y) - \tilde{a}_1(x)\tilde{a}_2(y))}, \text{ if } |A_2 - z| < 2\alpha,$$

and $\tilde{A}_2(z) = 0$ otherwise. According to the decomposition rule of fuzzy numbers into two separate parts, $\tilde{A}_2(z)$, $A_2 - 2\alpha < z \leq A_2$, is equal to the optimal value of the following mathematical programming problem:

$$\phi(x) \to \max$$

$$\text{subject to } \{a_1 - \alpha < x \leq a_1,\ a_2 - \alpha < z - x \leq a_2\},$$

where $\phi(x) =$

$$\frac{[1 - (a_1 - x)/\alpha][1 - (a_2 - z + x)/\alpha]}{\gamma + (1-\gamma)\{2 - (a_1 + a_2 - z)/\alpha - [1 - (a_1 - x)/\alpha][1 - (a_2 - z + x)/\alpha]\}}.$$

Using Lagrange's multipliers method for the solution of the above problem we get that its optimal value is

$$\frac{\left(1 - \dfrac{A_2 - z}{2\alpha}\right)^2}{1 + (\gamma - 1)\left(\dfrac{A_2 - z}{2\alpha}\right)^2}$$

and its unique solution is

$$x = \frac{a_1 - a_2 + z}{2},$$

where the derivative vanishes. Indeed, from the inequality

$$\frac{\left(1 - \dfrac{A_2 - z}{2\alpha}\right)^2}{1 + (\gamma - 1)\left(\dfrac{A_2 - z}{2\alpha}\right)^2} \geq 1 - \frac{A_2 - z}{\alpha},$$

for $A_2 - 2\alpha < z \leq A_2$, and

$$\phi''(\frac{1}{2}(a_1 - a_2 + z)) < 0$$

follows that the function $\phi$ attains its conditional maximum at the single stationary point

$$\frac{a_1 - a_2 + z}{2}.$$

If $A_2 \leq z < A_2 + 2\alpha$, then $\tilde{A}_2(z)$ is equal to the optimal value of the the following mathematical programming problem

$$\varphi(x) \to \max \tag{1.12}$$

$$\text{subject to } \{a_1 \leq x < a_1 + \alpha,\ a_2 \leq z - x < a_2 + \alpha\},$$

where $\varphi(x) =$

$$\frac{[1 - (x - a_1)/\alpha][1 - (z - x - a_2)/\alpha]}{\gamma + (1 - \gamma)\{2 - (z - a_1 - a_2)/\alpha - [1 - (x - a_1)/\alpha][1 - (z - x - a_2)/\alpha]\}}.$$

In a similar manner we get that the optimal value of (1.12) is

$$\frac{[1 - (z - A_2)/(2\alpha)]^2}{1 + (\gamma - 1)[(z - A_2)/(2\alpha)]^2}$$

and the unique solution of (1.12) is $x = (a_1 - a_2 + z)/2$ (where the derivative vanishes). Which ends the proof.

**Lemma 1.6.2** *[123] Let $2 < \gamma < \infty$ and $\tilde{a}_i = (a_i, \alpha)$, $i = 1, 2$. Then their $H_\gamma$-sum $\tilde{A}_2 := \tilde{a}_1 + \tilde{a}_2$ has the following membership function*

$$\tilde{A}_2(z) = \begin{cases} h_1(z) \text{ if } 1 - \dfrac{1}{\gamma - 1} \le \dfrac{|A_2 - z|}{\alpha} < 2, \\ h_2(z) \text{ if } \dfrac{|A_2 - z|}{\alpha} < 1 - \dfrac{1}{\gamma - 1}, \\ 0 \quad \text{otherwise,} \end{cases}$$

*where*

$$h_1(z) = \frac{[1 - (A_2 - z)/(2\alpha)]^2}{1 + (\gamma - 1)[(A_2 - z)/(2\alpha)]^2}, \quad h_2(z) = 1 - \frac{|A_2 - z|}{\alpha}$$

*and $A_2 = a_1 + a_2$.*

The following theorems can be interpreted as central limit theorems for mutually $H_\gamma$-related fuzzy variables of symmetric triangular form (see [274]).

**Theorem 1.6.1** *[123] Let $\gamma = 0$ and $\tilde{a}_i = (a_i, \alpha)$, $i \in \mathbb{N}$. Suppose that $A := \sum_{i=1}^{\infty} a_i$ exists and is finite, then with the notation*

$$\tilde{A}_n = \tilde{a}_1 + \cdots + \tilde{a}_n, \quad A_n = a_1 + \cdots + a_n$$

*we have*

$$\left(\lim_{n \to \infty} \tilde{A}_n\right)(z) = \frac{1}{1 + |A - z|/\alpha}, \quad z \in \mathbb{R}.$$

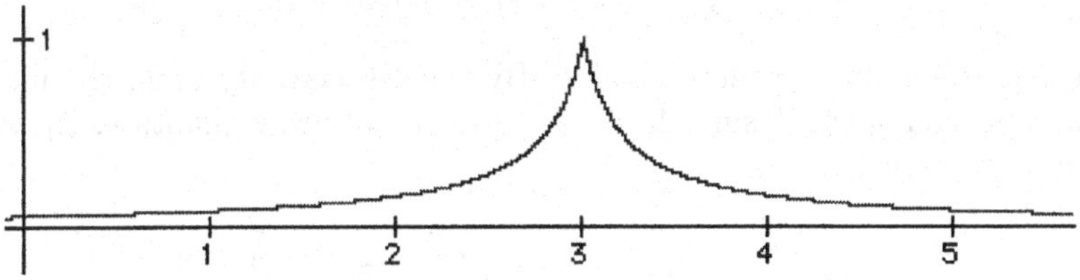


**Fig. 1.12.** The limit distribution of the $H_0$-sum of $\tilde{a}_i$'s.

**Theorem 1.6.2** *[123] (Einstein-sum). Let $\gamma = 2$ and $\tilde{a}_i = (a_i, \alpha)$, $i \in \mathbb{N}$. If $A := \sum_{i=1}^{\infty} a_i$ exists and is finite, then we have*

$$\left(\lim_{n \to \infty} \tilde{A}_n\right)(z) = \frac{2}{1 + \exp\left[\dfrac{-2|A - z|}{\alpha}\right]}, \quad z \in \mathbb{R}.$$

According to the decomposition rule of fuzzy numbers into two separate parts, the above theorems remain valid for sequences of non-symmetric fuzzy numbers of triangular form $\tilde{a}_1 = (a_1, \alpha, \beta)$, $\tilde{a}_2 = (a_2, \alpha, \beta)$, ... with the difference that in the membership function of their $H_\gamma$-sum instead of $\alpha$ we write $\beta$ if $z \geq A$.

## 1.7 t-norm-based addition of fuzzy numbers

Recall that a t-norm $T$ is Archimedean iff $T$ is continuous and $T(x, x) < x$ for all $x \in (0, 1)$. Every Archimedean t-norm $T$ is representable by a continuous and decreasing function $f\colon [0, 1] \to [0, \infty]$ with $f(1) = 0$ and

$$T(x, y) = f^{[-1]}(f(x) + f(y)),$$

where $f^{[-1]}$ is the pseudo-inverse of $f$, defined by

$$f^{[-1]}(y) = \begin{cases} f^{-1}(y) & \text{if } y \in [0, f(0)] \\ 0 & \text{otherwise.} \end{cases}$$

The function $f$ is the additive generator of $T$.

If $T$ is an Archimedean t-norm and $\tilde{a}_1$ and $\tilde{a}_2$ are fuzzy sets of the real line (i.e. fuzzy quantities) then their $T$-sum $\tilde{A}_2 := \tilde{a}_1 + \tilde{a}_2$ is defined by

$$\tilde{A}_2(z) = \sup_{x_1 + x_2 = z} T(\tilde{a}_1(x_1), \tilde{a}_2(x_2)), \ z \in \mathbb{R},$$

which expression can be written in the form

$$\tilde{A}_2(z) = f^{[-1]}(f(\tilde{a}_1(x_1)) + f(\tilde{a}_2(x_2))),$$

where $f$ is the additive generator of $T$. By the associativity of $T$, the membership function of the $T$-sum $\tilde{A}_n := \tilde{a}_1 + \cdots + \tilde{a}_n$ of fuzzy quantities $\tilde{a}_1, \ldots,$ $\tilde{a}_n$ can be written as

$$\tilde{A}_n(z) = \sup_{x_1 + \cdots + x_n = z} f^{[-1]}\left(\sum_{i=1}^{n} f(\tilde{a}_i(x_i))\right).$$

Since $f$ is continuous and decreasing, $f^{[-1]}$ is also continuous and non-increasing, we have

$$\tilde{A}_n(z) = f^{[-1]}\left(\inf_{x_1 + \cdots + x_n = z} \sum_{i=1}^{n} f(\tilde{a}_i(x_i))\right).$$

Following Fullér and Keresztfalvi [130] we shall determine a class of t-norms in which the addition of fuzzy numbers is very simple.

**Theorem 1.7.1** *[130] Let $T$ be an Archimedean t-norm with additive generator $f$ and let $\tilde{a}_i = (a_i, b_i, \alpha, \beta)_{LR}$, $i = 1, \dots, n$, be fuzzy numbers of LR-type. If $L$ and $R$ are twice differentiable, concave functions, and $f$ is twice differentiable, strictly convex function then the membership function of the $T$-sum $\tilde{A}_n = \tilde{a}_1 + \cdots + \tilde{a}_n$ is*

$$\tilde{A}_n(z) = \begin{cases} 1 & \text{if } A_n \le z \le B_n \\ f^{[-1]}\left(n \times f\left(L\left(\dfrac{A_n - z}{n\alpha}\right)\right)\right) & \text{if } A_n - n\alpha \le z \le A_n \\ f^{[-1]}\left(n \times f\left(R\left(\dfrac{z - B_n}{n\beta}\right)\right)\right) & \text{if } B_n \le z \le B_n + n\beta \\ 0 & \text{otherwise} \end{cases}$$

*where $A_n = a_1 + \cdots + a_n$ and $B_n = b_1 + \cdots + b_n$.*

It should be noted, that from the concavity of shape functions it follows that the fuzzy numbers in question can not have infinite support.

Theorem 1.7.1 has been improved and generalized later by Kawaguchi and Da-Te [204, 205], Hong [171, 178], Hong and Kim [176], Hong and Hwang [170, 172, 177, 179, 180], Marková [242], Mesiar [249, 250, 251], De Baets and Markova [4, 5].

Namely, in 1994 Hong and Hwang ([170]) proved that Theorem 1.7.1 remains valid for convex additive genrator $f$, and concave shape functions $L$ and $R$. In 1994 Hong and Hwang ([172]) provided an upper bound for the membership function of $T$-sum of $LR$-fuzzy numbers with different spreads. In 1996 Mesiar [249] showed that Theorem 1.7.1 remains valid if both $L \circ f$ and $R \circ f$ are convex functions. In 1997 Hong and Hwang [180] gave upper and lower bounds of $T$-sums of $LR$-fuzzy numbers $\tilde{a}_i = (a_i, \alpha_i, \beta_i)_{LR}$, $i = 1, \dots, n$, with different spreads where $T$ is an Archimedean t-norm.

We shall illustrate the Theorem 1.7.1 by Yager's, Dombi's and Hamacher's parametrized t-norms. For simplicity we shall restrict our consideration to the case of symmetric fuzzy numbers

$$\tilde{a}_i = (a_i, a_i, \alpha, \alpha)_{LL}, \quad i = 1, \dots, n.$$

Introducing the notation

$$\sigma_n := \frac{|A_n - z|}{n\alpha},$$

we get the following formulas for the membership function of t-norm-based sum

$$\tilde{A}_n = \tilde{a}_1 + \cdots + \tilde{a}_n,$$

(i) Yager's t-norm with $p > 1$:

$$T(x, y) = 1 - \min\left\{1, \sqrt[p]{(1-x)^p + (1-y)^p}\right\} \quad \text{with } f(x) = (1-x)^p$$

and then

$$\tilde{A}_n(z) = \begin{cases} 1 - n^{1/p}(1 - L(\sigma_n)) & \text{if } \sigma_n < L^{-1}(1 - n^{-1/p}) \\ 0 & \text{otherwise.} \end{cases}$$

(ii) Hamacher's t-norm with $p \leq 2$:

$$T(x,y) = \frac{xy}{p + (1-p)(x + y - xy)} \quad \text{with } f(x) = \ln \frac{p + (1-p)x}{x}.$$

Then

$$\tilde{A}_n(z) = \begin{cases} v(p,\sigma) & \text{if } \sigma_n < 1 \\ 0 & \text{otherwise.} \end{cases}$$

where

$$v(p,\sigma) = \frac{p}{[(p + (1-p)L(\sigma_n))/L(\sigma_n)]^n - 1 + p}.$$

Specially, for the product t-norm (that is $H_1$):

$$T(x,y) = xy \quad \text{with } f(x) = -\ln x.$$

Then

$$\tilde{A}_n(z) = L^n(\sigma_n), \quad z \in \mathbb{R}.$$

(iii) Dombi's t-norm with $p > 1$:

$$T(x,y) = \frac{1}{1 + \sqrt[p]{(1/x - 1)^p + (1/y - 1)^p}} \quad \text{with } f(x) = \left(\frac{1}{x} - 1\right)^p.$$

Then

$$\tilde{A}_n(z) = \begin{cases} \left(1 + n^{1/p}(1/L(\sigma_n) - 1)\right)^{-1} & \text{if } \sigma_n < 1 \\ 0 & \text{otherwise.} \end{cases}$$

## 1.8 A functional relationship between t-norm-based addition and multiplication

A fuzzy quantity $M$ of $\mathbb{R}$ is said to be positive if $\mu_M(x) = 0$ for all $x < 0$, and a fuzzy number is negative if $\mu_M(x) = 0$ for all $x > 0$. The following theorem (Fullér and Keresztfalvi, [133]) gives a functional relationship between the membership functions of fuzzy numbers $M_1 + \cdots + M_n$ and $M_1 \times \cdots \times M_n$, where $M_i$, $i = 1, \ldots, n$, are positive $LR$ fuzzy numbers of the same form $M_i = M = (a, b, \alpha, \beta)_{LR}$.

**Theorem 1.8.1** *[133] Let $T$ be an Archimedean t-norm with an additive generator $f$ and let $M_i = M = (a, b, \alpha, \beta)_{LR}$ be positive fuzzy numbers of LR type. If $L$ and $R$ are twice differentiable, concave functions, and $f$ is twice differentiable, strictly convex function, then*

$$(M_1 + \cdots + M_n)(nz) = (M_1 \times \cdots \times M_n)(z^n) = f^{[-1]}\Big(n \cdot f(M(z))\Big). \quad (1.13)$$

*Proof.* Let $z \geq 0$ be arbitrarily fixed. According to the decomposition rule of fuzzy numbers into two separate parts, we can assume without loss of generality that $z < a$. From Theorem 1.7.1 it follows that

$$(M_1 + \cdots + M_n)(nz) = f^{[-1]}\left(n \cdot f\left(L\left(\frac{na - nz}{n\alpha}\right)\right)\right) =$$

$$f^{[-1]}\left(n \cdot f\left(L\left(\frac{a-z}{\alpha}\right)\right)\right) = f^{[-1]}\Big(n \cdot f(M(z))\Big)$$

The proof will be complete if we show that

$$\begin{aligned}(M \times \cdots \times M)(z) &= \sup_{x_1 \cdot \ldots \cdot x_n = z} T\Big(M(x_1), \ldots, M(x_n)\Big) \\ &= T\Big(M(\sqrt[n]{z}), \ldots, M(\sqrt[n]{z})\Big) = f^{[-1]}\Big(n \cdot f(M(\sqrt[n]{z}))\Big) \quad (1.14)\end{aligned}$$

We shall justify it by induction:

(i) for $n = 1$ (1.14) is obviously valid;

(ii) Let us suppose that (1.14) holds for some $n = k$, i. e.

$$\begin{aligned}\left(M^k\right)(z) &= \sup_{x_1 \cdot \ldots \cdot x_k = z} T\Big(M(x_1), \ldots, M(x_k)\Big) \\ &= T\Big(M(\sqrt[k]{z}), \ldots, M(\sqrt[k]{z})\Big) \\ &= f^{[-1]}\Big(k \cdot f(M(\sqrt[k]{z}))\Big),\end{aligned}$$

and verify the case $n = k + 1$. It is clear that

$$\begin{aligned}\left(M^{k+1}\right)(z) &= \sup_{x \cdot y = z} T\Big(M^k(x), M(y)\Big) \\ &= \sup_{x \cdot y = z} T\Big(M(\sqrt[k]{x}), \ldots, M(\sqrt[k]{x}), M(y)\Big) \\ &= g^{[-1]}\left(\inf_{x \cdot y = z}\Big(k \cdot g(M(\sqrt[k]{x})) + g(M(y))\Big)\right) \\ &= g^{[-1]}\Big(\inf_x \Big(k \cdot g(M(\sqrt[k]{x})) + g(M(z/x))\Big)\Big).\end{aligned}$$

The support and the peak of $M^{k+1}$ are

$$[M^{k+1}]^1 = [M]^{1^{k+1}} = [a^{k+1}, b^{k+1}]$$
$$\operatorname{Supp}(M^{k+1}) \subset \Big(\operatorname{Supp}(M)\Big)^{k+1} = [(a-\alpha)^{k+1}, (a+\beta)^{k+1}].$$

According to the decomposition rule we can consider only the left hand side of $M$, that is let $z \in [(a-\alpha)^{k+1}, a^{k+1}]$. We need to find the minimum of the mapping

$$x \mapsto k \cdot g(M(\sqrt[k]{x})) + g(M(z/x)),$$

in the interval $[(a-\alpha)^k, a^k]$. Let us introduce the auxiliary variable $t = \sqrt[k]{x}$ and look for the minimum of the function

$$t \mapsto \varphi(t) := k \cdot f(M(t)) + f(M(z/t^k)),$$

in the interval $[a-\alpha, a]$. Dealing with the left hand side of $M$ we have

$$M(t) = L\left(\frac{a-t}{\alpha}\right) \qquad \text{and} \qquad M(z/t^k) = L\left(\frac{a - z/t^k}{\alpha}\right).$$

The derivative of $\varphi$ is equal to zero when

$$\varphi'(t) = kf'(M(t))L'\left(\frac{a-t}{\alpha}\right) \cdot \frac{-1}{\alpha}$$
$$+ f'(M(z/t^k))L'\left(\frac{a-z/t^k}{\alpha}\right) \cdot \frac{-1}{\alpha} \cdot \left(-k \cdot \frac{z}{t^{k+1}}\right) = 0,$$

i. e.

$$t \cdot f'(M(t)) \cdot L'\left(\frac{a-t}{\alpha}\right) = \frac{z}{t^k} \cdot f'(M(z/t^k)) \cdot L'\left(\frac{a-z/t^k}{\alpha}\right) \tag{1.15}$$

which obviously holds taking $t = z/t^k$. So $t_0 = \sqrt[k+1]{z}$ is a solution of (1.15), furthermore, from the strict monotony of

$$t \mapsto t \cdot f'(M(t)) \cdot L'\left(\frac{a-t}{\alpha}\right)$$

follows that there are no other solutions.

It is easy to check, that $\varphi''(t_0) > 0$, which means that $\varphi$ attains its absolute minimum at $t_0$. Finally, from the relations $\sqrt[k]{x_0} = \sqrt[k+1]{z}$ and $z/x_0 = \sqrt[k+1]{z}$, we get

$$\begin{aligned}(M^{k+1})(z) &= T\Big(M(\sqrt[k+1]{z}), \ldots, M(\sqrt[k+1]{z}), M(\sqrt[k+1]{z})\Big)\\ &= f^{[-1]}\Big(k \cdot f(M(\sqrt[k+1]{z})) + f(M(\sqrt[k+1]{z}))\Big)\\ &= f^{[-1]}\Big((k+1) \cdot g(M(\sqrt[k+1]{z}))\Big).\end{aligned}$$

Which ends the proof.

As an immediate consequence of Theorem 1.8.1 we can easily calculate the exact possibility distribution of expressions of the form

$$e_n^*(M) := \frac{M + \cdots + M}{n}$$

and the limit distribution of $e_n^*(M)$ as $n \to \infty$. Namely, from (1.13) we have

$$(e_n^*(M))(z) = \left(\frac{M + \cdots + M}{n}\right)(z) =$$

$$(M + \cdots + M)(n \cdot z) = f^{[-1]}\Big(n \cdot f(M(z))\Big)$$

therefore, from $f(x) > 0$ for $0 \leq x < 1$ and

$$\lim_{x \to \infty} f^{[-1]}(x) = 0,$$

we get

$$\Big[\lim_{n \to \infty} e_n^*(M)\Big](z) = \lim_{n \to \infty} (e_n^*(M))(z) =$$

$$\lim_{n \to \infty} f^{[-1]}\Big(n \cdot f(M(z))\Big) = \begin{cases} 1 \text{ if } z \in [a, b] \\ 0 \text{ if } z \notin [a, b], \end{cases}$$

that is

$$\lim_{n \to \infty} e_n^*(M) = [a, b], \tag{1.16}$$

which is the peak of $M$. It can be shown [86] that (1.16) remains valid for the (non-Archimedean) weak t-norm. It is easy to see [121] that when $T(x, y) = xy$:

$$(M_1 + \cdots + M_n)(nz) = (M_1 \times \cdots \times M_n)(z^n) = \big(M(z)\big)^n.$$

## 1.9 On generalization of Nguyen's theorems

In this Section we generalize Nguyen's theorem (Theorem 1.3.2 in Section 1.3) and following Fullér and Keresztfalvi [122], we give a necessary and sufficient condition for obtaining the equality

$$[f(A, B)]^\alpha = \bigcup_{T(\xi, \eta) \geq \alpha} f([A]^\xi, [B]^\eta), \ \alpha \in (0, 1], \tag{1.17}$$

where $f : X \times Y \to Z$, $T$ is a t-norm, $A$ and $B$ are fuzzy subsets of $X$ and $Y$, respectively, $f(A, B)$ is defined via sup-$T$-norm convolution, $[A]^\alpha$ and $[B]^\alpha$ are the $\alpha$-level sets of $A$ and $B$, respectively, and $[f(A, B)]^\alpha$ is the $\alpha$-level set of $f(A, B)$.

Furthermore, we shall define a class of fuzzy subsets in which this equality holds for all upper semicontinuous $T$ and continuous $f$. It should be noted that in the special case $T(x,y) = \min\{x,y\}$, the equation (1.17) yields

$$[f(A,B)]^\alpha = f([A]^\alpha, [B]^\alpha), \ \alpha \in (0,1],$$

which coincides with Nguyen's result. Additionally, since fuzzy logics are defined in terms of t-norms rather just min-max operators, the result of this Section can be useful for workers in the field in the implementation of algorithms.

The symbol $\mathcal{F}(X)$ denotes the family of all fuzzy subsets of a set $X$. When $X$ is a topological space, we denote by $\mathcal{F}(X,\mathcal{K})$ the set of all fuzzy subsets of $X$ having upper semicontinuous, compactly-supported membership function.

Recall that if $T$ is a t-norm, $f: X \times Y \to Z$, $A \in \mathcal{F}(X)$ and $B \in \mathcal{F}(Y)$ then the fuzzy set $f(A,B) \in \mathcal{F}(Z)$ is defined via the extension principle by

$$f(A,B)(z) = \sup_{f(x,y)=z} T(A(x), B(y)), \ z \in Z.$$

The following theorem illustrates that, if instead of min-norm in Zadeh's extension principle, we use an arbitrary t-norm, then we obtain results similar to those of Nguyen.

**Theorem 1.9.1** *[122] Let $X \neq \emptyset$, $Y \neq \emptyset$, $Z \neq \emptyset$ be sets and let $T$ be a t-norm. If $f: X \times Y \to Z$ is a two-place function and $A \in \mathcal{F}(X)$, $B \in \mathcal{F}(Y)$ then a necessary and sufficient condition for the equality*

$$[f(A,B)]^\alpha = \bigcup_{T(\xi,\eta)\geq\alpha} f([A]^\xi, [B]^\eta), \ \alpha \in (0,1], \tag{1.18}$$

*is, that for each $z \in Z$,*

$$\sup_{f(x,y)=z} T(A(x), B(y))$$

*is attained.*

The next theorem shows that the equality (1.17) holds for all upper semicontinuous $T$ and continuous $f$ in the class of upper semicontinuous and compactly-supported fuzzy subsets. In the following, $X$, $Y$, $Z$ are locally compact topological speces.

**Theorem 1.9.2** *[122] If $f: X \times Y \to Z$ is continuous and the t-norm $T$ is upper semicontinuous, then*

$$[f(A,B)]^\alpha = \bigcup_{T(\xi,\eta)\geq\alpha} f([A]^\xi, [B]^\eta), \ \alpha \in (0,1],$$

*holds for each $A \in \mathcal{F}(X,\mathcal{K})$ and $B \in \mathcal{F}(Y,\mathcal{K})$.*

The following examples illustrate that the $\alpha$-cuts of the fuzzy set $f(A, B)$ can be generated in a simple way when the t-norm in question has a simple form.

**Example 1.9.1** *If* $T(x, y) = \min(x, y)$*, then using the fact that* $\xi \geq \alpha$ *and* $\eta \geq \alpha$ *implies*

$$f([A]^\xi, [B]^\eta) \subset f([A]^\alpha, [B]^\alpha),$$

*equation (1.17) is reduced to the well-known form of Nguyen:*

$$[f(A, B)]^\alpha = f([A]^\alpha, [B]^\alpha) \; \alpha \in (0, 1],$$

**Example 1.9.2** *If* $T(x, y) = T_W(x, y)$*, where*

$$T_W(x, y) = \begin{cases} \min\{x, y\} \text{ if } \max\{x, y\} = 1 \\ 0 \qquad\qquad\quad \text{otherwise} \end{cases}$$

*is the weak t-norm, then (1.17) turns into*

$$[f(A, B)]^\alpha = f([A]^1, [B]^\alpha) \cup f([A]^\alpha, [B]^1) \; \alpha \in (0, 1],$$

*since* $T_W(\xi, \eta) \geq \alpha > 0$ *holds only if* $\xi = 1$ *or* $\eta = 1$.

*Thus if* $[A]^1 = \emptyset$ *or* $[B]^1 = \emptyset$*, then* $[f(A, B)]^\alpha = \emptyset$, $\forall \alpha \in (0, 1]$. *If there exist unique* $x_0$ *and* $y_0$ *such that* $A(x_0) = B(y_0) = 1$*, then we obtain*

$$[f(A, B)]^\alpha = f(x_0, [B]^\alpha) \cup f([A]^\alpha, y_0) \; \alpha \in (0, 1],$$

**Example 1.9.3** *If* $T(x, y) = xy$*, then the equation (1.17) yields*

$$[f(A, B)]^\alpha = \bigcup_{\xi \in [\alpha, 1]} f([A]^\xi, [B]^{\alpha/\xi}), \; \alpha \in (0, 1].$$

**Example 1.9.4** *If* $T(x, y) = \max\{0, x + y - 1\}$*, then*

$$[f(A, B)]^\alpha = \bigcup_{\xi \in [\alpha, 1]} f([A]^\xi, [B]^{\alpha+1-\xi}), \; \alpha \in (0, 1].$$

## 1.10 Measures of possibility and necessity

Fuzzy numbers can also be considered as possibility distributions [91]. If $A \in \mathcal{F}$ is a fuzzy number and $x \in \mathbb{R}$ a real number then $A(x)$ can be interpreted as the degree of possiblity of the statement "$x$ is $A$".

Let $A, B \in \mathcal{F}$ be fuzzy numbers. The degree of possibility that the proposition "$A$ is less than or equal to $B$" is true denoted by $\text{Pos}[A \leq B]$ and defined by the extension principle as

$$\text{Pos}[A \leq B] = \sup_{x \leq y} \min\{A(x), B(y)\} = \sup_{z \leq 0}(A - B)(z), \tag{1.19}$$

In a similar way, the degree of possibility that the proposition "$A$ is greater than or equal to $B$" is true, denoted by $\mathrm{Pos}[A \geq B]$, is defined by

$$\mathrm{Pos}[A \geq B] = \sup_{x \geq y} \min\{A(x), B(y)\} = \sup_{z \geq 0}(A - B)(z). \qquad (1.20)$$

Finally, the degree of possibility that the proposition is true "$A$ is equal to

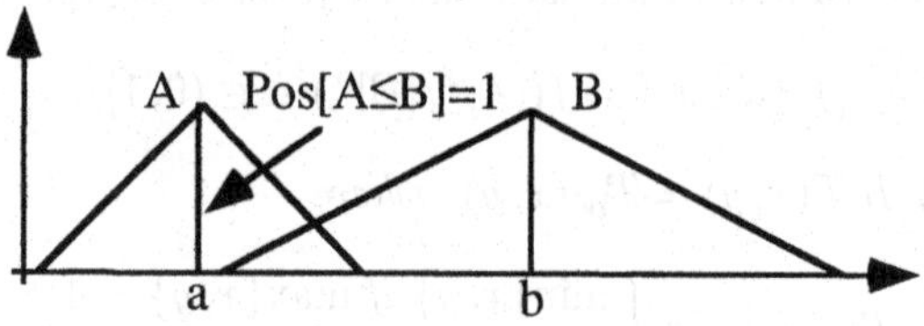


**Fig. 1.13.** $\mathrm{Pos}[A \leq B] = 1$, because $a \leq b$.

$B$" and denoted by $\mathrm{Pos}[A = B]$, is defined by

$$\mathrm{Pos}[A = B] = \sup_{x} \min\{A(x), B(x)\} = (A - B)(0), \qquad (1.21)$$

Let $A = (a, \alpha)$ and $B = (b, \beta)$ fuzzy numbers of symmetric triangular form. It is easy to compute that,

$$\mathrm{Pos}[A \leq B] = \begin{cases} 1 & \text{if } a \leq b \\ 1 - \dfrac{a - b}{\alpha + \beta} & \text{otherwise} \\ 0 & \text{if } a \geq b + \alpha + \beta \end{cases} \qquad (1.22)$$

The degree of necessity that the proposition "$A$ is less than or equal to $B$"

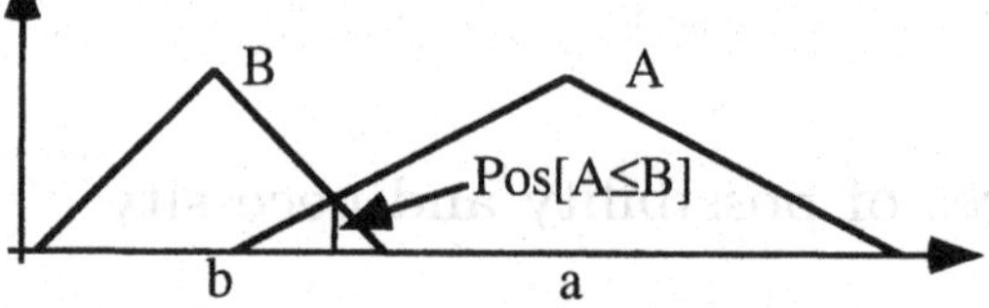


**Fig. 1.14.** $\mathrm{Pos}[A \leq B] < 1$, because $a > b$.

is true, denoted by $\mathrm{Pos}[A \leq B]$, is defined as

$$\mathrm{Nes}[A \leq B] = 1 - \mathrm{Pos}[A \geq B].$$

If $A = (a, \alpha)$ and $B = (b, \beta)$ are fuzzy numbers of symmetric triangular form

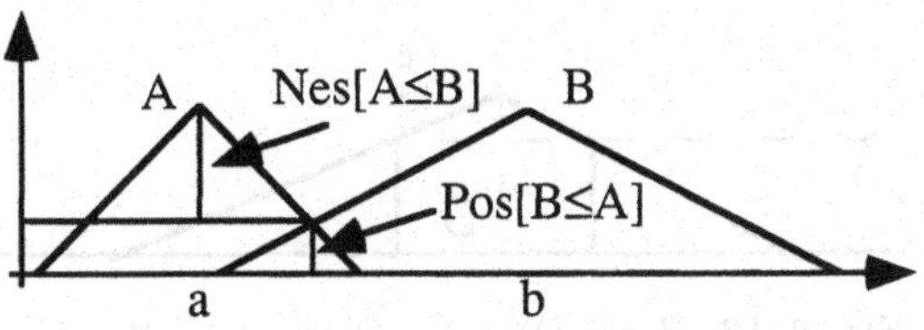


**Fig. 1.15.** $\text{Nes}[A \le B] < 1$, $(a < b,\ A \cap B \ne \emptyset)$.

then

$$\text{Nes}[A \le B] = \begin{cases} 1 & \text{if } a \le b - \alpha - \beta \\ \dfrac{b-a}{\alpha+\beta} & \text{otherwise} \\ 0 & \text{if } a \ge b \end{cases} \tag{1.23}$$

Let $\xi \in \mathcal{F}$ be a fuzzy number. Given a subset $D \subset \mathbb{R}$, the grade of possibility

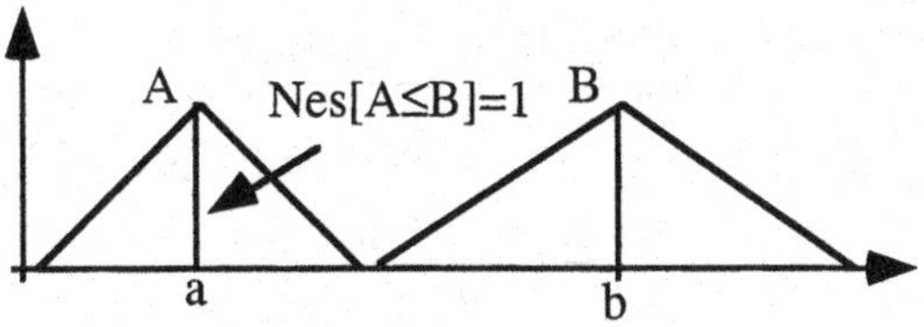


**Fig. 1.16.** $\text{Nes}[A \le B] = 1$, $(a < b$ and $A \cap B = \emptyset)$.

of the statement "D contains the value of $\xi$" is defined by

$$\text{Pos}(\xi \mid D) = \sup_{x \in D} \xi(x) \tag{1.24}$$

The quantity $1 - \text{Pos}(\xi \mid \bar{D})$, where $\bar{D}$ is the complement of $D$, is denoted by $Nes(\xi \mid D)$ and is interpreted as the grade of necessity of the statement "D contains the value of $\xi$". It satisfies dual property with respect to (1.24):

$$\text{Nes}(\xi \mid D) = 1 - \text{Pos}(\xi \mid \bar{D}).$$

If $D = [a, b] \subset \mathbb{R}$ then instead of $\text{Nes}(\xi \mid [a, b])$ we shall write $\text{Nes}(a \le \xi \le b)$ and if $D = \{x\}, x \in \mathbb{R}$ we write $\text{Nes}(\xi = x)$. Let $\xi_1, \xi_2, \dots$ be a sequence of fuzzy numbers. We say that $\{\xi_n\}$ converges pointwise to a fuzzy set $\xi$ (and write $\lim_{n\to\infty} \xi_n = \xi$) if

$$\lim_{n\to\infty} \xi_n(x) = \xi(x),$$

for all $x \in \mathbb{R}$.

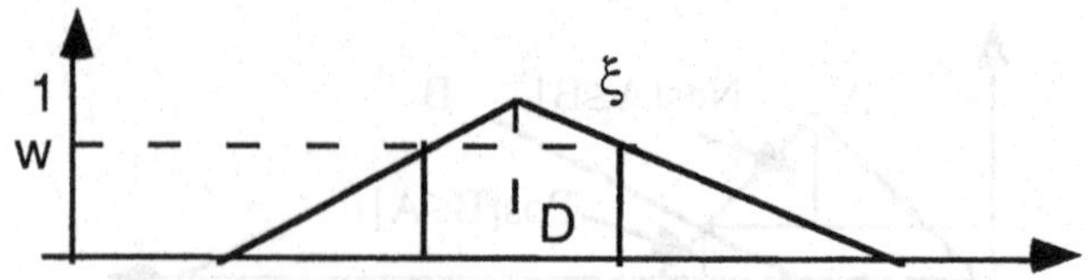


**Fig. 1.17.** $\text{Pos}(\xi|D) = 1$ és $\text{Nes}(\xi|D) = 1 - w$.

## 1.11 A law of large numbers for fuzzy numbers

Following Fullér [127, 132] we study the problem:

If $\xi_1, \xi_2, \ldots$ are fuzzy numbers with modal values $M_1, M_2, \ldots$, then what is the strongest $t$-norm for which

$$\lim_{n\to\infty} \text{Nes}\left(m_n - \epsilon \leq \frac{\xi_1 + \cdots + \xi_n}{n} \leq m_n + \epsilon\right) = 1,$$

for any $\epsilon > 0$, where

$$m_n = \frac{M_1 + \cdots + M_n}{n},$$

the arithmetic mean

$$\frac{\xi_1 + \cdots + \xi_n}{n}$$

is defined via sup-$t$-norm convolution and Nes denotes necessity. Given two fuzzy numbers, $\xi$ and $\eta$, their $T$-sum $\xi + \eta$ is defined by

$$(\xi + \eta)(z) = \sup_{x+y=z} T(\xi(x), \eta(y)), \; x, y, z \in \mathbb{R}$$

where $T$ t-norm. The function $H_0 : [0,1] \times [0,1] \to [0,1]$, defined by

$$H_0(u,v) = \frac{uv}{u + v - uv},$$

is called Hamacher-norm with parameter zero ($H_0$-norm for short) [157].

Let $T_1$, $T_2$ be t-norms. We say that $T_1$ is weaker than $T_2$ (and write $T_1 \leq T_2$) if $T_1(x,y) \leq T_2(x,y)$ for each $x, y \in [0,1]$. We shall provide a fuzzy analogue of Chebyshev's theorem [63].

**Theorem 1.11.1** *(Chebyshev's theorem.) If $\xi_1$, $\xi_2$,... is a sequence of pairwise independent random variables having finite variances bounded by the same constant*

$$D\xi_1 \leq C, \; D\xi_2 \leq C, \ldots, D\xi_n \leq C, \ldots$$

*and*

$$M = \lim_{n\to\infty} \frac{M_1 + \cdots + M_n}{n}$$

*exists, then for any positive constant* $\epsilon$

$$\lim_{n\to\infty} \text{Prob}\left(\left|\frac{\xi_1+\cdots+\xi_n}{n} - \frac{M_1+\cdots+M_n}{n}\right| < \epsilon\right) = 1$$

*where* $M_n = M\xi_n$ *and Prob denotes probability.*

In this section we shall prove that if $\xi_1 = (M_1, \alpha)$, $\xi_2 = (M_2, \alpha)$ ... is a sequence of symmetric triangular fuzzy numbers and $T$ is a t-norm (by which the sequence of arithmetic means

$$\left\{\frac{\xi_1+\cdots+\xi_n}{n}\right\},$$

is defined) then the relation

$$\lim_{n\to\infty} \text{Nes}\left(m_n - \epsilon \le \frac{\xi_1+\cdots+\xi_n}{n} \le m_n + \epsilon\right) = 1, \text{ for any } \epsilon > 0 \qquad (1.25)$$

holds for any $T \le H_0$; and the relation (1.25) is not valid for the "min"-norm.

**Definition 1.11.1** *Let* $T$ *be a t-norm and let* $\xi$, $\xi_2$, ... *be a sequence of fuzzy numbers. We shall say that the sequence* $\{\xi_n\}$ *obeys the law of large numbers if it satisfies the relation (1.25).*

**Lemma 1.11.1** *Let* $\xi$ *and* $\eta$ *be fuzzy sets of* $\mathbb{R}$. *If* $\xi \subseteq \eta$ *(i.e.* $\xi(x) \le \eta(x)$, *for each* $x \in \mathbb{R}$*) then*

$$\text{Nes}(\xi = x) \ge \text{Nes}(\eta = x), \textit{ for each } x \in \mathbb{R}.$$

*Proof.* From the definition of necessity we have

$$\begin{aligned}\text{Nes}(\xi = x) &= 1 - \text{Pos}(\xi|\mathbb{R} \setminus \{x\}) \\ &= 1 - \sup_{t\ne x} \xi(t) \ge 1 - \sup_{t \ne x} \eta(t) = \text{Nes}(\eta = x).\end{aligned}$$

Which ends the proof.

The proof of the next two lemmas follows from the definition of t-sum of fuzzy numbers.

**Lemma 1.11.2** *Let* $T_1$ *and* $T_2$ *be t-norms and let* $\xi_1$ *and* $\xi_2$ *be fuzzy numbers. If* $T_1 \le T_2$ *then*

$$(\xi_1 + \xi_2)_1 \subseteq (\xi_1 + \xi_2)_2$$

*where* $(\xi_1 + \xi_2)_i$ *denotes the* $T_i$*-sum of fuzzy numbers* $\xi_1$ *and* $\xi_2$, $i = 1, 2$.

**Lemma 1.11.3** *Let $T = H_0$ and $\xi_i = (a_i, \alpha)$, $i = 1, 2, \dots, n$. Then with the notations*

$$\eta_n = \xi_1 + \cdots + \xi_n, \quad A_n = a_1 + \cdots + a_n$$

*we have*

$$\text{(i)}\ \eta_n(z) = \begin{cases} \dfrac{1 - |A_n - z|(n\alpha)^{-1}}{1 + (n-1)|A_n - z|(n\alpha)^{-1}} & \textit{if } |A_n - z| \le n\alpha, \\ 0 & \textit{otherwise,} \end{cases}$$

$$\text{(ii)}\ \left(\frac{\eta_n}{n}\right)(z) = \begin{cases} \dfrac{1 - |A_n/n - z|\alpha^{-1}}{1 + (n-1)|A_n/n - z|\alpha^{-1}} & \textit{if } |A_n/n - z| \le \alpha, \\ 0 & \textit{otherwise,} \end{cases}$$

*Proof.* We prove (i) by making an induction argument on $n$. Let $n = 2$. Then we need to determine the value of $\eta_2(z)$ from the following relationship:

$$\eta_2(z) = \sup_{x+y=z} \frac{\xi_1(x)\xi_2(y)}{\xi_1(x) + \xi_2(y) - \xi_1(x)\xi_2(y)} = \sup_{x+y=z} \frac{1}{\dfrac{1}{\xi_1(x)} + \dfrac{1}{\xi_2(y)} - 1},$$

if $z \in (a_1 + a_2 - 2\alpha, a_1 + a_2 + 2\alpha)$ and $\eta_2(z) = 0$ otherwise.

According to the decomposition rule of fuzzy numbers into two separate parts, $\eta_2(z)$, $z \in (a_1 + a_2 - 2\alpha, a_1 + a_2]$, is equal to the value of the following mathematical programming problem

$$\frac{1}{\dfrac{1}{1 - \dfrac{a_1 - x}{\alpha}} + \dfrac{1}{1 - \dfrac{a_2 - z + x}{\alpha}} - 1} \to \max \tag{1.26}$$

$$\text{subject to } a_1 - \alpha < x \le a_1,$$

$$a_2 - \alpha < z - x \le a_2.$$

Using Lagrange's multipliers method for the solution of the problem (1.26) we get that its value is

$$\frac{1 - \dfrac{a_1 + a_2 - z}{2\alpha}}{1 + \dfrac{a_1 + a_2 - z}{2\alpha}} = \frac{1 - \dfrac{A_2 - z}{2\alpha}}{1 + \dfrac{A_2 - z}{2\alpha}}$$

and the solution of (1.26) is

$$x = \frac{a_1 - a_2 + z}{2}$$

(where the first derivative vanishes). If $a_1 + a_2 \le z < a_1 + a_2 + 2\alpha$ then we need to solve the following problem

$$\frac{1}{\dfrac{1}{1-\dfrac{x-a_1}{\alpha}}+\dfrac{1}{1-\dfrac{z-x-a_2}{\alpha}}-1} \longrightarrow \max \tag{1.27}$$

$$\text{subject to } a_1 < x < a_1 + \alpha,$$
$$a_2 < z - x < a_2 + \alpha.$$

In a similar manner we get that the value of (1.27) is

$$\frac{1-\dfrac{z-A_2}{2\alpha}}{1+\dfrac{z-A_2}{2\alpha}}$$

and the solution of (1.27) is

$$x = \frac{a_1 - a_2 + z}{2}$$

(where the first derivative vanishes). Let us assume that (i) holds for some $n \in \mathbb{N}$. Then,

$$\eta_{n+1}(z) = (\eta_n + \xi_{n+1})(z), \; z \in \mathbb{R},$$

and by similar arguments it can be shown that (i) holds for $\eta_{n+1}$. The statement (ii) can be proved directly using the relationship $(\eta_n/n)(z) = \eta_n(nz)$, $z \in \mathbb{R}$. This ends the proof.

The theorem in question can be stated as follows:

**Theorem 1.11.2** *(Law of large numbers for fuzzy numbers, [132]) Let $T \le H_0$ and let $\xi_i = (M_i, \alpha)$, $i \in \mathbb{N}$ be fuzzy numbers. If*

$$M = \lim_{n\to\infty} \frac{M_1 + \cdots + M_n}{n}$$

*exists, then for any $\epsilon > 0$,*

$$\lim_{n\to\infty} \operatorname{Nes}\left( m_n - \epsilon \le \frac{\xi_1 + \cdots + \xi_n}{n} \le m_n + \epsilon \right) = 1, \tag{1.28}$$

*where*

$$m_n = \frac{M_1 + \cdots + M_n}{n}.$$

*Proof.* If $\epsilon \geq \alpha$ then we get (1.28) trivially. Let $\epsilon < \alpha$, then from Lemma 1.11.1 and Lemma 1.11.2 it follows that we need to prove (1.28) only for $T = H_0$. Using Lemma 1.11.3 we get

$$\text{Nes}\left(m_n - \epsilon \leq \frac{\eta_n}{n} \leq m_n + \epsilon\right)$$

$$= 1 - \text{Pos}\left(\frac{\eta_n}{n} |(-\infty, m_n - \epsilon) \cup (m_n + \epsilon, \infty)|\right)$$

$$= - \sup_{x \notin [m_n - \epsilon, m_n + \epsilon]} \left(\frac{\eta_n}{n}\right)(x)$$

$$= 1 - \frac{1 - |m_n - (m_n + \epsilon)|/\alpha}{1 + (n-1)|m_n - (m_n \pm \epsilon)|/\alpha}$$

$$= 1 - \frac{1 - \epsilon/\alpha}{1 + (n-1)\epsilon/\alpha},$$

and, consequently,

$$\lim_{n \to \infty} \text{Nes}\left(m_n - \epsilon \leq \frac{\eta_n}{n} \leq m_n + \epsilon\right) = 1 - \lim_{n \to \infty} \frac{1 - \epsilon/\alpha}{1 + (n-1)\epsilon/\alpha} = 1.$$

Which ends the proof.

Theorem 1.11.2 can be interpreted as a law of large numbers for mutually T-related fuzzy variables. Strong laws of large numbers for fuzzy random variables were proved in [228, 256]. Especially, if $T(u, v) = H_1(u, v) = uv$ then we get [121]

$$\lim_{n \to \infty} \text{Nes}\left(m_n - \epsilon \leq \frac{\xi_1 + \cdots + \xi_n}{n} \leq m_n + \epsilon\right) = 1 - \frac{\eta_n}{n}(m_n - \epsilon)$$

$$= 1 - \lim_{n \to \infty} \left(1 - \frac{\epsilon}{\alpha}\right)^n = 1.$$

The following theorem shows that if $T =$ "min" then the sequence $\xi_1 = (M_i, \alpha)$, $\xi_2 = (M_2, \alpha)$ ... does not obey the law of large numbers for fuzzy numbers.

**Theorem 1.11.3** *Let* $T(u, v) = \min\{u, v\}$ *and* $\xi_i = (M_i, \alpha)$, $i \in \mathbb{N}$. *Then for any positive* $\epsilon$, *such that* $\epsilon < \alpha$ *we have*

$$\lim_{n \to \infty} \text{Nes}\left(m_n - \epsilon \leq \frac{\xi_1 + \cdots + \xi_n}{n} \leq m_n + \epsilon\right) = \frac{\epsilon}{\alpha}.$$

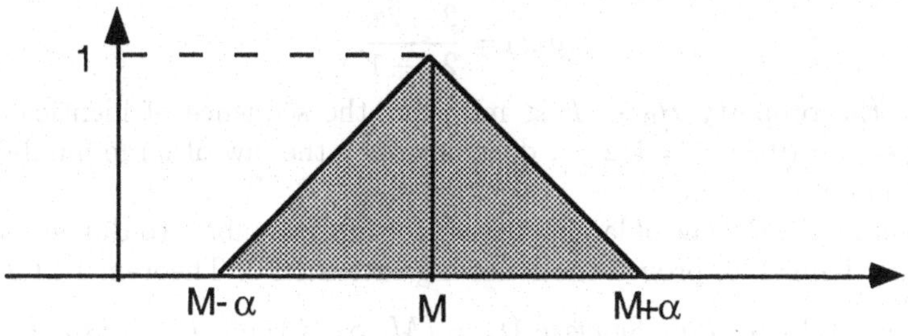


**Fig. 1.18.** The limit distribution of $\eta_n/n$ if $T$ ="min"

$$\text{Nes}\left(\lim_{n\to\infty}\frac{\eta_n}{n}=M\right)=0.$$

*Proof.* The proof of this theorem follows from the equalities $\eta_n/n=(m_n,\alpha)$, $n\in\mathbb{N}$ and

$$\lim_{n\to\infty}\frac{\eta_n}{n}=(M,\alpha).$$

From the addition rule of LR-type fuzzy numbers via sup-min convolution it follows that Theorem 1.11.2 remains valid for any sequence $\xi_1=(M_1,\alpha)_{LL}$, $\xi_2=(M_2,\alpha)_{LL}$, ..., of $LL$-type fuzzy numbers with continuous shape function $L$.

The results presented in this Section have been extended and improved by Triesch [297], Hong [173], Hong and Kim [176], and Jang and Kwon [188].

Namely, in 1993 Triesch [297] showed that the class of Archimedean t-norms can be characterised by the validity of a very general law of large numbers for sequences of $LR$ fuzzy numbers. The theorem in question is stated as follows:

**Theorem 1.11.4** *[297] Suppose that $T$ is a continuous t-norm. Then $T$ is Archimedean if and only if all sequences of fuzzy numbers $\xi_1=(M_1,\alpha_1,\beta_1)_{LR}$, $\xi_2=(M_2,\alpha_2,\beta_2)_{LR}$, ..., such that $\alpha_n\le C$ and $\beta_n\le C$ for all $n$ and some constant $C$ obey the law of large numbers with respect to $T$.*

In 1994 Hong [173] answered the following question stated in [132]

> Let $T$ be a t-norm such that $H_0<T<\min$ and let $\xi_1=(M_1,\alpha)$, $\xi_2=(M_2,\alpha)$ ..., be a sequence of symmetric triangular fuzzy numbers. Does this sequence obey the law of large numbers?

and showed that the t-norm defined by

$$T(u,v)=\begin{cases} g^{-1}(g(u)+g(v)) & \text{if } u,v\in(1/2,1]\\ \min\{u,v\} & \text{otherwise,}\end{cases}$$

where

$$g(x) = \frac{2-2x}{2x-1},$$

satisfies the property $H_0 < T < \min$, but the sequence of identical fuzzy numbers $\xi_i = (0,1)$, $i = 1, 2, \dots$ does not obey the law of large numbers for fuzzy numbers.

Generalizing the law of large numbers for fuzzy numbers to Banach spaces, Hong and Kim [176] proved the following extension of Theorem 1.11.2.

**Theorem 1.11.5** *[176] Suppose $\{\xi_i = (M_i, \alpha_i, \beta_i)_{LR}\}$, $i \in \mathbb{N}$ is a sequence of LR-fuzzy numbers with left and right spreads $\alpha_i$ and $\beta_i$, respectively, such that $\alpha_i \le C$ and $\beta_i \le C$ for all $i$ and some constant $C$. Suppose further that $T$ is an Archimedean t-norm. Then for any $\epsilon > 0$*

$$\lim_{n\to\infty} \mathrm{Nes}\left(m_n - \epsilon \le \frac{\xi_1 + \cdots + \xi_n}{n} \le m_n + \epsilon\right) = 1.$$

*Moreover, if $M = \lim_{n\to\infty} m_n$ exists and is finite, then*

$$\lim_{n\to\infty} \mathrm{Nes}\left(M - \epsilon \le \frac{\xi_1 + \cdots + \xi_n}{n} \le M + \epsilon\right) = 1.$$

## 1.12 Metrics for fuzzy numbers

Let $A$ and $B$ be fuzzy numbers with $[A]^\alpha = [a_1(\alpha), a_2(\alpha)]$ and $[B]^\alpha = [b_1(\alpha), b_2(\alpha)]$. We metricize the set of fuzzy numbers by the following metrics

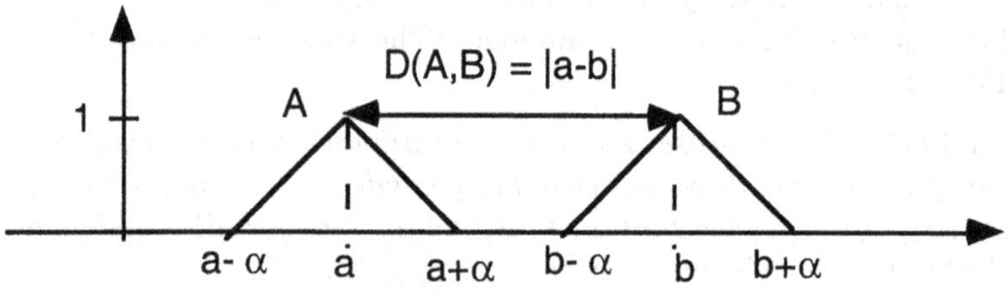


**Fig. 1.19.** Hausdorff distance between $A = (a, \alpha)$ and $B = (b, \alpha)$.

- **Hausdorff distance**

$$D(A,B) = \sup_{\alpha\in[0,1]} \max\{|a_1(\alpha) - b_1(\alpha)|, |a_2(\alpha) - b_2(\alpha)|\}.$$

i.e. $D(A,B)$ is the maximal distance between the $\alpha$-level sets of $A$ and $B$. For example, if $A = (a, \alpha)$ and $B = (b, \alpha)$ are fuzzy numbers of symmetric triangular form with the same width $\alpha > 0$ then

$$D(A,B) = |a - b|,$$

and if $A = (a, \alpha)$ and $B = (b, \beta)$ then

$$D(A,B) = |a - b| + |\alpha - \beta|.$$

- $C_\infty$ **distance**

$$C_\infty(A,B) = \sup\{|A(u) - B(u)| \, : \, u \in \mathbb{R}\}.$$

i.e. $C_\infty(A,B)$ is the maximal distance between the membership grades of $A$ and $B$. The following statement holds $0 \le C_\infty(A,B) \le 1$.
- **Hamming distance** Suppose $A$ and $B$ are fuzzy sets in $X$. Then their Hamming distance, denoted by $H(A,B)$, is defined by

$$H(A,B) = \int_X |A(x) - B(x)| \, dx.$$

- **Discrete Hamming distance** Suppose $A$ and $B$ are discrete fuzzy sets in $X = \{x_1, \dots, x_n\}$ defined by

$$A = \mu_1/x_1 + \cdots + \mu_n/x_n,$$

$$B = \nu_1/x_1 + \cdots + \nu_n/x_n.$$

Then their Hamming distance is defined by

$$H(A,B) = \sum_{j=1}^{n} |\mu_j - \nu_j|.$$

It should be noted that $D(A,B)$ is a better measure of *similarity* than $C_\infty(A,B)$, because $C_\infty(A,B) \le 1$ holds even though the supports of $A$ and $B$ are very far from each other.

We will use the following inequality relations between fuzzy numbers $[A]^\gamma = [a_1(\gamma), a_2(\gamma)]$ and $[B]^\gamma = [b_1(\gamma), b_2(\gamma)]$

$$A \le B \iff \max\{A, B\} = B \tag{1.29}$$

that is,

$$A \le B \iff a_1(\gamma) \le b_2(\gamma) \text{ and } a_2(\gamma) \le b_2(\gamma),$$

for all $\gamma \in [0,1]$, and [152],

$$A \le B \iff \mathcal{W}(A) = \int_0^1 \gamma(a_1(\gamma) + a_2(\gamma))d\gamma$$

$$\le \mathcal{W}(B) = \int_0^1 \gamma(b_1(\gamma) + b_2(\gamma))d\gamma \tag{1.30}$$

Equation (1.29) is derived directly from Zadeh' extension principle, and (1.30) compares fuzzy numbers based on their weighted center of gravity, where the weights are the membership degres.

## 1.13 Possibilistic mean value and variance of fuzzy numbers

In 1987 Dubois and Prade [90] defined an interval-valued expectation of fuzzy numbers, viewing them as consonant random sets. They also showed that this expectation remains additive in the sense of addition of fuzzy numbers.

Following Carlsson and Fullér [59] introducing the notations of *lower possibilistic* and *upper possibilistic* mean values we define the *interval-valued possibilistic mean, crisp possibilistic mean value* and *crisp (possibilistic) variance* of a continuous possibility distribution, which are consistent with the extension principle and with the well-known defintions of expectation and variance in probability theory. The theory developed in [59] is fully motivated by the principles introduced in [90] and by the possibilistic interpretation of the ordering introduced in [152].

Let $A$ and $B \in \mathcal{F}$ be fuzzy numbers with $[A]^\gamma = [a_1(\gamma), a_2(\gamma)]$ and $[B]^\gamma = [b_1(\gamma), b_2(\gamma)]$, $\gamma \in [0,1]$. In 1986 Goetschel and Voxman introduced a method for ranking fuzzy numbers as [152]

$$A \leq B \iff \int_0^1 \gamma(a_1(\gamma) + a_2(\gamma))\, d\gamma \leq \int_0^1 \gamma(b_1(\gamma) + b_2(\gamma))\, d\gamma \tag{1.31}$$

As was pointed out by Goetschel and Voxman this definition of ordering given in (1.31) was motivated in part by the desire to give less importance to the lower levels of fuzzy numbers.

We explain now the way of thinking that has led us to the introduction of notations of lower and upper possibilitistic mean values. First, we note that from the equality

$$\bar{M}(A) := \int_0^1 \gamma(a_1(\gamma) + a_2(\gamma)) d\gamma = \frac{\displaystyle\int_0^1 \gamma \cdot \frac{a_1(\gamma) + a_2(\gamma)}{2}\, d\gamma}{\displaystyle\int_0^1 \gamma\, d\gamma}, \tag{1.32}$$

it follows that $\bar{M}(A)$ is nothing else but the level-weighted average of the arithmetic means of all $\gamma$-level sets, that is, the weight of the arithmetic mean of $a_1(\gamma)$ and $a_2(\gamma)$ is just $\gamma$.

Second, we can rewrite $\bar{M}(A)$ as

$$\bar{M}(A) = \int_0^1 \gamma(a_1(\gamma) + a_2(\gamma))d\gamma$$

$$= \frac{2 \cdot \int_0^1 \gamma a_1(\gamma)d\gamma + 2 \cdot \int_0^1 \gamma a_2(\gamma)d\gamma}{2}$$

$$= \frac{1}{2}\left( \frac{\int_0^1 \gamma a_1(\gamma)d\gamma}{\frac{1}{2}} + \frac{\int_0^1 \gamma a_2(\gamma)d\gamma}{\frac{1}{2}} \right)$$

$$= \frac{1}{2}\left( \frac{\int_0^1 \gamma a_1(\gamma)d\gamma}{\int_0^1 \gamma d\gamma} + \frac{\int_0^1 \gamma a_2(\gamma)d\gamma}{\int_0^1 \gamma d\gamma} \right).$$

Third, let us take a closer look at the right-hand side of the equation for $\bar{M}(A)$. The first quantity, denoted by $M_*(A)$ can be reformulated as

$$M_*(A) = 2\int_0^1 \gamma a_1(\gamma)d\gamma = \frac{\int_0^1 \gamma a_1(\gamma)d\gamma}{\int_0^1 \gamma d\gamma}$$

$$= \frac{\int_0^1 \text{Pos}[A \le a_1(\gamma)]a_1(\gamma)d\gamma}{\int_0^1 \text{Pos}[A \le a_1(\gamma)]d\gamma}$$

$$= \frac{\int_0^1 \text{Pos}[A \le a_1(\gamma)] \times \min[A]^\gamma d\gamma}{\int_0^1 \text{Pos}[A \le a_1(\gamma)]d\gamma},$$

where Pos denotes possibility, i.e.

$$\text{Pos}[A \le a_1(\gamma)] = \Pi(-\infty, a_1(\gamma)) = \sup_{u \le a_1(\gamma)} A(u) = \gamma.$$

(since $A$ is continuous!) So $M_*(A)$ is nothing else but the lower possibility-weighted average of the minima of the $\gamma$-sets, and it is why we call it the lower possibilistic mean value of $A$.

In a similar manner we introduce $M^*(A)$ , the upper possibilistic mean value of $A$, as

$$M^*(A) = 2\int_0^1 \gamma a_2(\gamma)d\gamma = \frac{\int_0^1 \gamma a_2(\gamma)d\gamma}{\int_0^1 \gamma d\gamma}$$

$$= \frac{\int_0^1 \text{Pos}[A \geq a_2(\gamma)]a_2(\gamma)d\gamma}{\int_0^1 \text{Pos}[A \geq a_2(\gamma)]d\gamma}$$

$$= \frac{\int_0^1 \text{Pos}[A \geq a_2(\gamma)] \times \max[A]^\gamma d\gamma}{\int_0^1 \text{Pos}[A \leq a_2(\gamma)]d\gamma},$$

where we have used the equality

$$\text{Pos}[A \geq a_2(\gamma)] = \Pi(a_2(\gamma), \infty) = \sup_{u \geq a_2(\gamma)} A(u) = \gamma.$$

Let us introduce the notation

$$M(A) = [M_*(A), M^*(A)].$$

that is, $M(A)$ is a closed interval bounded by the lower and upper possibilistic mean values of $A$.

**Definition 1.13.1** *[59] We call $M(A)$ the interval-valued possibilistic mean of $A$.*

If $A$ is the characteristic function of the crisp interval $[a, b]$ then

$$M((a, b, 0, 0)) = [a, b],$$

that is, an interval is the possibilistic mean value of itself. We will now show that $M$ is a linear function on $\mathcal{F}$ in the sense of the extension principle.

**Theorem 1.13.1** *[59] Let $A$ and $B$ be two non-interactive fuzzy numbers and let $\lambda \in \mathbb{R}$ be a real number. Then*

$$M(A + B) = M(A) + M(B) \text{ and } M(\lambda A) = \lambda M(A),$$

*where the addition and multiplication by a scalar of fuzzy numbers is defined by the sup-min extension principle [332].*

The *crisp possibilistic mean value* of $A$ can be defined by (1.32) as the arithemtic mean of its lower possibilistic and upper possibilistic mean values, i.e.

$$\bar{M}(A) = \frac{M_*(A) + M^*(A)}{2}.$$

The following theorem [59] shows two very important properties of $\bar{M}\colon \mathcal{F} \to \mathbb{R}$.

**Theorem 1.13.2** *Let $[A]^\gamma = [a_1(\gamma), a_2(\gamma)]$ and $[B]^\gamma = [b_1(\gamma), b_2(\gamma)]$ be fuzzy numbers and let $\lambda \in \mathbb{R}$ be a real number. Then*

$$\bar{M}(A + B) = \bar{M}(A) + \bar{M}(B),$$

*and*

$$\bar{M}(\lambda A) = \lambda \bar{M}(A).$$

**Example 1.13.1** *Let $A = (a, \alpha, \beta)$ be a triangular fuzzy number with center $a$, left-width $\alpha > 0$ and right-width $\beta > 0$ then a $\gamma$-level of $A$ is computed by*

$$[A]^\gamma = [a - (1-\gamma)\alpha, a + (1-\gamma)\beta], \ \forall \gamma \in [0, 1],$$

*that is,*

$$M_*(A) = 2\int_0^1 \gamma[a - (1-\gamma)\alpha d\gamma = a - \frac{\alpha}{3},$$

$$M^*(A) = 2\int_0^1 \gamma[a + (1-\gamma)\beta]d\gamma = a + \frac{\beta}{3},$$

*and therefore,*

$$M(A) = \left[a - \frac{\alpha}{3}, a + \frac{\beta}{3}\right],$$

*and, finally,*

$$\bar{M}(A) = \int_0^1 \gamma[a - (1-\gamma)\alpha + a + (1-\gamma)\beta]d\gamma = a + \frac{\beta - \alpha}{6}.$$

*Specially, when $A = (a, \alpha)$ is a symmetric triangular fuzzy number we get $\bar{M}(A) = a$. If $A$ is a symmetric fuzzy number with peak $[q_-, q_+]$ then the equation*

$$\bar{M}(A) = \frac{q_- + q_+}{2}.$$

*always holds.*

We show now the relationship between the interval-valued expectation

$$E(A) = [E_*(A), E^*(A)],$$

introduced in [90] and the interval-valued possibilistic mean

$$M(A) = [M_*(A), M^*(A)]$$

for LR-fuzzy numbers with strictly decreasing shape functions.

An LR-type fuzzy number $A \in \mathcal{F}$ can be described with the following membership function [85]

$$A(u) = \begin{cases} L\left(\dfrac{q_- - u}{\alpha}\right) & \text{if } q_- - \alpha \le u \le q_- \\ 1 & \text{if } u \in [q_-, q_+] \\ R\left(\dfrac{u - q_+}{\beta}\right) & \text{if } q_+ \le u \le q_+ + \beta \\ 0 & \text{otherwise} \end{cases}$$

where $[q_-, q_+]$ is the peak of $A$; $q_-$ and $q_+$ are the lower and upper modal values; $L, R\colon [0,1] \to [0,1]$, with $L(0) = R(0) = 1$ and $L(1) = R(1) = 0$ are non-increasing, continuous mappings. We shall use the notation $A = (q_-, q_+, \alpha, \beta)_{LR}$. The closure of the support of $A$ is exactly $[q_- - \alpha, q_+ + \beta]$.

If $L$ and $R$ are strictly decreasing functions then we can easily compute the $\gamma$-level sets of $A$. That is,

$$[A]^\gamma = [q_- - \alpha L^{-1}(\gamma), q_+ + \beta R^{-1}(\gamma)],\ \gamma \in [0,1].$$

Following [90] (page 293) the lower and upper probability mean values of $A \in \mathcal{F}$ are computed by

$$E_*(A) = q_- - \alpha \int_0^1 L(u)du, \quad E^*(A) = q_+ + \beta \int_0^1 R(u)du,$$

(note that the support of $A$ is bounded) and the lower and upper possibilistic mean values are obtained as

$$M_*(A) = 2\int_0^1 \gamma(q_- - \alpha L^{-1}(\gamma))d\gamma = q_- - \alpha \int_0^1 \gamma L^{-1}(\gamma)d\gamma$$

$$M^*(A) = 2\int_0^1 \gamma(q_+ + \beta R^{-1}(\gamma))d\gamma = q_+ + \beta \int_0^1 \gamma R^{-1}(\gamma)d\gamma$$

Therefore, we can state the following lemma.

**Lemma 1.13.1** *If $A \in \mathcal{F}$ is a fuzzy number of LR-type with strictly decreasing (and continuous) shape functions then its interval-valued possibilistic mean is a proper subset of its interval-valued probabilistic mean,*

$$M(A) \subset E(A).$$

Lemma 1.13.1 reflects on the fact that points with small membership degrees are considered to be less important in the definition of lower and upper possibilistic mean values than in the definition of probabilistic ones. In the limit case, when $A = (q_-, q_+, 0, 0)$, the possibilistic and probablistic mean values are equal, and the equality

$$E(A) = M(A) = [q_-, q_+]$$

holds.

**Example 1.13.2** *Let $A = (a, \alpha, \beta)$ be a triangular fuzzy number with center $a$, left-width $\alpha > 0$ and right-width $\beta > 0$ then*

$$M(A) = \left[a - \frac{\alpha}{3}, a + \frac{\beta}{3}\right] \subset E(A) = \left[a - \frac{\alpha}{2}, a + \frac{\beta}{2}\right]$$

*and*

$$\bar{M}(A) = a + \frac{\beta - \alpha}{6} \neq \bar{E}(A) = \frac{E_*(A) + E^*(A)}{2} = a + \frac{\beta - \alpha}{4}.$$

*However, when $A$ is a symmetric fuzzy number then the equation*

$$\bar{M}(A) = \bar{E}(A).$$

*always holds.*

We introduce the (possibilistic) variance of $A \in \mathcal{F}$ as

$$\begin{aligned}\mathrm{Var}(A) = &\int_0^1 \mathrm{Pos}[A \leq a_1(\gamma)] \left(\left[\frac{a_1(\gamma) + a_2(\gamma)}{2} - a_1(\gamma)\right]^2\right) d\gamma \\ &+ \int_0^1 \mathrm{Pos}[A \geq a_2(\gamma)] \left(\left[\frac{a_1(\gamma) + a_2(\gamma)}{2} - a_2(\gamma)\right]^2\right) d\gamma \\ &= \frac{1}{2}\int_0^1 \gamma\big(a_2(\gamma) - a_1(\gamma)\big)^2 d\gamma.\end{aligned}$$

The variance of $A$ is defined as the expected value of the squared deviations between the arithmetic mean and the endpoints of its level sets, i.e. the lower possibility-weighted average of the squared distance between the left-hand endpoint and the arithmetic mean of the endpoints of its level sets plus the upper possibility-weighted average of the squared distance between the right-hand endpoint and the arithmetic mean of the endpoints their of its level sets.

*Note 1.13.1.* From a probabilistic viewpoint, the possibilistic mean and variance of a fuzzy number $A$ can be viewed as the expected values, when the level gamma is treated as a random variable having a beta distribution Beta(2,1) (for which the higher the level, the higher its weight or density), of the conditional mean value and variance given gamma, respectively, of the random variable taking on values $a_1(\gamma)$ and $a_2(\gamma)$ with probabilities 0.5. This could be an additional argument for the "coherence" between the definitions of $E(A)$ and $Var(A)$ introduced in [59].

The standard deviation of $A$ is defined by

$$\sigma_A = \sqrt{\mathrm{Var}(A)}.$$

**Example 1.13.3** *If $A = (a, \alpha, \beta)$ is a triangular fuzzy number then*

$$\begin{aligned}\mathrm{Var}(A) &= \frac{1}{2}\int_0^1 \gamma\big(a + \beta(1-\gamma) - (a - \alpha(1-\gamma))\big)^2 d\gamma \\ &= \frac{(\alpha+\beta)^2}{24}.\end{aligned}$$

*especially, if $A = (a, \alpha)$ is a symmetric triangular fuzzy number then*

$$\mathrm{Var}(A) = \frac{\alpha^2}{6}.$$

*In the limit case, when $A = (a, 0)$ is a fuzzy point, i.e.*

$$a_1(\gamma) = a_2(\gamma) = a = \text{const.}, \forall \gamma$$

*we get*

$$\mathrm{Var}(A) = 0.$$

If $A$ is the characteristic function of the crisp interval $[a, b]$ then

$$\mathrm{Var}(A) = \frac{1}{2}\int_0^1 \gamma(b-a)^2 d\gamma = \left(\frac{b-a}{2}\right)^2$$

that is,

$$\sigma_A = \frac{b-a}{2}, \quad \bar{M}(A) = \frac{a+b}{2}.$$

In probability theory, the corresponding result is: if the two possible outcomes of a probabilistic variable have equal probabilities then the expected value is their arithmetic mean and the standard deviation is the half of their distance.

We show now that the variance of a fuzzy number is invariant to shifting. Let $A \in \mathcal{F}$ and let $\theta$ be a real number. If $A$ is shifted by value $\theta$ then we get a fuzzy number, denoted by $B$, satisfying the property $B(x) = A(x - \theta)$ for all $x \in \mathbb{R}$. Then from the relationship

$$[B]^\gamma = [a_1(\gamma) + \theta, a_2(\gamma) + \theta]$$

we find

$$\begin{aligned}\mathrm{Var}(B) &= \frac{1}{2}\int_0^1 \gamma\big((a_2(\gamma) + \theta) - (a_1(\gamma) + \theta)\big)^2 d\gamma \\ &= \frac{1}{2}\int_0^1 \gamma\big(a_2(\gamma) - a_1(\gamma)\big)^2 d\gamma = \mathrm{Var}(A).\end{aligned}$$

The covariance between fuzzy numbers $A$ and $B$ is defined as

$$\text{Cov}(A, B) = \frac{1}{2}\int_0^1 \gamma(a_2(\gamma) - a_1(\gamma))(b_2(\gamma) - b_1(\gamma))d\gamma.$$

Let $A = (a, \alpha)$ and $B = (b, \beta)$ be symmetric trianglar fuzzy numbers. Then

$$\text{Cov}(A, B) = \frac{\alpha\beta}{6}.$$

The following theorem [59] shows that the variance of linear combinations of fuzzy numbers can easily be computed (in the same manner as in probability theory).

**Theorem 1.13.3** *Let $\lambda, \mu \in \mathbb{R}$ and let $A$ and $B$ be fuzzy numbers. Then*

$$\text{Var}(\lambda A + \mu B) = \lambda^2\text{Var}(A) + \mu^2\text{Var}(B) + 2|\lambda\mu|\text{Cov}(A, B)$$

*where the addition and multiplication by a scalar of fuzzy numbers is defined by the sup-min extension principle.*

As a special case of Theorem 1.13.3 we get $\text{Var}(\lambda A) = \lambda^2\text{Var}(A)$ for any $\lambda \in \mathbb{R}$ and

$$\text{Var}(A + B) = \text{Var}(A) + \text{Var}(B) + 2\text{Cov}(A, B).$$

Let $A = (a, \alpha)$ and $B = (b, \beta)$ be symmetric triangular fuzzy numbers and $\lambda$ $\mu$ be real numbers. Then

$$\text{Var}(\lambda A + \mu B) = \lambda^2\frac{\alpha^2}{6} + \mu^2\frac{\beta^2}{6} + 2|\lambda\mu|\frac{\alpha\beta}{6} = \frac{(|\lambda|\alpha + |\mu|\beta)^2}{6},$$

which coincides with the variance of the symmetric triangular fuzzy number

$$\lambda A + \mu B = (\lambda a + \mu b, |\lambda|\alpha + |\mu|\beta).$$

Another important question is the relationship between the subsethood and the variance of fuzzy numbers. One might expect that $A \subset B$ (that is $A(x) \leq B(x)$ for all $x \in \mathbb{R}$) should imply the relationship $\text{Var}(A) \leq \text{Var}(B)$ because $A$ is considered a "stronger restriction" than $B$. The following theorem [59] shows that subsethood does entail smaller variance.

**Theorem 1.13.4** *Let $A, B \in \mathcal{F}$ with $A \subset B$. Then* $\text{Var}(A) \leq \text{Var}(B)$.

## 1.14 Auxiliary lemmas

The following lemmas build up connections between $C_\infty$ and $D$ distances of fuzzy numbers.

**Lemma 1.14.1** *[203]. Let $\tilde{a}$, $\tilde{b}$, $\tilde{c}$ and $\tilde{d}$ be fuzzy numbers. Then*

$$D(\tilde{a}+\tilde{c},\tilde{b}+\tilde{d}) \leq D(\tilde{a},\tilde{b}) + D(\tilde{c},\tilde{d}),$$

$$D(\tilde{a}-\tilde{c},\tilde{b}-\tilde{d}) \leq D(\tilde{a},\tilde{b}) + D(\tilde{c},\tilde{d})$$

*and $D(\lambda\tilde{a},\lambda\tilde{b}) = |\lambda| D(\tilde{a},\tilde{b})$ for any $\lambda \in \mathbb{R}$.*

Let $\tilde{a} \in \mathcal{F}$ be a fuzzy number. Then for any $\theta \geq 0$ we define $\omega(\tilde{a},\theta)$, the modulus of continuity of $\tilde{a}$ as

$$\omega(\tilde{a},\theta) = \max_{|u-v|\leq\theta} |\tilde{a}(u) - \tilde{a}(v)|.$$

The following statements hold [161]:

$$\text{If } 0 \leq \theta \leq \theta' \text{ then } \omega(\tilde{a},\theta) \leq \omega(\tilde{a},\theta') \tag{1.33}$$

$$\text{If } \alpha > 0, \beta > 0, \text{ then } \omega(\tilde{a},\alpha+\beta) \leq \omega(\tilde{a},\alpha) + \omega(\tilde{a},\beta). \tag{1.34}$$

$$\lim_{\theta\to 0} \omega(\tilde{a},\theta) = 0 \tag{1.35}$$

Recall, if $\tilde{a}$ and $\tilde{b}$ are fuzzy numbers with $[\tilde{a}]^\alpha = [a_1(\alpha), a_2(\alpha)]$ and $[\tilde{b}]^\alpha = [b_1(\alpha), b_2(\alpha)]$ then

$$[\tilde{a}+\tilde{b}]^\alpha = [a_1(\alpha)+b_1(\alpha), a_2(\alpha)+b_2(\alpha)]. \tag{1.36}$$

**Lemma 1.14.2** *[105, 124] Let $\lambda \neq 0, \mu \neq 0$ be real numbers and let $\tilde{a}$ and $\tilde{b}$ be fuzzy numbers. Then*

$$\omega(\lambda\tilde{a},\theta) = \omega\left(\tilde{a}, \frac{\theta}{|\lambda|}\right), \tag{1.37}$$

$$\omega(\lambda\tilde{a}+\lambda\tilde{b},\theta) \leq \omega\left(\frac{\theta}{|\lambda|+|\mu|}\right), \tag{1.38}$$

*where*

$$\omega(\theta) := \max\{\omega(\tilde{a},\theta), \omega(\tilde{b},\theta)\},$$

*for $\theta \geq 0$.*

**Lemma 1.14.3** *Let $\tilde{a} \in \mathcal{F}$ be a fuzzy number and. Then $a_1\colon [0,1] \to \mathbb{R}$ is strictly increasing and*

$$a_1(\tilde{a}(t)) \leq t,$$

*for $t \in cl(\text{supp}\tilde{a})$, furthemore $\tilde{a}(a_1(\alpha)) = \alpha$, for $\alpha \in [0,1]$ and*

$$a_1(\tilde{a}(t)) \leq t \leq a_1(\tilde{a}(t)+0),$$

*for $a_1(0) \leq t < a_1(1)$, where*

$$a_1(\tilde{a}(t)+0) = \lim_{\epsilon\to+0} a_1(\tilde{a}(t)+\epsilon). \tag{1.39}$$

**Lemma 1.14.4** *Let $\tilde{a}$ and $\tilde{b}$ be fuzzy numbers. Then*

(i) $D(\tilde{a},\tilde{b}) \geq |a_1(\alpha+0) - b_1(\alpha+0)|$, *for* $0 \leq \alpha < 1$,
(ii) $\tilde{a}(a_1(\alpha+0)) = \alpha$, *for* $0 \leq \alpha < 1$,
(iii) $a_1(\alpha) \leq a_1(\alpha+0) < a_1(\beta)$, *for* $0 \leq \alpha < \beta \leq 1$.

*Proof.* (i) From the definition of the metric $D$ we have

$$\begin{aligned} |a_1(\alpha+0) - b_1(\alpha+0)| &= \lim_{\epsilon \to +0} |a_1(\alpha+\epsilon) - \lim_{\epsilon \to +0} b_1(\alpha+\epsilon)| \\ &= \lim_{\epsilon \to +0} |a_1(\alpha+\epsilon) - b_1(\alpha+\epsilon)| \\ &\leq \sup_{\gamma \in [0,1]} |a_1(\gamma) - b_1(\gamma)| \leq D(\tilde{a},\tilde{b}). \end{aligned}$$

(ii) Since $\tilde{a}(a_1(\alpha+\epsilon)) = \alpha+\epsilon$, for $\epsilon \leq 1-\alpha$, we have

$$\tilde{a}(a_1(\alpha+0)) = \lim_{\epsilon \to +0} A(a_1(\alpha+\epsilon)) = \lim_{\epsilon \to +0} (\alpha+\epsilon) = \alpha.$$

(iii) From strictly monotonity of $a_1$ it follows that $a_1(\alpha+\epsilon) < a_1(\beta)$, for $\epsilon < \beta - \alpha$. Therefore,

$$a_1(\alpha) \leq a_1(\alpha+0) = \lim_{\epsilon \to +0} a_1(\alpha+\epsilon) < a_1(\beta),$$

which completes the proof.

The following lemma shows that if all the $\alpha$-level sets of two (continuous) fuzzy numbers are close to each other, then there can be only a small deviation between their membership grades.

**Lemma 1.14.5** *Let $\delta \geq 0$ and let $\tilde{a}, \tilde{b}$ be fuzzy numbers. If $D(\tilde{a},\tilde{b}) \leq \delta$, then*

$$\sup_{t \in \mathbb{R}} |\tilde{a}(t) - \tilde{b}(t)| \leq \max\{\omega(\tilde{a},\delta), \omega(\tilde{b},\delta)\}. \tag{1.40}$$

*Proof.* Let $t \in \mathbb{R}$ be arbitrarily fixed. It will be sufficient to show that

$$|\tilde{a}(t) - \tilde{b}(t)| \leq \max\{\omega(\tilde{a},\delta), \omega(\tilde{b},\delta)\}.$$

If $t \notin \mathrm{supp}\tilde{a} \cup \mathrm{supp}\tilde{b}$ then we obtain (1.40) trivially. Suppose that $t \in \mathrm{supp}\tilde{a} \cup \mathrm{supp}\tilde{b}$. With no loss of generality we will assume $0 \leq \tilde{b}(t) < \tilde{a}(t)$. Then either of the following must occur:

(a) $t \in (b_1(0), b_1(1))$,
(b) $t \leq b_1(0)$,
(c) $t \in (b_2(1), b_2(0))$
(d) $t \geq b_2(0)$.

In this case of (a) from Lemma 1.14.4 (with $\alpha = \tilde{b}(t), \beta = \tilde{a}(t)$) and Lemma 1.14.3(iii) it follows that

$$\tilde{a}(a_1(\tilde{b}(t)+0)) = \tilde{b}(t), \quad t \geq a_1(\tilde{a}(t)) \geq a_1(\tilde{b}(t)+0)$$

and

$$D(\tilde{a},\tilde{b}) \geq |a_1(\tilde{b}(t)+0) - a_1(\tilde{b}(t)+0))|.$$

Therefore from continuity of $\tilde{a}$ we get

$$\begin{aligned}|\tilde{a}(t) - \tilde{b}(t)| &= |\tilde{a}(t) - \tilde{a}(a_1(\tilde{b}(t)+0))| \\ &= \omega(\tilde{a}, |t - a_1(\tilde{b}(t)+0)|) \\ &= \omega(\tilde{a}, t - a_1(\tilde{b}(t)+0)) \\ &\leq \omega(\tilde{a}, b_1(\tilde{b}(t)+0) - a_1(\tilde{b}(t)+0)) \leq \omega(\tilde{a},\delta).\end{aligned}$$

In this case of (b) we have $\tilde{b}(t) = 0$; therefore from Lemma 1.14.3(i) it follows that

$$\begin{aligned}|\tilde{a}(t) - \tilde{b}(t)| &= |\tilde{a}(t) - 0| \\ &= |\tilde{a}(t) - \tilde{a}(a_1(0))| \\ &\leq \omega(\tilde{a}, |t - a_1(0)|) \\ &\leq \omega(\tilde{a}, |b_1(0) - a_1(0)|) \leq \omega(\tilde{a},\delta).\end{aligned}$$

A similar reasoning yields in the cases of (c) and (d); instead of properties $a_1$ we use the properties of $a_2$.

Let $L > 0$ be a real number. By $\mathcal{F}(L)$ we denote the set of all fuzzy numbers $\tilde{a} \in \mathcal{F}$ with membership function satisfying the Lipschitz condition with constant $L$ , i.e.

$$|\tilde{a}(t) - \tilde{a}(t')| \leq L|t - t'|, \ \forall t, t' \in \mathbb{R}.$$

In the following lemma (which is a direct consequence of Lemma 1.14.2 and Lemma 1.14.5) we see that (i) linear combinations of Lipschitzian fuzzy numbers are also Lipschitzian ones, and (ii) if all the $\alpha$-level sets of two Lipschitzian fuzzy numbers are closer to each other than $\delta$, then there can be maximum $L\delta$ difference between their membership grades.

**Lemma 1.14.6** *Let $L > 0$, $\lambda \neq 0$, $\mu \neq 0$ be real numbers and let $\tilde{a}, \tilde{b} \in \mathcal{F}(L)$ be fuzzy numbers. Then*

$$\lambda\tilde{a} \in \mathcal{F}\left(\frac{L}{|\lambda|}\right),$$

$$\lambda\tilde{a} + \mu\tilde{b} \in \mathcal{F}\left(\frac{L}{|\lambda| + |\mu|}\right).$$

*Furthermore, if $D(\tilde{a},\tilde{b}) \leq \delta$, then*

$$\sup_t |\tilde{a}(t) - \tilde{b}(t)| \leq L\delta.$$

If the fuzzy $\tilde{a}$ and $\tilde{a}$ are of symmetric triangular form then Lemma 1.14.6 reads

**Lemma 1.14.7** *Let $\delta > 0$ be a real number and let $\tilde{a} = (a, \alpha)$ and $\tilde{b} = (b, \beta)$ be symmetric triangular fuzzy numbers. Then*

$$\lambda\tilde{a} \in \mathcal{F}\left[\frac{1}{\alpha|\lambda|}\right],$$

$$\lambda\tilde{a} + \mu\tilde{b} \in \mathcal{F}\left(\frac{\max\{1/\alpha, 1/\beta\}}{|\lambda| + |\mu|}\right).$$

*Furthermore, from the inequality $D(\tilde{a}, \tilde{b}) \le \delta$ it follows that*

$$\sup_t |\tilde{a}(t) - \tilde{b}(t)| \le \max\left\{\frac{\delta}{\alpha}, \frac{\delta}{\beta}\right\}.$$

## 1.15 Fuzzy implications

Let $p =$ "$x$ is in $A$" and $q =$ "$y$ is in $B$" be crisp propositions, where $A$ and $B$ are crisp sets for the moment. The implication $p \to q$ is interpreted as $\neg(p \wedge \neg q)$. The full interpretation of the material implication $p \to q$ is that the degree of truth of $p \to q$ quantifies to what extend $q$ is at least as true as $p$, i.e.

$$\tau(p \to q) = \begin{cases} 1 \text{ if } \tau(p) \le \tau(q) \\ 0 \text{ otherwise} \end{cases}$$

where $\tau(.)$ denotes the truth value of a proposition.

**Example 1.15.1** *Let $p =$ "$x$ is bigger than 10" and let $q =$ "$x$ is bigger than 9". It is easy to see that $p \to q$ is true, because it can never happen that $x$ is bigger than 10 and at the same time $x$ is not bigger than 9.*

Consider the implication statement: if "pressure is high" then "volume is small". The membership function of the fuzzy set $A =$ "big pressure" is defined by

$$A(u) = \begin{cases} 1 & \text{if } u \ge 5 \\ 1 - \dfrac{5-u}{4} & \text{if } 1 \le u \le 5 \\ 0 & \text{otherwise} \end{cases}$$

The membership function of the fuzzy set $B$, *small volume* is given by

$$B(v) = \begin{cases} 1 & \text{if } v \le 1 \\ 1 - \dfrac{v-1}{4} & \text{if } 1 \le v \le 5 \\ 0 & \text{otherwise} \end{cases}$$

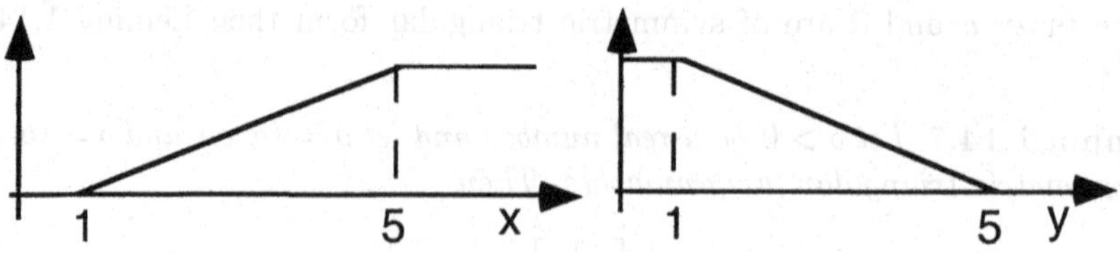


**Fig. 1.20.** "$x$ is big pressure" and "$y$ is small volume".

If $p$ is a proposition of the form "$x$ is $A$" where $A$ is a fuzzy set, for example, "big pressure" and $q$ is a proposition of the form "$y$ is $B$" for example, "small volume" then one encounters the following problem: *How to define the membership function of the fuzzy implication* $A \to B$*?* It is clear that $(A \to B)(x, y)$ should be defined *pointwise* i.e. $(A \to B)(x, y)$ should be a function of $A(x)$ and $B(y)$. That is

$$(A \to B)(u, v) = I(A(u), B(v)).$$

We shall use the notation $(A \to B)(u, v) = A(u) \to B(v)$. In our interpretation $A(u)$ is considered as the truth value of the proposition "$u$ is big pressure", and $B(v)$ is considered as the truth value of the proposition "$v$ is small volume".

$$u \text{ is big pressure} \to v \text{ is small volume} \equiv A(u) \to B(v)$$

One possible extension of material implication to implications with intermediate truth values is

$$A(u) \to B(v) = \begin{cases} 1 \text{ if } A(u) \le B(v) \\ 0 \text{ otherwise} \end{cases}$$

This implication operator is called *Standard Strict.*

$$\text{"4 is big pressure"} \to \text{"1 is small volume"}$$

$$= A(4) \to B(1) = 0.75 \to 1 = 1.$$

However, it is easy to see that this fuzzy implication operator is not appropriate for real-life applications. Namely, let $A(u) = 0.8$ and $B(v) = 0.8$. Then we have

$$A(u) \to B(v) = 0.8 \to 0.8 = 1.$$

Let us suppose that there is a small error of measurement or small rounding error of digital computation in the value of $B(v)$, and instead 0.8 we have to proceed with 0.7999. Then from the definition of Standard Strict implication operator it follows that

$$A(u) \to B(v) = 0.8 \to 0.7999 = 0.$$

This example shows that small changes in the input can cause a big deviation in the output, i.e. our system is very sensitive to rounding errors of digital computation and small errors of measurement.

A smoother extension of material implication operator can be derived from the equation

$$X \to Y = \sup\{Z | X \cap Z \subset Y\},$$

where $X, Y$ and $Z$ are classical sets. Using the above principle we can define the following fuzzy implication operator

$$A(u) \to B(v) = \sup\{z | \min\{A(u), z\} \leq B(v)\}$$

that is,

$$A(u) \to B(v) = \begin{cases} 1 & \text{if } A(u) \leq B(v) \\ B(v) & \text{otherwise} \end{cases}$$

This operator is called *Gödel* implication. Using the definitions of negation and union of fuzzy subsets the material implication $p \to q = \neg p \vee q$ can be extended by

$$A(u) \to B(v) = \max\{1 - A(u), B(v)\}$$

This operator is called *Kleene-Dienes* implication.

In many practical applications one uses Mamdani's implication operator to model causal relationship between fuzzy variables. This operator simply takes the minimum of truth values of fuzzy predicates

$$A(u) \to B(v) = \min\{A(u), B(v)\}$$

It is easy to see this is not a correct extension of material implications, because $0 \to 0$ yields zero. However, in knowledge-based systems, we are usually not interested in rules, in which the antecedent part is false. There are three important classes of fuzzy implication operators:

- **$S$-implications**: defined by

  $$x \to y = S(n(x), y)$$

  where $S$ is a t-conorm and $n$ is a negation on $[0, 1]$. These implications arise from the Boolean formalism

  $$p \to q = \neg p \vee q.$$

  Typical examples of $S$-implications are the Łukasiewicz and Kleene-Dienes implications.
- **$R$-implications**: obtained by residuation of continuous t-norm $T$, i.e.

  $$x \to y = \sup\{z \in [0, 1] \,|\, T(x, z) \leq y\}$$

  These implications arise from the *Intutionistic Logic* formalism. Typical examples of $R$-implications are the Gödel and Gaines implications.

- **t-norm implications**: if $T$ is a t-norm then

$$x \to y = T(x, y)$$

Although these implications do not verify the properties of material implication they are used as model of implication in many applications of fuzzy logic. Typical examples of t-norm implications are the Mamdani ($x \to y = \min\{x, y\}$) and Larsen ($x \to y = xy$) implications.

The most often used fuzzy implication operators are listed in Table 1.1.

| Name | Definition |
|---|---|
| Early Zadeh | $x \to y = \max\{1 - x, \min(x, y)\}$ |
| Łukasiewicz | $x \to y = \min\{1, 1 - x + y\}$ |
| Mamdani | $x \to y = \min\{x, y\}$ |
| Larsen | $x \to y = xy$ |
| Standard Strict | $x \to y = \begin{cases} 1 \text{ if } x \le y \\ 0 \text{ otherwise} \end{cases}$ |
| Gödel | $x \to y = \begin{cases} 1 \text{ if } x \le y \\ y \text{ otherwise} \end{cases}$ |
| Gaines | $x \to y = \begin{cases} 1 & \text{if } x \le y \\ y/x & \text{otherwise} \end{cases}$ |
| Kleene-Dienes | $x \to y = \max\{1 - x, y\}$ |
| Kleene-Dienes-Łukasiewicz | $x \to y = 1 - x + xy$ |
| Yager | $x \to y = y^x$ |

**Table 1.1.** Fuzzy implication operators.

## 1.16 Linguistic variables

The use of fuzzy sets provides a basis for a systematic way for the manipulation of vague and imprecise concepts. In particular, we can employ fuzzy sets to represent linguistic variables. A linguistic variable can be regarded either as a variable whose value is a fuzzy number or as a variable whose values are defined in linguistic terms.

**Definition 1.16.1** *A linguistic variable is characterized by a quintuple*

$$(x, T(x), U, G, M)$$

*in which $x$ is the name of variable; $T(x)$ is the term set of $x$, that is, the set of names of linguistic values of $x$ with each value being a fuzzy number defined on $U$; $G$ is a syntactic rule for generating the names of values of $x$; and $M$ is a semantic rule for associating with each value its meaning.*

For example, if *speed* is interpreted as a linguistic variable, then its term set $T$ (speed) could be

$$T = \{\text{slow, moderate, fast, very slow, more or less fast, sligthly slow, } \dots\}$$

where each term in $T$ (speed) is characterized by a fuzzy set in a universe of discourse $U = [0, 100]$. We might interpret

- *slow* as "a speed below about 40 mph"
- *moderate* as "a speed close to 55 mph"
- *fast* as "a speed above about 70 mph"

These terms can be characterized as fuzzy sets whose membership functions are

$$\text{slow}(v) = \begin{cases} 1 & \text{if } v \le 40 \\ 1 - (v-40)/15 & \text{if } 40 \le v \le 55 \\ 0 & \text{otherwise} \end{cases}$$

$$\text{moderate}(v) = \begin{cases} 1 - |v-55|/30 & \text{if } 40 \le v \le 70 \\ 0 & \text{otherwise} \end{cases}$$

$$\text{fast}(v) = \begin{cases} 1 & \text{if } v \ge 70 \\ 1 - \dfrac{70-v}{15} & \text{if } 55 \le v \le 70 \\ 0 & \text{otherwise} \end{cases}$$

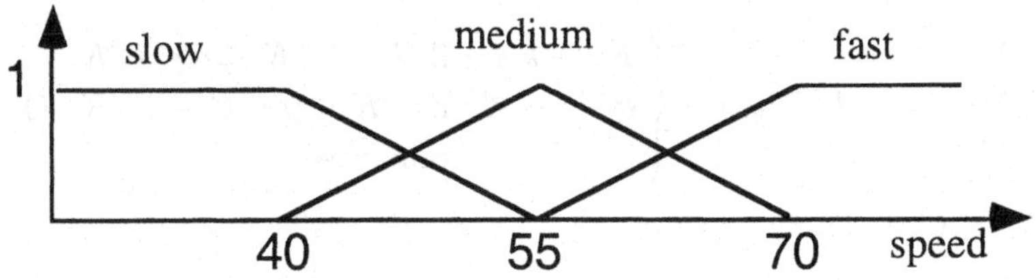


**Fig. 1.21.** Values of linguistic variable *speed.*

In many practical applications we normalize the domain of inputs and use the following type of fuzzy partition:

NVB (Negative Very Big)
NB (Negative Big),
NM (Negative Medium),
NS (Negative Small),
ZE (Zero),
PS (Positive Small),
PM (Positive Medium),
PB (Positive Big)
PVB (Positive Very Big)

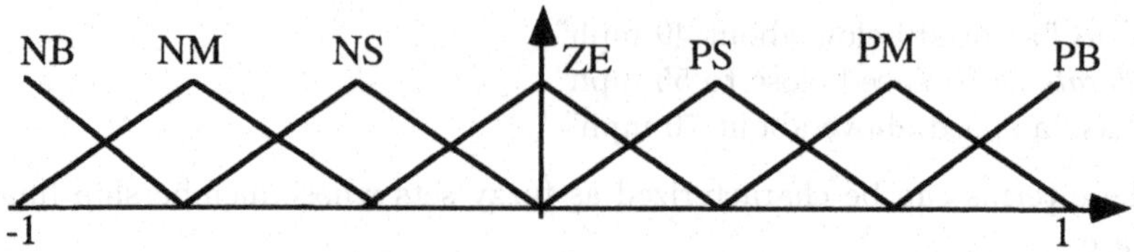


**Fig. 1.22.** A usual fuzzy partition of $[-1, 1]$.

We will use the following parametrized standard fuzzy partition of the unit inteval. Suppose that $U = [0, 1]$ and $\mathcal{T}(x)$ consists of $K + 1$, $K \geq 2$, terms,

$$\mathcal{T} = \{\text{small}_1, \text{around 1/K}, \text{around 2/K}, \dots, \text{around (K-1)/K}, \text{big}_K\}$$

which are represented by triangular membership functions $\{A_1, \dots, A_{K+1}\}$ of the form

$$A_1(u) = [\text{small}_1](u) = \begin{cases} 1 - Ku & \text{if } 0 \leq u \leq 1/K \\ 0 & \text{otherwise} \end{cases} \quad (1.41)$$

$$A_k(u) = [\text{around } k/K](u) = \begin{cases} Ku - k + 1 & \text{if } (k-1)/K \leq u \leq k/K \\ k + 1 - Ku & \text{if } k/K \leq u \leq (k+1)/K \\ 0 & \text{otherwise} \end{cases} \quad (1.42)$$

for $1 \leq k \leq (K - 1)$, and

$$A_{K+1}(u) = [\text{big}_K](u) = \begin{cases} Ku - K + 1 & \text{if } (K-1)/K \leq u \leq 1 \\ 0 & \text{otherwise} \end{cases} \quad (1.43)$$

If $K = 1$ then the fuzzy partition for the [0,1] interval consists of two linguistic terms {small, big} which are defined by

$$\text{small}(t) = 1 - t, \quad \text{big}(t) = t, \ t \in [0, 1]. \quad (1.44)$$

Suppose that $U = [0, 1]$ and $\mathcal{T}(x)$ consists of $2K + 1$, $K \geq 2$, terms,

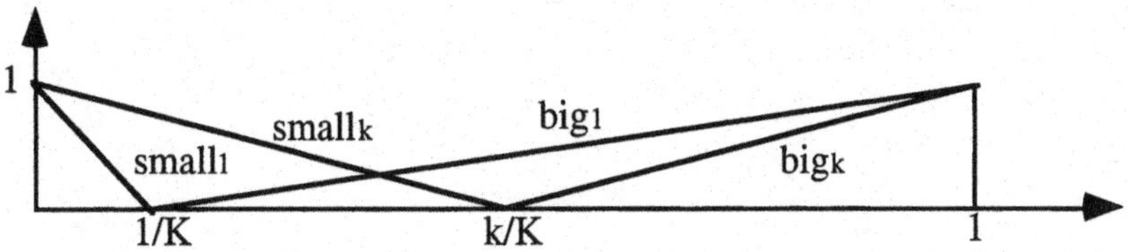


**Fig. 1.23.** Fuzzy partition of [0,1] with monotone membership functions.

$$\mathcal{T} = \{\text{small}_1, \ldots, \text{small}_K = \text{small}, \text{big}_0 = \text{big}, \text{big}_1, \ldots, \text{big}_K\}$$

which are represented by triangular membership functions as

$$\text{small}_k(u) = \begin{cases} 1 - \dfrac{K}{k}u & \text{if } 0 \leq u \leq k/K \\ 0 & \text{otherwise} \end{cases} \tag{1.45}$$

for $k \leq k \leq K$,

$$\text{big}_k(u) = \begin{cases} \dfrac{u - k/K}{1 - k/K} & \text{if } k/K \leq u \leq 1 \\ 0 & \text{otherwise} \end{cases} \tag{1.46}$$

for $0 \leq k \leq K - 1$.

# 2. Fuzzy Multicriteria Decision Making

## 2.1 Averaging operators

Fuzzy set theory provides a host of attractive aggregation connectives for integrating membership values representing uncertain information. These connectives can be categorized into the following three classes *union, intersection* and *compensation* connectives.

Union produces a high output whenever any one of the input values representing degrees of satisfaction of different features or criteria is high. Intersection connectives produce a high output only when all of the inputs have high values. Compensative connectives have the property that a higher degree of satisfaction of one of the criteria can compensate for a lower degree of satisfaction of another criteria to a certain extent. In the sense, union connectives provide full compensation and intersection connectives provide no compensation. In a decision process the idea of *trade-offs* corresponds to viewing the global evaluation of an action as lying between the *worst* and the *best* local ratings. This occurs in the presence of conflicting goals, when a compensation between the corresponding compabilities is allowed. Averaging operators realize trade-offs between objectives, by allowing a positive compensation between ratings.

**Definition 2.1.1** *An averaging operator $M$ is a function $M\colon [0,1]\times[0,1]\to[0,1]$, satisfying the following properties*

- *Idempotency*

$$M(x,x)=x,\ \forall x\in[0,1],$$

- *Commutativity*

$$M(x,y)=M(y,x),\ \forall x,y\in[0,1],$$

- *Extremal conditions*

$$M(0,0)=0,\quad M(1,1)=1$$

- *Monotonicity*

$$M(x,y)\le M(x',y')\ \textit{if}\ x\le x'\ \textit{and}\ y\le y',$$

- *$M$ is continuous.*

Averaging operators represent a wide class of aggregation operators. We prove that whatever is the particular definition of an averaging operator, $M$, the global evaluation of an action will lie between the *worst* and the *best* local ratings:

**Lemma 2.1.1** *If $M$ is an averaging operator then*

$$\min\{x, y\} \leq M(x, y) \leq \max\{x, y\}, \ \forall x, y \in [0, 1]$$

*Proof.* From idempotency and monotonicity of $M$ it follows that

$$\min\{x, y\} = M(\min\{x, y\}, \min\{x, y\}) \leq M(x, y)$$

and $M(x, y) \leq M(\max\{x, y\}, \max\{x, y\}) = \max\{x, y\}$. Which ends the proof.

Averaging operators have the following interesting properties [87]:

**Property 2.1.1** *A strictly increasing averaging operator cannot be associative.*

**Property 2.1.2** *The only associative averaging operators are defined by*

$$M(x, y, \alpha) = med(x, y, \alpha) = \begin{cases} y \text{ if } x \leq y \leq \alpha \\ \alpha \text{ if } x \leq \alpha \leq y \\ x \text{ if } \alpha \leq x \leq y \end{cases}$$

*where $\alpha \in (0, 1)$.*

An important family of averaging operators is formed by quasi-arithmetic means

$$M(a_1, \ldots, a_n) = f^{-1}\left(\frac{1}{n}\sum_{i=1}^{n} f(a_i)\right)$$

This family has been characterized by Kolmogorov as being the class of all decomposable continuous averaging operators. For example, the quasi-arithmetic mean of $a_1$ and $a_2$ is defined by

$$M(a_1, a_2) = f^{-1}\left(\frac{f(a_1) + f(a_2)}{2}\right).$$

The next table shows the most often used mean operators.

The process of information aggregation appears in many applications related to the development of intelligent systems. One sees aggregation in neural networks, fuzzy logic controllers, vision systems, expert systems and multi-criteria decision aids. In [317] Yager introduced a new aggregation technique based on the ordered weighted averaging (OWA) operators.

| Name | $M(x,y)$ |
|---|---|
| harmonic mean | $2xy/(x+y)$ |
| geometric mean | $\sqrt{xy}$ |
| arithmetic mean | $(x+y)/2$ |
| dual of geometric mean | $1-\sqrt{(1-x)(1-y)}$ |
| dual of harmonic mean | $(x+y-2xy)/(2-x-y)$ |
| median | $\mathrm{med}(x,y,\alpha),\ \alpha \in (0,1)$ |
| generalized $p$-mean | $((x^p+y^p)/2)^{1/p},\ p \geq 1$ |

**Table 2.1.** Mean operators.

**Definition 2.1.2** *An OWA operator of dimension n is a mapping* $F\colon \mathbb{R}^n \to \mathbb{R}$*, that has an associated weighting vector* $W = (w_1, w_2, \dots, w_n)^T$ *such as* $w_i \in [0,1]$*,* $1 \leq i \leq n$*, and*

$$w_1 + \dots + w_n = 1.$$

*Furthermore*

$$F(a_1, \dots, a_n) = w_1 b_1 + \dots + w_n b_n = \sum_{j=1}^{n} w_j b_j,$$

*where* $b_j$ *is the* $j$*-th largest element of the bag* $\langle a_1, \dots, a_n \rangle$*.*

**Example 2.1.1** *Assume* $W = (0.4, 0.3, 0.2, 0.1)^T$ *then*

$$F(0.7, 1, 0.2, 0.6) = 0.4 \times 1 + 0.3 \times 0.7 + 0.2 \times 0.6 + 0.1 \times 0.2 = 0.75.$$

A fundamental aspect of this operator is the re-ordering step, in particular an aggregate $a_i$ is not associated with a particular weight $w_i$ but rather a weight is associated with a particular ordered position of aggregate. When we view the OWA weights as a column vector we shall find it convenient to refer to the weights with the low indices as weights at the top and those with the higher indices with weights at the bottom.

It is noted that different OWA operators are distinguished by their weighting function. In [317] Yager pointed out three important special cases of OWA aggregations:

- $F^*$: In this case $W = W^* = (1, 0 \dots, 0)^T$ and
$$F^*(a_1, \dots, a_n) = \max\{a_1, \dots, a_n\},$$
- $F_*$: In this case $W = W_* = (0, 0 \dots, 1)^T$ and
$$F_*(a_1, \dots, a_n) = \min\{a_1, \dots, a_n\},$$

- $F_A$: In this case $W = W_A = (1/n, \dots, 1/n)^T$ and

$$F_A(a_1, \dots, a_n) = \frac{a_1 + \dots + a_n}{n}.$$

A number of important properties can be associated with the OWA operators. We shall now discuss some of these. For any OWA operator $F$ holds

$$F_*(a_1, \dots, a_n) \le F(a_1, \dots, a_n) \le F^*(a_1, \dots, a_n).$$

Thus the upper an lower star OWA operator are its boundaries. From the above it becomes clear that for any $F$

$$\min\{a_1, \dots, a_n\} \le F(a_1, \dots, a_n) \le \max\{a_1, \dots, a_n\}.$$

The OWA operator can be seen to be *commutative*. Let $\langle a_1, \dots, a_n \rangle$ be a bag of aggregates and let $\{d_1, \dots, d_n\}$ be any *permutation* of the $a_i$. Then for any OWA operator

$$F(a_1, \dots, a_n) = F(d_1, \dots, d_n).$$

A third characteristic associated with these operators is *monotonicity*. Assume $a_i$ and $c_i$ are a collection of aggregates, $i = 1, \dots, n$ such that for each $i$, $a_i \ge c_i$. Then

$$F(a_1, \dots, a_n) \ge F(c_1, c_2, \dots, c_n)$$

where $F$ is some fixed weight OWA operator.

Another characteristic associated with these operators is *idempotency*. If $a_i = a$ for all $i$ then for any OWA operator

$$F(a_1, \dots, a_n) = a.$$

From the above we can see the OWA operators have the basic properties associated with an *averaging operator.*

**Example 2.1.2** *A window type OWA operator takes the average of the $m$ arguments around the center. For this class of operators we have*

$$w_i = \begin{cases} 0 & \text{if } i < k \\ \dfrac{1}{m} & \text{if } k \le i < k+m \\ 0 & \text{if } i \ge k+m \end{cases} \tag{2.1}$$

In order to classify OWA operators in regard to their location between *and* and *or*, a measure of *orness*, associated with any vector $W$ is introduce by Yager [317] as follows

$$\text{orness}(W) = \frac{1}{n-1} \sum_{i=1}^{n} (n-i) w_i.$$

It is easy to see that for any $W$ the orness($W$) is always in the unit interval. Furthermore, note that the nearer $W$ is to an *or*, the closer its measure is to one; while the nearer it is to an *and*, the closer is to zero.

**Lemma 2.1.2** *Let us consider the the vectors*

$$W^* = (1,0\dots,0)^T,\ W_* = (0,0\dots,1)^T,\ W_A = (1/n,\dots,1/n)^T.$$

*Then it can easily be shown that* $\mathrm{orness}(W^*) = 1, \mathrm{orness}(W_*) = 0$ *and* $\mathrm{orness}(W_A) = 0.5$.

A measure of *andness* is defined as

$$\mathrm{andness}(W) = 1 - \mathrm{orness}(W).$$

Generally, an OWA operator with much of nonzero weights near the top will be an *orlike* operator, that is,

$$\mathrm{orness}(W) \geq 0.5$$

and when much of the weights are nonzero near the bottom, the OWA operator will be *andlike*, that is,

$$\mathrm{andness}(W) \geq 0.5.$$

**Example 2.1.3** *Let* $W = (0.8, 0.2, 0.0)^T$. *Then*

$$\mathrm{orness}(W) = \frac{1}{3}(2 \times 0.8 + 0.2) = 0.6,$$

*and*

$$\mathrm{andness}(W) = 1 - \mathrm{orness}(W) = 1 - 0.6 = 0.4.$$

*This means that the OWA operator, defined by*

$$F(a_1, a_2, a_3) = 0.8b_1 + 0.2b_2 + 0.0b_3 = 0.8b_1 + 0.2b_2,$$

*where* $b_j$ *is the* $j$*-th largest element of the bag* $\langle a_1, a_2, a_3 \rangle$, *is an* orlike *aggregation.*

The following theorem shows that as we move weight up the vector we increase the orness, while moving weight down causes us to decrease $orness(W)$.

**Theorem 2.1.1** *[318] Assume* $W$ *and* $W'$ *are two* $n$*-dimensional OWA vectors such that*

$$W = (w_1, \dots, w_n)^T,$$

*and*

$$W' = (w_1, \dots, w_j + \epsilon, \dots, w_k - \epsilon, \dots, w_n)^T$$

*where* $\epsilon > 0$, $j < k$. *Then* $orness(W') > orness(W)$.

In [317] Yager defined the measure of dispersion (or entropy) of an OWA vector by

$$\text{disp}(W) = -\sum_{i=1}^{n} w_i \ln w_i.$$

We can see when using the OWA operator as an averaging operator disp($W$) measures the degree to which we use all the aggregates equally. If $F$ is an OWA aggregation with weights $w_i$ the *dual* of $F$ denoted $F^R$, is an OWA aggregation of the same dimention where with weights $w_i^R$

$$w_i^R = w_{n-i+1}.$$

We can easily see that if $F$ and $F^R$ are duals then

$$\text{disp}(F^R) = \text{disp}(F), \quad \text{orness}(F^R) = 1 - \text{orness}(F) = \text{andness}(F).$$

Thus is $F$ is orlike its dual is andlike.

**Example 2.1.4** *Let* $W = (0.3, 0.2, 0.1, 0.4)^T$ *and* $W^R = (0.4, 0.1, 0.2, 0.3)^T$. *Then*

$$\text{orness}(F) = 1/3(3 \times 0.3 + 2 \times 0.2 + 0.1) \approx 0.466,$$
$$\text{orness}(F^R) = 1/3(3 \times 0.4 + 2 \times 0.1 + 0.2) \approx 0.533.$$

An important application of the OWA operators is in the area of quantifier guided aggregations [317]. Assume

$$\{A_1, \dots, A_n\},$$

is a collection of criteria. Let $x$ be an object such that for any criterion $A_i$, $A_i(x) \in [0, 1]$ indicates the degree to which this criterion is satisfied by $x$. If we want to find out the degree to which $x$ satisfies "*all* the criteria" denoting this by $D(x)$, we get following Bellman and Zadeh [7]:

$$D(x) = \min\{A_1(x), \dots, A_n(x)\}. \tag{2.2}$$

In this case we are essentially requiring $x$ to satisfy "$A_1$ and $A_2$ and $\cdots$ and $A_n$".

If we desire to find out the degree to which $x$ satisfies "*at least one* of the criteria", denoting this $E(x)$, we get

$$E(x) = \max\{A_1(x), \dots, A_n(x)\}.$$

In this case we are requiring $x$ to satisfy "$A_1$ or $A_2$ or $\cdots$ or $A_n$".

In many applications rather than desiring that a solution satisfies one of these extreme situations, "all" or "at least one", we may require that $x$ satisfies *most* or *at least half* of the criteria. Drawing upon Zadeh's concept [339] of linguistic quantifiers we can accomplish these kinds of quantifier guided aggregations.

**Definition 2.1.3** *A quantifier $Q$ is called*

- regular monotonically non-decreasing *if*

$$Q(0) = 0, \quad Q(1) = 1, \quad \text{if } r_1 > r_2 \text{ then } Q(r_1) \geq Q(r_2).$$

- regular monotonically non-increasing *if*

$$Q(0) = 1, \quad Q(1) = 0, \quad \text{if } r_1 < r_2 \text{ then } Q(r_1) \geq Q(r_2).$$

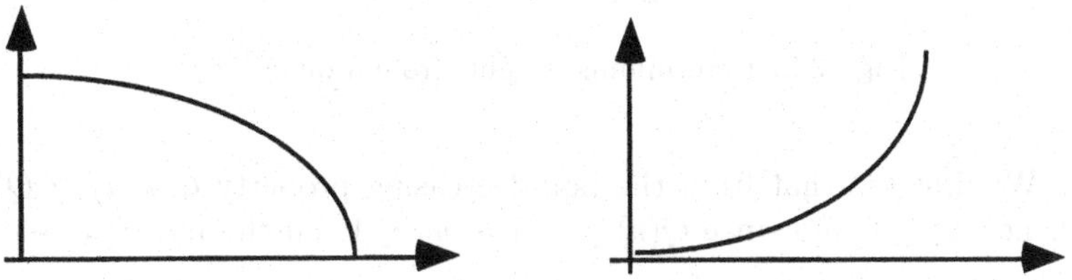

**Fig. 2.1.** Monoton linguistic quantifiers.

- regular unimodal *if*

$$Q(r) = \begin{cases} 0 & \text{if } r = 0 \\ \text{monotone increasing} & \text{if } 0 \leq r \leq a \\ 1 & \text{if } a \leq r \leq b, \ 0 < a < b < 1 \\ \text{monotone decreasing} & \text{if } b \leq r \leq 1 \\ 0 & \text{if } r = 1 \end{cases}$$

With $a_i = A_i(x)$ the overall valuation of $x$ is $F_Q(a_1, \dots, a_n)$ where $F_Q$ is an OWA operator. The weights associated with this quantified guided aggregation are obtained as follows

$$w_i = Q\left(\frac{i}{n}\right) - Q\left(\frac{i-1}{n}\right), \quad i = 1, \dots, n. \tag{2.3}$$

The next figure graphically shows the operation involved in determining the OWA weights directly from the quantifier guiding the aggregation.

**Theorem 2.1.2** *[318] If we construct $w_i$ via the method (2.3) we always get $w_1 + \cdots + w_n = 1$ and $w_i \geq 0$ for any function*

$$Q\colon [0,1] \to [0,1],$$

*satisfying the conditions of a regular nondecreasing quantifier.*

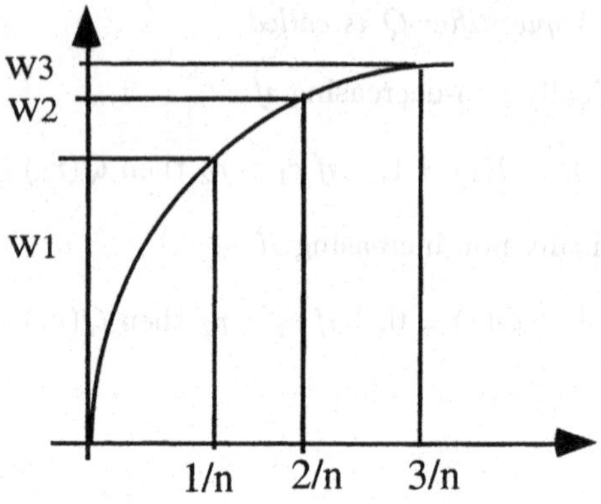


**Fig. 2.2.** Determining weights from a quantifier.

*Proof.* We first see that from the non-decreasing property $Q(i/n) \geq Q(i - 1/n)$ hence $w_i \geq 0$ and since $Q(r) \leq 1$ then $w_i \leq 1$. Furthermore we see

$$\sum_{i=1}^{n} w_i = \sum_{i=1}^{n} \left[ Q\left(\frac{i}{n}\right) - Q\left(\frac{i-1}{n}\right) \right] = Q\left[\frac{n}{n}\right] - Q\left[\frac{0}{n}\right] = 1 - 0 = 1.$$

Which proves the theorem.

We call any function satisfying the conditions of a regular non-decreasing quantifier an *acceptable OWA weight generating function.* Let us look at the weights generated from some basic types of quantifiers. The quantifier, *for all* $Q_*$, is defined such that

$$Q_*(r) = \begin{cases} 0 \text{ for } r < 1, \\ 1 \text{ for } r = 1. \end{cases}$$

Using our method for generating weights $w_i = Q_*(i/n) - Q_*((i-1)/n)$ we get

$$w_i = \begin{cases} 0 \text{ for } i < n, \\ 1 \text{ for } i = n. \end{cases}$$

This is exactly what we previously denoted as $W_*$. For the quantifier *there exists* we have

$$Q^*(r) = \begin{cases} 0 \text{ for } r = 0, \\ 1 \text{ for } r > 0. \end{cases}$$

In this case we get

$$w_1 = 1, \quad w_i = 0, \text{ for } i \neq 1.$$

This is exactly what we denoted as $W^*$.

Consider next the quantifier defined by $Q(r) = r$. This is *an identity* or *linear type* quantifier. In this case we get

$$w_i = Q\left(\frac{i}{n}\right) - Q\left(\frac{i-1}{n}\right) = \frac{i}{n} - \frac{i-1}{n} = \frac{1}{n}.$$

This gives us the pure averaging OWA aggregation operator. Recapitulating using the approach suggested by Yager if we desire to calculate

$$F_Q(a_1, \dots, a_n)$$

for $Q$ being a regular non-decreasing quantifier we proceed as follows:

- Calculate
$$w_i = Q\left[\frac{i}{n}\right] - Q\left[\frac{i-1}{n}\right],$$
- Calculate
$$F_Q(a_i, \dots, a_n) = w_1 b_1 + \cdots + w_n b_n.$$

where $b_i$ is the $i$-th largest of the $a_j$. For example, the weights of the window-

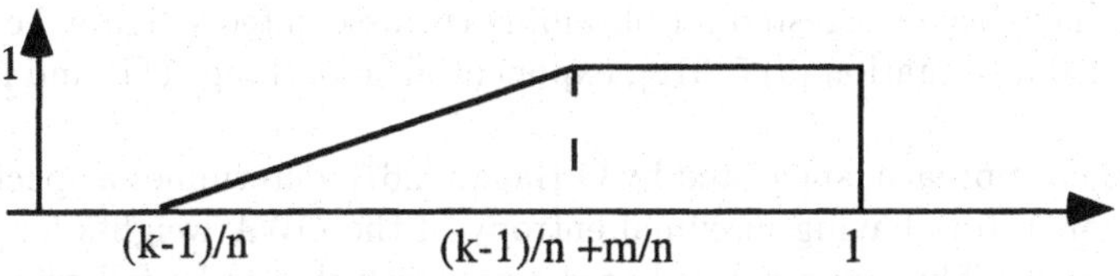


**Fig. 2.3.** Quantifier for a window-type OWA operator.

type OWA operator given by equation (2.1) can be derived from the quantifier

$$Q(r) = \begin{cases} 0 & \text{if } r \leq (k-1)/n \\ 1 - \dfrac{(k-1+m) - nr}{m} & \text{if } (k-1)/n \leq r \leq (k-1+m)/n \\ 1 & \text{if } (k-1+m)/n \leq r \leq 1 \end{cases}$$

## 2.2 Obtaining maximal entropy OWA operator weights

One important issue in the theory of OWA operators is the determination of the associated weights. One of the first approaches, suggested by O'Hagan [267], determines a special class of OWA operators having maximal entropy of the OWA weights for a given level of *orness*; algorithmically it is based on the solution of a constrained optimization problem. In this Section, using the method of Lagrange multipliers, we shall solve this constrained optimization problem analytically and derive a polinomial equation which is then solved to determine the optimal weighting vector.

In [317], Yager introduced two characterizing measures associated with the weighting vector $W$ of an OWA operator. The first one, the measure of *orness* of the aggregation, is defined as

$$\text{orness}(W) = \frac{1}{n-1}\sum_{i=1}^{n}(n-i)w_i.$$

and it characterizes the degree to which the aggregation is like an *or* operation. It is clear that $\text{orness}(W) \in [0,1]$ holds for any weighting vector.

The second one, the measure of *dispersion* of the aggregation, is defined as

$$\text{disp}(W) = -\sum_{i=1}^{n} w_i \ln w_i$$

and it measures the degree to which $W$ takes into account all information in the aggregation.

It is clear that the actual type of aggregation performed by an OWA operator depends upon the form of the weighting vector. A number of approaches have been suggested for obtaining the associated weights, i.e., quantifier guided aggregation [317, 318], exponential smoothing [111] and learning [327].

Another approach, suggested by O'Hagan [267], determines a special class of OWA operators having maximal entropy of the OWA weights for a given level of *orness*. This approach is based on the solution of he following mathematical programming problem:

$$\begin{aligned} &\text{maximize} && \text{disp}(W) = -\sum_{i=1}^{n} w_i \ln w_i \\ &\text{subject to } \text{orness}(W) = && \sum_{i=1}^{n} \frac{n-i}{n-1}\cdot w_i = \alpha,\ 0 \le \alpha \le 1 \\ & && w_1 + \dots + w_n = 1,\ 0 \le w_i \le 1,\ i = 1,\dots,n. \end{aligned} \tag{2.4}$$

Following [146] we shall transfer problem (2.4) to a polinomial equation which is then solved to determine the optimal weighting vector.

First we note that $\text{disp}(W)$ is meaningful if $w_i > 0$ and by letting $w_i \ln w_i$ to zero if $w_i = 0$, problem (2.4) turns into

$$\text{disp}(W) \to \max;$$

$$\text{subject to } \{\text{orness}(W) = \alpha,\ w_1 + \dots + w_n = 1,\ 0 \le \alpha \le 1\}.$$

If $n = 2$ then from $\text{orness}(w_1, w_2) = \alpha$ we get $w_1 = \alpha$ and $w_2 = 1 - \alpha$. Furthemore, if $\alpha = 0$ or $\alpha = 1$ then the associated weighting vectors are uniquely defined as $(0, 0, \dots, 0, 1)^T$ and $(1, 0, \dots, 0, 0)^T$, respectively, with value of dispersion zero.

Suppose now that $n \geq 3$ and $0 < \alpha < 1$. Let us

$$L(W, \lambda_1, \lambda_2) = -\sum_{i=1}^{n} w_i \ln w_i + \lambda_1 \left( \sum_{i=1}^{n} \frac{n-i}{n-1} w_i - \alpha \right) + \lambda_2 \left( \sum_{i=1}^{n} w_i - 1 \right).$$

denote the Lagrange function of constrained optimization problem (2.4), where $\lambda_1$ and $\lambda_2$ are real numbers. Then the partial derivatives of $L$ are computed as

$$\frac{\partial L}{\partial w_j} = -\ln w_j - 1 + \lambda_1 + \frac{n-j}{n-1}\lambda_2 = 0, \; \forall j \tag{2.5}$$

$$\frac{\partial L}{\partial \lambda_1} = \sum_{i=1}^{n} w_i - 1 = 0$$

$$\frac{\partial L}{\partial \lambda_2} = \sum_{i=1}^{n} \frac{n-i}{n-1} w_i - \alpha = 0.$$

For $j = n$ equation (2.5) turns into

$$-\ln w_n - 1 + \lambda_1 = 0 \iff \lambda_1 = \ln w_n + 1,$$

and for $j = 1$ we get

$$-\ln w_1 - 1 + \lambda_1 + \lambda_2 = 0,$$

and, therefore,

$$\lambda_2 = \ln w_1 + 1 - \lambda_1 = \ln w_1 + 1 - \ln w_n - 1 = \ln w_1 - \ln w_n.$$

For $1 \leq j \leq n$ we find

$$\ln w_j = \frac{j-1}{n-1} \ln w_n + \frac{n-j}{n-1} \ln w_1 \Rightarrow w_j = \sqrt[n-1]{w_1^{n-j} w_n^{j-1}}. \tag{2.6}$$

If $w_1 = w_n$ then (2.6) gives

$$w_1 = w_2 = \cdots = w_n = \frac{1}{n} \Rightarrow \text{disp}(W) = \ln n,$$

which is the optimal solution to (2.4) for $\alpha = 0.5$ (actually, this is the global optimal value for the dispersion of all OWA operators of dimension $n$). Suppose now that $w_1 \neq w_n$. Let us introduce the notations

$$u_1 = w_1^{\frac{1}{n-1}}, u_n = w_n^{\frac{1}{n-1}}.$$

Then we may rewrite (2.6) as $w_j = u_1^{n-j} u_n^{j-1}$, for $1 \leq j \leq n$. From the first condition, orness$(W) = \alpha$, we find

$$\sum_{i=1}^{n} \frac{n-i}{n-1} w_i = \alpha \iff \sum_{i=1}^{n} (n-i) u_1^{n-i} u_n^{i-1} = (n-1)\alpha,$$

and

$$\frac{u_n}{u_1} = \frac{(n-1)\alpha + 1 - nw_1}{(n-1)\alpha}. \tag{2.7}$$

From the second condition, $w_1 + \cdots + w_n = 1$, we find

$$\sum_{j=1}^{n} u_1^{n-j} u_n^{j-1} = 1 \iff u_1^n - u_n^n = u_1 - u_n \tag{2.8}$$

$$\iff u_1^{n-1} - \frac{u_n}{u_1} \times u_n^{n-1} = 1 - \frac{u_n}{u_1} \tag{2.9}$$

Comparing equations (2.7) and (2.9) we find

$$w_n = \frac{((n-1)\alpha - n)w_1 + 1}{(n-1)\alpha + 1 - nw_1}. \tag{2.10}$$

Let us rewrite equation (2.8) as

$$w_1[(n-1)\alpha + 1 - nw_1]^n = ((n-1)\alpha)^{n-1}[((n-1)\alpha - n)w_1 + 1]. \tag{2.11}$$

So the optimal value of $w_1$ should satisfy equation (2.11). Once $w_1$ is computed then $w_n$ can be determined from equation (2.10) and the other weights are obtained from equation (2.6).

*Note 2.2.1.* If $n = 3$ then from (2.6) we get

$$w_2 = \sqrt{w_1 w_3}$$

independently of the value of $\alpha$, which means that the optimal value of $w_2$ is always the geometric mean of $w_1$ and $w_3$.

Let us introduce the notations

$$f(w_1) = w_1[(n-1)\alpha + 1 - nw_1]^n,$$
$$g(w_1) = ((n-1)\alpha)^{n-1}[((n-1)\alpha - n)w_1 + 1].$$

Then to find the optimal value for the first weight we have to solve the following equation

$$f(w_1) = g(w_1),$$

where $g$ is a line and $f$ is a polinom of $w_1$ of dimension $n + 1$.

Without loss of generality we can assume that $\alpha < 0.5$, because if a weighting vector $W$ is optimal for problem (2.4) under some given degree of orness, $\alpha < 0.5$, then its reverse, denoted by $W^R$, and defined as

$$w_i^R = w_{n-i+1}$$

is also optimal for problem (2.4) under degree of orness $(1-\alpha)$. Really, as was shown by Yager [318], we find that

$$\text{disp}(W^R) = \text{disp}(W) \text{ and } \text{orness}(W^R) = 1 - \text{orness}(W).$$

Therefore, for any $\alpha > 0.5$, we can solve problem (2.4) by solving it with level of orness $(1-\alpha)$ and then taking the reverse of that solution.

From the equations

$$f\left(\frac{1}{n}\right) = g\left(\frac{1}{n}\right) \text{ and } f'\left(\frac{1}{n}\right) = g'\left(\frac{1}{n}\right)$$

we get that $g$ is always a tangency line to $f$ at the point $w_1 = 1/n$. But if $w_1 = 1/n$ then $w_1 = \cdots = w_n = 1/n$ also holds, and that is the optimal solution for $\alpha = 0.5$.

Consider the the graph of $f$. It is clear that $f(0) = 0$ and by solving the equation

$$f'(w_1) = [(n-1)\alpha + 1 - nw_1]^n - n^2 w_1[(n-1)\alpha + 1 - nw_1]^{n-1} = 0$$

we find that its unique solution is

$$\hat{w}_1 = \frac{(n-1)\alpha + 1}{n(n+1)} < \frac{1}{n},$$

and its second derivative, $f''(\hat{w}_1)$ is negative, which means that $\hat{w}_1$ is the only maximizing point of $f$ on the segment $[0, 1/n]$.

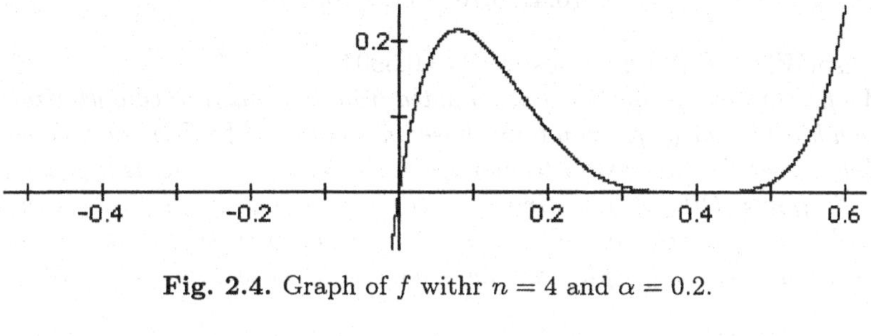


**Fig. 2.4.** Graph of $f$ withr $n = 4$ and $\alpha = 0.2$.

We prove now that $g$ can intersect $f$ only once in the open interval $(0, 1/n)$. It will guarantee the uniqueness of the optimal solution of problem (2.4). Really, from the equation

$$f''(w_1) = -2n^2[(n-1)\alpha+1-nw_1]^{n-1} + n^3(n-1)w_1[(n-1)\alpha+1-nw_1]^{n-2} = 0$$

we find that its unique solution is

$$\bar{w}_1 = 2\frac{(n-1)\alpha+1}{n(n+1)} = 2\hat{w}_1 < \frac{1}{n}, \text{ (since } \alpha < 0.5).$$

with the meaning that $f$ is strictly concave on $(0, \bar{w}_1)$, has an inflextion point at $\bar{w}_1$, and $f$ is strictly convex on $(\bar{w}_1, 1/n)$. Therefore, the graph of $g$ should lie *below* the graph of $g$ if $\hat{w}_1 < w_1 < 1/n$ and $g$ can cross $f$ only once in the interval $(0, \hat{w}_1)$.

**Example 2.2.1** *Let us suppose that* $n = 5$ *and* $\alpha = 0.6$. *Then from the equation*

$$w_1[4 \times 0.6 + 1 - 5w_1]^5 = (4 \times 0.6)^4[1 - (5 - 4 \times 0.6)w_1].$$

*we find*

$$w_1^* = 0.2884$$
$$w_5^* = \frac{(4 \times 0.6) - 5)w_1^* + 1}{4 \times 0.6 + 1 - 5w_1^*} = 0.1278$$
$$w_2^* = \sqrt[4]{(w_1^*)^3 w_5^*} = 0.2353,$$
$$w_3^* = \sqrt[4]{(w_1^*)^2 (w_5^*)^2} = 0.1920,$$
$$w_4^* = \sqrt[4]{(w_1^*)(w_5^*)^3} = 0.1566.$$

*and,* $\mathrm{disp}(W^*) = 1.5692$.

*Using exponential smoothing [13], Filev and Yager [111] obtained the following weighting vector*

$$W' = (0.41, 0.10, 0.13, 0.16, 0.20),$$

*with* $\mathrm{disp}(W') = 1.48$ *and* $\mathrm{orness}(W') = 0.5904$.

*We first note that the weights computed from the constrained optimization problem have better dispersion than those ones obtained by Filev and Yager in [111], however the (heuristic) technology suggested in [111] needs less computational efforts. Other interesting property here is that small changes in the required level of orness,* $\alpha$*, can cause a big variation in weighting vectors of near optimal dispersity, (for example, compare the weighting vectors* $W^*$ *and* $W'$*).*

## 2.3 OWA Operators for Ph.D. student selection

Following Carlsson and Fullér [43, 45] we illustrate the applicability of OWA operators to a doctoral student selection problem at the Graduate School of *Turku Centre for Computer Science* (TUCS).

TUCS offers a programme for gaining the Doctoral (PhD) degree in Computer Science and Information Systems. It is open for students from everywhere. The teaching language of the school is English. Prerequisites are either a Master's or a Bachelor's degree in Computer Science or in a closely related field. Study time is expected to be 4 years when starting from Master's level and 6 years from Bachelor's level.

The Graduate School offers advanced level courses in Computer Science and supervision of students within existing research projects. The main areas of research are *Algorithmics, Discrete Mathematics, Embedded Systems, Information Systems, Software Engineering.* Students are expected to take courses from at least two of these areas. Each student is assigned a supervisor from one of the fields indicated above.

The Graduate School is open for applications. There are no specific application forms. Applicants to TUCS graduate school should write a letter to the Director of TUCS. The letter should contain a formal application to the school, together with the following enclosures:

- Curriculum vitae
- Financing plan for studies
- Application for financial support, if requested
- Two letters of recommendation with referees' full contact addresses
- Official copy of examinations earned with official English translation
- Certificate of knowledge of English
- Short description of research interests

As certificate of knowledge of English, TOEFL test (minimum 550 points) or corresponding knowledge in English is required for applicants outside Finland.

Since the number of applicants (usually between 20 and 40) is much greater than the number of available scholarhips (around 6) we have to rank the candidates based on their performances. It can also happen that only a part of available scholarships will be awarded, because the number of *good* candidates is smaller than the number of available places.

The problem of selecting *young promising doctoral researchers* can be seen to consist of three components. The first component is a collection

$$X = \{x_1, \ldots, x_p\}$$

of applicants for the Ph.D. program.

The second component is a collection of 6 criteria (see Table 3) which are considered relevant in the ranking process.

For simplicity we suppose that all applicants are *young* and have Master's degree acquired more than one year before. In this case all the criteria are meaningful, and are of approximately the same importance.

For applicants with Bachelor's degree the first three criteria *Fit in research groups*, *Contributions* and *On the frontier of research* are meaningless,

| **Research interests** | (excellent) | (average) | (weak) |
|---|---|---|---|
| - Fit in research groups | ○ | ○ | ○ |
| - On the frontier of research | ○ | ○ | ○ |
| - Contributions | ○ | ○ | ○ |
| **Academic background** | | | |
| - University | ○ | ○ | ○ |
| - Grade average | ○ | ○ | ○ |
| - Time for acquiring degree | ○ | ○ | ○ |
| Letters of recommendation | Y | N | |
| Knowledge of English | Y | N | |

**Table 2.2.** Evaluation sheet.

because we have an undergraduate student without any research record. An applicant with Bachelor's degree or *just acquired* Master's degree should have excellent university record from a good university to be competitive.

For *old* applicants we encounter the problem of trade-offs between the age and the research record, and in this case their ratings on the last three criteria *University*, *Grade average* and *Time for acquiring degree* do not really matter. An *old* applicant should have a very good research record and a history of scientific cooperation with a TUCS research group to be competitive.

The third component is a group of 11 experts whose opinions are solicited in ranking the alternatives. The experts are selected from the following 9 research groups

- Algorithmics Group
- Coding Theory Group
- Computational Intelligence for Business
- Information Systems Research group
- Institute for Advanced Management Systems Research
- Probabilistic Algorithms and Software Quality
- Programming Methodology Group
- Strategic Information Systems Planning
- Theory Group: Mathematical Structures in Computer Science

So we have a Multi Expert-Multi Criteria Decision Making (ME-MCDM) problem. The ranking system described in the following is a two stage process. In the first stage, individual experts are asked to provide an evaluation of the alternatives. This evaluation consists of a rating for each alternative on each of the criteria, where the ratings are chosen from the scale $\{1, 2, 3\}$, where 3 stands for *excellent*, 2 stands for *average* and 1 means *weak* performance. Each expert provides a 6-tuple

$$(a_1, \dots, a_6)$$

for each applicant, where $a_i \in \{1, 2, 3\}$, $i = 1, \dots, 6$. The next step in the process is to find the overall evaluation for an alternative by a given expert.

In the second stage we aggregate the individual experts evaluations to obtain an overall value for each applicant.

In [317] Yager suggested an approach to the aggregation of criteria satisfactions guided by a regular non-decreasing quantifier $Q$. If $Q$ is Regular Increasing Monotone (RIM) quantifier then we measure the overall success of the alternative $x = (a_1, \dots, a_n)$ by

$$F_Q(a_1, \dots, a_n)$$

where $F_Q$ is an OWA operator derived from $Q$, i.e. the weights associated with this quantified guided aggregation are obtained as follows

$$w_i = Q\left(\frac{i}{n}\right) - Q\left(\frac{i-1}{n}\right)$$

for $i = 1, \dots, n$. The standard degree of orness associated with a (RIM) linguistic quantifier $Q$

$$\text{orness}(Q) = \int_0^1 Q(r)\, dr$$

is equal to the area under the quantifier [322]. This definition for the measure of orness of quantifier provides a simple useful method for obtaining this measure.

Consider the family of RIM quantifiers

$$Q_\alpha(r) = r^\alpha, \ \alpha \geq 0. \tag{2.12}$$

It is clear that

$$\text{orness}(Q_\alpha) = \int_0^1 r^\alpha\, dr = \frac{1}{\alpha + 1}$$

and $\text{orness}(Q_\alpha) < 0.5$ for $\alpha > 1$, $\text{orness}(Q_\alpha) = 0.5$ for $\alpha = 1$ and $\text{orness}(Q_\alpha) > 0.5$ for $\alpha < 1$.

Taking into consideration that we have 6 criteria (see Table 3) the weights derived from $Q_\alpha$ are determined as

$$w_1 = \left[\frac{1}{6}\right]^\alpha - 0,$$

$$w_2 = \left[\frac{2}{6}\right]^\alpha - \left[\frac{1}{6}\right]^\alpha,$$

$$w_3 = \left[\frac{3}{6}\right]^\alpha - \left[\frac{2}{6}\right]^\alpha$$

$$w_4 = \left[\frac{4}{6}\right]^\alpha - \left[\frac{3}{6}\right]^\alpha,$$

$$w_5 = \left[\frac{5}{6}\right]^\alpha - \left[\frac{4}{6}\right]^\alpha,$$

$$w_6 = 1 - \left[\frac{5}{6}\right]^\alpha$$

Furthermore, whatever is the linguistic quantifier, $Q_\alpha$, representing the statement *most criteria are satisfied by* $x$, we see that

$$1 \leq F_\alpha(a_1, \ldots, a_6) \leq 3$$

holds for each alternative $x = (a_1, \ldots, a_6)$ since $a_i \in \{1, 2, 3\}$, $i = 1, \ldots, 6$.

We search for an index $\alpha \geq 0$ such that the associated linguistic quantifier $Q_\alpha$ from the family (2.12) approximates the experts' preferences as much as possible. After interviewing the experts we found that all of them agreed on the following principles

1. if an applicant has more than two weak performances then his overall performance should be less than two,
2. if an applicant has maximum two weak performances then his overall performance should be more than two,
3. if an applicant has all but one excellent performances then his overall performance should be about 2.75,
4. if an applicant has three weak performances and one of them is on the criterion *on the frontier of research* then his overall performance should not be above 1.5,

From (1) we get

$$F_\alpha(3, 3, 3, 1, 1, 1) = 3 \times (w_1 + w_2 + w_3) + w_4 + w_5 + w_6 < 2,$$

that is,

$$3 \times \left[\frac{3}{6}\right]^\alpha + 1 - \left[\frac{3}{6}\right]^\alpha < 2 \iff \left[\frac{1}{2}\right]^\alpha < \left[\frac{1}{2}\right] \iff \alpha > 1,$$

and from (*ii*) we obtain

$$F_\alpha(3,3,3,2,1,1) = 3 \times (w_1 + w_2 + w_3) + 2 \times w_4 + w_5 + w_6 > 2$$

that is,

$$3 \times \left[\frac{3}{6}\right]^\alpha + 2 \times \left(\left[\frac{4}{6}\right]^\alpha - \left[\frac{3}{6}\right]^\alpha\right) + 1 - \left[\frac{4}{6}\right]^\alpha > 2 \iff \left[\frac{1}{2}\right]^\alpha + \left[\frac{2}{3}\right]^\alpha > 1$$

which holds if $\alpha < 1.293$. So from (1) and (2) we get

$$1 < \alpha \leq 1.293,$$

which means that $Q_\alpha$ should be *andlike* (or risk averse) quantifier with a degree of compensation just below the arithmetic average.

It is easy to verify that (6.10) and (iv) can not be satisfied by any quantifier $Q_\alpha$, $1 < \alpha \leq 1.293$, from the family (2.12). In fact, (6.10) requires that $\alpha \approx 0.732$ which is smaller than 1 and (iv) can be satisfied if $\alpha \geq 2$ which is bigger than 1.293. Rules (6.10) and (4) have priority whenever they are applicable.

In the second stage the technique for combining the expert's evaluation to obtain an overall evaluation for each alternative is based upon the OWA operators. Each applicant is represented by an 11-tuple

$$(b_1, \dots, b_{11})$$

where $b_i \in [1,3]$ is the unit score derived from the $i$-th expert's ratings. We suppose that the $b_i$'s are organized in descending order, i.e. $b_i$ can be seen as the worst of the $i$-th top scores.

Taking into consideration that the experts are selected from 9 different research groups there exists no applicant that scores overall well on the first criterion "Fit in research group". After a series of negotiations all experts agreed that the support of at least four experts is needed for qualification of the applicant.

Since we have 11 experts, applicants are evaluated based on their top four scores

$$(b_1, \dots, b_4)$$

and if at least three experts agree that the applicant is excellent then his final score should be 2.75 which is a cut-off value for the best student. That is

$$F_\alpha(3,3,3,1) = 3 \times (w_1 + w_2 + w_3) + w_4 = 2.75,$$

that is,

$$3 \times \left[\frac{3}{4}\right]^\alpha + 1 - \left[\frac{3}{4}\right]^\alpha = 2.75 \iff \left[\frac{3}{4}\right]^\alpha = 0.875 \iff \alpha \approx 0.464$$

So in the second stage we should choose an *orlike* OWA operator with $\alpha \approx 0.464$ for aggregating the top six scores of the applicant to find the final score.

If the final score is less than 2 then the applicant is disqualified and if the final score is at least 2.5 then the scholarship should be awarded to him. If the final score is between 2 and 2.5 then the scholarship can be awarded to the applicant pending on the total number of scholarships available.

We have presented a two stage process for doctoral student selection problem. In the first stage we have used an *andlike* OWA operator to implement some basic rules derived from certain (extremal) situations. In the second stage we have applied an *orlike* OWA operator, because the final score of applicants should be high if at least three experts find his record attractive (we do not require support from *all experts*).

It can happen (and it really happened) that some experts (a minority) forms a coalition and deliberately *overrate* some candidates in order to qualify them even though the majority of experts finds these candidates overall weak. We can resolve this problem by adding an extra criterion to the set of criteria measuring the competency of individual experts, or we issue an alarm message about the attempted cheating.

To determine the most appropriate linguistic quantifier in the first stage we can also try to *identify* interdependences between criteria [30, 35].

**Example 2.3.1** *Let us choose $\alpha = 1.2$ for the aggregation of the ratings in the first stage. Consider some applicant with the following scores (after re-ordering the scores in descending order):*

| | | | | | | | Unit score |
|---|---|---|---|---|---|---|---|
| *Expert 1* | *3* | *3* | *3* | *2* | *2* | *1* | *2.239* |
| *Expert 2* | *3* | *3* | *3* | *2* | *2* | *2* | *2.435* |
| *Expert 3* | *3* | *2* | *2* | *2* | *2* | *1* | *1.920* |
| *Expert 4* | *3* | *3* | *3* | *3* | *2* | *2* | *2.615* |
| *Expert 5* | *3* | *3* | *2* | *2* | *2* | *1* | *2.071* |
| *Expert 6* | *3* | *3* | *3* | *2* | *2* | *1* | *2.239* |
| *Expert 7* | *3* | *3* | *2* | *2* | *2* | *1* | *2.071* |
| *Expert 8* | *3* | *3* | *2* | *2* | *1* | *1* | *1.882* |
| *Expert 9* | *3* | *2* | *2* | *2* | *2* | *1* | *1.920* |
| *Expert 10* | *3* | *3* | *2* | *2* | *1* | *1* | *1.882* |
| *Expert 11* | *2* | *2* | *2* | *2* | *1* | *1* | *1.615* |

*The weights associated with this linguistic quantifier are*

$$(0.116, 0.151, 0.168, 0.180, 0.189, 0.196)$$

*In the second stage we choose $\alpha = 0.464$ and obtain the following weights*

$$(0.526, 0.199, 0.150, 0.125).$$

*The best four scores of the applicant are*

$$(2.615, 2.435, 2.239, 2.239).$$

*The final score is computed as*

$$F_\alpha(2.615, 2.435, 2.239, 2.239) = 2.475.$$

*So the applicant has good chances to get the scholarship.*

## 2.4 Possibility and necessity in weighted aggregation

Yager [321] discussed the issue of weighted min and max aggregations and provided for a formalization of the process of importance weighted transformation. Following Carlsson and Fullér [32, 42] we introduce fuzzy implication operators for importance weighted transformation. It should be noted that this new class of transfer functions contains as a subset those ones introduced by Yager in 1994. First we provide the definitions of terms needed in the process of weighted aggregation. Recall the three important classes of fuzzy implication operators:

- $S$-**implications**: defined by

$$x \to y = S(n(x), y) \tag{2.13}$$

  where $S$ is a t-conorm and $n$ is a negation on $[0, 1]$. We shall use the following $S$-implications: $x \to y = \min\{1 - x + y, 1\}$ (Łukasiewicz) and $x \to y = \max\{1 - x, y\}$ (Kleene-Dienes).
- $R$-**implications**: obtained by residuation of continuous t-norm $T$, i.e.

$$x \to y = \sup\{z \in [0, 1] \mid T(x, z) \leq y\}$$

  We shall use the following $R$-implication: $x \to y = 1$ if $x \leq y$ and $x \to y = y$ if $x > y$ (Gödel), $x \to y = \min\{1 - x + y, 1\}$ (Łukasiewicz)
- **t-norm implications**: if $T$ is a t-norm then

$$x \to y = T(x, y)$$

  We shall use the minimum-norm as t-norm implication (Mamdani).

Let $A$ and $B$ be two fuzzy predicates defined on the real line $\mathbb{R}$. Knowing that '$X$ is $B$' is true, the degree of possibility that the proposition '$X$ is $A$' is true, denoted by $\text{Pos}[A|B]$ or $\text{Pos}[A = B]$, is given by

$$\text{Pos}[A|B] = \sup_{t \in \mathbb{R}} A(t) \wedge B(t), \tag{2.14}$$

the degree of necessity that the proposition '$X$ is $A$' is true, $N[A|B]$, is given by

$$\text{Nes}[A|B] = 1 - \text{Pos}[\neg A|B],$$

where $A$ and $B$ are the possibility distributions defined by the predicates $A$ and $B$, respectively, and

$$(\neg A)(t) = 1 - A(t)$$

for any $t$. We can use any t-norm $T$ in (2.14) to model the logical connective *and*:

$$\text{Pos}[A|B] = \sup\{T(A(t), B(t)) | t \in \mathbb{R}\}, \tag{2.15}$$

Then for the measure of necessity of $A$, given $B$ we get

$$\text{Nes}[A|B] = 1 - \text{Pos}[\neg A|B] = 1 - \sup_t T(1 - A(t), B(t)).$$

Let $S$ be a t-conorm derived from t-norm $T$, then

$$1 - \sup_t T(1 - A(t), B(t)) = \inf_t \{1 - T(1 - A(t), B(t))\} =$$

$$\inf_t \{S(1 - B(t), A(t))\} = \inf_t \{B(t) \to A(t)\},$$

where the implication operator is defined in the sense of (2.13). That is,

$$\text{Nes}[A|B] = \inf_t \{B(t) \to A(t)\}.$$

Let $A$ and $W$ be discrete fuzzy sets in the unit interval, such that

$$A = a_1/(1/n) + a_2/(2/n) + \cdots + a_n/1,$$

and

$$W = w_1/(1/n) + w_2/(2/n) + \cdots + w_n/1,$$

where $n > 1$, and the terms $a_j/(j/n)$ and $w_j/(j/n)$ signify that $a_j$ and $w_j$ are the grades of membership of $j/n$ in $A$ and $W$, respectively, i.e.

$$A(j/n) = a_j, \quad W(j/n) = w_j$$

for $j = 1, \dots, n$, and the plus sign represents the union. Then we get the following simple formula for the measure of necessity of $A$, given $W$

$$\text{Nes}[A|W] = \min_{j=1,\dots,n} \{W(j/n) \to A(j/n)\} = \min_{j=1,\dots,n} \{w_j \to a_j\} \tag{2.16}$$

and we use the notation

$$\text{Nes}[A|W] = N[(a_1, a_2, \dots, a_n)|(w_1, w_2, \dots, w_n)]$$

A classical MADM problem can be expressed in a matrix format. A decision matrix is an $m \times n$ matrix whose element $x_{ij}$ indicates the performance rating of the $i$-th alternative, $x_i$, with respect to the $j$-th attribute, $c_j$:

$$\begin{pmatrix} x_{11} & x_{12} & \dots & x_{1n} \\ x_{21} & x_{22} & \dots & x_{2n} \\ \vdots & \vdots & & \vdots \\ x_{m1} & x_{m2} & \dots & x_{mn} \end{pmatrix}$$

In fuzzy case the values of the decision matrix are given as degrees of "how an alternative satisfies a certain attribute". Let $x$ be an alternative such that for any criterion $C_j(x) \in [0,1]$ indicates the degree to which this criterion is satisfied by $x$. So, in fuzzy case we have the following decision matrix

$$\begin{pmatrix} a_{11} & a_{12} & \dots & a_{1n} \\ a_{21} & a_{22} & \dots & a_{2n} \\ \vdots & \vdots & & \vdots \\ a_{m1} & a_{m2} & \dots & a_{mn} \end{pmatrix}$$

where $a_{ij} = C_j(x_{ij})$, for $i = 1,\dots,m$ and $j = 1,\dots,n$. Let $x$ be an alternative and let

$$(a_1, a_2, \dots, a_n)$$

denote the degrees to which $x$ satisfies the criteria, i.e.

$$a_j = C_j(x), \ i = 1,\dots,n.$$

In many applications of fuzzy sets as multi-criteria decision making, pattern recognition, diagnosis and fuzzy logic control one faces the problem of weighted aggregation. The issue of weighted aggregation has been studied by Carlsson and Fullér [32], Dubois and Prade [87, 88, 89], Fodor and Roubens [112] and Yager [315, 317, 318, 319, 320, 321].

Assume associated with each fuzzy set $C_j$ is a weight $w_j \in [0,1]$ indicating its importance in the aggregation procedure, $j = 1,\dots,n$. The general process for the inclusion of importance in the aggregation involves the transformation of the fuzzy sets under the importance. Let **Agg** indicate an aggregation operator, max or min, to find the weighted aggregation. Yager [321] first transforms each of the membership grades using the weights

$$g(w_i, a_i) = \hat{a}_i,$$

for $i = 1,\dots,n$, and then obtain the weighted aggregate

$$\mathbf{Agg}\langle \hat{a}_1, \dots, \hat{a}_n \rangle.$$

The form of $g$ depends upon the type of aggregation being performed, the operation **Agg**.

As discussed by Yager in incorporating the effect of the importances in the min operation we are interested in reducing the effect of the elements which have low importance. In performing the min aggregation it is the elements with low values that play the most significant role in this type of aggregation, one way to reduce the effect of elements with low importance is to transform them into big values, values closer to one. Yager introduced a class of functions which can be used for the inclusion of importances in the min aggregation

$$g(w_i, a_i) = S(1 - w_i, a_i),$$

where $S$ is a t-conorm, and then obtain the weighted aggregate

$$\min\{\hat{a}_1, \dots, \hat{a}_n\} = \min\{S(1 - w_1, a_1), \dots S(1 - w_n, a_n)\} \tag{2.17}$$

We first note that if $w_i = 0$ then from the basic property of t-conorms it follows that

$$S(1 - w_i, a_i) = S(1, w_i) = 1.$$

Thus, zero importance gives us one. Yager notes that the formula can be seen as a measure of the degree to which an alternative satisfies the following proposition:

*All important criteria are satisfied*

**Example 2.4.1** *Let*

$$(0.3, 0.2, 0.7, 0.6)$$

*be the vector of weights and let*

$$(0.4, 0.6, 0.6, 0.4)$$

*be the vector of aggregates. If* $g(w_i, a_i) = \max\{1 - w_i, a_i\}$ *then we get*

$$g(w_1, a_1) = (1 - 0.3) \vee 0.4 = 0.7,$$

$$g(w_2, a_2) = (1 - 0.2) \vee 0.6 = 0.8,$$

$$g(w_3, a_3) = (1 - 0.7) \vee 0.6 = 0.6,$$

$$g(w_4, a_4) = (1 - 0.6) \vee 0.4 = 0.4.$$

*That is*

$$\min\{g(w_1, a_1), \dots, g(w_4, a_4)\} = \min\{0.7, 0.8, 0.6, 0.4\} = 0.4.$$

As for the max aggregation operator: Since it is the large values that play the most important role in the aggregation we desire to transform the low importance elements into small values and thus have them not play a significant role in the max aggregation. Yager suggested a class of functions which can be used for importance transformation in max aggregation

$$g(w_i, a_i) = T(w_i, a_i),$$

where $T$ is a t-norm. We see that if $w_i = 0$ then $T(w_i, a_i) = 0$ and the element plays no rule in the max.

Let **Agg** indicate any aggregation operator and let

$$(a_1, a_2, \dots, a_n),$$

denote the vector of aggregates. We define the weighted aggregation as

$$\mathbf{Agg}\,\langle g(w_1, a_1), \dots, g(w_n, a_n)\rangle.$$

where the function $g$ satisfies the following properties

- if $a > b$ then $g(w, a) \geq g(w, b)$,
- $g(w, a)$ is monotone in $w$,
- $g(0, a) = id, \;\; g(1, a) = a$,

where the identity element, $id$, is such that if we add it to our aggregates it doesn't change the aggregated value. Let us recall formula (2.16)

$$\text{Nes}[(a_1, a_2, \dots, a_n)|(w_1, w_2, \dots, w_n)] = \min\{w_1 \to a_1, \dots, w_n \to a_n\}, \quad (2.18)$$

where

$$A = a_1/(1/n) + a_2/(2/n) + \cdots + a_n/1,$$

is the fuzzy set of performances and

$$W = w_1/(1/n) + w_2/(2/n) + \cdots + w_n/1,$$

is the fuzzy set of weights; and the formula for weighted aggregation by the minimum operator

$$\min\{\hat{a}_1, \dots, \hat{a}_n\},$$

where

$$\hat{a}_i = g(w_i, a_i) = S(1 - w_i, a_i),$$

and $S$ is a t-conorm.

It is easy to see that if the implication operator in (2.18) is an $S$-implication then from the equality

$$w_j \to a_j = S(1 - w_j, a_j),$$

it follows that the weighted aggregation of the $a_i$'s is nothing else, but

$$\text{Nes}[(a_1, a_2, \dots, a_n)|(w_1, w_2, \dots, w_n)],$$

the necessity of performances, given weights.

This observation leads us to a new class of transfer functions introduced by Carlsson and Fullér [32, 42] (which contains Yager's functions as a subset):

$$\hat{a}_i = g(w_i, a_i) = w_i \to a_i, \tag{2.19}$$

where $\to$ is an arbitrary implication operator. Then we combine the $\hat{a}_i$'s with an appropriate aggregation operator **Agg**.

However, we first select the implication operator, and then the aggregation operator **Agg** to combine the $\hat{a}_i$'s. If we choose a t-norm implication in (2.19) then we will select the max operator, and if we choose an $R$- or $S$-implication then we will select the min operator to aggregate the $\hat{a}_i$'s.

It should be noted that if we choose an $R$-implication in (2.19) then the equation

$$\min\{w_1 \to a_1, \dots, w_n \to a_n\} = 1,$$

holds iff $w_i \leq a_i$ for all $i$, i.e. when each performance rating is at least as big as its associated weight. In other words, if a performance rating with respect to an attribute exceeds the value of the weight of this attribute then this rating does not matter in the overall rating. However, ratings which are well below of the corresponding weights play a significant role in the overall rating. Thus the formula (2.18) with an $R$-implication can be seen as a measure of the degree to which an alternative satisfies the following proposition:

*All scores are bigger than or equal to the importances*

It should be noted that the min aggregation operator does not allow any compensation, i.e. a higher degree of satisfaction of one of the criteria can not compensate for a lower degree of satisfaction of another criteria. Averaging operators realize *trade-offs* between objectives, by allowing a positive compensation between ratings.

Another possibility is to use an *andlike* or an *orlike* OWA-operator to aggregate the elements of the bag

$$\langle w_1 \to a_1, \dots, w_n \to a_n \rangle.$$

Let $A$ and $W$ be discrete fuzzy sets in $[0,1]$, where $A(t)$ denotes the performance rating and $W(t)$ denotes the weight of a criterion labeled by $t$. Then the weighted aggregation of $A$ can be defined by,

- a t-norm-based measure of necessity of $A$, given $W$:

$$\text{Nes}[A|W] = \min_t \{W(t) \to A(t)\}.$$

For example, the Kleene-Dienes implication operator,

$$w_i \to a_i = \max\{1 - w_i, a_i\},$$

implements Yager's approach to fuzzy screening [318].

- a t-norm-based measure of possibility of $A$, given $W$:

$$\text{Pos}[A|W] = \max_t \{T(A(t), W(t))\}.$$

- an OWA-operator defined on the bag

$$\langle W(t) \to A(t) \,|\, t \rangle.$$

Other possibility is to take the value

$$\frac{\int_0^1 A(t) \wedge W(t)\, dt}{\int_0^1 W(t)\, dt},$$

for the overall score of $A$. If $A(t) \geq W(t)$ for all $t \in [0,1]$ then the overall score of $A$ is equal to one. However, the bigger the set

$$\{t \in [0,1] | A(t) \leq W(t)\},$$

the smaller the overall rating of $A$.

**Example 2.4.2** *Let* $(0.3, 0.2, 0.7, 0.6)$ *be the vector of weights and let* $(0.4, 0.6, 0.6, 0.4)$ *be the vector of aggregates. If*

$$g(w_i, a_i) = \min\{1, 1 - w_i + a_i\},$$

*is the Łukasiewicz implication then we compute*

$$g(w_1, a_1) = 0.3 \to 0.4 = 1,$$
$$g(w_2, a_2) = 0.2 \to 0.6 = 1,$$
$$g(w_3, a_3) = 0.7 \to 0.6 = 0.9,$$
$$g(w_4, a_4) = 0.6 \to 0.4 = 0.8.$$

*That is*

$$\min\{g(w_1, a_1), \dots, g(w_4, a_4)\} = \min\{1, 1, 0.9, 0.8\} = 0.8.$$

*If* $g(w_i, a_i)$ *is implemented by the Gödel implication then we get*

$$g(w_1, a_1) = 0.3 \to 0.4 = 1,$$
$$g(w_2, a_2) = 0.2 \to 0.6 = 1,$$
$$g(w_3, a_3) = 0.7 \to 0.6 = 0.6,$$
$$g(w_4, a_4) = 0.6 \to 0.4 = 0.4.$$

*That is*

$$\min\{g(w_1, a_1), \dots, g(w_4, a_4)\} = \min\{1, 1, 0.6, 0.4\} = 0.4.$$

*If* $g(w_i, a_i) = w_i a_i$ *is the Larsen implication then we have*

$$g(w_1, a_1) = 0.3 \times 0.4 = 0.12,$$
$$g(w_2, a_2) = 0.2 \times 0.6 = 0.12,$$
$$g(w_3, a_3) = 0.7 \times 0.6 = 0.42,$$
$$g(w_4, a_4) = 0.6 \times 0.4 = 0.24.$$

*That is*

$$\max\{g(w_1, a_1), \ldots, g(w_4, a_4)\} = \max\{0.12, 0.12, 0.42, 0.24\} = 0.42.$$

Generalizing Yager's principles for weighted min and max aggregations we introduced fuzzy implication operators as a means for importance weighted transformation. Weighted aggregations are important in decision problems where we have multiple attributes to consider and where the outcome is to be judged in terms of attributes which are not equally important for the decision maker. The importance is underscored if there is a group of decision makers with varying value judgments on the attributes and/or if this group has factions promoting some subset of attributes.

## 2.5 Benchmarking in linguistic importance weighted aggregations

In this Section we concentrate on the issue of weighted aggregations and provide a possibilistic approach to the process of importance weighted transformation when both the importances (interpreted as *benchmarks*) and the ratings are given by symmetric triangular fuzzy numbers. Following Carlsson and Fullér [48, 55] we will show that using the possibilistic approach

(i) small changes in the membership function of the importances can cause only small variations in the weighted aggregate;
(ii) the weighted aggregate of fuzzy ratings remains stable under small changes in the *nonfuzzy* importances;
(iii) the weighted aggregate of crisp ratings still remains stable under small changes in the crisp importances whenever we use a continuous implication operator for the importance weighted transformation.

In many applications of fuzzy sets such as multi-criteria decision making, pattern recognition, diagnosis and fuzzy logic control one faces the problem of weighted aggregation. The issue of weighted aggregation has been studied extensively by Carlsson and Fullér [30, 42, 43], Delgado et al [80], Dubois and Prade [87, 88, 89], Fodor and Roubens [112], Herrera et al [162, 163, 165, 166, 167] and Yager [315, 317, 318, 319, 320, 321, 324, 326].

Unlike Herrera and Herrera-Viedma [166] who perform direct computation on a finite and totally ordered term set, we use the membership functions to aggregate the values of the linguistic variables *rate* and *importance*. The main problem with finite term sets is that the impact of small changes in the weighting vector can be disproportionately large on the weighted aggregate (because the set of possible output values is finite, but the set of possible weight vectors is a subset of $\mathbb{R}^n$). For example, the *rounding* operator in the *convex combination of linguistic labels*, defined by Delgado et al. [80], is very sensitive to the values around 0.5 ($round(0.499) = 0$ and $round(0.501) = 1$).

Following Carlsson and Fullér [55] we consider the process of importance weighted aggregation when both the aggregates and the importances are given by an infinite term set, namely by the values of the linguistic variables "rate" and "importance". In this approach the importances are considered as benchmark levels for the performances, i.e. an alternative performs well on all criteria if the degree of satisfaction to each of the criteria is at least as big as the associated benchmark.

The proposed "stable" method in [55] ranks the alternatives by measuring the degree to which they satisfy the proposition:

"All ratings are larger than or equal to their importance".

We will also use OWA operators to measure the degree to which an alternative satisfies the proposition:

"Most ratings are larger than or equal to their importance",

where the OWA weights are derived from a well-chosen lingusitic quantifier.

Recall that a fuzzy set $A$ is called a symmetric triangular fuzzy number with center $a$ and width $\alpha > 0$ if its membership function has the following form

$$A(t) = \begin{cases} 1 - \dfrac{|a-t|}{\alpha} & \text{if } |a-t| \leq \alpha \\ 0 & \text{otherwise} \end{cases}$$

and we use the notation $A = (a, \alpha)$. If $\alpha = 0$ then $A$ collapses to the characteristic function of $\{a\} \subset \mathbb{R}$ and we will use the notation $A = \bar{a}$.

We will use symmetric triangular fuzzy numbers to represent the values of linguistic variables [334] *rate* and *importance* in the universe of discourse $I = [0, 1]$. The set of all symmetric triangular fuzzy numbers in the unit interval will be denoted by $\mathcal{F}(I)$.

Let $A = (a, \alpha)$ and $B = (b, \beta)$. The degree of possibility that the proposition "$A$ is less than or equal to $B$" is true, denoted by $\text{Pos}[A \leq B]$, is defined by (1.19) and computed by

$$\text{Pos}[A \leq B] = \begin{cases} 1 & \text{if } a \leq b \\ 1 - \dfrac{a-b}{\alpha+\beta} & \text{if } 0 < a-b < \alpha+\beta \\ 0 & \text{otherwise} \end{cases} \tag{2.20}$$

Let $A$ be an alternative with ratings $(A_1, A_2, \dots, A_n)$, where $A_i = (a_i, \alpha_i) \in \mathcal{F}(I)$, $i = 1, \dots, n$. For example, the symmetric triangular fuzzy number $A_j = (0.8, \alpha)$ when $0 < \alpha \leq 0.2$ can represent the property

"the rating on the $j$-th criterion is around 0.8"

and if $\alpha = 0$ then $A_j = (0.8, \alpha)$ is interpreted as "the rating on the $j$-th criterion is equal to 0.8"

and finally, the value of $\alpha$ can not be bigger than 0.2 because the domain of $A_j$ is the unit interval.

Assume that associated with each criterion is a weight $W_i = (w_i, \gamma_i)$ indicating its importance in the aggregation procedure, $i = 1, \dots, n$. For example, the symmetric triangular fuzzy number $W_j = (0.5, \gamma) \in \mathcal{F}(I)$ when $0 < \gamma \leq 0.5$ can represent the property

"the importance of the $j$-th criterion is approximately 0.5"

and if $\gamma = 0$ then $W_j = (0.5, \gamma)$ is interpreted as

"the importance of the $j$-th criterion is equal to 0.5"

and finally, the value of $\gamma$ can not be bigger than 0.5 becuase the domain of $W_j$ is the unit interval.

The general process for the inclusion of importance in the aggregation involves the transformation of the ratings under the importance. Following Carlsson and Fullér [55] we suggest the use of the transformation function

$$g\colon \mathcal{F}(I) \times \mathcal{F}(I) \to [0, 1],$$

where,

$$g(W_i, A_i) = \mathrm{Pos}[W_i \leq A_i],$$

for $i = 1, \dots, n$, and then obtain the weighted aggregate,

$$\phi(A, W) = \mathbf{Agg}\langle \mathrm{Pos}[W_1 \leq A_1], \dots, \mathrm{Pos}[W_n \leq A_n] \rangle. \tag{2.21}$$

where **Agg** denotes an aggregation operator.

For example if we use the min function for the aggregation in (2.21), that is,

$$\phi(A, W) = \min\{\mathrm{Pos}[W_1 \leq A_1], \dots, \mathrm{Pos}[W_n \leq A_n]\} \tag{2.22}$$

then the equality

$$\phi(A, W) = 1$$

holds iff $w_i \leq a_i$ for all $i$, i.e. when the mean value of each performance rating is at least as large as the mean value of its associated weight. In other words, if a performance rating with respect to a criterion exceeds the importance of this criterion with possibility one, then this rating does not matter in the overall rating. However, ratings which are well below the corresponding importances (in possibilistic sense) play a significant role in the overall rating. In this sense the importance can be considered as *benchmark* or *reference level* for the performance. Thus, formula (2.21) with the min operator can be seen as a measure of the degree to which an alternative satisfies the following proposition:

"All ratings are larger than or equal to their importance".

It should be noted that the min aggregation operator does not allow any compensation, i.e. a higher degree of satisfaction of one of the criteria can not compensate for a lower degree of satisfaction of another criterion.

Averaging operators realize *trade-offs* between criteria, by allowing a positive compensation between ratings. We can use an *andlike* or an *orlike* OWA-operator [319] to aggregate the elements of the bag

$$\langle \text{Pos}[W_1 \leq A_1], \dots, \text{Pos}[W_n \leq A_n] \rangle.$$

In this case (2.21) becomes,

$$\phi(A, W) = \mathbf{OWA}\langle \text{Pos}[W_1 \leq A_1], \dots, \text{Pos}[W_n \leq A_n] \rangle,$$

where **OWA** denotes an Ordered Weighted Averaging Operator. Formula (2.21) does not make any difference among alternatives whose performance ratings exceed the value of their importance with respect to all criteria with possibility one: the overall rating will always be equal to one. Penalizing ratings that are "larger than the associated importance, but not large enough" (that is, their intersection is not empty) we can modify formula (2.21) to measure the degree to which an alternative satisfies the following proposition:

"All ratings are essentially larger than their importance".

In this case the transformation function can be defined as

$$g(W_i, A_i) = \text{Nes}[W_i \leq A_i] = 1 - \text{Pos}[W_i > A_i],$$

for $i = 1, \dots, n$, and then obtain the weighted aggregate,

$$\phi(A, W) = \min\{\text{Nes}[W_1 \leq A_1], \dots, \text{Nes}[W_n \leq A_n]\}. \tag{2.23}$$

If we do allow a positive compensation between ratings then we can use OWA-operators in (2.23). That is,

$$\phi(A, W) = \mathbf{OWA}\langle \text{Nes}[W_1 \leq A_1], \dots, \text{Nes}[W_n \leq A_n] \rangle.$$

The following theorem shows that if we choose the min operator for **Agg** in (2.21) then small changes in the membership functions of the weights can cause only a small change in the weighted aggregate, i.e. the weighted aggregate depends continuously on the weights.

**Theorem 2.5.1** *[55] Let $A_i = (a_i, \alpha) \in \mathcal{F}(I)$, $\alpha_i > 0$, $i = 1, \dots, n$ and let $\delta > 0$ such that*

$$\delta < \alpha := \min\{\alpha_1, \dots, \alpha_n\}$$

*If* $W_i = (w_i, \gamma_i)$ *and* $W_i^\delta = (w_i^\delta, \gamma^\delta) \in \mathcal{F}(I)$, $i = 1, \dots, n$, *satisfy the relationship*

$$\max_i D(W_i, W_i^\delta) \leq \delta \tag{2.24}$$

*then the following inequality holds,*

$$|\phi(A, W) - \phi(A, W^\delta)| \leq \frac{\delta}{\alpha} \tag{2.25}$$

*where* $\phi(A, W)$ *is defined by (2.22) and*

$$\phi(A, W^\delta) = \min\{Pos[W_1^\delta \leq A_1], \dots, Pos[W_n^\delta \leq A_n]\}.$$

From (2.24) and (2.25) it follows that

$$\lim_{\delta \to 0} \phi(A, W^\delta) = \phi(A, W)$$

for any $A$, which means that if $\delta$ is small enough then $\phi(A, W^\delta)$ can be made arbitrarily close to $\phi(A, W)$.

As an immediate consequence of (2.25) we can see that Theorem 2.5.1 remains valid for the case of crisp weighting vectors, i.e. when $\gamma_i = 0$, $i = 1, \dots, n$. In this case

$$\mathrm{Pos}[\bar{w}_i \leq A_i] = \begin{cases} 1 & \text{if } w_i \leq a_i \\ A(w_i) & \text{if } 0 < w_i - a_i < \alpha_i \\ 0 & \text{otherwise} \end{cases}$$

where $\bar{w}_i$ denotes the characteristic function of $w_i \in [0, 1]$; and the weighted aggregate, denoted by $\phi(A, w)$, is computed as

$$\phi(A, w) = \mathbf{Agg}\{\mathrm{Pos}[\bar{w}_1 \leq A_1], \dots, \mathrm{Pos}[\bar{w}_n \leq A_n]\}$$

If **Agg** is the minimum operator then we get

$$\phi(A, w) = \min\{\mathrm{Pos}[\bar{w}_1 \leq A_1], \dots, \mathrm{Pos}[\bar{w}_n \leq A_n]\} \tag{2.26}$$

If both the ratings and the importances are given by crisp numbers (i.e. when $\gamma_i = \alpha_i = 0$, $i = 1, \dots, n$) then $\mathrm{Pos}[\bar{w}_i \leq \bar{a}_i]$ implements the *standard strict* implication operator, i.e.,

$$\mathrm{Pos}[\bar{w}_i \leq \bar{a}_i] = w_i \to a_i = \begin{cases} 1 \text{ if } w_i \leq a_i \\ 0 \text{ otherwise} \end{cases}$$

It is clear that whatever is the aggregation operator in

$$\phi(a, w) = \mathbf{Agg}\{\mathrm{Pos}[\bar{w}_1 \leq \bar{a}_1], \dots, \mathrm{Pos}[\bar{w}_n \leq \bar{a}_n]\},$$

the weighted aggregate, $\phi(a, w)$, can be very sensitive to small changes in the weighting vector $w$.

However, we can still sustain the *benchmarking character* of the weighted aggregation if we use an $R$-implication operator to transform the ratings under importance [30, 42]. For example, for the operator

$$\phi(a, w) = \min\{w_1 \to a_1, \ldots, w_n \to a_n\}. \tag{2.27}$$

where $\to$ is an $R$-implication operator, the equation

$$\phi(a, w) = 1,$$

holds iff $w_i \leq a_i$ for all $i$, i.e. when the value of each performance rating is at least as big as the value of its associated weight. However, the crucial question here is: Does the

$$\lim_{w^\delta \to w} \phi(a, w^\delta) = \phi(a, w), \ \forall a \in I,$$

relationship still remain valid for any $R$-implication?

The answer is negative. $\phi$ will be continuous in $w$ if and only if the implication operator is continuous. For example, if we choose the Gödel implication in (2.27) then $\phi$ will not be continuous in $w$, because the Gödel implication is not continuous.

To illustrate the sensitivity of $\phi$ defined by the Gödel implication (5.2) consider (2.27) with $n = 1$, $a_1 = w_1 = 0.6$ and $w_1^\delta = w_1 + \delta$. In this case

$$\phi(a_1, w_1) = \phi(w_1, w_1) = \phi(0.6, 0.6) = 1,$$

but

$$\phi(a, w_1^\delta) = \phi(w_1, w_1 + \delta) = \phi(0.6, 0.6 + \delta) = (0.6 + \delta) \to 0.6 = 0.6,$$

that is,

$$\lim_{\delta \to 0} \phi(a_1, w_1^\delta) = 0.6 \neq \phi(a_1, w_1) = 1.$$

But if we choose the (continuous) Łukasiewicz implication in (2.27) then $\phi$ will be continuous in $w$, and therefore, small changes in the importance can cause only small changes in the weighted aggregate. Thus, the following formula

$$\phi(a, w) = \min\{(1 - w_1 + a_1) \wedge 1, \ldots, (1 - w_n + a_n) \wedge 1\}. \tag{2.28}$$

not only keeps up the benchmarking character of $\phi$, but also implements a stable approach to importance weighted aggregation in the nonfuzzy case.

If we do allow a positive compensation between ratings then we can use an OWA-operator for aggregation in (2.28). That is,

$$\phi(a, w) = \mathbf{OWA}\,\langle(1 - w_1 + a_1) \wedge 1, \ldots, (1 - w_n + a_n) \wedge 1\rangle. \tag{2.29}$$

Taking into consideration that OWA-operators are usually continuous, equation (2.29) also implements a stable approach to importance weighted aggregation in the nonfuzzy case.

**Example 2.5.1** *We illustrate our approach by several examples.*

- Crisp importance and crisp ratings. *Consider the aggregation problem with*

$$a = \begin{pmatrix} 0.7 \\ 0.5 \\ 0.8 \\ 0.9 \end{pmatrix} \quad and \quad w = \begin{pmatrix} 0.8 \\ 0.7 \\ 0.9 \\ 0.6 \end{pmatrix}.$$

*Using formula (2.28) for the weighted aggregate we find*

$$\phi(a,w) = \min\{0.8 \to 0.7, 0.7 \to 0.5, 0.9 \to 0.8, 0.6 \to 0.9\} =$$
$$\min\{0.9, 0.8, 0.9, 1\} = 0.8$$

- Crisp importance and fuzzy ratings. *Consider the aggregation problem with*

$$a = \begin{pmatrix} (0.7, 0.2) \\ (0.5, 0.3) \\ (0.8, 0.2) \\ (0.9, 0.1) \end{pmatrix} \quad and \quad w = \begin{pmatrix} 0.8 \\ 0.7 \\ 0.9 \\ 0.6 \end{pmatrix}.$$

*Using formula (2.26) for the weighted aggregate we find*

$$\phi(A,w) = \min\{1/2, 1/3, 1/2, 1\} = 1/3.$$

*The essential reason for the low performance of this object is that it performed low on the second criterion which has a high importance. If we allow positive compensations and use an OWA operator with weights, for example,* $(1/6, 1/3, 1/6, 1/3)$ *then we find*

$$\phi(A,w) = \mathbf{OWA}\langle 1/2, 1/3, 1/2, 1\rangle =$$

$$1/6 + 1/2 \times (1/3 + 1/6) + 1/3 \times 1/3 = 19/36 \approx 0.5278$$

- Fuzzy importance and fuzzy ratings. *Consider the aggregation problem with*

$$A = \begin{pmatrix} (0.7, 0.2) \\ (0.5, 0.3) \\ (0.8, 0.2) \\ (0.9, 0.1) \end{pmatrix} \quad and \quad W = \begin{pmatrix} (0.8, 0.2) \\ (0.7, 0.3) \\ (0.9, 0.1) \\ (0.6, 0.2) \end{pmatrix}.$$

*Using formula (2.22) for the weighted aggregate we find*

$$\phi(A,W) = \min\{3/4, 2/3, 2/3, 1\} = 2/3.$$

*The reason for the relatively high performance of this object is that, even though it performed low on the second criterion which has a high importance, the second importance has a relatively large tolerance level, 0.3.*

In this Section we have introduced a possibilistic approach to the process of importance weighted transformation when both the importances and the aggregates are given by triangular fuzzy numbers. In this approach the importances have been considered as benchmark levels for the performances, i.e. an alternative performs well on all criteria if the degree of satisfaction to each of the criteria is at least as big as the associated benchmark. We have suggested the use of measure of necessity to be able to distinguish alternatives with overall rating one (whose performance ratings exceed the value of their importance with respect to all criteria with possibility one).

We have showon that using the possibilistic approach (i) small changes in the membership function of the importances can cause only small variations in the weighted aggregate; (ii) the weighted aggregate of fuzzy ratings remains stable under small changes in the *nonfuzzy* importances; (iii) the weighted aggregate of crisp ratings still remains stable under small changes in the crisp importances whenever we use a continuous implication operator for the importance weighted transformation.

These results have further implications in several classes of multiple criteria decision making problems, in which the aggregation procedures are rough enough to make the finely tuned formal selection of an optimal alternative meaningless.

# 3. Fuzzy Reasoning

## 3.1 The theory of approximate reasoning

In 1979 *Zadeh* introduced the theory of approximate reasoning [337]. This theory provides a powerful framework for reasoning in the face of imprecise and uncertain information. Central to this theory is the representation of propositions as statements assigning fuzzy sets as values to variables. Suppose we have two interactive variables $x \in X$ and $y \in Y$ and the causal relationship between $x$ and $y$ is completely known. Namely, we know that $y$ is a function of $x$, that is $y = f(x)$. Then we can make inferences easily

$$"y = f(x)" \ \& \ "x = x_1" \longrightarrow "y = f(x_1)".$$

This inference rule says that if we have $y = f(x)$, for all $x \in X$ and we observe that $x = x_1$ then $y$ takes the value $f(x_1)$. More often than not we do not know the complete causal link $f$ between $x$ and $y$, only we now the values of $f(x)$ for some particular values of $x$, that is

$$\begin{array}{ll}\Re_1: & \text{If } x = x_1 \text{ then } y = y_1\\ \Re_2: & \text{If } x = x_2 \text{ then } y = y_2\\ & \dots\\ \Re_n: & \text{If } x = x_n \text{ then } y = y_n\end{array}$$

If we are given an $x' \in X$ and want to find an $y' \in Y$ which correponds to $x'$ under the rule-base $\Re = \{\Re_1, \dots, \Re_m\}$ then we have an interpolation problem.

Let $x$ and $y$ be linguistic variables, e.g. "$x$ is high" and "$y$ is small". The basic problem of approximate reasoning is to find the membership function of the consequence $C$ from the rule-base $\{\Re_1, \dots, \Re_n\}$ and the fact $A$.

$$\begin{array}{ll}\Re_1: & \text{if } x \text{ is } A_1 \text{ then } y \text{ is } C_1,\\ \Re_2: & \text{if } x \text{ is } A_2 \text{ then } y \text{ is } C_2,\\ & \dots\dots\dots\dots\\ \Re_n: & \text{if } x \text{ is } A_n \text{ then } y \text{ is } C_n\\ \text{fact:} & \quad x \text{ is } A\\ \hline \text{consequence:} & \qquad\qquad y \text{ is } C\end{array}$$

In fuzzy logic and approximate reasoning, the most important fuzzy inference rule is the *Generalized Modus Ponens* (GMP).

The classical *Modus Ponens* inference rule says:

| | | |
|---|---|---|
| premise | if $p$ then | $q$ |
| fact | $p$ | |
| consequence | | $q$ |

This inference rule can be interpreted as: If $p$ is true and $p \to q$ is true then $q$ is true.

If we have fuzzy sets, $A \in \mathcal{F}(U)$ and $B \in \mathcal{F}(V)$, and a fuzzy implication operator in the premise, and the fact is also a fuzzy set, $A' \in \mathcal{F}(U)$, (usually $A \neq A'$) then the consequnce, $B' \in \mathcal{F}(V)$, can be derived from the premise and the fact using the compositional rule of inference suggested by Zadeh [333]. The *Generalized Modus Ponens* inference rule says

| | | |
|---|---|---|
| premise | if $x$ is $A$ then | $y$ is $B$ |
| fact | $x$ is $A'$ | |
| consequence: | | $y$ is $B'$ |

where the consequence $B'$ is determined as a composition of the fact and the fuzzy implication operator

$$B' = A' \circ (A \to B)$$

that is,

$$B'(v) = \sup_{u \in U} \min\{A'(u), (A \to B)(u,v)\}, \ v \in V.$$

The consequence $B'$ is nothing else but the shadow of $A \to B$ on $A'$. The *Generalized Modus Ponens*, which reduces to classical modus ponens when $A' = A$ and $B' = B$, is closely related to the forward data-driven inference which is particularly useful in the *Fuzzy Logic Control*.

In many practical cases instead of sup-min composition we use sup-$T$ composition, where $T$ is a t-norm.

**Definition 3.1.1** *(sup-$T$ compositional rule of inference)*

| | | |
|---|---|---|
| *premise* | *if $x$ is $A$ then* | *$y$ is $B$* |
| *fact* | *$x$ is $A'$* | |
| *consequence:* | | *$y$ is $B'$* |

*where the consequence $B'$ is determined as a composition of the fact and the fuzzy implication operator*

$$B' = A' \circ (A \to B)$$

*that is,*

$$B'(v) = \sup\{T(A'(u), (A \to B)(u, v)) \mid u \in U\}, \; v \in V.$$

*It is clear that $T$ can not be chosen independently of the implication operator.*

**Example 3.1.1** *The GMP with Larsen's product implication, where the membership function of the consequence $B'$ is defined by*

$$B'(y) = \sup \min\{A'(x), A(x)B(y)\},$$

*for all $y \in \mathbb{R}$.*

The classical *Modus Tollens inference rule* says: If $p \to q$ is true and $q$ is false then $p$ is false. The *Generalized Modus Tollens*, inference rule says,

| | | |
|---|---|---|
| premise | if $x$ is $A$ then | $y$ is $B$ |
| fact | | $y$ is $B'$ |
| consequence: | $x$ is $A'$ | |

which reduces to "Modus Tollens" when $B = \neg B$ and $A' = \neg A$, is closely related to the backward goal-driven inference which is commonly used in expert systems, especially in the realm of *medical diagnosis.*

Suppose that $A$, $B$ and $A'$ are fuzzy numbers. The GMP should satisfy some rational properties

**Property 3.1.1** *Basic property:*

$$\frac{\begin{array}{ll} \textit{if} \;\; x \textit{ is } A \textit{ then} & y \textit{ is } B \\ \;\;\;\; x \textit{ is } A & \end{array}}{\qquad\qquad y \textit{ is } B}$$

**Property 3.1.2** *Total indeterminance:*

$$\frac{\begin{array}{ll} \textit{if } x \textit{ is } A \textit{ then} & y \textit{ is } B \\ x \textit{ is } \neg A & \end{array}}{\qquad\qquad y \textit{ is unknown}}$$

**Property 3.1.3** *Subset:*

$$\frac{\begin{array}{ll} \textit{if } x \textit{ is } A \textit{ then} & y \textit{ is } B \\ x \textit{ is } A' \subset A & \end{array}}{\qquad\qquad y \textit{ is } B}$$

**Property 3.1.4** *Superset:*

$$\frac{\begin{array}{ll} \textit{if} \;\; x \textit{ is } A \textit{ then} & y \textit{ is } B \\ \;\;\;\; x \textit{ is } A' & \end{array}}{\qquad\qquad y \textit{ is } B' \supset B}$$

Suppose that $A$, $B$ and $A'$ are fuzzy numbers. The GMP with Mamdani implication inference rule says

$$\begin{array}{rl} \text{if} \quad x \text{ is } A \text{ then} & y \text{ is } B \\ x \text{ is } A' & \\ \hline & y \text{ is } B' \end{array}$$

where the membership function of the consequence $B'$ is defined by

$$B'(y) = \sup\{A'(x) \wedge A(x) \wedge B(y) | x \in \mathbb{R}\}, \; y \in \mathbb{R}.$$

It can be shown that the GMP with Mamdani implication operator does not satisfy all the four properties listed above. However, the GMP with Gödel implication does satisfy all the four properties listed above [145].

## 3.2 Aggregation in fuzzy system modeling

Many applications of fuzzy set theory involve the use of a fuzzy rule base to model complex and perhaps ill-defined systems. These applications include fuzzy logic control, fuzzy expert systems and fuzzy systems modeling. Typical of these situations are set of $n$ rules of the form

$$\begin{aligned} \Re_1 &: \text{if } x \text{ is } A_1 \text{ then } y \text{ is } C_1 \\ \Re_2 &: \text{if } x \text{ is } A_2 \text{ then } y \text{ is } C_2 \\ &\cdots\cdots\cdots\cdots \\ \Re_n &: \text{if } x \text{ is } A_n \text{ then } y \text{ is } C_n \end{aligned}$$

The fuzzy inference process consists of the following four step algorithm [320]:

- Determination of the relevance or matching of each rule to the current input value.
- Determination of the output of each rule as fuzzy subset of the output space. We shall denote these individual rule outputs as $R_j$.
- Aggregation of the individual rule outputs to obtain the overall fuzzy system output as fuzzy subset of the output space. We shall denote this overall output as $R$.
- Selection of some action based upon the output set.

Our purpose here is to investigate the requirements for the operations that can be used to implement this reasoning process. We are particularly concerned with the third step, the rule output aggregation.

Let us look at the process for combining the individual rule outputs. A basic assumption we shall make is that the operation is *pointwise* and *likewise*. By pointwise we mean that for every $y$, $R(y)$ just depends upon

$R_j(y)$, $j = 1, \ldots, n$. By likewise we mean that the process used to combine the $R_j$ is the same for all of the $y$.

Let us denote the pointwise process we use to combine the individual rule outputs as

$$F(y) = \mathbf{Agg}(R_1(y), \ldots, R_n(y))$$

In the above **Agg** is called the aggregation operator and the $R_j(y)$ are the arguments. More generally, we can consider this as an operator

$$a = \mathbf{Agg}(a_1, \ldots, a_n)$$

where the $a_i$ and $a$ are values from the membership grade space, normally the unit interval.

Let us look at the minimal requirements associated with **Agg**. We first note that the combination of of the individual rule outputs should be independent of the choice of indexing of the rules. This implies that a required property that we must associate with th Agg operator is that of commutativity, the indexing of the arguments does not matter. We note that the commutativity property allows to represent the arguments of the **Agg** operator, as an unordered collection of possible duplicate values; such an object is a **bag**.

For an individual rule output, $R_j$, the membership grade $R_j(y)$ indicates the degree or sterength to which this rule suggests that $y$ is the appropriate solution. In particular if for a pair of elements $y'$ and $y''$ it is the case that $R_i(y') \geq R_i(y'')$, then we are saying that rule $j$ is preferring $y'$ as the system output over $y''$. From this we can reasonably conclude that if all rules prefer $y'$ over $y''$ as output then the overall system output should prefer $y'$ over $y''$. This observation requires us to impose a monotonicity condition on the **Agg** operation. In particular if

$$R_j(y') \geq R_j(y''),$$

for all $j$, then $R(y') \geq R(y'')$.

There appears one other condition we need to impose upon the aggregation operator. Assume that there exists some rule whose firing level is zero. The implication of this is that the rule provides no information regarding what should be the output of the system. It should not affect the final $R$. The first observation we can make is that whatever output this rule provides should not make make any distinction between the potential outputs. Thus, we see that the aggregation operator needs an identy element.

In summary, we see that the aggregation operator, **Agg** must satisfy three conditions: *commutativity, monotonicity, must contain a fixed identity.* These conditions are based on the three requirements: that the indexing of the rules be unimportant, a positive association between individual rule output and total system output, and non-firing rules play no role in the decision process.

These operators are called MICA (Monotonic Identity Commutative Aggregation) operators introduced by Yager [320]. MICA operators are the most general class for aggregation in fuzzy modeling. They include t-norms, t-conorms, averaging and compensatory operators.

Assume $X$ is a set of elements. A bag drawn from $X$ is any collection of elements which is contained in $X$. A bag is different from a subset in that it allows multiple copies of the same element. A bag is similar to a set in that the ordering of the elements in the bag does not matter. If $A$ is a bag consisiting of $a$, $b$, $c$, $d$ we denote this as $A =< a, b, c, d >$. Assume $A$ and $B$ are two bags. We denote the sum of the bags $C = A \oplus B$ where $C$ is the bag consisting of the members of both $A$ and $B$.

**Example 3.2.1** *Let* $A = \langle a, b, c, d \rangle$ *and* $B = \langle b, c, c \rangle$ *then*

$$A \oplus B = \langle a, b, c, d, b, c, c \rangle$$

In the following we let $\text{Bag}(X)$ indicate the set of all bags of the set $X$.

**Definition 3.2.1** *A function*

$$F \colon \text{Bag}(X) \to X$$

*is called a bag mapping from* $\text{Bag}(X)$ *into the set* $X$.

An important property of bag mappings are that they are commutative in the sense that the ordering of the elements does not matter.

**Definition 3.2.2** *Assume* $A = \langle a_1, \ldots, a_n \rangle$ *and* $B = \langle b_1, \ldots, b_n \rangle$ *are two bags of the same cardinality* $n$. *If the elements in* $A$ *and* $B$ *can be indexed in such way that* $a_i \geq b_i$ *for all* $i$ *then we shall denote this* $A \geq B$.

**Definition 3.2.3** *(MICA operator) [320] A bag mapping* $M \colon \text{Bag}([0,1]) \to [0,1]$ *is called MICA operator if it has the following two properties*

- *If* $A \geq B$ *then* $M(A) \geq M(B)$ *(monotonicity)*
- *For every bag* $A$ *there exists an element,* $u \in [0,1]$, *called the identity of* $A$ *such that if* $C = A \oplus < u >$ *then* $M(C) = M(A)$ *(identity)*

Thus the MICA operator is endowed with two properties in addition to the inherent commutativity of the bag operator, monotonicity and identity: (i) the requirement of *monotonicity* appears natural for an aggregation operator in that it provides some connection between the arguments and the aggregated value; (ii) the property of identity allows us to have the facility for aggregating data which does not affect the overall result. This becomes useful for enabling us to include importances among other characteristics.

## 3.3 Multiple fuzzy reasoning schemes

Suppose we are given one block of fuzzy rules of the form

$$\begin{array}{lll}\Re_1: & \text{if } x \text{ is } A_1 \text{ then } z \text{ is } C_1, & \\ \Re_2: & \text{if } x \text{ is } A_2 \text{ then } z \text{ is } C_2, & \\ & \cdots\cdots\cdots & \\ \Re_n: & \text{if } x \text{ is } A_n \text{ then } z \text{ is } C_n & \\ \text{fact:} & \quad x \text{ is } A & \\ \hline \text{consequence:} & & z \text{ is } C\end{array}$$

where the rules are connected with the (hidden) sentence connective *also*. The $i$-th fuzzy rule $\Re_i$, from this rule-base, $\Re = \{\Re_1, \dots, \Re_n\}$, is implemented by a *fuzzy implication* $R_i$ and is defined as

$$R_i(u, w) = A_i(u) \to C_i(w)$$

There are two main approaches to determine the consequence $C$:

1. *Combine the rules first.* In this approach, we first combine all the rules by an aggregation operator **Agg** into one rule which used to obtain $C$ from $A$.

$$R = \mathbf{Agg}\,(\Re_1, \Re_2, \cdots, \Re_n)$$

If the implicite sentence connective *also* is interpreted as *and* then we get

$$R(u, w) = \bigcap_{i=1}^{n} R_i(u, w) = \min(A_i(u) \to C_i(w))$$

or by using a t-norm $T$ for modeling the connective *and*

$$R(u, w) = T(R_1(u, w), \dots, R_n(u, w))$$

If the implicite sentence connective *also* is interpreted as *or* then we get

$$R(u, w) = \bigcup_{i=1}^{n} R_i(u, v, w) = \max(A_i(u) \to C_i(w))$$

or by using a t-conorm $S$ for modeling the connective *or*

$$R(u, w) = S(R_1(u, w), \dots, R_n(u, w))$$

Then we compute $C$ from $A$ by the compositional rule of inference as

$$C = A \circ R = A \circ \mathbf{Agg}\,(R_1, R_2, \cdots, R_n).$$

2. *Fire the rules first.* Fire the rules individually, given $A$, and then combine their results into $C$. We first compose $A$ with each $R_i$ producing intermediate result
$$C_i' = A \circ R_i$$
for $i = 1, \dots, n$ and then combine the $C_i'$ component wise into $C'$ by some aggregation operator **Agg**
$$C' = \mathbf{Agg}\,(C_1', \dots, C_n') = \mathbf{Agg}\,(A \circ R_1, \dots, A \circ R_n).$$

**Lemma 3.3.1** *Consider one block of fuzzy rules of the form*

$$\Re_i\text{: } \textit{if } x \textit{ is } A_i \textit{ then } z \textit{ is } C_i, \;\; 1 \le i \le n$$

*and suppose that the input to the system is a fuzzy singleton. Then the consequence, $C$, inferred from the complete set of rules is equal to the aggregated result, $C'$, derived from individual rules. This statements holds for any kind of aggregation operators used to combine the rules.*

If several linguistic variables are involved in the antecedents and the conclusions of the rules then the system will be referred to as a multi-input-multi-output fuzzy system. For example, the case of two-input-single-output (MISO) fuzzy systems is of the form

$$\Re_i : \text{if } x \text{ is } A_i \text{ and } y \text{ is } B_i \text{ then} z \text{ is } C_i$$

where $x$ and $y$ are the process state variables, $z$ is the control variable, $A_i$, $B_i$, and $C_i$ are linguistic values of the linguistic vatiables $x$, $y$ and $z$ in the universes of discourse $U$, $V$, and $W$, respectively, and an implicit sentence connective *also* links the rules into a rule set or, equivalently, a rule-base. The procedure for obtaining the fuzzy output of such a knowledge base consists from the following three steps:

- Find the firing level of each of the rules.
- Find the output of each of the rules.
- Aggregate the individual rule outputs to obtain the overall system output.

To infer the output $z$ from the given process states $x$, $y$ and fuzzy relations $R_i$, we apply the compositional rule of inference:

$$\begin{array}{ll}
\Re_1 : & \text{if } x \text{ is } A_1 \text{ and } y \text{ is } B_1 \text{ then } z \text{ is } C_1 \\
\Re_2 : & \text{if } x \text{ is } A_2 \text{ and } y \text{ is } B_2 \text{ then } z \text{ is } C_2 \\
 & \cdots\cdots\cdots\cdots \\
\Re_n : & \text{if } x \text{ is } A_n \text{ and } y \text{ is } B_n \text{ then } z \text{ is } C_n \\
\text{fact :} & \quad x \text{ is } \bar{x}_0 \text{ and } y \text{ is } \bar{y}_0 \\
\hline
\text{consequence :} & \qquad\qquad\qquad\qquad\quad z \text{ is } C
\end{array}$$

where the consequence is computed by

$$\text{consequence} = \text{Agg}\,\langle \text{fact} \circ \Re_1, \ldots, \text{fact} \circ \Re_n \rangle.$$

That is,

$$C = \text{Agg}(\bar{x}_0 \times \bar{y}_0 \circ R_1, \ldots, \bar{x}_0 \times \bar{y}_0 \circ R_n)$$

taking into consideration that $\bar{x}_0(u) = 0,\ u \neq x_0$ and $\bar{y}_0(v) = 0,\ v \neq y_0$, the computation of the membership function of $C$ is very simple:

$$C(w) = \text{Agg}\{A_1(x_0) \times B_1(y_0) \to C_1(w), \ldots, A_n(x_0) \times B_n(y_0) \to C_n(w)\}$$

for all $w \in W$. The procedure for obtaining the fuzzy output of such a knowledge base can be formulated as

- The firing level of the $i$-th rule is determined by

$$A_i(x_0) \times B_i(y_0).$$

- The output of of the $i$-th rule is calculated by

$$C_i'(w) := A_i(x_0) \times B_i(y_0) \to C_i(w)$$

  for all $w \in W$.
- The overall system output, $C$, is obtained from the individual rule outputs $C_i'$ by

$$C(w) = \text{Agg}\{C_1', \ldots, C_n'\}$$

  for all $w \in W$.

**Example 3.3.1** *If the sentence connective* also *is interpreted as anding the rules by using minimum-norm then the membership function of the consequence is computed as*

$$C = (\bar{x}_0 \times \bar{y}_0 \circ R_1) \cap \ldots \cap (\bar{x}_0 \times \bar{y}_0 \circ R_n).$$

*That is,*

$$C(w) = \min\{A_1(x_0) \times B_1(y_0) \to C_1(w), \ldots, A_n(x_0) \times B_n(y_0) \to C_n(w)\},$$

*for all $w \in W$.*

**Example 3.3.2** *If the sentence connective* also *is interpreted as oring the rules by using minimum-norm then the membership function of the consequence is computed as*

$$C = (\bar{x}_0 \times \bar{y}_0 \circ R_1) \cup \ldots \cup (\bar{x}_0 \times \bar{y}_0 \circ R_n).$$

*That is,*

$$C(w) = \max\{A_1(x_0) \times B_1(y_0) \to C_1(w), \ldots, A_n(x_0) \times B_n(y_0) \to C_n(w)\},$$

*for all $w \in W$.*

**Example 3.3.3** *Suppose that the Cartesian product and the implication operator are implemented by the t-norm $T(u, v) = uv$. If the sentence connective also is interpreted as oring the rules by using minimum-norm then the membership function of the consequence is computed as*

$$C = (\bar{x}_0 \times \bar{y}_0 \circ R_1) \cup \ldots \cup (\bar{x}_0 \times \bar{y}_0 \circ R_n).$$

*That is,*

$$C(w) = \max\{A_1(x_0)B_1(y_0)C_1(w), \ldots, A_n(x_0)B_n(y_0)C_n(w)\}$$

*for all $w \in W$.*

We present three well-known inference mechanisms in MISO fuzzy systems. For simplicity we assume that we have two fuzzy rules of the form

| | |
|---|---|
| $\Re_1$ : | if $x$ is $A_1$ and $y$ is $B_1$ then $z$ is $C_1$ |
| $\Re_2$ : | if $x$ is $A_2$ and $y$ is $B_2$ then $z$ is $C_2$ |
| fact : | $x$ is $\bar{x}_0$ and $y$ is $\bar{y}_0$ |
| consequence : | $z$ is $C$ |

**Tsukamoto** [299] All linguistic terms are supposed to have monotonic membership functions. The firing levels of the rules are computed by

$$\alpha_1 = A_1(x_0) \wedge B_1(y_0), \quad \alpha_2 = A_2(x_0) \wedge B_2(y_0).$$

In this mode of reasoning the individual crisp control actions $z_1$ and $z_2$ are computed from the equations

$$\alpha_1 = C_1(z_1), \quad \alpha_2 = C_2(z_2),$$

and the overall crisp control action is expressed as

$$z_0 = \frac{\alpha_1 z_1 + \alpha_2 z_2}{\alpha_1 + \alpha_2} = \frac{\alpha_1 C_1^{-1}(\alpha_1) + \alpha_2 C_2^{-1}(\alpha_2)}{\alpha_1 + \alpha_2},$$

i.e. $z_0$ is computed by the discrete Center-of-Gravity method.
**Sugeno and Takagi** [293] use the following architecture:

| | |
|---|---|
| $\Re_1$ : | if $x$ is $A_1$ and $y$ is $B_1$ then $z_1 = a_1 x + b_1 y$ |
| $\Re_2$ : | if $x$ is $A_2$ and $y$ is $B_2$ then $z_2 = a_2 x + b_2 y$ |
| fact : | $x$ is $\bar{x}_0$ and $y$ is $\bar{y}_0$ |
| consequence : | $z_0$ |

The firing levels of the rules are computed by

$$\alpha_1 = A_1(x_0) \wedge B_1(y_0), \quad \alpha_2 = A_2(x_0) \wedge B_2(y_0), \tag{3.1}$$

then the individual rule outputs are derived from the relationships

$$z_1^* = a_1x_0 + b_1y_0, \quad z_2^* = a_2x_0 + b_2y_0,$$

and the crisp control action is expressed as

$$z_0 = \frac{\alpha_1 z_1^* + \alpha_2 z_2^*}{\alpha_1 + \alpha_2}$$

If we have $m$ rules in our rule-base then the crisp control action is computed as

$$z_0 = \frac{\alpha_1 z_1^* + \cdots + \alpha_m z_m^*}{\alpha_1 + \cdots + \alpha_m},$$

where $\alpha_i$ denotes the firing level of the $i$-th rule, $i = 1, \dots, m$.
**Simplified fuzzy reasoning.** [257] In this context, the word *simplified* means that the individual rule outputs are given by crisp numbers, and therefore, we can use their weighted sum (where the weights are the firing strengths of the corresponding rules) to obtain the overall system output:

| | | |
|---|---|---|
| $\Re_1$: | if $x$ is $A_1$ and $y$ is $B_1$ | then $z = z_1$ |
| $\Re_2$: | if $x$ is $A_2$ and $y$ is $B_2$ | then $z = z_2$ |
| fact: | $x$ is $u_1$ and $y$ is $u_2$ | |
| consequence: | | $z_0$ |

where $A_1$, $A_2$, $B_1$ and $B_2$ are values of the linguistc variables $x$ and $y$, respectively. We derive $z_0$ from the initial content of the data base, $\{u_1, u_2\}$, and from the fuzzy rule base $\Re = \{\Re_1, \Re_2\}$ by the simplified fuzzy reasoning scheme as

$$z_0 = \frac{z_1\alpha_1 + z_2\alpha_2}{\alpha_1 + \alpha_2}$$

where $\alpha_i$ denotes the firing level of the $i$-th rule computed by (3.1).

## 3.4 Some properties of the compositional rule of inference

In this Section following Fullér and Zimmermann [126, 134], and Fullér and Werners [131] we show two very important features of the compositional rule of inference under triangular norms. Namely, we prove that (i) if the t-norm defining the composition and the membership function of the observation are continuous, then the conclusion depends continuously on the observation; (ii) if the t-norm and the membership function of the relation are continuous, then the observation has a continuous membership function. We consider the compositional rule of inference with different observations $P$ and $P'$:

| | |
|---|---|
| Observation: | $X$ has property $P$ |
| Relation: | $X$ and $Y$ are in relation $R$ |
| Conclusion: | $Y$ has property $Q$ |

| | |
|---|---|
| Observation: | $X$ has property $P'$ |
| Relation m: | $X$ and $Y$ are in relation $R$ |
| Conclusion: | $Y$ has property $Q'$ |

According to Zadeh's compositional rule of inference, $Q$ and $Q'$ are computed as

$$Q = P \circ R, \qquad Q' = P' \circ R$$

i.e.,

$$\mu_Q(y) = \sup_{x \in \mathbb{R}} T(\mu_P(x), \mu_R(x,y)), \quad \mu_{Q'}(y) = \sup_{x \in \mathbb{R}} T(\mu_{P'}(x), \mu_R(x,y)).$$

The following theorem shows that when the observations are close to each other in the metric $D$, then there can be only a small deviation in the membership functions of the conclusions.

**Theorem 3.4.1** [134] *Let $\delta \geq 0$ and $T$ be a continuous triangular norm, and let $P$, $P'$ be fuzzy intervals. If $D(P, P') \leq \delta$ then*

$$\sup_{y \in \mathbb{R}} |\mu_Q(y) - \mu_{Q'}(y)| \leq \omega_T(\max\{\omega_P(\delta), \omega_{P'}(\delta)\}).$$

*where $\omega_P(\delta)$ and $\omega_{P'}(\delta)$ denotes the modulus of continuity of $P$ and $P'$ at $\delta$.*

It should be noted that the stability property of the conclusion $Q$ with respect to small changes in the membership function of the observation $P$ in the compositional rule of inference scheme is independent from the relation $R$ (it's membership function can be discontinuous). Since the membership function of the conclusion in the compositional rule of inference can have unbounded support, it is possible that the maximal distance between the $\alpha$-level sets of $Q$ and $Q'$ is infinite, but their membership grades are arbitrarily close to each other.

The following theorem establishes the continuity property of the conclusion in the compositional rule of inference scheme.

**Theorem 3.4.2** [134] *Let $R$ be continuous fuzzy relation, and let $T$ be a continuous t-norm. Then $Q$ is continuous and*

$$\omega_Q(\delta) \leq \omega_T(\omega_R(\delta)),$$

*for each $\delta \geq 0$.*

From Theorem 3.4.2 it follows that the continuity property of the membership function of the conclusion $Q$ in the compositional rule of inference scheme is independent from the observation $P$ (it's membership function can be discontinuous). The next theorem shows that the stability property of the conclusion under small changes in the membership function of the observation holds in the discrete case, too.

**Theorem 3.4.3** [134] *Let $T$ be a continuous t-norm. If the observation $P$ and the relation matrix $R$ are finite, then*

$$H(Q, Q') \leq \omega_T(H(P, P')) \tag{3.2}$$

*where $H$ denotes the Hamming distance and the conclusions $Q$ and $Q'$ are computed as*

$$\mu_Q(y_j) = \max_{i=1,\dots,m} T(\mu_P(x_i), \mu_R(x_i, y_j)),$$

$$\mu_{Q'}(y_j) = \max_{i=1,\dots,m} T(\mu_{P'}(x_i), \mu_R(x_i, y_j)),$$

*for $j = 1, \dots, n$, $\text{supp}(\mu_Q) = \text{supp}(\mu_{Q'}) = \{y_1, \dots, y_n\}$ and $\text{supp}(\mu_P) = \text{supp}(\mu_{P'}) = \{x_1, \dots, x_m\}$.*

The proof of this theorem is carried out analogously to the proof of Theorem 3.4.1. It should be noted that in the case of $T(u, v) = \min\{u, v\}$ (3.2) yields

$$H(Q, Q') \leq H(P, P').$$

Theorems 3.4.1 and 3.4.2 can be easily extended to the compositional rule of inference with several relations:

| | |
|---|---|
| Observation: | $X$ has property $P$ |
| Relation 1: | $X$ and $Y$ are in relation $W_1$ |
| ... | |
| Relation m: | $X$ and $Y$ are in relation $W_m$ |
| Conclusion: | $Y$ has property $Q$ |

| | |
|---|---|
| Observation: | $X$ has property $P'$ |
| Relation 1: | $X$ and $Y$ are in relation $W_1$ |
| ... | |
| Relation m: | $X$ and $Y$ are in relation $W_m$ |
| Conclusion: | $Y$ has property $Q'$. |

According to Zadeh's compositional rule of inference, $Q$ and $Q'$ are computed by sup-$T$ composition as follows

$$Q = \bigcap_{i=1}^{m} P \circ W_i \quad \text{and} \quad Q' = \bigcap_{i=1}^{m} P' \circ W_i. \tag{3.3}$$

Generalizing Theorems 3.4.1 and 3.4.2 about the case of single relation, we show that when the observations are close to each other in the metric $D$, then there can be only a small deviation in the membership function of the conclusions even if we have several relations.

**Theorem 3.4.4** [131] *Let $\delta \geq 0$ and $T$ be a continuous triangular norm, and let $P$, $P'$ be continuous fuzzy intervals. If*

$$D(P, P') \leq \delta$$

*then*

$$\sup_{y \in \mathbb{R}} |\mu_Q(y) - \mu_{Q'}(y)| \leq \omega_T(\max\{\omega_P(\delta), \omega_{P'}(\delta)\})$$

*where $Q$ and $Q'$ are computed by (3.3).*

In the following theorem we establish the continuity property of the conclusion under continuous fuzzy relations $W_i$ and continuous t-norm $T$.

**Theorem 3.4.5** [131] *Let $W_i$ be continuous fuzzy relation, i=1,...,m and let $T$ be a continuous t-norm. Then $Q$ is continuous and*

$$\omega_Q(\delta) \leq \omega_T(\omega(\delta)) \quad \textit{for each } \delta \geq 0$$

*where* $\omega(\delta) = \max\{\omega_{W_1}(\delta), \ldots, \omega_{W_m}(\delta)\}$.

The above theorems are also valid for Multiple Fuzzy Reasoning (MFR) schemes:

| | | |
|---|---|---|
| Observation: | $P$ | $P'$ |
| Implication 1: | $P_1 \to Q_1$ | $P'_1 \to Q'_1$ |
| | $\ldots$ | $\ldots$ |
| Implication $m$: | $P_m \to Q_m$ | $P'_m \to Q'_m$ |
| Conclusion: | $Q$ | $Q'$ |

where $Q$ and $Q'$ are computed by sup-$T$ composition as follows

$$Q = P \circ \bigcap_{i=1}^{m} P_i \to Q_i, \quad Q' = P' \circ \bigcap_{i=1}^{m} P'_i \to Q'_i,$$

i.e.,

$$\mu_Q(y) = \sup_{x \in \mathbb{R}} T(\mu_P(x), \min_{i=1,\ldots,m} \mu_{P_i}(x) \to \mu_{Q_i}(y)),$$

$$\mu_{Q'}(y) = \sup_{x \in \mathbb{R}} T(\mu_{P'}(x), \min_{i=1,\ldots,m} \mu_{P'_i(x)} \to \mu_{Q'_i}(y)).$$

Then the following theorems hold.

**Theorem 3.4.6** [131] *Let $\delta \geq 0$, let $T$ be a continuous triangular norm, let $P$, $P'$, $P_i$, $P'_i$, $Q_i$, $Q'_i$, $i = 1, \dots, m$, be fuzzy intervals and let $\to$ be a continuous fuzzy implication operator. If*

$$\max\{D(P, P'), \max_{i=1,\dots,m} D(P_i, P'_i), \max_{i=1,\dots,m} D(Q_i, Q'_i)\} \leq \delta,$$

*then*

$$\sup_{y \in \mathbb{R}} |\mu_Q(y) - \mu_{Q'}(y)| \leq \omega_T(\max\{\omega(\delta), \omega_{\to}(\omega(\delta))\}),$$

*where*

$$\omega(\delta) = max\{\omega_{P_i}(\delta), \omega_{P'_i}(\delta), \omega_{Q_i}(\delta), \omega_{Q'_i}(\delta)\},$$

*and $\omega_{\to}$ denotes the modulus of continuity of the fuzzy implication operator.*

**Theorem 3.4.7** [131] *Let $\to$ be a continuous fuzzy implication operator, let $P$, $P'$, $P_i$, $P'_i$, $Q_i$, $Q'_i$, $i = 1, \dots, m$, be fuzzy intervals and let $T$ be a continuous t-norm. Then $Q$ is continuous and*

$$\omega_Q(\delta) \leq \omega_T(\omega_{\to}(\omega(\delta)) \quad \textit{for each } \delta \geq 0,$$

*where*

$$\omega(\delta) = \max\{\omega_{P_i}(\delta), \omega_{P'_i}(\delta), \omega_{Q_i}(\delta), \omega_{Q'_i}(\delta)\},$$

*and $\omega_{\to}$ denotes the modulus of continuity of the fuzzy implication operator.*

From $\lim_{\delta \to 0} \omega(\delta) = 0$ and Theorem 3.4.6 it follows that

$$\|\mu_Q - \mu_{Q'}\|_\infty = \sup_y |\mu_Q(y) - \mu_{Q'}(y)| \to 0$$

whenever $D(P, P') \to 0$, $D(P_i, P'_i) \to 0$ and $D(Q_i, Q'_i) \to 0$, $i = 1, \dots, m$, which means the stability of the conclusion under small changes of the observation and rules.

The stability property of the conclusion under small changes of the membership function of the observation and rules guarantees that small rounding errors of digital computation and small errors of measurement of the input data can cause only a small deviation in the conclusion, i.e. every successive approximation method can be applied to the computation of the linguistic approximation of the exact conclusion.

## 3.5 Computation of the compositional rule of inference under t-norms

In approximate reasoning there are several kinds of inference rules, which deal with the problem of deduction of conclusions in an imprecise setting. An important problem is the (approximate) computation of the membership function of the conclusion in these schemes. Throughout this Section shall use $\phi$-functions [160] for the representation of linguistic terms in the compositional rule of inference.

**Definition 3.5.1** *A $\phi$-function is defined by*

$$\phi(x;a,b,c,d)=\begin{cases}1 & \text{if } b\le x\le c\\ \phi_1\left(\dfrac{x-a}{b-c}\right) & \text{if } a\le x\le b,\ a<b,\\ \phi_2\left(\dfrac{x-c}{d-c}\right) & \text{if } c\le x\le d,\ c<d,\\ 0 & \text{otherwise}\end{cases} \tag{3.4}$$

*where $\phi_1\colon [0,1]\to[0,1]$ is continuous, monoton increasing function and $\phi_1(0)=0$, $\phi_1(1)=1$; $\phi_2:[0,1]\to[0,1]$ is continuous, monoton decreasing function and $\phi_2(0)=1$, $\phi_2(1)=0$ So $\phi$ is a function which is 0 left of $a$, increases to 1 in $(a,b)$, is 1 in $[b,c]$, decreases to 0 in $(c,d)$ and is 0 right of $d$ (for the sake of simplicity, we do not consider the cases $a=b$ or $c=d$).*

It should be noted that $\phi$ can be considered as the membership function of the fuzzy interval $\tilde{a}=(b,c,b-a,d-c)_{LR}$, with $R(x)=\phi_2(x)$ and $L(x)=\phi_1(1-x)$.

In [160] Hellendoorn showed the closure property of the compositional rule of inference under sup-min composition and presented exact calculation formulas for the membership function of the conclusion when both the observation and relation parts are given by $S$-, $\pi$-, or $\phi$-function. Namely, he proved the following theorem.

**Theorem 3.5.1** *[160] In the compositional rule of inference under minimum norm,*

| | |
|---|---|
| *Observation:* | *X has property P* |
| *Relation:* | *X and Y are in relation W* |
| *Conclusion:* | *Y has property Q* |

*is true that, when $\mu_P(x)=\phi(x;a_1,a_2,a_3,a_4)$ and $\mu_W(x,y)=\phi(y-x;b_1,b_2,b_3,b_4)$ then*

$$\mu_Q(y)=\phi(y;a_1+b_1,a_2+b_2,a_3+b_3,a_4+b_4),$$

*where the function $\phi$ is defined by (3.4) .*

In this Section, following Fullér and Werners [128], and Fullér and Zimmermann [129], generalizing Hellendoorn's results, we derive exact calculation formulas for the compositional rule of inference under triangular norms when both the observation and the part of the relation (rule) are given by concave $\phi$-function [160]; and the t-norm is Archimedean with a strictly convex additive generator function. The efficiency of this method stems from the fact that the distributions, involved in the relation and observation, are represented by a parametrized $\phi$-function. The deduction process then consists of some simple computations performed on the parameters.

We consider the compositional rule of inference, where, the membership functions of $P$ and $W$ are defined by means of a particular $\phi$-function, and the membership function of the conclusion $Q$ is defined by sup-$T$ composition of $P$ and $W$

$$Q(y) = (P \circ W)(y) = \sup_x T(P(x), W(x,y)), y \in \mathbb{R}.$$

The following theorem presents an efficient method for the exact computation of the membership function of the conclusion.

**Theorem 3.5.2** *[129] Let $T$ be an Archimedean t-norm with additive generator $f$ and let $P(x) = \phi(x; a, b, c, d)$ and $W(x,y) = \phi(y - x; a + u, b + u, c + v, d + v)$. If $\phi_1$ and $\phi_2$ are twice differentiable, concave functions, and $f$ is a twice differentiable, strictly convex function, then*

$$Q(y) = \begin{cases} 1 & \text{if } 2b + u \le y \le 2c + v \\ f^{[-1]}\left(2f\left(\phi_1\left[\dfrac{y - 2a - u}{2(b-a)}\right]\right)\right) & \text{if } 2a + u \le y \le 2b + u \\ f^{[-1]}\left(2f\left(\phi_2\left[\dfrac{y - 2c - v}{2(d-c)}\right]\right)\right) & \text{if } 2c + v \le y \le 2d + v \\ 0 & \text{otherwise.} \end{cases}$$

It should be noted that we have calculated the membership function of $Q$ under the assumption that the left and right spreads of $P$ do not differ from the left and right spreads of $W$ (the lengths of their tops can be different). To determine the exact membership function of $Q$ in the general case: $P(x) = \phi(x; a_1, a_2, a_3, a_4)$ and $W(x,y) = \phi(y-x; b_1, b_2, b_3, b_4)$ can be very tricky (see [172]).

Using Theorem 3.5.2 we shall compute the exact membership function of the conclusion $Q$ in the case of Yager's, Dombi's and Hamacher's parametrized t-norm. Let us consider the following scheme

$$\begin{array}{lcl} P(x) & = & \phi(x; a, b, c, d) \\ W(y,x) & = & \phi(y - x; a + u, b + u, c + v, d + v) \\ \hline Q(y) & = & (P \circ W)(y) \end{array}$$

Denoting

$$\sigma := \frac{(y - 2a - u)}{2(b-a)}, \quad \theta := \frac{y - 2c - v}{2(d-c)},$$

we get the following formulas for the membership function of the conclusion $Q$.

- Yager's t-norm with $p > 1$. Here

$$T(x,y) = 1 - \min\left\{1, \sqrt[p]{(1-x)^p + (1-y)^p}\right\}.$$

with generator $f(t) = (1-t)^p$, and

$$Q(y) = \begin{cases} 1 - 2^{1/p}(1-\phi_1(\sigma)) & \text{if } 0 < \sigma < \phi_1^{-1}(2^{-1/p}), \\ 1 & \text{if } 2b + u \le y \le 2c + v, \\ 1 - 2^{1/p}(1-\phi_2(\theta)) & \text{if } 0 < \theta < \phi_2^{-1}(1 - 2^{1/p}), \end{cases} \tag{3.5}$$

- Hamacher's t-norm with $p \le 2$. Here

$$T(x,y) = \frac{xy}{p + (1-p)(x+y-xy)}$$

with generator

$$f(t) = \ln \frac{p + (1-p)t}{t},$$

and

$$Q(y) = \begin{cases} \dfrac{p}{\tau_1^2 - 1 + p} & \text{if } 0 < \sigma < 1, \\ 1 & \text{if } 2b + u \le y \le 2c + v, \\ \dfrac{p}{\tau_2^2 - 1 + p} & \text{if } 0 < \theta < 1, \end{cases}$$

where

$$\tau_1 = \frac{p + (1-p)\phi_1(\sigma)}{\phi_1(\sigma)}, \quad \tau_2 = \frac{p + (1-p)\phi_2(\sigma)}{\phi_2(\sigma)}$$

- Dombi's t-norm with $p > 1$. Here

$$T(x,y) = \frac{1}{1 + \sqrt[p]{(1/x-1)^p + (1/y-1)^p}}$$

with additive generator

$$f(t) = \left(\frac{1}{t} - 1\right)^p,$$

and

$$Q(y) = \begin{cases} \dfrac{1}{1 + 2^{1/p}\tau_3} & \text{if } 0 < \sigma < 1, \\ 1 & \text{if } 2b + u \le y \le 2c + v, \\ \dfrac{1}{1 + 2^{1/p}\tau_4} & \text{if } 0 < \theta < 1, \end{cases}$$

where

$$\tau_3 = \frac{1}{\phi_1(\sigma)} - 1, \quad \tau_4 = \frac{1}{\phi_2(\sigma)} - 1$$

We have used the membership function $\phi(y-x; -2, 0, 0, 3)$ to describe "$x$ and $y$ are approximately equal". This means that the membership degree is one, iff $x$ and y are equal in the classical sense. If $y - x > 2$ or $x - y > 3$, then the degree of membership is 0. The conclusion $Q$ has been called "$y$ is more or less close to [3, 4]", because $P(t) = Q(T) = 1$, when $t \in [3,4]$ and $P(t) < Q(t)$ otherwise.

## 3.6 On the generalized method-of-case inference rule

In this Section we will deal with the generalized method-of-case (GMC) inference scheme with fuzzy antecedents, which has been introduced by Da in [72]. We show that when the fuzzy numbers involved in the observation part of the scheme have continuous membership functions; and the t-norm, t-conorm used in the definition of the membership function of the conclusion are continuous, then the conclusion defined by the compositional rule of inference depends continuously on the observation.

When the predicates are crisp then the method of cases reads

| | | | | |
|---|---|---|---|---|
| Observation: | | $A$ | or | $B$ |
| Antecedent 1: | if | $A$ | then | $C$ |
| Antecedent 2: | if | $B$ | then | $C$ |
| Conclusion: | | $C$ | | |

This equivalent to saying that the formula is a tautology in binary logic where $A$, $B$ and $C$ are propositional variables. The proof of many theorems in conventional mathematics is based on this scheme, e.g. theorems involving the absolute value of a real variable are usually proved by considering separately positive and nonpositive values of the variable, and the conclusion is derived in each of these cases.

We will investigate the effect of small changes of the observation to the conclusion of similar deduction schemes when the antecedents involve fuzzy concepts.

Let $X$, $Y$ and $Z$ be variables taking values in universes $U$, $V$ and $W$, respectively and let $A, A' \in \mathcal{F}(U)$, $B, B' \in \mathcal{F}(U)$, and $C \in \mathcal{F}(W)$, then the generalized method of cases reads:

| | | |
|---|---|---|
| Observation: | | $X$ is $A'$ OR $Y$ is $B'$ |
| Antecedent 1: | IF | $X$ is $A$ THEN $Z$ is |
| Antecedent 2: | IF | $Y$ is $B$ THEN $Z$ is $C$ |
| Conclusion: | | $Z$ is $C'$ |

The conclusion $C'$ is given by applying the general compositional rule of inference

$$C'(w) = \sup_{(u,v)\in U\times V} T(S(A'(u), B'(v)), I(A(u), C(w)), I(B(v), C(w))) \quad (3.6)$$

where $T$ is an arbitrary triangular norm, $S$ is an arbitrary conorm and $I$ represents an arbitrary fuzzy implication operator. For instance,

| | |
|---|---|
| Observation: | This bunch of grapes is fairly sweet OR this bunch of grapes is more or less yellow |
| Antecedent 1: | IF a bunch of grapes is yellow THEN the bunch of grapes is ripe |
| Antecedent 2: | IF a bunch of grapes is sweet THEN the bunch of grapes is ripe |
| Conclusion: | This bunch of grapes is more or less ripe |

Consider now the generalized method-of-case scheme with different fuzzy observations $A'$, $A''$, $B'$, $B''$:

$$\begin{array}{ll} & X \text{ is } A' \text{ OR } Y \text{ is } B' \\ \text{IF} & X \text{ is } A \text{ THEN } Z \text{ is } C \\ \text{IF} & Y \text{ is } B \text{ THEN } Z \text{ is } C \\ \hline & Z \text{ is } C' \end{array} \qquad \begin{array}{ll} & X \text{ is } A'' \text{ OR } Y \text{ is } B'' \\ \text{IF} & X \text{ is } A \text{ THEN } Z \text{ is } C \\ \text{IF} & Y \text{ is } B \text{ THEN } Z \text{ is } C \\ \hline & Z \text{ is } C'' \end{array}$$

where $C'$ and $C''$ are defined by the compositional rule of inference, in the sense of (3.6), i.e.

$$C'(w) = \sup_{(u,v)\in U\times V} T(S(A'(u), B'(v)), I(A(u), C(w)), I(B(v), C(w))) \quad (3.7)$$

$$C''(w) = \sup_{(u,v)\in U\times V} T(S(A''(u), B''(v)), I(A(u), C(w)), I(B(v), C(w))) \quad (3.8)$$

The following theorem gives an upper estimation for the distance between the conclusions $C'$ and $C''$ obtained from GMC schemes above.

**Theorem 3.6.1** *[125] Let $T$ and $S$ be continuous functions and let $A'$, $A''$, $B'$ and $B''$ be continuous fuzzy numbers. Then with the notation*

$$\Delta = max\{\omega_{A'}(D(A', A'')), \omega_{A''}(D(A', A'')), \omega_{B'}(D(B', B'')), \omega_{B''}(D(B', B''))\}$$

*we have*

$$\sup_{w\in W} |C'(w) - C''(w)| \leq \omega_T(\omega_S(\Delta)), \quad (3.9)$$

*where the conclusions $C'$, $C''$ are defined by (3.7) and (3.8),respectively.*

It should be noted that: (i) from (3.9) it follows that $C' \to C''$ uniformly as $\Delta \to 0$, which means the stability (in the classical sense) of the conclusion under small changes of the fuzzy terms; (ii) the stability or instability of the conclusion does not depend on the implication operator $I$.

*Note 3.6.1.* In 1992 Fedrizzi and Fullér [104] considered a Group Decision Support System (GDSS) logic architecture in which linguistic variables and fuzzy production rules were used for reaching consensus, and showed that the degrees of consensus (defined by a certain similarity measure) relative to each alternative are stable under small changes in the experts' opinions.

**Example 3.6.1** *For illustration consider the following schemes with arbitrary continuous fuzzy numbers $A$, $B$ and $C$:*

$$\begin{array}{ll} & X \text{ is } A \text{ OR } Y \text{ is } B \\ \text{IF} & X \text{ is } A \text{ THEN } Z \text{ is } C \\ \text{IF} & Y \text{ is } B \text{ THEN } Z \text{ is } C \\ \hline & Z \text{ is } C' \end{array}$$

$$\begin{array}{ll} & X \text{ is } A \text{ OR } Y \text{ is more or less } B \\ \text{IF} & X \text{ is } A \text{ THEN } Z \text{ is } C \\ \text{IF} & Y \text{ is } B \text{ THEN } Z \text{ is } C \\ \hline & Z \text{ is } C'' \end{array}$$

*where*

$$(\text{more or less } B)(y) := \sqrt{B(y)},$$

*for* $y \in \mathbb{R}$,

$$T(u, v) = \min\{u, v\},$$

*(minimum norm);*

$$S(x, y) = \max\{u, v\},$$

*(maximum conorm);*

$$I(x, y) = \begin{cases} 1 \text{ if } x \leq y \\ y \text{ otherwise} \end{cases}$$

*(Gödel's implication operator).*

*Following Da ([72], p.125), we get* $C' = C$ *and* $C'' = \text{more or less}\, C'$, *i.e.*

$$C''(w) = \sqrt{C(w)}, \ w \in \mathbb{R}.$$

*So,*

$$\sup_{w \in \mathbb{R}} |C'(w) - C''(w)| = \sup_{w \in \mathbb{R}} |C(w) - \sqrt{C(w)}| = 1/4$$

*On the other hand, using the relationships,*

$$D(A, A) = 0, \ D(B, \text{more or less} B) \leq 1/4;$$

$$\omega_S(\Delta) = \Delta, \omega_T(\Delta) = \Delta, \ \Delta > 0;$$

*Theorem 3.6.1 gives*

$$\sup_{w \in R} |C'(w) - C''(w)| \leq \max\{\omega_B(1/4), \omega_{\{\text{more or less} B\}}(1/4)\} \leq 1/4$$

*which means, that our estimation (3.9) is sharp, i.e. there exist* $C'$ *and* $C''$, *such that*

$$\sup_{w \in \mathbb{R}} |C'(w) - C''(w)| = \omega_T(\omega_S(\Delta)).$$

# 4. Fuzzy Optimization

## 4.1 Possibilistic linear equality systems

Modelling real world problems mathematically we often have to find a solution to a linear equality system

$$a_{i1}x_1 + \cdots + a_{in}x_n = b_i, \ i = 1, \ldots, m, \tag{4.1}$$

or shortly,

$$Ax = b,$$

where $a_{ij}$, $b_i$ and $x_j$ are real numbers. It is known that system (4.1) generally belongs to the class of ill-posed problems, so a small perturbation of the parameters $a_{ij}$ and $b_i$ may cause a large deviation in the solution.

A possibilistic linear equality system is

$$\tilde{a}_{i1}x_1 + \cdots + \tilde{a}_{in}x_n = \tilde{b}_i, \ i = 1, \ldots, m, \tag{4.2}$$

or shortly,

$$\tilde{A}x = \tilde{b},$$

where $\tilde{a}_{ij}$, $\tilde{b}_i \in \mathcal{F}(\mathbb{R})$ are fuzzy quantities, $x \in \mathbb{R}^n$, the operations addition and multiplication by a real number of fuzzy quantities are defined by Zadeh's extension principle and the equation is understood in possibilistic sense. Recall the truth value of the assertion "$\tilde{a}$ is equal to $\tilde{b}$", written as $\tilde{a} = \tilde{b}$, denoted by $\text{Pos}(\tilde{a} = \tilde{b})$, is defined as

$$\text{Pos}(\tilde{a} = \tilde{b}) = \sup_t \{\tilde{a}(t) \wedge \tilde{b}(t)\} = (\tilde{a} - \tilde{b})(0). \tag{4.3}$$

We denote by $\mu_i(x)$ the degree of satisfaction of the $i$-th equation in (4.2) at the point $x \in \mathbb{R}^n$, i.e.

$$\mu_i(x) = \text{Pos}(\tilde{a}_{i1}x_1 + \cdots + \tilde{a}_{in}x_n = \tilde{b}_i).$$

Following Bellman and Zadeh [7] the fuzzy solution (or the fuzzy set of feasible solutions) of system (4.2) can be viewed as the intersection of the $\mu_i$'s such that

$$\mu(x) = \min\{\mu_1(x), \ldots, \mu_m(x)\}. \tag{4.4}$$

A measure of consistency for the possibilistic equality system (4.2) is defined as

$$\mu^* = \sup\{\mu(x) \mid x \in \mathbb{R}^n\}. \tag{4.5}$$

Let $X^*$ be the set of points $x \in \mathbb{R}^n$ for which $\mu(x)$ attains its maximum, if it exists. That is

$$X^* = \{x^* \in \mathbb{R}^n \mid \mu(x^*) = \mu^*\}$$

If $X^* \neq \emptyset$ and $x^* \in X^*$, then $x^*$ is called a maximizing (or best) solution of (4.2).

If $\tilde{a}$ and $\tilde{b}$ are fuzzy numbers with $[a]^\alpha = [a_1(\alpha), a_2(\alpha)]$ and $[b]^\alpha = [b_1(\alpha), b_2(\alpha)]$ then their Hausdorff distance is defined as

$$D(\tilde{a}, \tilde{b}) = \sup_{\alpha \in [0,1]} \max\{|a_1(\alpha) - b_1(\alpha)|, |a_2(\alpha) - b_2(\alpha)|\}.$$

i.e. $D(\tilde{a}, \tilde{b})$ is the maximal distance between the $\alpha$-level sets of $\tilde{a}$ and $\tilde{b}$.

Let $L > 0$ be a real number. By $\mathcal{F}(L)$ we denote the set of all fuzzy numbers $\tilde{a} \in \mathcal{F}$ with membership function satisfying the Lipschitz condition with constant $L$ , i.e.

$$|\tilde{a}(t) - \tilde{a}(t')| \leq L|t - t'|, \ \forall t, t' \in \mathbb{R}.$$

In many important cases the fuzzy parameters $\tilde{a}_{ij}$, $\tilde{b}_i$ of the system (4.2) are not known exactly and we have to work with their approximations $\tilde{a}_{ij}^\delta$, $\tilde{b}_i^\delta$ such that

$$\max_{i,j} D(\tilde{a}_{ij}, \tilde{a}_{ij}^\delta) \leq \delta, \quad \max_i D(\tilde{b}_i, \tilde{b}_i^\delta) \leq \delta, \tag{4.6}$$

where $\delta \geq 0$ is a real number. Then we get the following system with perturbed fuzzy parameters

$$\tilde{a}_{i1}^\delta x_1 + \cdots + \tilde{a}_{in}^\delta x_n = \tilde{b}_i^\delta, \ i = 1, \ldots, m \tag{4.7}$$

or shortly,

$$\tilde{A}^\delta x = \tilde{b}^\delta.$$

In a similar manner we define the solution

$$\mu^\delta(x) = \min\{\mu_1^\delta(x), \ldots \mu_m^\delta(x)\},$$

and the measure of consistency

$$\mu^*(\delta) = \sup\{\mu^\delta(x) \mid x \in \mathbb{R}^n\},$$

of perturbed system (4.7), where

$$\mu_i^\delta(x) = \mathrm{Pos}(\tilde{a}_{i1}^\delta x_1 + \cdots + \tilde{a}_{in}^\delta x_n = \tilde{b}_i^\delta)$$

denotes the degree of satisfaction of the $i$-th equation at $x \in \mathbb{R}^n$. Let $X^*(\delta)$ denote the set of maximizing solutions of the perturbed system (4.7).

Kovács [224] showed that the fuzzy solution to system (4.2) with symmetric triangular fuzzy numbers is a stable with respect to small changes of centres of fuzzy parameters. Following Fullér [120] in the next theorem we establish a stability property (with respect to perturbations (4.6)) of the solution of system (4.2).

**Theorem 4.1.1** *[120] Let $L > 0$ and $\tilde{a}_{ij}$, $\tilde{a}^{\delta}_{ij}$, $\tilde{b}_i$, $\tilde{b}^{\delta}_i \in \mathcal{F}(L)$. If (4.6) holds, then*

$$\|\mu - \mu^{\delta}\|_{\infty} = \sup_{x \in \mathbb{R}^n} |\mu(x) - \mu^{\delta}(x)| \leq L\delta, \tag{4.8}$$

*where $\mu(x)$ and $\mu^{\delta}(x)$ are the (fuzzy) solutions to systems (4.2) and (4.7), respectively.*

*Proof.* It is sufficient to show that

$$|\mu_i(x) - \mu_i^{\delta}(x)| \leq L\delta$$

for each $x \in \mathbb{R}^n$ and $i = 1, \dots, m$. Let $x \in \mathbb{R}^n$ and $i \in \{1, \dots, m\}$ be arbitrarily fixed. From (4.3) it follows that

$$\mu_i(x) = \left( \sum_{j=1}^{n} \tilde{a}_{ij} x_j - \tilde{b}_i \right)(0) \quad \text{and} \quad \mu_i^{\delta}(x) = \left( \sum_{j=1}^{n} \tilde{a}^{\delta}_{ij} x_j - \tilde{b}^{\delta}_i \right)(0).$$

Applying Lemma 1.14.1 we have

$$D\left( \sum_{j=1}^{n} \tilde{a}_{ij} x_j - \tilde{b}_i, \sum_{j=1}^{n} \tilde{a}^{\delta}_{ij} x_j - \tilde{b}^{\delta}_i \right) \leq$$

$$\sum_{j=1}^{n} |x_j| D(\tilde{a}_{ij}, \tilde{a}^{\delta}_{ij}) + D(\tilde{b}_i, \tilde{b}^{\delta}_i) \leq \delta(|x|_1 + 1),$$

where $|x|_1 = |x_1| + \cdots + |x_n|$. Finally, by Lemma 1.14.6 we have

$$\sum_{j=1}^{n} \tilde{a}_{ij} x_j - \tilde{b}_i \in \mathcal{F}\left( \frac{L}{|x|_1 + 1} \right) \quad \text{and} \quad \sum_{j=1}^{n} \tilde{a}^{\delta}_{ij} x_j - \tilde{b}^{\delta}_i \in \mathcal{F}\left( \frac{L}{|x|_1 + 1} \right)$$

therefore,

$$\begin{aligned}
|\mu_i(x) - \mu_i^{\delta}(x)| &= \left| \left( \sum_{j=1}^{n} \tilde{a}_{ij} x_j - \tilde{b}_i \right)(0) - \left( \sum_{j=1}^{n} \tilde{a}^{\delta}_{ij} x_j - \tilde{b}^{\delta}_i \right)(0) \right| \\
&\leq \sup_{t \in \mathbb{R}} \left| \left( \sum_{j=1}^{n} \tilde{a}_{ij} x_j - \tilde{b}_i \right)(t) - \left( \sum_{j=1}^{n} \tilde{a}^{\delta}_{ij} x_j - \tilde{b}^{\delta}_i \right)(t) \right| \\
&\leq \frac{L}{|x|_1 + 1} \times \delta(|x|_1 + 1) = L\delta.
\end{aligned}$$

Which proves the theorem.

From (4.8) it follows that

$$|\mu^* - \mu^*(\delta)| \leq L\delta,$$

where $\mu^*$, $\mu^*(\delta)$ are the measures of consistency for the systems (4.2) and (4.7), respectively. It is easily checked that in the general case $\tilde{a}_{ij}, \tilde{b}_i \in \mathcal{F}(\mathbb{R})$ the solution to possibilistic linear equality system (4.2) may be unstable (in metric $C_\infty$) under small variations in the membership function of fuzzy parameters (in metric D).

When the problem is to find a maximizing solution to a possibilistic linear equality system (4.2), then according to Negoita [259], we are led to solve the following optimization problem

$$\begin{aligned} &\text{maximize} \quad \lambda \\ &\mu_1(x_1, \dots, x_n) \geq \lambda, \\ &\dots \\ &\mu_m(x_1, \dots, x_n) \geq \lambda, \\ &x \in \mathbb{R}^n, \; 0 \leq \lambda \leq 1. \end{aligned} \tag{4.9}$$

Finding the solutions of problem (4.9) generally requires the use of nonlinear programming techniques, and could be tricky. However, if the fuzzy numbers in (4.2) are of trapezoidal form, then the problem (4.9) turns into a quadratically constrained programming problem.

Even though the fuzzy solution and the measure of consistency of system (4.2) have a stability property with respect to changes of the fuzzy parameters, the behavior of the maximizing solution towards small perturbations of the fuzzy parameters can be very fortuitous, i.e. supposing that, $X^*$, the set of maximizing solutions to system (4.2) is not empty, the distance between $x^*(\delta)$ and $X^*$ can be very big, where $x^*(\delta)$ is a maximizing solution of the perturbed possibilistic equality system (4.7).

Consider now the possiblistic equality system (4.2) with fuzzy numbers of symmetric triangular form

$$(a_{i1}, \alpha)x_1 + \cdots + (a_{in}, \alpha)x_n = (b_i, \alpha), \; i = 1, \dots, m,$$

or shortly,

$$(A, \alpha)x = (b, \alpha) \tag{4.10}$$

Then following Kovács and Fullér [226] the fuzzy solution of (4.10) can be written in a compact form

$$\mu(x) = \begin{cases} 1 & \text{if } Ax = b \\ 1 - \dfrac{||Ax - b||_\infty}{\alpha(|x|_1 + 1)} & \text{if } 0 < ||Ax - b||_\infty \leq \alpha(|x|_1 + 1) \\ 0 & \text{if } ||Ax - b||_\infty > \alpha(|x|_1 + 1) \end{cases}$$

where

$$||Ax - b||_\infty = \max\{|\langle a_1, x\rangle - b_1|, \dots, |\langle a_m, x\rangle - b_m|\}.$$

If

$$[\mu]^1 = \{x \in \mathbb{R}^n \mid \mu(x) = 1\} \neq \emptyset$$

then the set of maximizing solutions, $X^* = [\mu]^1$, of (4.10) coincides with the solution set, denoted by $X^{**}$, of the crisp system $Ax = b$. The stability theorem for system (4.10) reads

**Theorem 4.1.2** [224] *If*

$$D(\tilde{A}, \tilde{A}^\delta) = \max_{i,j} |a_{ij} - a^\delta_{ij}| \leq \delta, \; D(\tilde{b}, \tilde{b}^\delta) = \max_i |b_i - b^\delta_i| \leq \delta$$

*hold, then*

$$||\mu - \mu^\delta||_\infty = \sup_x |\mu(x) - \mu^\delta(x)| \leq \frac{\delta}{\alpha},$$

*where $\mu(x)$ and $\mu^\delta(x)$ are the fuzzy solutions to possibilistic equality systems*

$$(A, \alpha)x = (b, \alpha),$$

*and*

$$(A^\delta, \alpha)x = (b^\delta, \alpha),$$

*respectively.*

Theorem 4.1.1 can be extended to possibilistic linear equality systems with (continuous) fuzzy numbers.

**Theorem 4.1.3** [124] *Let $\tilde{a}_{ij}$, $\tilde{a}^\delta_{ij}$, $\tilde{b}_i$, $\tilde{b}^\delta_i \in \mathcal{F}$ be fuzzy numbers. If (4.6) holds, then*

$$||\mu - \mu^\delta||_\infty \leq \omega(\delta),$$

*where $\omega(\delta)$ denotes the maximum of modulus of continuity of all fuzzy coefficients at $\delta$ in (4.2) and (4.7).*

In 1992 Kovács [227] showed a wide class of fuzzified systems that are well-posed extensions of ill-posed linear equality and inequality systems.

Consider the following two-dimensional possibilistic equality system

$$(1, \alpha)x_1 + (1, \alpha)x_2 = (0, \alpha) \tag{4.11}$$

$$(1, \alpha)x_1 - (1, \alpha)x_2 = (0, \alpha)$$

Then its fuzzy solution is

$$\mu(x) = \begin{cases} 1 & \text{if } x = 0 \\ \tau_2(x) & \text{if } 0 < \max\{|x_1 - x_2|, |x_1 + x_2|\} \leq \alpha(|x_1| + |x_2| + 1) \\ 0 & \text{if } \max\{|x_1 - x_2|, |x_1 + x_2|\} > \alpha(|x_1| + |x_2| + 1) \end{cases}$$

**Fig. 4.1.** The graph of fuzzy solution of system (4.11) with $\alpha = 0.4$.

where

$$\tau_2(x) = 1 - \frac{\max\{|x_1 - x_2|, |x_1 + x_2|\}}{\alpha(|x_1| + |x_2| + 1)},$$

and the only maximizing solution of system (4.11) is $x^* = (0,0)$. There is no problem with stability of the solution even for the crisp system

$$\begin{bmatrix} 1 & 1 \\ 1 & -1 \end{bmatrix} \begin{pmatrix} x_1 \\ x_2 \end{pmatrix} = \begin{pmatrix} 0 \\ 0 \end{pmatrix}$$

because $\det(A) \neq 0$.

The fuzzy solution of possibilistic equality system

$$\begin{aligned} (1,\alpha)x_1 + (1,\alpha)x_2 &= (0,\alpha) \\ (1,\alpha)x_1 + (1,\alpha)x_2 &= (0,\alpha) \end{aligned} \tag{4.12}$$

is

$$\mu(x) = \begin{cases} 1 & \text{if } |x_1 + x_2| = 0 \\ 1 - \dfrac{|x_1 + x_2|}{\alpha(|x_1| + |x_2| + 1)} & \text{if } 0 < |x_1 + x_2| \leq \alpha(|x_1| + |x_2| + 1) \\ 0 & \text{if } |x_1 + x_2| > \alpha(|x_1| + |x_2| + 1) \end{cases}$$

and the set of its maximizing solutions is

$$X^* = \{x \in \mathbb{R}^2 \mid x_1 + x_2 = 0\}.$$

In this case we have

**Fig. 4.2.** The graph of fuzzy solution of system (4.12) with $\alpha = 0.4$.

$$X^* = X^{**} = \{x \in \mathbb{R}^2 \mid Ax = b\}.$$

We might experience problems with the stability of the solution of the crisp system

$$\begin{bmatrix} 1 & 1 \\ 1 & 1 \end{bmatrix} \begin{pmatrix} x_1 \\ x_2 \end{pmatrix} = \begin{pmatrix} 0 \\ 0 \end{pmatrix}$$

because $\det(A) = 0$.

Really, the fuzzy solution of possibilistic equality system

$$(1, \alpha)x_1 + (1, \alpha)x_2 = (\delta_1, \alpha) \tag{4.13}$$

$$(1, \alpha)x_1 + (1, \alpha)x_2 = (\delta_2, \alpha)$$

where $\delta_1 = 0.3$ and $\delta_2 = -0.3$, is

$$\mu(x) =$$

$$\begin{cases} \tau_1(x) \text{ if } 0 < \max\{|x_1 + x_2 - 0.3|, |x_1 + x_2 + 0.3|\} \leq \alpha(|x_1| + |x_2| + 1) \\ 0 \qquad \text{ if } \max\{|x_1 + x_2 - 0.3|, |x_1 + x_2 + 0.3|\} > \alpha(|x_1| + |x_2| + 1) \end{cases}$$

where

$$\tau_1(x) = 1 - \frac{\max\{|x_1 + x_2 - 0.3|, |x_1 + x_2 + 0.3|\}}{\alpha(|x_1| + |x_2| + 1)}$$

and the set of the maximizing solutions of (4.13) is empty, and $X^{**}$ is also empty. Even though the set of maximizing solution of systems (4.12) and (4.13) varies a lot under small changes of the centers of fuzzy numbers of the right-hand side, $\delta_1$ and $\delta_2$, their fuzzy solutions can be made arbitrary close to each other by letting

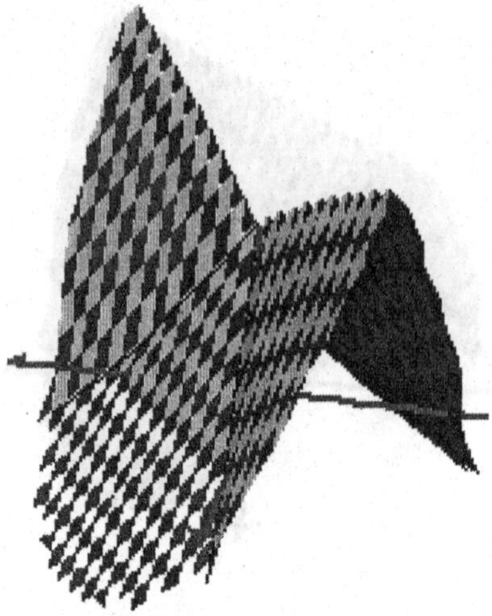

**Fig. 4.3.** The graph of fuzzy solution of system (4.13) with $\alpha = 0.4$.

$$\frac{\max\{\delta_1, \delta_2\}}{\alpha}$$

to tend to zero.

## 4.2 Sensitivity analysis of $\tilde{a}x = \tilde{b}$ and $\tilde{a}^\delta x = \tilde{b}^\delta$.

We illustrate Theorem 4.1.1 by a very simple possibilistic equality system

$$\tilde{a}x = \tilde{b}, \tag{4.14}$$

where $\tilde{a} = (a, \alpha) \in \mathcal{F}(1/\alpha)$ and $\tilde{b} = (b, \alpha) \in \mathcal{F}(1/\alpha)$ are (Lipschitzian) fuzzy numbers of symmetric triangular form with the same width $\alpha > 0$.

It is easy to check that the fuzzy solution to system (4.14) is

$$\begin{aligned} \mu(x) &= \mathrm{Pos}(\tilde{a}x = \tilde{b}) \\ &= \mathrm{Pos}[(ax, \alpha|x|) = (b, \alpha)] \\ &= 1 - \frac{|ax - b|}{\alpha(|x| + 1)}, \end{aligned}$$

if $|ax - b| \leq \alpha(|x| + 1)$ and $\mu(x) = 0$ otherwise. If $a \neq 0$ then the only maximizing solution is

$$x^* = \frac{b}{a}$$

which is also the unique solution, denoted by $x^{**}$, of the crisp equation $ax = b$. Suppose we are given the following perturbed possibilistic equality system

$$\tilde{a}^\delta x = \tilde{b}^\delta, \tag{4.15}$$

where $\tilde{a}^\delta = (a^\delta, \alpha) \in \mathcal{F}(1/\alpha)$ and $\tilde{b}^\delta = (b^\delta, \alpha) \in \mathcal{F}(1/\alpha)$ are (Lipschitzian) fuzzy numbers of symmetric triangular form with the original (exact) width $\alpha > 0$.

The fuzzy solution to system (4.15) is

$$\begin{aligned}\mu^\delta(x) &= \text{Pos}(\tilde{a}^\delta x = \tilde{b}^\delta)\\ &= \text{Pos}[(a^\delta x, \alpha|x|) = (b^\delta, \alpha)]\\ &= 1 - \frac{|a^\delta x - b^\delta|}{\alpha(|x|+1)},\end{aligned}$$

if $|a^\delta x - b^\delta| \le \alpha(|x|+1)$ and $\mu(x) = 0$ otherwise. If $a^\delta \neq 0$ then the only maximizing solution is

$$x^*(\delta) = \frac{b^\delta}{a^\delta}$$

which is also the unique solution, denoted by $x^{**}(\delta)$, of the crisp equation $a^\delta x = b^\delta$.

Suppose, furthermore, that $\tilde{a}$, $\tilde{a}^\delta$, $\tilde{b}$ and $\tilde{b}^\delta$ satisfy the following inequalities

$$D(\tilde{a}, \tilde{a}^\delta) = |a - a^\delta| \le \delta, \quad D(\tilde{b}, \tilde{b}^\delta) = |b - b^\delta| \le \delta,$$

where $\delta > 0$ is a small positive number. Then we can easily give an upper bound for the $C_\infty$ distance between the fuzzy solutions $\mu$ and $\mu^\delta$ by

$$\begin{aligned}|\mu(x) - \mu^\delta(x)| &= \left|1 - \frac{|ax-b|}{\alpha(|x|+1)} - \left(1 - \frac{|a^\delta x - b^\delta|}{\alpha(|x|+1)}\right)\right|\\ &= \left|\frac{|ax-b| - |a^\delta x - b^\delta|}{\alpha(|x|+1)}\right|\\ &\le \left|\frac{|x||a-a^\delta| + |b-b^\delta|}{\alpha(|x|+1)}\right|\\ &\le \left|\frac{|x|\delta + \delta}{\alpha(|x|+1)}\right| \le \frac{\delta}{\alpha}.\end{aligned}$$

for any $x \in \mathbb{R}$, which coincides with the upper bound derived from Theorem 4.1.1 with $L = 1/\alpha$.

What if $a = 0$ and $b = 0$? In this case the crisp system becomes

$$0x = 0,$$

and its solution set is the whole real line. However, depending on the values of $a^\delta$ and $b^\delta$, the perturbed crisp system

$$a^\delta x = b^\delta,$$

either has no solution (if $a^\delta = 0$ and $b^\delta \neq 0$), has the unique solution $b^\delta/a^\delta$ (if $a^\delta \neq 0$) or its solution set is the whole real line (if $a^\delta = 0$ and $b^\delta = 0$). So, even a very small change in the crisp coefficients can cause a very large deviation in the solution.

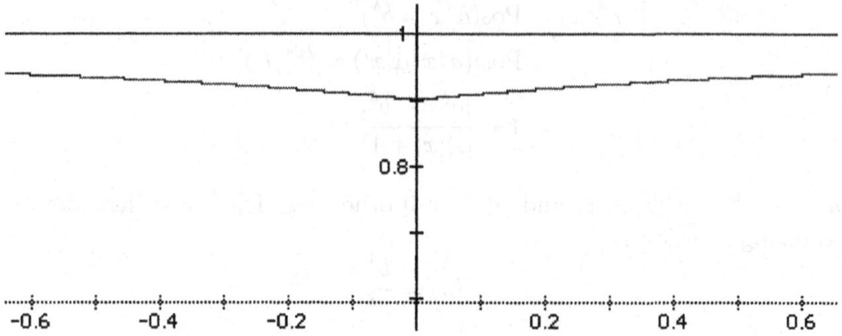


**Fig. 4.4.** Fuzzy solution of $(0, \alpha)x = (b^\delta, \alpha)$ with $\alpha = 0.2$ and $\delta = 0.02$.

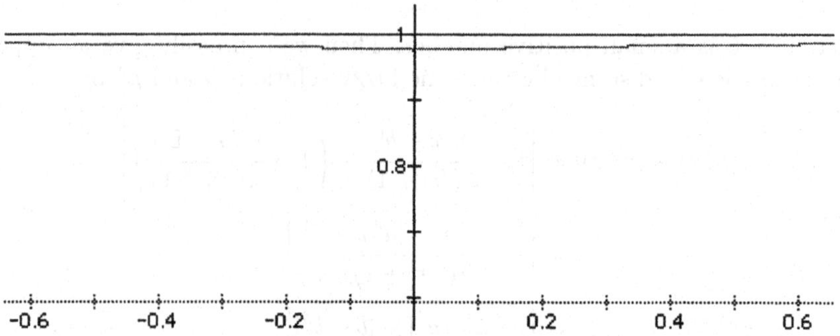


**Fig. 4.5.** Fuzzy solution of $(0, \alpha)x = (b^\delta, \alpha)$ with $\alpha = 0.2$ and $\delta = 0.005$.

The fuzzified systems, however, behave totally differently. Consider the possibilistic systems

$$(0, \alpha)x = (0, \alpha), \tag{4.16}$$

and

$$(a^\delta, \alpha)x = (b^\delta, \alpha), \tag{4.17}$$

where $|a^\delta| \leq \delta$ and $|b^\delta| \leq \delta$ are small numbers. Then the fuzzy solution of (4.16) is

$$\mu(x) = 1 - \frac{|0x - 0|}{\alpha(|x| + 1)} = 1,$$

for all $x \in \mathbb{R}$, so $\mu$ is the universal fuzzy set in $\mathbb{R}$, and the fuzzy solution of (4.17) is

$$\mu^\delta(x) = 1 - \frac{|a^\delta x - b^\delta|}{\alpha(|x|+1)},$$

and in the sense of Theorem 4.1.1 we get that

$$\|\mu - \mu^\delta\| = \sup_x |\mu(x) - \mu^\delta(x)| \le \frac{\delta}{\alpha},$$

which means that the fuzzy solutions of the original and the perturbed systems can be made arbitrarily close to each other if $\delta$ is sufficiently small. If

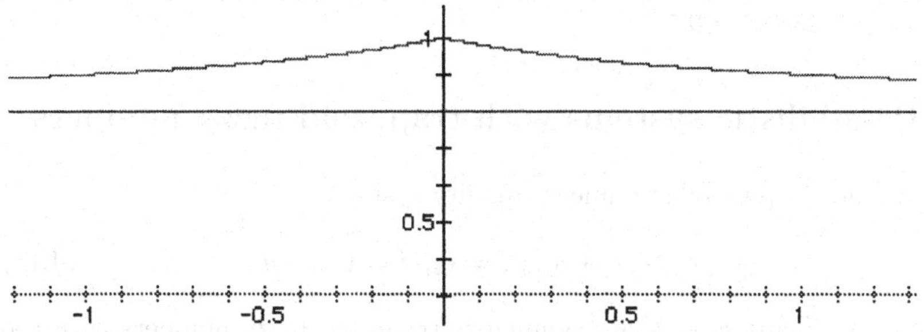


**Fig. 4.6.** Fuzzy solution of $(a^\delta, \alpha)x = (0, \alpha)$ with $\alpha = 0.05$ and $\delta = 0.01$.

$b^\delta = 0$ but $a^\delta \ne 0$ then the fuzzy solution of

$$(a^\delta, \alpha)x = (0, \alpha)$$

is computed as

$$\mu^\delta(x) = 1 - \frac{|a^\delta x|}{\alpha(|x|+1)},$$

and its unique maximizing solution is zero.

Finally, if $a \ne 0$, $b \ne 0$, $a^\delta \ne 0$ and $b^\delta \ne 0$ then the solutions

$$x^* = \frac{b}{a} \text{ and } x^*(\delta) = \frac{b^\delta}{a^\delta},$$

of the crisp systems $ax = b$ and $a^\delta x = b^\delta$ can be very far from each other even for very small $\delta$. However, the fuzzy solutions of $(a^\delta, \alpha)x = (b^\delta, \alpha)$ and $(a, \alpha)x = (b, \alpha)$ can be made arbitrarily close to each other (depending on the relationship between $\delta$ and $\alpha$).

Even though the fuzzy solutions are very close to each other, the distance between the maximizing solutions can be very big, because the maximizing solutions of the fuzzy system with triangular fuzzy numbers coincide with the solutions of the crisp systems.

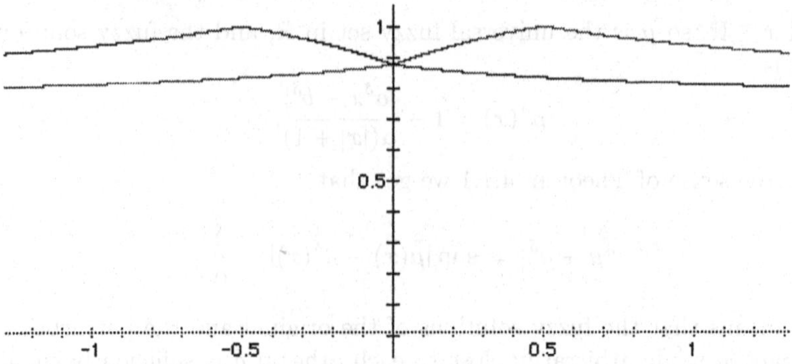


**Fig. 4.7.** Fuzzy solutions of $(a^\delta, \alpha)x = (b^\delta, \alpha)$ and $(a, \alpha)x = (b, \alpha)$ with $a^\delta = -0.01$, $a = 0.01$, $b^\delta = b = 0.005$, $\alpha = 0.04$ and $\delta = 0.02$. The maximizing solutions are $x^*(\delta) = -0.5$ and $x^* = 0.5$.

## 4.3 Possibilistic systems with trapezoid fuzzy numbers

Consider now a possibilistic linear equality system

$$\tilde{a}_{i1}x_1 + \cdots + \tilde{a}_{in}x_n = \tilde{b}_i, \ i = 1, \dots, m, \tag{4.18}$$

where $\tilde{a}_{ij} \in \mathcal{F}$ and $\tilde{b}_i \in \mathcal{F}$ are symmetric trapezoid fuzzy numbers with the same width $\alpha > 0$ and tolerance intervals $[a_{ij} - \theta, a_{ij} + \theta]$ and $[b_i - \theta, b_i + \theta]$, respectively, and represented by (1.1) as

$$\tilde{a}_{ij} = (a_{ij} - \theta, a_{ij} + \theta, \alpha, \alpha) \text{ and } \tilde{b}_i = (b_i - \theta, b_i + \theta, \alpha, \alpha).$$

Suppose that we are given the following perturbed possibilistic linear equality

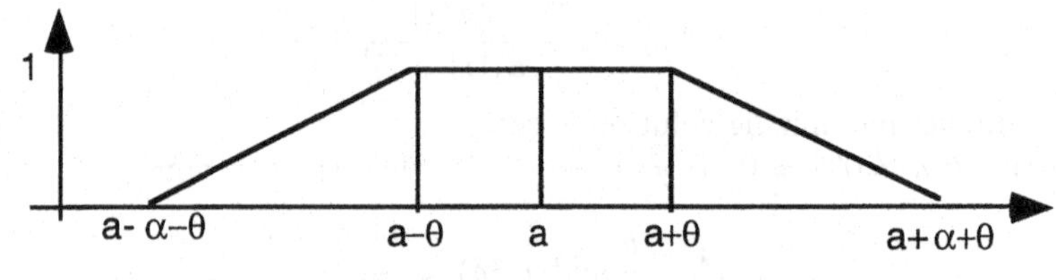


**Fig. 4.8.** A symmetric trapezoid fuzzy number with center $a$.

system

$$\tilde{a}^\delta_{i1}x_1 + \cdots + \tilde{a}^\delta_{in}x_n = \tilde{b}^\delta_i, \ i = 1, \dots, m, \tag{4.19}$$

where

$$\tilde{a}^\delta_{ij} = (a^\delta_{ij} - \theta, a^\delta_{ij} + \theta, \alpha, \alpha) \text{ and } \tilde{b}^\delta_i = (b^\delta_i - \theta, b^\delta_i + \theta, \alpha, \alpha).$$

Following Kovács, Vasiljev and Fullér [119] the fuzzy solutions to system (4.18) and (4.19) can be written as

$$\mu(x) = \begin{cases} 1 & \text{if } \|Ax - b\|_\infty \le \theta(|x|_1 + 1) \\ 1 + \dfrac{\theta}{\alpha} - \dfrac{\|Ax - b\|_\infty}{\alpha(|x|_1 + 1)} & \text{if } \theta(|x|_1 + 1) < \|Ax - b\|_\infty \le (\theta + \alpha)(|x|_1 + 1) \\ 0 & \text{if } \|Ax - b\|_\infty > (\theta + \alpha)(|x|_1 + 1) \end{cases}$$

and

$$\mu^\delta(x) = \begin{cases} 1 & \text{if } \|A^\delta x - b^\delta\|_\infty \le \theta(|x|_1 + 1) \\ 1 + \dfrac{\theta}{\alpha} - \dfrac{\|A^\delta x - b^\delta\|_\infty}{\alpha(|x|_1 + 1)} & \text{if } \theta(|x|_1 + 1) < \|A^\delta x - b^\delta\|_\infty \le (\theta + \alpha)(|x|_1 + 1) \\ 0 & \text{if } \|A^\delta x - b^\delta\|_\infty > (\theta + \alpha)(|x|_1 + 1) \end{cases}$$

The following theorem [119] shows that the stability property of fuzzy solutions of systems (4.18) and (4.19) does not depend on $\theta$.

**Theorem 4.3.1** *[119] Let $\delta > 0$ and let $\mu$ and $\mu^\delta$ be the solutions of possibilistic equality systems (4.18) and (4.19), respectively. If $a_{ij}$, $a^\delta_{ij}$, $b_i$ and $b^\delta_i$ satisfy the inequalities*

$$D(\tilde{a}_{ij}, \tilde{a}^\delta_{ij}) = |a_{ij} - a^\delta_{ij}| \le \delta, \quad D(\tilde{b}_i, \tilde{b}^\delta_i) = |b_i - b^\delta_i| \le \delta, \tag{4.20}$$

*then*

$$\|\mu - \mu^\delta\|_\infty = \sup_{x \in R^n} |\mu(x) - \mu^\delta(x)| \le \frac{\delta}{\alpha}. \tag{4.21}$$

To find a maximizing solution to (4.18) we have to solve the following nonlinear programming problem

$$\gamma \to \max; \ (x, \gamma) \in Z,$$

$$Z = \left\{ (x, \gamma) \mid 1 + \frac{\theta}{\alpha} - \frac{\|Ax - b\|_\infty}{\alpha(|x|_1 + 1)} \ge \gamma, \ 0 \le \gamma \le 1 \right\}.$$

The next theorem shows that if the crisp equality system $Ax = b$ has a solution and $\theta > 0$ then the sets of maximizing solutions of systems (4.18) and (4.19) can be made close to each other.

**Theorem 4.3.2** [119] *Suppose the set $X^{**} = \{x \in \mathbb{R}^n | Ax = b\}$ is not empty. If $a^\delta_{ij}$ and $b^\delta_i$ satisfy the relationships (4.20) and $0 \le \delta \le \theta$ then*

$$\rho(x, X^*) = \inf_{y \in X^*} |x - y| \le C_0(\delta + \theta)(|x|_1 + 1), \ x \in X^*(\delta),$$

*where $X^*$ is the set of maximizing solutions of (4.18) and*

$$X^*(\delta) = \{x \in \mathbb{R}^n \mid \mu^\delta(x) = 1\},$$

*is the set of maximizing solutions of (4.19) and $C_0$ is a positive constant depending only on the $a_{ij}$'s.*

Theorem 4.3.2 states nothing else but if the maximizing solutions of possibilistic equality systems (4.18) and (4.19) can be made close to each other supposing the sets $X^*(\delta)$, $\forall\delta > 0$ are uniformly bounded.

**Example 4.3.1** *Specially, the fuzzy solution of a possibilistic equation*

$$(a-\theta, a+\theta, \alpha, \alpha)x = (b-\theta, b+\theta, \alpha, \alpha), \qquad (4.22)$$

*can be written as*

$$\mu(x) = \begin{cases} 1 & \text{if } |ax-b| \le \theta(|x|+1) \\ 1 + \dfrac{\theta}{\alpha} - \dfrac{|ax-b|}{\alpha(|x|+1)} & \text{if } \theta(|x|+1) < |ax-b| \le (\theta+\alpha)(|x|+1) \\ 0 & \text{if } |ax-b| > (\theta+\alpha)(|x|+1) \end{cases}$$

*It is clear that the set of maximizing solutions of (4.22)*

$$X^* = \{x \in \mathbb{R} : |ax-b| \le \theta(|x|+1)\}$$

*always contains the solution set, $X^{**}$, of the equality $ax = b$.*

## 4.4 Flexible linear programming

The conventional model of linear programming (LP) can be stated as

$$\langle a_0, x\rangle \to \min$$

$$\text{subject to } Ax \le b.$$

In many real-world problems instead of minimization of the objective function $\langle a_0, x\rangle$ it may be sufficient to determine an $x$ such that

$$a_{01}x_1 + \cdots + a_{0n}x_n \le b_0; \text{ subject to } Ax \le b. \qquad (4.23)$$

where $b_0$ is a predetermined aspiration level.

Assume that all parameters in (4.23) are fuzzy quantities and are described by symmetric triangular fuzzy numbers. Then the following flexible (or fuzzy) linear programming (FLP) problem can be obtained by replacing crisp parameters $a_{ij}$, $b_i$ with symmetric triangular fuzzy numbers $\tilde{a}_{ij} = (a_{ij}, \alpha)$ and $\tilde{b}_i = (b_i, d_i)$ respectively,

$$(a_{i1}, \alpha)x_1 + \cdots + (a_{in}, \alpha)x_n \leq (b_i, d_i), \quad i = 0, \ldots, m. \tag{4.24}$$

Here $d_0$ and $d_i$ are interpreted as the tolerance levels for the objective function and the $i$-th constraint, respectively. The parameter $\alpha > 0$ will guarantee the stability property of the solution of (4.24) under small changes in the coefficients $a_{ij}$ and $b_i$.

We denote by $\mu_i(x)$ the degree of satisfaction of the $i$-th restriction at the point $x \in R^n$ in (4.24), i.e.

$$\mu_i(x) = \text{Pos}(\tilde{a}_{i1}x_1 + \cdots + \tilde{a}_{in}x_n \leq \tilde{b}_i).$$

Then the (fuzzy) solution of the FLP problem (4.24) is defined as a fuzzy set on $R^n$ whose membership function is given by

$$\mu(x) = \min\{\mu_0(x), \mu_1(x), \ldots, \mu_m(x)\},$$

and the maximizing solution $x^*$ of the FLP problem (4.24) satisfies the equation

$$\mu(x^*) = \mu^* = \max_x \mu(x).$$

From (1.22) it follows that the degree of satisfaction of the $i$-th restriction at $x$ in (4.24) is the following:

$$\mu_i(x) = \begin{cases} 1 & \text{if } \langle a_i, x\rangle \leq b_i, \\ 1 - \dfrac{\langle a_i, x\rangle - b_i}{\alpha|x|_1 + d_i} & \text{otherwise,} \\ 0 & \text{if } \langle a_i, x\rangle > b_i + \alpha|x|_1 + d_i, \end{cases} \tag{4.25}$$

where $|x|_1 = |x_1| + \cdots + |x_n|$ and $\langle a_i, x\rangle = a_{i1}x_1 + \cdots + a_{in}x_n$, $i = 0, 1, \ldots, m$.

In the extremal case $\alpha = 0$ but $d_i > 0$ in (4.25), we get a linear membership function for $\mu_i$, i.e. Zimmermann's principle [345]. Really, for $\alpha = 0$ we get

$$(a_{i1}, 0)x_1 + \cdots + (a_{in}, 0)x_n \leq (b_i, d_i), \tag{4.26}$$

and the $\mu_i$'s have a very simple form

$$\mu_i(x) = \begin{cases} 1 & \text{if } \langle a_i, x\rangle \leq b_i, \\ 1 - \dfrac{\langle a_i, x\rangle - b_i}{d_i} & \text{if } b_i < \langle a_i, x\rangle \leq b_i + d_i, \\ 0 & \text{if } \langle a_i, x\rangle > b_i + d_i, \end{cases}$$

for $i = 0, 1, \ldots, m$.

If $\alpha = 0$ then $\mu_i$ has an easy interpretation: If for an $x \in \mathbb{R}^n$ the value of $\langle a_i, x\rangle$ is less or equal than $b_i$ then $x$ satisfies the $i$-th constraint with the maximal conceivable degree one; if $b_i < \langle a_i, x\rangle < b_i + d_i$ then $x$ is not feasible in classical sense, but the decision maker can still tolerate the violation of the

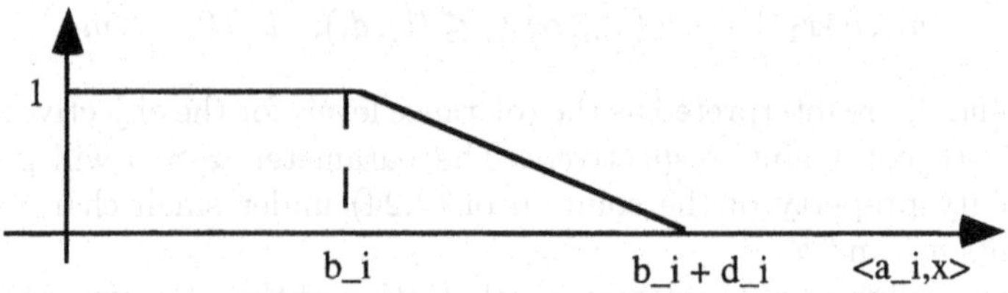


**Fig. 4.9.** The graph of $\mu_i$ if $\alpha = 0$.

crisp constraint, and accept $x$ as a solution with a positive degree, however, the bigger the violation the less is the degree of acceptance; and if $\langle a_i, x\rangle > b_i + d_i$ then the violation of the $i$-th costraint is untolerable by the decision maker, that is, $\mu_i(x) = 0$.

Sensitivity analysis in FLP problems (with crisp parameters and soft constraints) was first considered in [156], where a functional relationship between changes of parameters of the right-hand side and those of the optimal value of the primal objective function was derived for almost all conceivable cases. In [295] a FLP problem (with symmetric triangular fuzzy numbers) was formulated and the value of information was discussed via sensitivity analysis.

Following Fullér [118] we investigate the stability of the solution in FLP problems (with symmetric triangular fuzzy numbers and extended operations and inequalities) with respect to changes of fuzzy parameters and show that the solution to these problems is stable (in metric $C_\infty$) under small variations in the membership functions of the fuzzy coefficients.

Consider now the perturbed FLP problem

$$(a_{i1}^\delta, \alpha)x_1 + \cdots + (a_{in}^\delta, \alpha)x_n \leq (b_i^\delta, d_i),\ i = 0, \ldots, m. \tag{4.27}$$

where $a_{ij}^\delta$ and $b_i^\delta$ satisfy the inequalities

$$\max_{i,j} |a_{ij} - a_{ij}^\delta| \leq \delta, \quad \max_i |b_i - b_i^\delta| \leq \delta. \tag{4.28}$$

In a similar manner we can define the solution of FLP problem (4.27) by

$$\mu^\delta(x) = \min\{\mu_0^\delta(x), \mu_1^\delta(x), \ldots, \mu_m^\delta(x)\},\ x \in \mathbb{R}^n,$$

where $\mu_i^\delta(x)$ denotes the degree of satisfaction of the $i$-th restriction at $x \in \mathbb{R}^n$ and the maximizing solution $x^*(\delta)$ of FLP problem (4.27) satisfies the equation

$$\mu^\delta(x^*(\delta)) = \mu^*(\delta) = \sup_x \mu^\delta(x). \tag{4.29}$$

In the following theorem we establish a stability property of the fuzzy solution of FLP problem (4.24).

**Theorem 4.4.1** [118] *Let $\mu(x)$ and $\mu^\delta(x)$ be solution of FLP problems (4.24) and (4.27) respectively. Then*

$$||\mu - \mu^\delta||_\infty = \sup_{x \in R^n} |\mu(x) - \mu^\delta(x)| \le \delta \left[\frac{1}{\alpha} + \frac{1}{d}\right] \tag{4.30}$$

*where* $d = \min\{d_0, d_1, \ldots, d_m\}$.

*Proof.* First let $\delta \ge \min\{\alpha, d\}$. Then from $|\mu(x) - \mu^\delta(x)| \le 1$, $\forall x \in \mathbb{R}^n$ and

$$\frac{\delta}{\alpha + d} \ge 1,$$

we obtain (4.30). Suppose that

$$0 < \delta < \min\{\alpha, d\}.$$

It will be sufficient to show that

$$|\mu_i(x) - \mu_i^\delta(x)| \le \delta \left[\frac{1}{\alpha} + \frac{1}{d}\right], \ \forall x \in \mathbb{R}^n, \ i = 0, \ldots, m, \tag{4.31}$$

because from (4.31) follows (4.30). Let $x \in \mathbb{R}^n$ and $i \in \{0, \ldots, m\}$ be arbitrarily fixed.

Consider the following cases:

(1) $\mu_i(x) = \mu_i^\delta(x)$. In this case (4.31) is trivially obtained.

(2) $0 < \mu_i(x) < 1$ and $0 < \mu_i^\delta(x) < 1$. In this case from (4.25), (4.28) we have

$$\begin{aligned}
|\mu_i(x) - \mu_i^\delta(x)| &= \left|1 - \frac{\langle a_i, x\rangle - b_i}{\alpha|x|_1 + d_i} - \left(1 - \frac{\langle a_i^\delta, x\rangle - b_i^\delta}{\alpha|x|_1 + d_i}\right)\right| \\
&= \frac{|b_i - b_i^\delta| + \langle a_i^\delta, x\rangle - \langle a_i, x\rangle|}{\alpha|x|_1 + d_i} \\
&\le \frac{|b_i - b_i^\delta| + |\langle a_i^\delta - a_i, x\rangle|}{\alpha|x|_1 + d_i} \\
&\le \frac{\delta + |a_i^\delta - a_i|_\infty |x|_1}{\alpha|x|_1 + d_i} \\
&\le \frac{\delta + \delta|x|_1}{\alpha|x|_1 + d_i} \\
&\le \delta\left[\frac{1}{\alpha} + \frac{1}{d_i}\right] \le \delta\left[\frac{1}{\alpha} + \frac{1}{d}\right],
\end{aligned}$$

where $a_i^\delta = (a_{i1}^\delta, \ldots, a_{in}^\delta)$ and $|a_i^\delta - a_i|_\infty = \max_j |a_{ij}^\delta - a_{ij}|$.

(3) $\mu_i(x) = 1$ and $0 < \mu_i^\delta(x) < 1$. In this case we have $\langle a_i, x\rangle \le b_i$. Hence

$$|\mu_i(x) - \mu_i^\delta(x)| = \left|1 - \left[1 - \frac{\langle a_i^\delta, x\rangle - b_i^\delta}{\alpha|x|_1 + d_i}\right]\right|$$
$$= \frac{\langle a_i^\delta, x\rangle - b_i^\delta}{\alpha|x|_1 + d_i}$$
$$\leq \frac{(\langle a_i^\delta, x\rangle - b_i^\delta) - (\langle a_i, x\rangle - b_i)}{\alpha|x|_1 + d_i}$$
$$\leq \delta\left[\frac{1}{\alpha} + \frac{1}{d}\right].$$

(4) $0 < \mu_i(x) < 1$ and $\mu_i^\delta(x) = 1$. In this case the proof is carried out analogously to the proof of the preceding case.

(5) $0 < \mu_i(x) < 1$ and $\mu_i^\delta(x) = 0$. In this case from

$$\langle a_i^\delta, x\rangle - b_i^\delta > \alpha|x|_1 + d_i$$

it follows that

$$|\mu_i(x) - \mu_i^\delta(x)| = \left|1 - \frac{\langle a_i, x\rangle - b_i}{\alpha|x|_1 + d_i}\right|$$
$$= \frac{1}{\alpha|x|_1 + d_i} \times \left|\alpha|x|_1 + d_i - (\langle a_i, x\rangle - b_i)\right|$$
$$\leq \frac{|\langle a_i(\delta), x\rangle - b_i(\delta) - (\langle a_i, x\rangle - b_i)|}{\alpha|x|_1 + d_i}$$
$$\leq \delta\left[\frac{1}{\alpha} + \frac{1}{d}\right].$$

(6) $\mu_i(x) = 0$ and $0 < \mu_i^\delta(x) < 1$. In this case the proof is carried out analogously to the proof of the preceding case.

(7) $\mu_i(x) = 1$ $\mu_i^\delta(x) = 0$, or $\mu_i(x) = 0$, $\mu_i^\delta(x) = 1$. These cases are not reasonable. For instance suppose that case $\mu_i(x) = 1$, $\mu_i^\delta(x) = 0$ is conceivable. Then from (4.28) it follows that

$$|\langle a_i, x\rangle - b_i - (\langle a_i(\delta), x\rangle - b_i(\delta))| \leq |b_i - b_i^\delta| + |a_i^\delta - a_i|_\infty |x|_1$$
$$\leq \delta(|x|_1 + 1).$$

On the other hand we have

$$|\langle a_i, x\rangle - b_i - (\langle a_i^\delta, x\rangle - b_i^\delta)| \geq |\langle a_i^\delta, x\rangle - b_i^\delta| \geq \alpha|x|_1 + d_i$$
$$> \delta|x|_1 + \delta = \delta(|x|_1 + 1).$$

So we arrived at a contradiction, which ends the proof.

From (4.30) it follows that

$$|\mu^* - \mu^*(\delta)| \le \delta\left[\frac{1}{\alpha} + \frac{1}{d}\right]$$

and

$$||\mu - \mu^\delta||_C \to 0 \text{ if } \delta/\alpha \to 0 \text{ and } \delta/d \to 0,$$

which means stability with respect to perturbations (4.28) of the solution and the measure of consistency in FLP problem (4.24).

To find a maximizing solution to FLP problem (4.24) we have to solve the following nonlinear programming problem

$$\max \lambda$$

$$\lambda(\alpha|x|_1 + d_0) - \alpha|x|_1 + \langle a_0, x\rangle \le b_0 + d_0,$$

$$\lambda(\alpha|x|_1 + d_1) - \alpha|x|_1 + \langle a_1, x\rangle \le b_1 + d_1,$$

$$\dots\dots$$

$$\lambda(\alpha|x|_1 + d_m) - \alpha|x|_1 + \langle a_m, x\rangle \le b_m + d_m,$$

$$0 \le \lambda \le 1,\ x \in \mathbb{R}^n.$$

It is easily checked that in the extremal case $\alpha = 0$ but $d_i > 0$, the solution of FLP problem (4.24) may be unstable with respect to changes of the crisp parameters $a_{ij}$, $b_i$.

As an example consider the following simple FLP

$$(1, \alpha)x \to \min \tag{4.32}$$

$$\text{subject to } (-1, \alpha)x \le (-1, d_1),\ x \in \mathbb{R},$$

with $b_0 = 0.5$, $\alpha = 0.4$, $d_0 = 0.6$ and $d_1 = 0.5$.

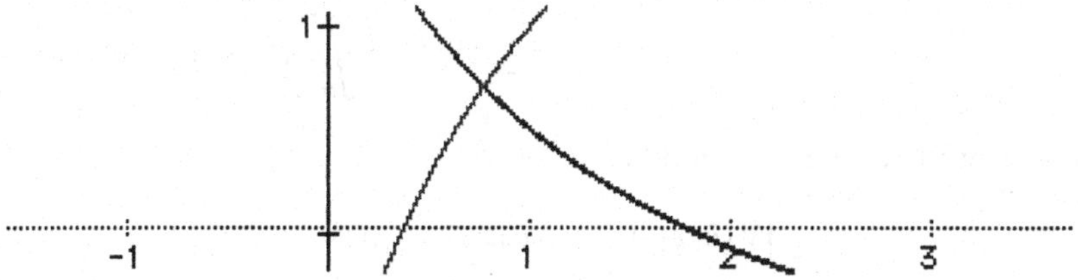


**Fig. 4.10.** $\mu_0$ and $\mu_1$.

That is,

$$(1, 0.4)x \le (0.5, 0.6)$$

$$(-1, 0.4)x \le (-1, 0.5),\ x \in \mathbb{R},$$

and

$$\mu_0(x) = \begin{cases} 1 & \text{if } x \le 0.5 \\ 1 - \dfrac{x - 0.5}{0.4|x| + 0.6} & \text{if } 0.5 \le x \le 1.1 \\ 0 & \text{if } x > 1.1 \end{cases}$$

$$\mu_1(x) = \begin{cases} 1 & \text{if } -x \le -1 \\ 1 - \dfrac{-x + 1}{0.4|x| + 0.5} & \text{if } -1 < -x \le -0.5 \\ 0 & \text{if } -x > -0.5 \end{cases}$$

The uniqe maximizing solution of (4.32) is $x^* = 0.764$ and the degree of consistency is $\mu^* = 0.707$. The degree of consistency is smaller than one, because the aspiration level, $b_0 = 0.5$, is set below one, the minimum of the crisp goal function, $1 \times x$ under the crisp constraint $x \ge 1$.

## 4.5 Fuzzy linear programming with crisp relations

Following Fullér [115, 116] we consider LP problems, in which all of the coefficients are fuzzy numbers

$$\tilde{c}_1 x_1 + \cdots + \tilde{c}_n x_n \to \max \tag{4.33}$$

$$\tilde{a}_{i1} x_1 + \cdots + \tilde{a}_{in} x_n \le \tilde{b}_i, \ i = 1, \dots, m, \ x \in \mathbb{R}^n.$$

Suppose that the crisp inequlity relation between fuzzy numbers is defined by (1.30), i.e. if $[\tilde{a}]^\gamma = [a_1(\gamma), a_2(\gamma)]$ and $[\tilde{b}]^\gamma = [b_1(\gamma), b_2(\gamma)]$ then

$$\tilde{a} \le \tilde{b} \iff \mathcal{W}(\tilde{a}) = \int_0^1 \gamma(a_1(\gamma) + a_2(\gamma))d\gamma$$

$$\le \mathcal{W}(\tilde{b}) = \int_0^1 \gamma(b_1(\gamma) + b_2(\gamma))d\gamma.$$

In this way (4.33) can be stated as follows

$$\mathcal{W}(\tilde{c}_1 x_1 + \cdots + \tilde{c}_n x_n) \to \max \tag{4.34}$$

$$\mathcal{W}(\tilde{a}_{i1} x_1 + \cdots + \tilde{a}_{in} x_n) \le \mathcal{W}(\tilde{b}_i), \ i = 1, \dots, m, \ x \in \mathbb{R}^n.$$

First we observe that $\mathcal{W}\colon \mathcal{F} \to \mathbb{R}$ is a linear mapping, in the sense that

$$\mathcal{W}(\tilde{a} + \tilde{b}) = \mathcal{W}(\tilde{a}) + \mathcal{W}(\tilde{b}),$$

and

$$\mathcal{W}(\lambda\tilde{a}) = \lambda\mathcal{W}(\tilde{a}). \tag{4.35}$$

for any $\lambda \in \mathbb{R}$. Really, from the equation

$$[\tilde{a} + \tilde{b}]^\gamma = [a_1(\gamma) + b_1(\gamma), a_2(\gamma) + b_2(\gamma)],$$

we have

$$\mathcal{W}(\tilde{a} + \tilde{b}) = \int_0^1 \gamma(a_1(\gamma) + b_1(\gamma) + a_2(\gamma) + b_2(\gamma))d\gamma =$$

$$\int_0^1 \gamma(a_1(\gamma) + a_2(\gamma))d\gamma + \int_0^1 \gamma(b_1(\gamma) + b_2(\gamma))d\gamma = \mathcal{W}(\tilde{a}) + \mathcal{W}(\tilde{b}),$$

and (4.35) follows from the relationship $[\lambda\tilde{a}]^\gamma = \lambda[\tilde{a}]^\gamma$ by

$$\begin{aligned} \mathcal{W}(\lambda\tilde{a}) &= \int_0^1 \gamma(\lambda a_1(\gamma) + \lambda a_2(\gamma))d\gamma \\ &= \int_0^1 \gamma(\lambda a_2(\gamma) + \lambda a_1(\gamma))d\gamma = \lambda\mathcal{W}(\tilde{a}). \end{aligned}$$

Using the linearity of $\mathcal{W}$ the LP problem (4.34) with fuzzy number coefficients turns into the following crisp LP problem

$$\mathcal{W}(\tilde{c}_1)x_1 + \cdots + \mathcal{W}(\tilde{c}_n)x_n \to \max \tag{4.36}$$

$$\mathcal{W}(\tilde{a}_{i1})x_1 + \cdots + \mathcal{W}(\tilde{a}_{in})x_n \le \mathcal{W}(\tilde{b}_i), \; i = 1, \dots, m, \; x \in \mathbb{R}^n.$$

or shortly,

$$\langle \mathcal{W}(\tilde{c}), x\rangle \to \max; \text{ subject to } \mathcal{W}(\tilde{A})x \le \mathcal{W}(\tilde{b}), \; x \in \mathbb{R}^n. \tag{4.37}$$

Consider (4.34) with symmetric fuzzy quasi-triangular fuzzy number coefficients (1.2) of the form

$$\tilde{a}_{ij} = (a_{ij}, \alpha_{ij})_{LL}, \quad \tilde{b}_i = (b_i, \beta_i)_{LL}, \quad \tilde{c}_j = (c_j, \theta_j)_{LL}.$$

Then from the representations

$$[\tilde{a}_{ij}]^\gamma = [a_{ij} - \alpha_{ij}L^{-1}(1-\gamma), a_{ij} + \alpha_{ij}L^{-1}(1-\gamma)],$$

$$[\tilde{b}_i]^\gamma = [b_i - \beta_i L^{-1}(1-\gamma), b_i + \beta_i L^{-1}(1-\gamma)],$$

$$[\tilde{c}_j]^\gamma = [c_j - \theta_j L^{-1}(1-\gamma), c_j + \theta_j L^{-1}(1-\gamma)],$$

we get

$$\mathcal{W}(\tilde{a}_{ij}) = \int_0^1 \gamma(a_{ij} - \alpha_{ij}L^{-1}(1-\gamma) + a_{ij} + \alpha_{ij}L^{-1}(1-\gamma))d\gamma = a_{ij},$$

$$\mathcal{W}(\tilde{b}_i) = \int_0^1 \gamma(b_i - \beta_i L^{-1}(1-\gamma) + b_i + \beta_i L^{-1}(1-\gamma))d\gamma = b_i,$$

$$\mathcal{W}(\tilde{c}_j) = \int_0^1 \gamma(c_j - \theta_j L^{-1}(1-\gamma) + c_j + \theta_j L^{-1}(1-\gamma))d\gamma = c_j,$$

in this way FLP problem (4.37) turns into the crisp LP

$$\langle c, x\rangle \rightarrow \max; \text{ subject to } Ax \leq b,\ x \in \mathbb{R}^n.$$

where the coefficients are the centres of the corresponding fuzzy coefficients.

## 4.6 Possibilistic linear programming

We consider certain possibilistic linear programming problems, which have been introduced by Buckley in [14]. In contrast to classical linear programming (where a small error of measurement may produce a large variation in the objective function), we show that the possibility distribution of the objective function of a possibilistic linear program with continuous fuzzy number parameters is stable under small perturbations of the parameters. First, we will briefly review possibilistic linear programming and set up notations. A possibilitic linear program is

$$\max/\min\ Z = x_1\tilde{c}_1 + \cdots + x_n\tilde{c}_n, \tag{4.38}$$

$$\text{subject to}\quad x_1\tilde{a}_{i1} + \cdots + x_n\tilde{a}_{in} * \tilde{b}_i,\ 1 \leq i \leq m,\ x \geq 0.$$

where $\tilde{a}_{ij}$, $\tilde{b}_i$, $\tilde{c}_j$ are fuzzy numbers, $x = (x_1, \ldots, x_n)$ is a vector of (nonfuzzy) decision variables, and $*$ denotes $<$, $\leq$, $=$, $\geq$ or $>$ for each $i$.

We will assume that all fuzzy numbers $\tilde{a}_{ij}$, $\tilde{b}_i$ and $\tilde{c}_j$ are non-interactive. Non-interactivity means that we can find the joint possibility distribution of all the fuzzy variables by calculating the min-intersection of their possibility distributions. Following Buckley [14], we define $\mathrm{Pos}[Z = z]$, the possibility distribution of the objective function $Z$. We first specify the possibility that $x$ satisfies the $i$-th constraints. Let

$$\Pi(a_i, b_i) = \min\{\tilde{a}_{i1}(a_{i1}), \ldots, \tilde{a}_{in}(a_{in}), \tilde{b}_i(b_i\},$$

where $a_i = (a_{i1}, \ldots, a_{in})$, which is the joint distribution of $\tilde{a}_{ij}$, $j = 1, \ldots, n$, and $\tilde{b}_i$. Then

$$\mathrm{Pos}[x \in \mathcal{F}_i] = \sup_{a_i, b_i}\{\, \Pi(a_i, b_i) \mid a_{i1}x_1 + \cdots + a_{in}x_n * b_i \,\},$$

which is the possibility that $x$ is feasible with respect to the $i$-th constraint. Therefore, for $x \geq 0$,

$$\mathrm{Pos}[x \in \mathcal{F}] = \min_{1 \le i \le m} \mathrm{Pos}[x \in \mathcal{F}_i],$$

which is the possibility that $x$ is feasible. We next construct $\mathrm{Pos}[Z = z|x]$ which is the conditional possibility that $Z$ equals $z$ given $x$. The joint distribution of the $\tilde{c}_j$ is

$$\Pi(c) = \min\{\tilde{c}_1(c_1), \dots, \tilde{c}_n(c_n)\}$$

where $c = (c_1, \dots, c_n)$. Therefore,

$$\mathrm{Pos}[Z = z|x] = \sup_c\{\Pi(c)|c_1x_1 + \cdots + c_nx_n = z\}.$$

Finally, applying Bellman and Zadeh's method for fuzzy decision making [7], the possibility distribution of the objective function is defined as

$$\mathrm{Pos}[Z = z] = \sup_{x \ge 0} \min\{\mathrm{Pos}[Z = z|x], \mathrm{Pos}[x \in \mathcal{F}]\}.$$

It should be noted that Buckley [15] showed that the solution to an appropriate linear program gives the correct $z$ values in $\mathrm{Pos}[Z = z] = \alpha$ for each $\alpha \in [0, 1]$.

An important question [90, 156, 347] is the influence of the perturbations of the fuzzy parameters to the possibility distribution of the objective function. We will assume that there is a collection of fuzzy parameters $\tilde{a}^\delta_{ij}$, $\tilde{b}^\delta_i$ and $\tilde{c}^\delta_j$ available with the property

$$D(\tilde{A}, \tilde{A}^\delta) \le \delta,\ D(\tilde{b}, \tilde{b}^\delta) \le \delta,\ D(\tilde{c}, \tilde{c}^\delta) \le \delta, \tag{4.39}$$

where

$$D(\tilde{A}, \tilde{A}^\delta) = \max_{i,j} D(\tilde{a}_{ij}, \tilde{a}^\delta_{ij}),$$
$$D(\tilde{b}, \tilde{b}^\delta) = \max_{i} D(\tilde{b}_i, \tilde{b}^\delta_i),$$
$$D(\tilde{c}, \tilde{c}^\delta) = \max_{j} D(\tilde{c}_j, \tilde{c}^\delta_j).$$

Then we have to solve the following perturbed problem:

$$\max/\min\ Z^\delta = x_1\tilde{c}^\delta_1 + \cdots + x_n\tilde{c}^\delta_n \tag{4.40}$$
$$\text{subject to}\quad x_1\tilde{a}^\delta_{i1} + \cdots + x_n\tilde{a}^\delta_{in} * \tilde{b}^\delta_i,\ 1 \le i \le m,\ x \ge 0.$$

Let us denote by $\mathrm{Pos}[x \in \mathcal{F}^\delta_i]$ the possibility that $x$ is feasible with respect to the $i$-th constraint in (4.40). Then the possibility distribution of the objective function $Z^\delta$ is defined as follows:

$$\mathrm{Pos}[Z^\delta = z] = \sup_{x \ge 0}(\min\{\mathrm{Pos}[Z^\delta = z \mid x], \mathrm{Pos}[x \in \mathcal{F}^\delta]\}).$$

The next theorem shows a stability property (with respect to perturbations (4.39) of the possibility dostribution of the objective function of the possibilistic linear programming problems (4.38) and (4.40).

**Theorem 4.6.1** *Let $\delta \geq 0$ be a real number and let $\tilde{a}_{ij}$, $\tilde{b}_i$, $\tilde{a}^{\delta}_{ij}$, $\tilde{c}_j$, $\tilde{c}^{\delta}_j$ be (continuous) fuzzy numbers. If (4.39) hold, then*

$$\sup_{z\in\mathbb{R}} \mid \mathrm{Pos}[Z^{\delta} = z] - \mathrm{Pos}[Z = z] \mid \leq \omega(\delta) \tag{4.41}$$

*where*

$$\omega(\delta) = \max_{i,j}\{\omega(\tilde{a}_{ij}, \delta), \omega(\tilde{a}^{\delta}_{ij}, \delta), \omega(\tilde{b}_i, \delta), \omega(b^{\delta}_i, \delta), \omega(\tilde{c}_j, \delta), \omega(\tilde{c}^{\delta}_j, \delta)\}.$$

From (4.41) follows that $\sup_z |\mathrm{Pos}[Z^{\delta} = z] - \mathrm{Pos}[Z = z]| \to 0$ as $\delta \to 0$, which means the stability of the possiibility distribution of the objective function with respect to perturbations (4.39). As an immediate consequence of this theorem we obtain the following result: If the fuzzy numbers in (4.38) and (4.40) satisfy the Lipschitz condition with constant $L > 0$, then

$$\sup_{z\in\mathbb{R}} \mid \mathrm{Pos}[Z^{\delta} = z] - \mathrm{Pos}[Z = z] \mid \leq L\delta$$

Furthermore, similar estimations can be obtained in the case of symmetric trapezoidal fuzzy number parameters [225] and in the case of symmetric triangular fuzzy number parameters [118, 224]. It is easy to see that in the case of non-continuous fuzzy parameters the possibility distribution of the objective function may be unstable under small changes of the parameters.

**Example 4.6.1** *Consider the following possibilistic linear program*

$$max/min\ \tilde{c}x \tag{4.42}$$

$$\text{subject to} \quad \tilde{a}x \leq \tilde{b},\ x \geq 0.$$

*where $\tilde{a} = (1, 1)$, $\tilde{b} = (2, 1)$ and $\tilde{c} = (3, 1)$ are fuzzy numbers of symmetric triangular form. Here $x$ is one-dimensional ($n = 1$) and there is only one constraint ($m = 1$). We find*

$$\mathrm{Pos}[x \in \mathcal{F}] = \begin{cases} 1 & \text{if } x \leq 2, \\ \dfrac{3}{x+1} & \text{if } x > 2. \end{cases}$$

*and*

$$\mathrm{Pos}[Z = z|x] = \mathrm{Pos}[\tilde{c}x = z] = \begin{cases} 4 - z/x \text{ if } z/x \in [3, 4], \\ z/x - 2 \text{ if } z/x \in [2, 3], \\ 0 \qquad \text{otherwise}, \end{cases}$$

*for $x \neq 0$, and*

$$\mathrm{Pos}[Z = z|0] = \mathrm{Pos}[0 \times \tilde{c} = z] = \begin{cases} 1 \text{ if } z = 0, \\ 0 \text{ otherwise.} \end{cases}$$

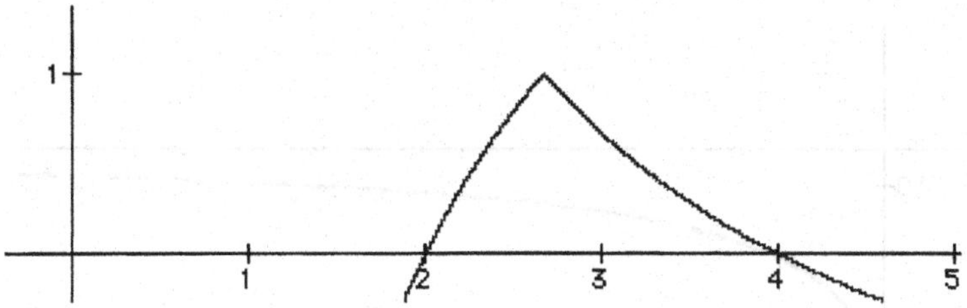


**Fig. 4.11.** The graph of $\text{Pos}[Z = z|x]$ for $z = 8$.

*Therefore,*

$$\text{Pos}[Z = z] = \sup_{x \geq 0} \min \left\{ \frac{3}{x+1}, 1 - \left| \frac{z}{x} - 3 \right| \right\}$$

*if* $z > 6$ *and* $\text{Pos}[Z = z] = 1$ *if* $0 \leq z \leq 6$. *That is,*

$$\text{Pos}[Z = z] = \begin{cases} 1 & \textit{if } 0 \leq z \leq 6, \\ v(z) & \textit{otherwise.} \end{cases}$$

*where*

$$v(z) = \frac{24}{z + 7 + \sqrt{z^2 + 14z + 1}}.$$

*This result can be understood if we consider the crisp LP problem with the centers of the fuzzy numbers*

$$\max / \min 3x; \ \textit{subject to } x \leq 2, \ x \geq 0.$$

*All negative values as possible solutions to the crisp problem are excluded by the constraint* $x \geq 0$, *and the possible values of the objective function are in the interval* $[0, 6]$. *However, due to the fuzziness in (4.42), the objective function can take bigger values than six with a non-zero degrees of possibility. Therefore to find an optimal value of the problem*

$$(3,1)x \to \max \tag{4.43}$$

$$\textit{subject to } (1,1)x \leq (2,1), \ x \geq 0.$$

*requires a determination a trade-off between the increasing value of* $z$ *and the decreasing value of* $\text{Pos}[Z = z]$. *If we take the product operator for modeling the trade-offs then we see that the resulting problem*

$$z \times \text{Pos}[Z = z] = \frac{24z}{z + 7 + \sqrt{z^2 + 14z + 1}} \to \max$$

$$\textit{subject to } z \geq 0.$$

*does not have a finite solution, because the function* $z \times \text{Pos}[Z = z]$ *is strictly increasing if* $z \geq 0$.

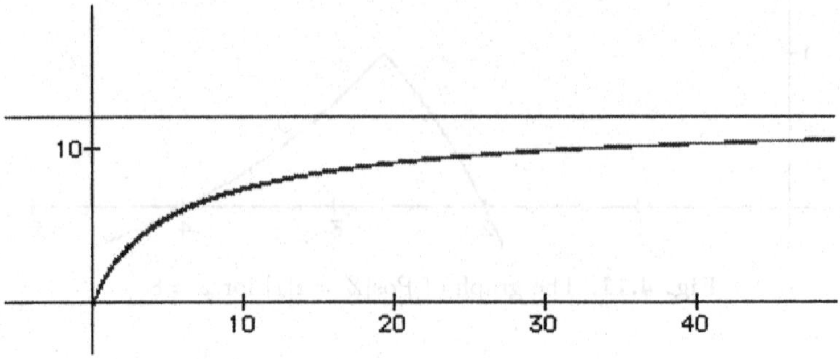


**Fig. 4.12.** $z \times \text{Pos}[Z = z]$ tends to 12 as $z \to \infty$.

## 4.7 Possibilistic quadratic programming

A possibilistic quadratic program is

$$\begin{array}{ll} \text{maximize} & Z := x^T \tilde{C} x + \langle \tilde{d}, x \rangle \\ \text{subject to } \langle \tilde{a}_i, x \rangle \le \tilde{b}_i,\ 1 \le i \le m,\ x \ge 0 & \end{array} \tag{4.44}$$

where $\tilde{C} = (\tilde{c}_{kj})$ is a matrix of fuzzy numbers, $\tilde{a}_i = (\tilde{a}_{ij})$ and $\tilde{d} = (\tilde{d}_j)$ are vectors of fuzzy numbers, $\tilde{b}_i$ is a fuzzy number and

$$\langle \tilde{d}, x \rangle = \tilde{d}_1 x_1 + \cdots + \tilde{d}_n x_n.$$

We will assume that all fuzzy numbers are non-interactive. We define, $\text{Pos}[Z = z]$, the possibility distribution of the objective function $Z$. We first specify the possibility that $x$ satisfies the $i$-th constraint. Let

$$\Pi(a_i, b_i) = \min\{\tilde{a}_{i1}(a_{i1}), \ldots, \tilde{a}_{in}(a_{in}), \tilde{b}_i(b_i)\}$$

where $a_i = (a_{i1}, \ldots, a_{in})$, which is the joint possibility distribution of $\tilde{a}_i$, $1 \le j \le n$ and $\tilde{b}_i$. Then

$$\text{Pos}[x \in \mathcal{F}_i] = \sup_{a_i, b_i} \{\Pi(a_i, b_i) \mid a_{i1} x_1 + \cdots + a_{in} x_n \le b_i\}$$

which is the possibility that $x$ is feasible with respect to th $i$-th constraint. Therefore, for $x \ge 0$,

$$\text{Pos}[x \in \mathcal{F}] = \min\{\text{Pos}[x \in \mathcal{F}_1], \ldots, \text{Pos}[x \in \mathcal{F}_m]\}.$$

We next construct $\text{Pos}[Z = z|x]$ which is the conditional possibility that $Z$ equals $z$ given $x$. The joint possibility distribution of $\tilde{C}$ and $\tilde{d}$ is

$$\Pi(C, d) = \min_{k,j}\{\tilde{C}_{kj}(c_{kj}), \tilde{d}_j(d_j)\}$$

where $C = (c_{kj})$ is a crisp matrix and $d = (d_j)$ a crisp vector. Therefore,

$$\mathrm{Pos}[Z = z|x] = \sup_{C,d}\{\Pi(C,d) \mid x^T Cx + \langle d, x\rangle = z\}.$$

Finally, the possibility distribution of the objective function is defined as

$$\mathrm{Pos}[Z = z] = \sup_{x\geq 0} \min\{\mathrm{Pos}[Z = z|x], \mathrm{Pos}[x \in \mathcal{F}]\}.$$

We show that possibilistic quadratic programs with crisp decision variables and continuous fuzzy number coefficients are well-posed, i.e. small changes in the membership function of the coefficients may cause only a small deviation in the possibility distribution of the objective function. We will assume that there is a collection of fuzzy parameters $\tilde{A}^\delta$, $\tilde{b}^\delta$, $\tilde{C}^\delta$ and $\tilde{d}^\delta$ are available with the property

$$D(\tilde{A}, \tilde{A}^\delta) \leq \delta,\ D(\tilde{C}, \tilde{C}^\delta) \leq \delta,\ D(\tilde{b}, \tilde{b}^\delta) \leq \delta,\ D(\tilde{d}, \tilde{d}^\delta) \leq \delta, \tag{4.45}$$

Then we have to solve the following perturbed problem:

$$\begin{aligned} &\text{maximize } x^T \tilde{C}^\delta x + \langle \tilde{d}^\delta, x\rangle \\ &\text{subject to } \tilde{A}^\delta x \leq \tilde{b}^\delta,\ x \geq 0 \end{aligned} \tag{4.46}$$

Let us denote by $\mathrm{Pos}[x \in \mathcal{F}_i^\delta]$ that $x$ is feasible with respect to the $i$-th constraint in (4.46). Then the possibility distribution of the objective function $Z^\delta$ is defined as follows

$$\mathrm{Pos}[Z^\delta = z] = \sup_{x\geq 0} \min\{\mathrm{Pos}[Z^\delta = z|x], \mathrm{Pos}[x \in \mathcal{F}^\delta]\}.$$

The next theorem shows a stability property of the possibility distribution of the objective function of the possibilistic quadratic programs (4.44) and (4.46).

**Theorem 4.7.1** *[20] Let $\delta > 0$ be a real number and let $\tilde{c}_{kj}$, $\tilde{a}_{ij}$, $\tilde{d}_j$, $\tilde{b}_i$, $\tilde{c}^\delta_{kj}$, $\tilde{a}^\delta_{ij}$, $\tilde{d}^\delta_j$, $\tilde{b}^\delta_i \in \mathcal{F}$ be fuzzy numbers. If (4.45) hold then*

$$\sup_{z\in\mathbb{R}} |\mathrm{Pos}[Z^\delta = z] - \mathrm{Pos}[Z = z]| \leq \omega(\delta)$$

*where $\omega(\delta)$ denotes the maximum of modulus of continuity of all fuzzy number coefficients at $\delta$ in (4.44) and (4.46).*

From Theorem 4.7.1 it follows that $\sup_z |\mathrm{Pos}[Z^\delta = z] - \mathrm{Pos}[Z = z]| \to$ as $\delta \to 0$ which means the stability of the possibility distribution of the objective function with respect to perturbations (4.45).

## 4.8 Multiobjective possibilistic linear programming

Stability and sensitivity analysis becomes more and more attractive also in the area of multiple objective mathematical programming (for excellent surveys see e.g. Gal [147] and Rios Insua [278]). Publications on this topic usually investigate the impact of parameter changes (in the righthand side or/and the objective functions or/and the 'A-matrix' or/and the domination structure) on the solution in various models of vector maximization problems, e.g. linear or nonlinear, deterministic or stochastic, static or dynamic [82, 279].

Following Fullér and Fedrizzi [137], in this Section we show that the possibility distribution of the objectives of an multiobjective possibilistic linear program (MPLP) with (continuous) fuzzy number coefficients is stable under small changes in the membership function of the fuzzy parameters.

A multiobjective possibilistic linear program (MPLP) is

$$\max/\min\ Z = (\tilde{c}_{11}x_1 + \cdots + \tilde{c}_{1n}x_n, \dots, \tilde{c}_{k1}x_1 + \cdots + \tilde{c}_{kn}x_n) \qquad (4.47)$$

$$\text{subject to} \quad \tilde{a}_{i1}x_1 + \cdots \tilde{a}_{in}x_n * \tilde{b}_i,\ i = 1, \dots, m,\ x \geq 0,$$

where $\tilde{a}_{ij}$, $\tilde{b}_i$, and $\tilde{c}_{lj}$ are fuzzy quantities, $x = (x_1, \dots, x_n)$ is a vector of (non-fuzzy) decision variables and $|ast$ denotes $<$, $\leq$, $=$, $\geq$ or $>$ for each $i$, $i = 1, \dots, m$.

Even though $*$ may vary from row to row in the constraints, we will rewrite the MPLP (4.47) as

$$\max/\min\ Z = (\tilde{c}_1 x, \dots, \tilde{c}_k x)$$

$$\text{subject to} \quad \tilde{A}x * \tilde{b}, x \geq 0,$$

where $\tilde{a} = \{\tilde{a}_{ij}\}$ is an $m \times n$ matrix of fuzzy numbers and $\tilde{b} = (\tilde{b}_1, ..., \tilde{b}_m)$ is a vector of fuzzy numbers. The fuzzy numbers are the possibility distributions associated with the fuzzy variables and hence place a restriction on the possible values the variable may assume [334, 335]. For example, $\text{Pos}[\tilde{a}_{ij} = t] = \tilde{a}_{ij}(t)$. We will assume that all fuzzy numbers $\tilde{a}_{ij}$, $\tilde{b}_i$, $\tilde{c}_l$ are non-interactive.

Following Buckley [16], we define $\text{Pos}[Z = z]$, the possibility distribution of the objective function $Z$. We first specify the possibility that $x$ satisfies the $i$-th constraints. Let

$$\Pi(a_i, b_i) = \min\{\tilde{a}_{i1}(a_{i1}), \dots, \tilde{a}_{in}(a_{in}), \tilde{b}_i(b_i\},$$

where $a_i = (a_{i1}, \dots, a_{in})$, which is the joint distribution of $\tilde{a}_{ij}, j = 1, \dots, n$, and $\tilde{b}_i$. Then

$$\text{Pos}[x \in \mathcal{F}_i] = \sup_{a_i, b_i}\{\Pi(a_i, b_i) \mid a_{i1}x_1 + \cdots + a_{in}x_n * b_i\},$$

which is the possibility that $x$ is feasible with respect to the $i$-th constraint. Therefore, for $x \geq 0$,

$$\text{Pos}[x \in \mathcal{F}] = \min\{\text{Pos}[x \in \mathcal{F}_1], \dots, \text{Pos}[x \in \mathcal{F}_m]\}.$$

which is the possibility that $x$ is feasible. We next construct $\text{Pos}[Z = z|x]$ which is the conditional possibility that $Z$ equals $z$ given $x$. The joint distribution of the $\tilde{c}_{lj},\ j = 1, \dots, n$, is

$$\Pi(c_l) = \min\{\tilde{c}_{l1}(c_{l1}), \dots, \tilde{c}_{ln}(c_{ln})\}$$

where $c_l = (c_{l1}, \dots, c_{ln}),\ l = 1, \dots, k$. Therefore,

$$\text{Pos}[Z = z|x] = \text{Pos}[\tilde{c}_1 x = z_1, \dots, \tilde{c}_k x = z_k] = \min_{1 \le l \le k} \text{Pos}[\tilde{c}_l x = z_l] =$$

$$\min_{1 \le l \le k} \sup_{c_{l1}, \dots, c_{lk}} \{\Pi(c_l) \mid c_{l1}x_1 + \dots + c_{ln}x_n = z_l\}.$$

Finally, the possibility distribution of the objective function is defined as

$$\text{Pos}[Z = z] = \sup_{x \ge 0} \min\{\text{Pos}[Z = z|x], \text{Pos}[x \in \mathcal{F}]\}$$

We will assume that there is a collection of fuzzy parameters $\tilde{a}^{\delta}_{ij}$, $\tilde{b}^{\delta}_{i}$, $\tilde{c}^{\delta}_{lj}$ available with the property

$$\max_{i,j} D(\tilde{a}_{ij}, \tilde{a}^{\delta}_{ij}) \le \delta, \quad \max_{i} D(\tilde{b}_i, \tilde{b}^{\delta}_i) \le \delta, \quad \max_{l,j} D(\tilde{c}_{lj}, \tilde{c}^{\delta}_{lj}) \le \delta. \tag{4.48}$$

Then we have to solve the following problem:

$$\max/\min\ Z^{\delta} = (\tilde{c}^{\delta}_1 x, \dots, \tilde{c}^{\delta}_k x) \tag{4.49}$$

$$\text{subject to}\quad \tilde{A}^{\delta} x * \tilde{b}^{\delta},\ x \ge 0.$$

Let us denote by $\text{Pos}[x \in \mathcal{F}^{\delta}_i]$ the possibility that $x$ is feasible with respect to the $i$-th constraint in (4.49). Then the possibility distribution of the objective function $Z^{\delta}$ in (4.49) is defined as:

$$\text{Pos}[Z^{\delta} = z] = \sup_{x \ge 0}(\min\{\text{Pos}[Z^{\delta} = z \mid x], \text{Pos}[x \in \mathcal{F}^{\delta}]\}).$$

The next theorem shows a stability property (with respect to perturbations (4.48) of the possibility distribution of the objective function, $Z$, of multiobjective possibilistic linear programming problems (4.47) and (4.49).

**Theorem 4.8.1** *[137] Let $\delta \ge 0$ be a real number and let $\tilde{a}_{ij}$, $\tilde{b}_i$, $\tilde{a}^{\delta}_{ij}$, $\tilde{c}_{lj}$, $\tilde{c}^{\delta}_{lj}$ be (continuous) fuzzy numbers. If (4.48) hold, then*

$$\sup_{z \in \mathbb{R}^k} \mid \text{Pos}[Z^{\delta} = z] - \text{Pos}[Z = z] \mid \le \omega(\delta)$$

*where $\omega(\delta)$ is the maximum of moduli of continuity of all fuzzy numbers at $\delta$.*

From Theorem 4.8.1 it follows that

$$\sup_{z \in \mathbb{R}^k} \mid \mathrm{Pos}[Z^\delta = z] - \mathrm{Pos}[Z = z] \mid \to 0 \text{ as } \delta \to 0$$

which means the stability of the possibility distribution of the objective function with respect to perturbations (4.48). It is easy to see that in the case of non-continuous fuzzy parameters the possibility distribution of the objective function may be unstable under small changes of the parameters.

**Example 4.8.1** *As an example, consider the following biobjective possibilistic linear program*

$$\begin{aligned} & max/min \ (\tilde{c}x, \tilde{c}x) \\ & subject\ to \quad \tilde{a}x \le \tilde{b}, \ x \ge 0. \end{aligned} \tag{4.50}$$

*where* $\tilde{a} = (1,1)$, $\tilde{b} = (2,1)$ *and* $\tilde{c} = (3,1)$ *are fuzzy numbers of symmetric triangular form. Here* $x$ *is one-dimensional* ($n = 1$) *and there is only one constraint* ($m = 1$). *We find*

$$\mathrm{Pos}[x \in \mathcal{F}] = \begin{cases} 1 & if\ x \le 2, \\ \dfrac{3}{x+1} & if\ x > 2. \end{cases}$$

*and*

$$\mathrm{Pos}[Z = (z_1, z_2)|x] = \min\{\mathrm{Pos}[\tilde{c}x = z_1], \mathrm{Pos}[\tilde{c}x = z_2]\}$$

*where*

$$\mathrm{Pos}[\tilde{c}x = z_i] = \begin{cases} 4 - \dfrac{z_i}{x} \ if\ z_i/x \in [3,4], \\ \dfrac{z_i}{x} - 2 \ if\ z_i/x \in [2,3], \\ 0 \qquad otherwise, \end{cases}$$

*for* $i = 1,2$ *and* $x \neq 0$, *and*

$$\mathrm{Pos}[Z = (z_1, z_2)|0] = \mathrm{Pos}[0 \times \tilde{c} = z] = \begin{cases} 1 \ if\ z = 0, \\ 0 \ otherwise. \end{cases}$$

*Both possibilities are nonlinear functions of* $x$, *however the calculation of* $\mathrm{Pos}[Z = (z_1, z_2)]$ *is easily performed and we obtain*

$$\mathrm{Pos}[Z = (z_1, z_2)] = \begin{cases} \theta_1 & if\ z \in M_1, \\ \min\{\theta_1, \theta_2, \theta_3\} & if\ z \in M_2, \\ 0 & otherwise, \end{cases}$$

*where*

$$M_1 = \{z \in \mathbb{R}^2 \mid |z_1 - z_2| \le \min\{z_1, z_2\}, z_1 + z_2 \le 12\},$$

$$M_2 = \{z \in \mathbb{R}^2 \mid |z_1 - z_2| \leq \min\{z_1, z_2\}, z_1 + z_2 > 12\},$$

*and*

$$\theta_i = \frac{24}{z_i + 7 + \sqrt{z_i^2 + 14z_i + 1}}.$$

*for* $i = 1, 2$ *and*

$$\theta_3 = \frac{4\min\{z_1, z_2\} - 2\max\{z_1, z_2\}}{z_1 + z_2}.$$

*Consider now a perturbed biobjective problem with two different objectives (derived from (4.50) by a simple* $\delta$*-shifting of the centres of* $\tilde{a}$ *and* $\tilde{c}$*):*

$$max/min\ (\tilde{c}x, \tilde{c}^\delta x) \tag{4.51}$$

$$subject\ to\quad \tilde{a}^\delta x \leq \tilde{b},\ x \geq 0.$$

*where* $\tilde{a} = (1 + \delta, 1)$, $\tilde{b} = (2, 1)$, $\tilde{c} = (3, 1)$, $\tilde{c}^\delta = (3 - \delta, 1)$ *and* $\delta \geq 0$ *is the error of measurement. Then*

$$\mathrm{Pos}[x \in \mathcal{F}^\delta] = \begin{cases} 1 & if\ x \leq \dfrac{2}{1+\delta}, \\ \dfrac{3 - \delta x}{x+1} & if\ x > \dfrac{2}{1+\delta}. \end{cases}$$

*and*

$$\mathrm{Pos}[Z^\delta = (z_1, z_2)|x] = \min\{\mathrm{Pos}[\tilde{c}x = z_1], \mathrm{Pos}[\tilde{c}^\delta x = z_2]\}$$

*where*

$$\mathrm{Pos}[\tilde{c}x = z_1] = \begin{cases} 4 - \dfrac{z_1}{x}\ if\ z_1/x \in [3, 4], \\ \dfrac{z_1}{x} - 2\ if\ z_1 i/x \in [2, 3], \\ 0 \qquad otherwise, \end{cases}$$

$$\mathrm{Pos}[\tilde{c}^\delta x = z_2] = \begin{cases} 4 - \delta - \dfrac{z_2}{x}\ if\ z_2/x \in [3 - \delta, 4 - \delta], \\ \dfrac{z_2}{x} - 2 + \delta\ if\ z_2/x \in [2 - \delta, 3 - \delta], \\ 0 \qquad otherwise, \end{cases}$$

$x \neq 0$, *and*

$$\mathrm{Pos}[Z^\delta = (z_1, z_2)|0] = \mathrm{Pos}[0 \times \tilde{c} = z] = \begin{cases} 1\ if\ z = 0, \\ 0\ otherwise. \end{cases}$$

*So,*

$$\mathrm{Pos}[Z^\delta = (z_1, z_2)] = \begin{cases} \theta_1(\delta) & \text{if } z \in M_1(\delta), \\ \min\{\theta_1(\delta), \theta_2(\delta), \theta_3(\delta)\} & \text{if } z \in M_2(\delta), \\ 0 & \text{otherwise,} \end{cases}$$

*where*

$$M_1(\delta) = \left\{ z \in \mathbb{R}^2 \mid |z_1 - z_2| \le (1 - 0.5\delta) \min\{z_1, z_2\}, z_1 + z_2 \le \frac{2(6-\delta)}{1+\delta} \right\},$$

$$M_2(\delta) = \left\{ z \in \mathbb{R}^2 \mid |z_1 - z_2| \le (1 - 0.5\delta) \min\{z_1, z_2\}, z_1 + z_2 > \frac{2(6-\delta)}{1+\delta} \right\},$$

$$\theta_1(\delta) = \frac{24 + \delta\left(7 - z_1 - \sqrt{z_1^2 + 14z_1 + 1 + 4z_1\delta}\right)}{z_1 + 7 + \sqrt{z_1^2 + 14z_1 + 1 + 4z_1\delta} + 2\delta}$$

$$\theta_2(\delta) = \frac{24 - \delta\left(\delta + z_2 - 1 + \sqrt{(1 - \delta - z_2)^2 + 16z_2}\right)}{z_2 + 7 + \sqrt{(1 - \delta - z_2)^2 + 16z_2} + \delta}$$

*and*

$$\theta_3(\delta) = \frac{(4-\delta)\min\{z_1, z_2\} - 2\max\{z_1, z_2\}}{z_1 + z_2}.$$

*It is easy to check that*

$$\sup_{x \ge 0} |\mathrm{Pos}[x \in \mathcal{F}] - \mathrm{Pos}[x \in \mathcal{F}^\delta]| \le \delta,$$

$$\sup_{z} |\mathrm{Pos}[Z = z|x] - \mathrm{Pos}[Z^\delta = z|x]| \le \delta, \ \forall x \ge 0,$$

$$\sup_{z} |\mathrm{Pos}[Z = z] - \mathrm{Pos}[Z^\delta = z]| \le \delta.$$

*On the other hand, from the definition of metric $D$ the modulus of continuity and Theorem 4.8.1 it follows that*

$$D(\tilde{a}, \tilde{a}^\delta) = \delta, D(\tilde{c}, \tilde{c}^\delta) = \delta, D(\tilde{c}, \tilde{c}) = 0, D(\tilde{b}, \tilde{b}) = 0, \omega(\delta) = \delta,$$

*and, therefore,*

$$\sup_{z} |\mathrm{Pos}[Z = z] - \mathrm{Pos}[Z^\delta = z]| \le \delta.$$

Assume now that all fuzzy numbers $\tilde{a}_{ij}$, $\tilde{b}_i$, $\tilde{a}_{ij}^\delta$, $\tilde{b}_i^\delta$, $\tilde{c}_{lj}$ and $\tilde{c}_{lj}^\delta$ in (4.47) and (4.49) are weakly non-interactive [334]. Weakly-noninteractivity means that there exists a triangular norm $T$, such that we can find the joint possibility distribution of all the fuzzy variables by calculating the $T$-intersection of their possibility distributions.

The next theorem shows a stability property of the possibility distribution of the objective functions of multiobjective possibilistic linear programs with $T$-weakly non-interactive fuzzy number coefficients (4.47) and (4.49).

**Theorem 4.8.2** *[97] Let $\delta \geq 0$ be a real number and let $\tilde{a}_{ij}$, $\tilde{b}_i$, $\tilde{a}^{\delta}_{ij}$, $\tilde{b}^{\delta}_i$, $\tilde{c}_{lj}$ and $\tilde{c}^{\delta}_{lj}$ be T-weakly-noninteractivity fuzzy numbers. If (4.48) hold, and T is a continuous t-norm then*

$$\sup_{z \in \mathbb{R}^k} |\mathrm{Pos}[Z^{\delta} = z] - \mathrm{Pos}[Z = z]| \leq \omega(T, \Omega(\delta))$$

*where $\Omega(\delta)$ is the maximum of modulus of continuity of all fuzzy number coefficients at $\delta$ in (4.47) and (4.49), and $\omega(T, .)$ denotes the modulus of continuity of T.*

# 5. Fuzzy Reasoning for Fuzzy Optimization

## 5.1 Fuzzy reasoning for FMP

Following Fullér and Zimmermann [135], we interpret fuzzy linear programming (FLP) problems with fuzzy coefficients and fuzzy inequality relations as multiple fuzzy reasoning schemes (MFR), where the antecedents of the scheme correspond to the constraints of the FLP problem and the fact of the scheme is the objective of the FLP problem.

Then the solution process consists of two steps: first, for every decision variable $x \in \mathbb{R}^n$, we compute the (fuzzy) value of the objective function, $\text{MAX}(x)$, via sup-min convolution of the antecedents/constraints and the fact/objective, then an (optimal) solution to FLP problem is any point which produces a maximal element of the set

$$\{\text{MAX}(x) \mid x \in \mathbb{R}^n\}$$

(in the sense of the given inequality relation). We show that this solution process for a classical (crisp) LP problem results in a solution in the classical sense, and (under well-chosen inequality relations and objective function) coincides with those suggested by Buckley [15], Delgado et al. [77, 78], Negoita [258], Ramik and Rimanek [275], Verdegay [302, 303] and Zimmermann [344].

We consider FLP problems of the form

$$\tilde{c}_1 x_1 + \cdots + \tilde{c}_n x_n \to \max \tag{5.1}$$

$$\tilde{a}_{i1} x_1 + \cdots + \tilde{a}_{in} x_n \lesssim \tilde{b}_i, \quad i = 1, \ldots, m,$$

or, shortly,

$$\langle \tilde{c}, x \rangle \to \max$$

$$\text{subject to } \tilde{A}x \lesssim \tilde{b},$$

where $x \in \mathbb{R}^n$ is the vector of decision variables, $\tilde{a}_{ij}$, $\tilde{b}_i$ and $\tilde{c}_j$ are fuzzy quantities, the operations addition and multiplication by a real number of fuzzy quantities are defined by Zadeh's extension principle, the inequality relation, $\lesssim$, for the constraints is given by a certain fuzzy relation and the objective function is to be maximized in the sense of a given crisp inequality relation, $\leq$, between fuzzy quantities.

The FLP problem (5.1) can be stated as follows: Find $x^* \in \mathbb{R}^n$ such that

$$\tilde{c}_1 x_1 + \cdots + \tilde{c}_n x_n \leq \tilde{c}_1 x_1^* + \cdots + \tilde{c}_n x_n^*$$

$$\tilde{a}_{i1} x_1 + \cdots + \tilde{a}_{in} x_n \lesssim \tilde{b}_i, \; i = 1, \ldots, m,$$

i.e. we search for an alternative, $x^*$, which maximizes the objective function subject to constraints. Now we set up the notations and recall some fuzzy inference rules needed for the proposed solution principle.

In the following $\bar{a}$ denotes the characteristic function of the singleton $a \in \mathbb{R}$, i.e

$$\bar{a}(t) = \begin{cases} 1 \text{ if } t = a \\ 0 \text{ otherwise.} \end{cases}$$

Let $X$ be a non-empty set. The empty fuzzy set in $X$, denoted by $\emptyset_X$, is defined as $\emptyset_X(x) = 0, \forall x \in X$. A binary fuzzy relation $W$ in $X$ is a fuzzy subset of the Certesian product $X \times X$ and defined by its membership function $\mu_W$ (or simply $W$ if not confusing). If $\mu_W(u, v) \in \{0, 1\}, \forall u, v \in X$ then $W$ is called a crisp relation in $X$. Throughout this Section we shall use the terms relation and inequality relation interchangeably, i.e. we do not require any additional property for the later. However, we can get unexpected solutions if we use unjustifiable inequality relations to compare fuzzy quantities.

Let $\leq$ be a crisp inequality relation in $\mathcal{F}$. Then for all pairs $\tilde{a}, \tilde{b} \in \mathcal{F}$ it induces a crisp binary relation in $\mathbb{R}$ defined by

$$(\tilde{a} \leq \tilde{b})(u, v) = \begin{cases} 1 \text{ if } u = v, \text{ and } \tilde{a} \text{ and } \tilde{b} \text{ are in relation } \leq, \\ 0 \text{ otherwise.} \end{cases}$$

It is clear that $(\tilde{a} \leq \tilde{b}) = \emptyset$ iff and $\tilde{a}$ and $\tilde{b}$ are not in relation $\leq$. If the inequality relation $\leq$ is modeled by a fuzzy implication operator $I$ then for all pairs $\tilde{a}, \tilde{b} \in \mathcal{F}$ it induces a fuzzy binary relation in $\mathbb{R}$ defined by

$$(\tilde{a} \leq \tilde{b})(u, v) = I(\tilde{a}(u), \tilde{b}(v)),$$

e.g. if $\leq$ is given by the Gödel implication operator then we have

$$(\tilde{a} \leq \tilde{b})(u, v) = \begin{cases} 1 & \text{if } \tilde{a}(u) \leq \tilde{b}(v), \\ \tilde{b}(v) & \text{otherwise.} \end{cases} \tag{5.2}$$

If an inequality relation $\leq$ in $\mathcal{F}$ is not crisp then we will usually write $\lesssim$ instead . We will use the following crisp inequality relations in $\mathcal{F}$:

$$\tilde{a} \leq \tilde{b} \iff \tilde{\max}\left\{\tilde{a}, \tilde{b}\right\} = \tilde{b} \tag{5.3}$$

where $\tilde{\max}$ is the ordinary extension of the two-placed max function defined as

$$\tilde{a} \leq \tilde{b} \iff \tilde{a} \subseteq \tilde{b}, \tag{5.4}$$

where $\tilde{a} \subseteq \tilde{b}$ if $\tilde{a}(u) \leq \tilde{b}(u)$, for all $u \in \mathbb{R}$,

$$\tilde{a} \leq \tilde{b} \iff \text{peak}(\tilde{a}) \leq \text{peak}(\tilde{b}) \tag{5.5}$$

where $\tilde{a}$ and $\tilde{b}$ are fuzzy numbers, and peak($\tilde{a}$) and peak($\tilde{b}$) denote their peaks,

$$\bar{a} \leq \bar{b} \iff a \leq b, \tag{5.6}$$

where $\bar{a}$ and $\bar{b}$ are fuzzy singletons. Let $\Gamma$ be an index set, $\tilde{a}_\gamma \in \mathcal{F}$, $\gamma \in \Gamma$, and let $\leq$ a crisp inequality relation in $\mathcal{F}$. We say that $\tilde{a}$ is a maximal element of the set

$$\mathcal{G} := \{\tilde{a}_\gamma \mid \gamma \in \Gamma\} \tag{5.7}$$

if $\tilde{a}_\gamma \leq \tilde{a}$ for all $\gamma \in \Gamma$ and $\tilde{a} \in \mathcal{G}$. A fuzzy quantity $\tilde{A}$ is called an upper bound of $\mathcal{G}$ if $\tilde{a}_\gamma \leq \tilde{A}$ for all $\gamma \in \Gamma$. A fuzzy quantity $\tilde{A}$ is called a least upper bound (supremum) of $\mathcal{G}$ if it is an upper bound and if there exists an upper bound $\tilde{B}$, such that $\tilde{B} \leq \tilde{A}$, then $\tilde{A} \leq \tilde{B}$. If $\tilde{A}$ is a least upper bound of $\mathcal{G}$, then we write

$$\tilde{A} = \sup\{\tilde{a}_\gamma \mid \gamma \in \Gamma\}$$

It is easy to see that, depending on the definition of the inequality relation, the set (5.7) may have many maximal elements (suprema) or the set of maximal elements (suprema) may be empty. For example, (i) if $\{\text{peak}(\tilde{a}) \mid \gamma \in \Gamma\}$ is a bounded and closed subset of the real line then $\mathcal{G}$ has at least one maximal element in the sense of relation (5.5); (ii) $\mathcal{G}$ always has a unique supremum in relation (5.4), but usually does not have maximal elements; (iii) if there exists $u \in \mathbb{R}$, such that $\tilde{a}_\gamma(v) = 0$, for all $v \geq u$ and $\gamma \in \Gamma$ then $\mathcal{G}$ has infinitely many suprema in relation (5.3).
The degree of possibility of the statement "$\tilde{a}$ is smaller or equal to $\tilde{b}$", which we write Pos[$\tilde{a} \leq \tilde{b}$], induces the following relation in $\mathbb{R}$

$$(\tilde{a} \lesssim \tilde{b})(u,v) = \begin{cases} \text{Pos}[\tilde{a} \leq \tilde{b}] & \text{if } u = v \\ 0 & \text{otherwise} \end{cases} \tag{5.8}$$

We shall use the compositional rule of inference scheme with several relations (called Multiple Fuzzy Reasoning Scheme) [333] which has the general form

| | |
|---|---|
| Fact | $X$ has property $P$ |
| Relation 1: | $X$ and $Y$ are in relation $W_1$ |
| ... | ... |
| Relation m: | $X$ and $Y$ are in relation $W_m$ |
| Consequence: | $Y$ has property $Q$ |

where $X$ and $Y$ are linguistic variables taking their values from fuzzy sets in classical sets $U$ and $V$, respectively, $P$ and $Q$ are unary fuzzy predicates in $U$

and $V$, respectively, and $W_i$ is a binary fuzzy relation in $U \times V$, i=1,...,m. The consequence $Q$ is determined by

$$Q = P \circ \bigcap_{i=1}^{m} W_i$$

or in detail,

$$\mu_Q(y) = \sup_{x \in U} \min \{\mu_P(x), \mu_{W_1}(x,y), \ldots, \mu_{W_1}(x,y)\}.$$

We consider FLP problems as MFR schemes, where the antecedents of the scheme correspond to the constraints of the FLP problem and the fact of the scheme is interpreted as the objective function of the FLP problem. Then the solution process consists of two steps: first, for every decision variable $x \in \mathbb{R}^n$, we compute the value of the objective function, MAX($x$), via sup-min convolution of the antecedents/constraints and the fact/objective, then an (optimal) solution to the FLP problem is any point which produces a maximal element of the set

$$\{\mathrm{MAX}(x) | x \in \mathbb{R}^n\} \tag{5.9}$$

in the sense of the given inequality relation. We interpret the FLP problem (5.1) as MFR schemes of the form

| | |
|---|---|
| Antecedent 1 | $\mathrm{Constraint}_1(x) := \tilde{a}_{11}x_1 + \cdots + \tilde{a}_{1n}x_n \lesssim \tilde{b}_1$ |
| ... | ... |
| Antecedent m | $\mathrm{Constraint}_m(x) := \tilde{a}_{m1}x_1 + \cdots + \tilde{a}_{mn}x_n \lesssim \tilde{b}_m$ |
| Fact | $\mathrm{Goal}(x) := \tilde{c}_1x_1 + \cdots + \tilde{c}_nx_n$ |
| Consequence | MAX(x) |

where $x \in \mathbb{R}^n$ and the consequence (i.e. the value of the objective function subject to constraints at $x$) $MAX(x)$ is computed as follows

$$\mathrm{MAX}(x) = \mathrm{Goal}(x) \circ \bigcap_{i=1}^{m} \mathrm{Constraint}_i(x),$$

i.e.

$$\mu_{MAX(x)}(v) = \sup_u \min \{\mu_{\mathrm{Goal}(x)}(u), \\ \mu_{\mathrm{Constraint}_1(x)}(u,v), \ldots, \mu_{\mathrm{Constraint}_m}(u,v)\}. \tag{5.10}$$

Then an optimal value of the objective function of problem (5.1), denoted by $M$, is defined as

$$M := \sup \{MAX(x) | x \in \mathbb{R}^n\}, \tag{5.11}$$

where sup is understood in the sense of the given crisp inequality relation for the objective function. Finally, a solution $x^* \in \mathbb{R}^n$ to problem (5.1) is obtained from the equation

$$\mathrm{MAX}(x^*) = M.$$

The set of solutions of problem (5.1) is non-empty iff the set of maximizing elements of (5.9) is non-empty. Apart from the deterministic LP,

$$\langle c, x \rangle \to \max$$
$$\text{subject to } Ax \leq b,$$

where we simply compute the value of the objective function as

$$c_1 y_1 + \cdots + c_n y_n$$

at any feasible point $y \in \mathbb{R}^n$ and do not care about non-feasible points, in FLP problem (5.1) we have to consider the whole decision space, because each $y$ from $\mathbb{R}^n$ has a (fuzzy) degree of feasibility (given by the fuzzy relations $\mathrm{Constraint}_i(y)$, $i = 1, \dots, m$). We have a right to compute the value of the objective function of (5.1) at $y \in \mathbb{R}^n$ as $\tilde{c}_1 y_1 + \cdots + \tilde{c}_n x_n$ if there are no constraints at all (if there are no rules in a fuzzy reasoning scheme then the consequence takes the value of the observation automatically).

To determine a maximal element of the set (5.9) even for a *crisp* inequality relation is usually a very complicated process. However, this problem can lead to a crisp LP problem (see Zimmermann [345], Buckley [15]), crisp multiple criteria parametric linear programming problem (see Delgado et al. [77, 78], Verdegay [302, 303]) or nonlinear mathematical programming problem (see Zimmermann [349]). If the inequality relation for the objective function is not crisp but fuzzy, then we somehow have to find an element from the set (5.9) which can be considered as a best choice in the sense of the given fuzzy inequality relation (see Ovchinnikov [271], Orlovski [268], Ramik and Rimanek [275], Rommelfanger [280], Roubens and Vincke [283], Tanaka and Asai [294]).

### 5.1.1 Extension to nonlinear FMP

We show how the proposed approach can be extended to nonlinear FMP problems with fuzzy coefficients. Generalizing the classical mathematical programming (MP) problem

$$\begin{aligned} &\text{maximize } g(c, x) \\ &\text{subject to } f_i(a_i, x) \leq b_i, \ i = 1, \dots, m, \end{aligned}$$

where $x \in \mathbb{R}^n$, $c = (c_i, \dots, c_k)$ and $a_i = (a_{i1}, \dots, a_{il})$ are vectors of crisp coefficients, we consider the following FMP problem

$$\begin{aligned}&\text{maximize } g(\tilde{c}_1, \dots \tilde{c}_k, x)\\&\text{subject to } f_i(\tilde{a}_{i1}, \dots \tilde{a}_{il}, x) \lesssim \tilde{b}_i,\ i = 1, \dots, m,\end{aligned}$$

where $x \in \mathbb{R}^n$, $\tilde{c}_h$, $h = 1, \dots, k$, $\tilde{a}_{is}$, $s = 1, \dots, l$, and $\tilde{b}_i$ are fuzzy quantities, the functions $g(\tilde{c}, x)$ and $f_i(\tilde{a}_i, x)$ are defined by Zadeh's extension principle, and the inequality relation $\lesssim$ is defined by a certain fuzzy relation. We interpret the above FMP problem as MFR schemes of the form

$$\begin{array}{ll}\text{Antecedent 1:} & \text{Constraint}_1(x) := f_i(\tilde{a}_{11}, \dots \tilde{a}_{1l}, x) \lesssim \tilde{b}_1\\ \dots & \dots\\ \text{Antecedent m:} & \text{Constraint}_m(x) := f_m(\tilde{a}_{m1}, \dots \tilde{a}_{ml}, x) \lesssim \tilde{b}_m\\ \text{Fact:} & \text{Goal}(x) := g(\tilde{c}_1, \dots, \tilde{c}_k, x)\\ \hline \text{Consequence} & \text{MAX}(x)\end{array}$$

Then the solution process is carried out analogously to the linear case, i.e an optimal value of the objective function, $M$, is defined by (5.11), and a solution $x^* \in \mathbb{R}^n$ is obtained by solving the equation $\text{MAX}(x^*) = M$.

### 5.1.2 Relation to classical LP problems

We show that our solution process for classical LP problems results in a solution in the classical sense. A classical LP problem can be stated as follows

$$\max\langle c, x\rangle;\ \text{subject to } Ax \le b,\ x \in \mathbb{R}^n. \tag{5.12}$$

Let $X^*$ be the set of solutions and if $X^* \ne \emptyset$ then let $v^* = \langle c, x^*\rangle$ denote the optimal value of the objective function of (5.12). An element $x$ from $\mathbb{R}^n$ is said to be feasible if it satisfies the inequality $Ax \le b$. Generalizing the crisp LP problem (5.12) we consider the FLP problem (5.1) with fuzzy singletons and crisp inequality relations (5.6)

$$\begin{aligned}\text{maximize}\quad & \text{Goal}(x) := \bar{c}_1 x_1 + \dots + \bar{c}_k x_n\\ \text{subject to}\quad & \text{Constraint}_1(x) := \bar{a}_{11} x_1 + \dots + \bar{a}_{1n} x_n \le \bar{b}_i\\ & \dots\\ & \text{Constraint}_m(x) := \bar{a}_{m1} x_1 + \dots + \bar{a}_{mn} x_n \le \bar{b}_m\end{aligned} \tag{5.13}$$

where $\bar{a}_{ij}, \bar{b}_i$ and $\bar{c}_j$ denote the characteristic function of the crisp coefficients $a_{ij}, b_i$ and $c_j$, respectively, and the inequality relation $\le$ is defined by

$$\bar{a}_{i1} x_1 + \dots + \bar{a}_{in} x_n \le \bar{b}_i \iff a_{i1} x_1 + \dots + a_{in} x_n \le b_i,$$

i.e.

$$(\bar{a}_{i1} x_1 + \dots + \bar{a}_{in} x_n \le \bar{b}_i)(u, v) = \begin{cases} 1 \text{ if } u = v \text{ and } \langle a_i, x\rangle \le b_i\\ 0 \text{ otherwise}\end{cases} \tag{5.14}$$

Then from (5.10) we get

$$\mu_{MAX(x)}(v) = \begin{cases} 1 \text{ if } v = \langle c, x\rangle \text{ and } Ax \le b \\ 0 \text{ otherwise,} \end{cases}$$

which can be written in the form

$$MAX(x) = \begin{cases} \overline{\langle c, x\rangle} \text{ if } x \text{ is feasible} \\ 0 \quad\quad \text{otherwise,} \end{cases}$$

consequently, if $x$ and $x'$ are feasible then

$$\mathrm{MAX}(x) \le \mathrm{MAX}(x') \iff \langle c, x\rangle \le \langle c, x'\rangle,$$

and if $x'$ is feasible, but $x''$ is not feasible then

$$\mathrm{MAX}(x'') \le \mathrm{MAX}(x'),$$

since $\mathrm{MAX}(x'')$ is empty. Therefore from (5.11) we get $M = \overline{v^*}$, and $x^*$ satisfies the equality $\mathrm{MAX}(x^*) = M$ if and only if $v^* = \langle c, x^*\rangle$, i.e. $x^* \in X^*$. This means that LP problem (5.12) and FLP problem (5.13) have the same solution-set, and the optimal value of the FLP problem is the characteristic function of the optimal value of the LP problem.

### 5.1.3 Crisp objective and fuzzy coefficients in constraints

FLP problems with crisp inequality relations in fuzzy constraints and crisp objective function can be formulated as follows (see Negoita's robust programming [258], Ramik and Rimanek [275], and Werners [311])

$$\begin{aligned} &\max && \langle c, x\rangle \\ &\text{subject to } && \tilde{a}_{i1}x_1 + \cdots + \tilde{a}_{in}x_n \le \tilde{b}_i, \; i = 1, \ldots, m. \end{aligned} \tag{5.15}$$

It is easy to see that problem (5.15) is equivalent to the crisp MP problem

$$\max\langle c, x\rangle; \text{ subject to } x \in X, \tag{5.16}$$

where,

$$X = \bigcap_{i=1}^{m} X_i = \bigcap_{i=1}^{m} \left\{ x \in \mathbb{R}^n \mid \tilde{a}_{i1}x_1 + \cdots + \tilde{a}_{in}x_n \le \tilde{b}_i \right\}.$$

Now we show that our approach leads to the same crisp MP problem (5.15). Consider problem (5.1) with fuzzy singletons in the objective function

$$\begin{aligned} &\max && \langle \bar{c}, x\rangle \\ &\text{subject to } && \tilde{a}_{i1}x_1 + \cdots + \tilde{a}_{in}x_n \le \tilde{b}_i, \; i = 1, \ldots, m. \end{aligned}$$

where the inequality relation $\leq$ is defined by

$$(\tilde{a}_{i1}x_1 + \cdots + \tilde{a}_{in}x_n \leq \tilde{b}_i)(u, v) = \begin{cases} 1 \text{ if } u = v \text{ and } x \in X_i \\ 0 \text{ otherwise} \end{cases}$$

Then we have

$$\mu_{MAX(x)}(v) = \begin{cases} 1 \text{ if } v = \langle c, x \rangle \text{ and } x \in X \\ 0 \text{ otherwise} \end{cases}$$

Thus, to find a maximizing element of the set $\{MAX(x) \mid x \in \mathbb{R}^n\}$ in the sense of the given inequality relation we have to solve the crisp problem (5.16).

### 5.1.4 Fuzzy objective function and crisp constraints

Consider the FLP problem (5.1) with fuzzy coefficients in the objective function and fuzzy singletons in the constraints

$$\begin{aligned} &\text{maximize } \tilde{c}_1x_1 + \cdots + \tilde{c}_nx_n \\ &\text{subject to } \bar{a}_{i1}x_1 + \cdots + \bar{a}_{in}x_n \leq \bar{b}_i, \; i = 1, \ldots, m, \end{aligned} \tag{5.17}$$

where the inequality relation for constraints is defined by (5.14) and the objective function is to be maximized in relation (5.3), i.e.

$$\text{MAX}(x') \leq \text{MAX}(x'') \iff \tilde{\max}\{\text{MAX}(x'), \text{MAX}(x'')\} = \text{MAX}(x'').$$

Then $\mu_{MAX(x)}(v)$, $\forall v \in \mathbb{R}$, is the optimal value of the following crisp MP problem

$$\begin{aligned} &\text{maximize } (\tilde{c}_1x_1 + \cdots + \tilde{c}_nx_n)(v) \\ &\text{subject to } Ax \leq b, \; x \in \mathbb{R}^n \end{aligned}$$

and the problem of computing a solution to FLP problem (5.17) leads to the same crisp multiple objective parametric linear programming problem obtained by Delgado et al. [77, 78] and Verdegay [302, 303].

### 5.1.5 Relation to Zimmermann's soft constraints

Consider Zimmermann's LP with crisp coefficients and soft constraints: Find $x$ such that

$$\langle c, x \rangle \lesssim z; \; \langle a_i, x \rangle \lesssim b_i, \; i = 1, \ldots, m, \tag{5.18}$$

where the inequality relation $\lesssim$ is defined by

$$\langle a_i, x \rangle \lesssim b_i = \begin{cases} 1 & \text{if } \langle a_i, x \rangle \leq b_i \\ 1 - \dfrac{b_i - \langle a_i, x \rangle}{d_i} & \text{if } b_i \leq \langle a_i, x \rangle \leq b_i + d_i \\ 0 & \text{otherwise} \end{cases} \tag{5.19}$$

for $i = 1, \dots, m$, and

$$\langle c, x\rangle \lesssim z = \begin{cases} 1 & \text{if } \langle c, x\rangle \le z \\ 1 - \dfrac{z - \langle c, x\rangle}{d_0} & \text{if } z \le \langle c, x\rangle \le z + d_0 \\ 0 & \text{otherwise} \end{cases} \tag{5.20}$$

An optimal solution $x^*$ to (5.18) is determined from the crisp LP

$$\lambda \to \max \tag{5.21}$$

$$1 - \frac{z - \langle c, x\rangle}{d_0} \ge \lambda,$$

$$1 - \frac{z - \langle a_i, x\rangle}{d_i} \ge \lambda,$$

$$x \in \mathbb{R}^n,\ 0 \le \lambda \le 1, i = 1, \dots, m.$$

The following theorem can be proved directly by using the definitions (5.4) and (5.11).

**Theorem 5.1.1** *The FLP problem*

$$\begin{array}{ll} \text{maximize} & 1_{\mathbb{R}}(x) \\ \text{subject to} & \bar{c}_1 x_1 + \cdots + \bar{c}_n x_n \lesssim \bar{z} \\ & \bar{a}_{i1} x_1 + \cdots + \bar{a}_{in} x_n \lesssim \bar{b}_i, \ \ i = 1, \dots, m. \end{array} \tag{5.22}$$

*where* $1_{\mathbb{R}}(u) = 1$, $\forall u \in \mathbb{R}$, *the objective function is to be maximized in relation (5.4) and* $\lesssim$ *is defined by (5.19) and (5.20), i.e.*

$$(\langle a_i, x\rangle \lesssim b_i)(u, v) = \begin{cases} 1 & \textit{if } \langle a_i, x\rangle \le b_i \\ 1 - \dfrac{b_i - \langle a_i, x\rangle}{d_i} & \textit{if } b_i \le \langle a_i, x\rangle \le b_i + d_i \\ 0 & \textit{otherwise} \end{cases}$$

*for* $i = 1, \dots, m$, *and*

$$(\langle c, x\rangle \lesssim z)(u, v) = \begin{cases} 1 & \textit{if } \langle c, x\rangle \le z \\ 1 - \dfrac{z - \langle c, x\rangle}{d_0} & \textit{if } z \le \langle c, x\rangle \le z + d_0 \\ 0 & \textit{otherwise} \end{cases}$$

*has the same solution-set as problem (5.21).*

### 5.1.6 Relation to Buckley's possibilistic LP

We show that when the inequality relations in an FLP problem are defined in a possibilistic sense then the optimal value of the objective function is equal to the possibility distribution of the objective function defined by Buckley [14]. Consider a possibilistic LP

$$\begin{aligned} &\text{maximize } Z := \tilde{c}_1 x_1 + \cdots + \tilde{c}_n x_n \\ &\text{subject to } \tilde{a}_{i1} x_1 + \cdots + \tilde{a}_{in} x_n \leq \tilde{b}_i, \ i = 1, \dots, m. \end{aligned} \tag{5.23}$$

The possibility distribution of the objective function $Z$, denoted by $\text{Pos}[Z = z]$, is defined by [14]

$$\text{Pos}[Z = z] =$$

$$\sup_x \min \left\{ \text{Pos}[Z = z \mid x], \text{Pos}[\langle \tilde{a}_1, x \rangle \leq \tilde{b}_1], \dots, \text{Pos}[\langle \tilde{a}_m, x \rangle \leq \tilde{b}_m] \right\},$$

where $\text{Pos}[Z = z \mid x]$, the conditional possibility that $Z = z$ given $x$, is defined by

$$\text{Pos}[Z = z \mid x] = (\tilde{c}_1 x_1 + \cdots + \tilde{c}_n x_n)(z).$$

The following theorem can be proved directly by using the definitions of $\text{Pos}[Z = z]$ and $\mu_M(v)$.

**Theorem 5.1.2** *For the FLP problem*

$$\begin{aligned} &\text{maximize } \tilde{c}_1 x_1 + \cdots + \tilde{c}_n x_n \\ &\text{subject to } \tilde{a}_{i1} x_1 + \cdots + \tilde{a}_{in} x_n \lesssim \tilde{b}_i, \ i = 1, \dots, m. \end{aligned} \tag{5.24}$$

*where the inequality relation $\lesssim$ is defined by (5.8) and the objective function is to be maximized in relation (5.4), i.e.*

$$\text{MAX}(x') \leq \text{MAX}(x'') \iff \text{MAX}(x') \subseteq \text{MAX}(x''),$$

*the following equality holds*

$$\mu_M(v) = \text{Pos}[Z = v],$$

*for all $v \in \mathbb{R}$, where $M$ is defined by (5.11).*

So, if the inequality relations for constraints are defined in a possibilistic sense and the objective function is to be maximized in relation (5.4) then the optimal value of the objective function of FLP problem (5.24) is equal to the possibility distribution of the objective function of possibilistic LP (5.23).

We illustrate our approach by two simple FMP problems. Consider first the FLP problem

$$\begin{aligned} &\text{maximize } \tilde{c}x \\ &\text{subject to } \tilde{a} \lesssim \tilde{a}, \ 0 \leq x \leq 4, \end{aligned} \tag{5.25}$$

where $\tilde{c} = (1,1)$ is a fuzzy number of symmetric triangular form, $\tilde{a}$ is a fuzzy number with membership function

$$\tilde{a}(u) = \begin{cases} 1 - u/4 & \text{if } 0 \le x \le 4 \\ 0 & \text{otherwise,} \end{cases}$$

the inequality relation for the constraint is defined by

$$(\tilde{a} \lesssim \tilde{a})(u,v) = \begin{cases} 1 & \text{if } \tilde{a}(u) \le \tilde{a}(v) \\ \tilde{a}(v) & \text{otherwise} \end{cases}$$

and the inequality relation for the objective function is given by (5.4). Then the corresponding fuzzy reasoning scheme is

| | |
|---|---|
| Antecedent | $\tilde{a} \lesssim \tilde{a}$ |
| Fact | $\tilde{c}x$ |
| Consequence | MAX$(x)$ |

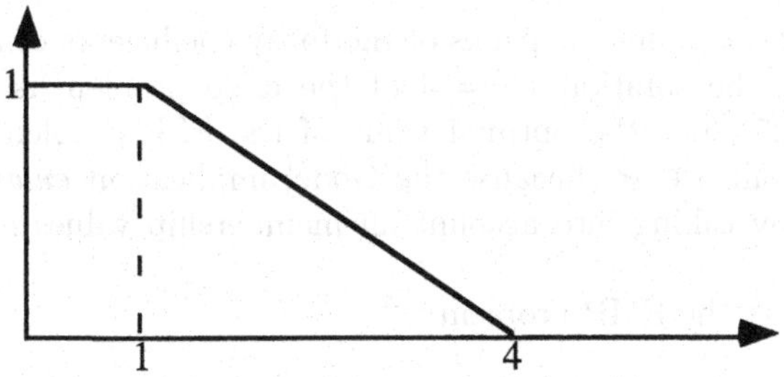


**Fig. 5.1.** The membership function of MAX(1).

It is easy to compute that for $0 \le x \le 2$

$$\mu_{MAX(x)}(v) = \begin{cases} 1 & \text{if } 0 \le v \le x \\ \dfrac{4-v}{4-x} & \text{if } x < v \le 4 \\ 0 & \text{otherwise} \end{cases}$$

and for $2 \le x \le 4$

$$\mu_{MAX(x)}(v) = \begin{cases} 1 & \text{if } 0 \le v \le x \\ (1/x - 4/x^2)v + 4/x & \text{if } x < v \le 2x \\ 2 - 4/x & \text{otherwise} \end{cases}$$

So, if $0 \le x' \le x'' \le 4$ then from (5.4) we get

$$\text{MAX}(x') \le \text{MAX}(x'') \le \text{MAX}(4) = 1_{\mathbb{R}}.$$

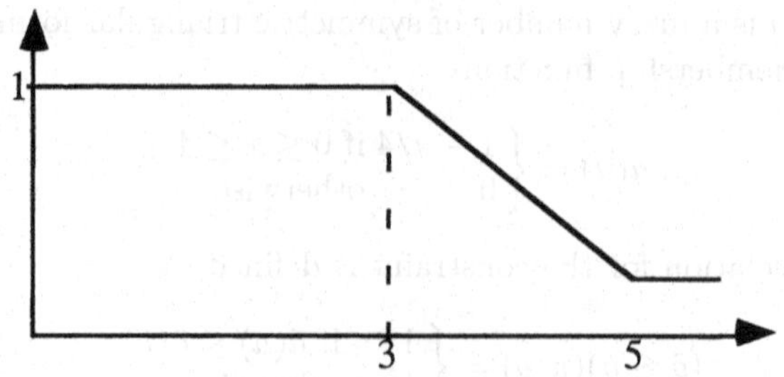


**Fig. 5.2.** The membership function of MAX(2.5).

This means that $x^* = 4$ is the unique solution and $1_{\mathbb{R}}$ is the optimal value of (5.25).

It differs from the *defuzzified* case

$$\begin{aligned}&\text{maximize } x\\&\text{subject to } 0 \leq 0,\ 0 \leq x \leq 4\end{aligned}$$

where the coefficients are the peaks of the fuzzy coefficients of FLP problem (5.25), because the solution $x^* = 4$ of the crisp problem is equal to the solution of (5.25), but the optimal value of the FLP problem is too large $\mu_M(v) = 1$ for all $v \in \mathbb{R}$ (because the Gödel implication *enlarges* MAX$(x)$ for all $x \in \mathbb{R}$ by taking into account all membership values $\tilde{a}(u)$ and $\tilde{a}(v)$ separately).

Consider next the FMP problem

$$\begin{aligned}&\text{maximize } \tilde{c}x\\&\text{subject to } (\tilde{a}x)^2 \lesssim \tilde{b},\ x \geq 0,\end{aligned} \tag{5.26}$$

where $\tilde{a} = (2,1)$, $\tilde{b} = (1,1)$ and $\tilde{c} = (3,1)$ are fuzzy numbers of symmetric triangular form, the inequality relation $\lesssim$ is defined in a possibilistic sense, i.e.

$$(\tilde{a}x \lesssim \tilde{b})(u,v) = \begin{cases}\text{Pos}[\tilde{a}x \leq \tilde{b}] & \text{if } u = v,\\ 0 & \text{otherwise}\end{cases}$$

and the inequality relation for the values of the objective function is defined by (5.5) (with the difference that subnormal values of the objective function are considered smaller than normal ones), i.e.

$$\text{MAX}(x') \leq \text{MAX}(x'') \iff \text{peak}(\text{MAX}(x')) \leq \text{peak}(\text{MAX}(x'')),$$

where MAX$(x')$ and MAX$(x'')$ are fuzzy numbers, and MAX$(x') \leq$ MAX$(x'')$ if MAX$(x')$ is subnormal fuzzy quantity and MAX$(x'')$ is a fuzzy number. It is easy to compute that

$$\text{Pos}[(\tilde{a}x)^2 \lesssim \tilde{b}] = \begin{cases} 1 & \text{if } x \le 1/2, \\ \dfrac{-1 - 2x^2 + \sqrt{1+12x^2}}{2x^2} & \text{if } 1/2 \le x \le \sqrt{2} \\ 0 & \text{if } x \ge \sqrt{2} \end{cases}$$

and $MAX(x)$ is a fuzzy number if $0 \le x \le 1/2$. Therefore, the unique

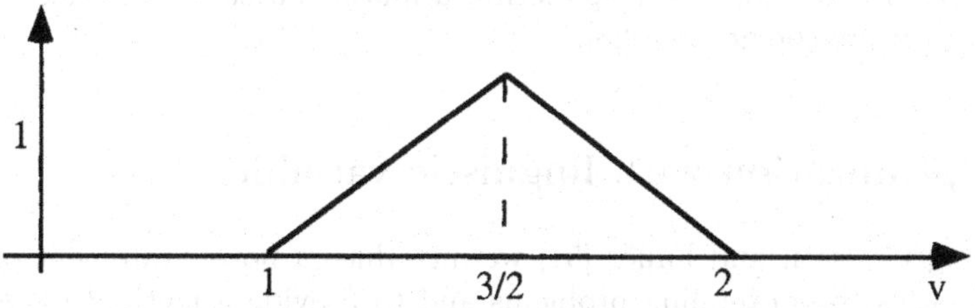


**Fig. 5.3.** "$v$ is approximately equal to 3/2".

solution to FMP problem (5.26) is $x^* = 1/2$ and the optimal value of the objective function is

$$\mu_{MAX(x)}(v) = \mu_{MAX(1/2)}(v) = \begin{cases} 4 - 2v & \text{if } 3/2 \le v \le 2, \\ 2v - 2 & \text{if } 1 \le v \le 3/2 \\ 0 & \text{otherwise} \end{cases}$$

So, the optimal solution to FMP problem (5.26) is equal to the optimal solution of crisp problem

$$\begin{aligned} &\text{maximize } 3x \\ &\text{subject to } (2x)^2 \le 1,\ x \ge 0, \end{aligned}$$

where the coefficients are the peaks of the fuzzy coefficients of problem (5.26), and the optimal value of problem (5.26), which can be called "$v$ is approximately equal to 3/2", can be considered as an approximation of the optimal value of the crisp problem $v^* = 3/2$.

We have interpreted FLP problems with fuzzy coefficients and fuzzy inequality relations as MFR schemes and shown a method for finding an optimal value of the objective function and an optimal solution. In the general case the computerized implementation of the proposed solution principle is not easy. To compute MAX($x$) we have to solve a generally non-convex and non-differentiable mathematical programming problem. However, the stability property of the consequence in MFR schemes under small changes of the membership function of the antecedents [121] guarantees that small rounding errors of digital computation and small errors of measurement in membership functions of the coefficients of the FLP problem can cause only a small deviation in the membership function of the consequence, MAX($x$), i.e. every successive approximation method can be applied to the computation of the linguistic approximation of the exact $\text{MAX}(x)$.

However, to find an optimal value of the objective function, $M$, from the equation $\text{MAX}(x) = M$ can be a very complicated process (for related works see [258, 268, 302, 303, 347, 349]) and very often we have to put up with a compromise solution [280]. An efficient fuzzy-reasoning-based method is needed for the exact computation of $M$. The solution principle described above can be applied to multiple criteria mathematical programming problems with fuzzy coefficients [28].

## 5.2 Optimization with linguistic variables

Following Carlsson and Fullér [51] we introduce a novel statement of fuzzy mathematical programming problems and to provide a method for findig a fair solution to these problems. Suppose we are given a mathematical programming problem in which the functional relationship between the decision variables and the objective function is not completely known. Our knowledge-base consists of a block of fuzzy if-then rules, where the antecedent part of the rules contains some linguistic values of the decision variables, and the consequence part consists of a linguistic value of the objective function. We suggest the use of Tsukamoto's fuzzy reasoning method to determine the crisp functional relationship between the objective function and the decision variables, and solve the resulting (usually nonlinear) programming problem to find a fair optimal solution to the original fuzzy problem.

When Bellman and Zadeh [7], and a few years later Zimmermann [344], introduced fuzzy sets into optimization problems, they cleared the way for a new family of methods to deal with problems which had been inaccessible to and unsolvable with standard mathematical programming techniques.

Fuzzy optimization problems can be stated and solved in many different ways (for good surveys see [185, 353]). Usually the authors consider optimization problems of the form

$$\max/\min\ f(x);\ \text{subject to}\ x \in X,$$

where $f$ or/and $X$ are defind by fuzzy terms. Then they are searching for a crisp $x^*$ which (in certain) sense maximizes $f$ under the (fuzzy) constraints $X$. For example, fuzzy linear programming (FLP) problems are stated as [282]

$$\begin{array}{l} \max/\min\ \ f(x) := \tilde{c}_1 x_1 + \cdots + \tilde{c}_n x_n \\ \text{subject to}\ \tilde{a}_{i1} x_1 + \cdots + \tilde{a}_{in} x_n \lesssim \tilde{b}_i,\ i = 1, \ldots, m, \end{array} \tag{5.27}$$

where $x \in \mathbb{R}^n$ is the vector of crisp decision variables, $\tilde{a}_{ij}$, $\tilde{b}_i$ and $\tilde{c}_j$ are fuzzy quantities, the operations addition and multiplication by a real number of fuzzy quantities are defined by Zadeh's extension principle [334], the inequality relation, $\lesssim$, is given by a certain fuzzy relation, $f$ is to be maximized in the sense of a given crisp inequality relation between fuzzy quantities, and the (implicite) $X$ is a fuzzy set describing the concept "$x$ satisfies all the constraints".

Unlike in (5.27) the fuzzy value of the objective function $f(x)$ may not be known for any $x \in \mathbb{R}^n$. In many cases we are able to describe the causal link between $x$ and $f(x)$ linguistically using fuzzy if-then rules. Following Carlsson and Fullér [51] we consider a new statement of constrained fuzzy optimization problems, namely

$$\max/\min f(x); \text{subject to } \{\Re(x) \mid x \in X\}, \tag{5.28}$$

where $x_1, \dots, x_n$ are linguistic variables, $X \subset \mathbb{R}^n$ is a (crisp or fuzzy) set of constrains on the domains of $x_1, \dots, x_n$, and $\Re(x) = \{\Re_1(x), \dots, \Re_m(x)\}$ is a fuzzy rule base, and

$$\Re_i(x) : \text{if } x_1 \text{ is } A_{i1} \text{ and } \dots \text{and } x_n \text{ is } A_{in} \text{ then } f(x) \text{ is } C_i,$$

constitutes the only knowledge available about the (linguistic) values of $f(x)$, and $A_{ij}$ and $C_i$ are fuzzy numbers.

Generalizing the fuzzy reasoning approach introduced by Carlsson and Fullér [28] we shall determine the crisp value of $f$ at $y \in X$ by Tsukamoto's fuzzy reasoning method, and obtain an optimal solution to (5.28) by solving the resulting (usually nonlinear) optimization problem max/min $f(y)$, subject to $y \in X$.

The use of fuzzy sets provides a basis for a systematic way for the manipulation of vague and imprecise concepts. In particular, we can employ fuzzy sets to represent linguistic variables. A linguistic variable [334] can be regarded either as a variable whose value is a fuzzy number or as a variable whose values are defined in linguistic terms. Fuzzy points are used to represent crisp values of linguistic variables. If $x$ is a linguistic variable in the universe of discourse $X$ and $y \in X$ then we simple write "$x = y$" or "$x$ is $\bar{y}$" to indicate that $y$ is a crisp value of the linguistic variable $x$.

Recall the three basic t-norms: (i) minimum: $T(a, b) = \min\{a, b\}$, (ii) Łukasiewicz: $T(a, b) = \max\{a + b - 1, 0\}$, and (iii) product (or probabilistic): $T(a, b) = ab$.

We briefly describe Tsukamoto's fuzzy reasoning method [299]. Consider the following fuzzy inference system,

| | | | |
|---|---|---|---|
| $\Re_1$: | if | $x_1$ is $A_{11}$ and ... and $x_n$ is $A_{1n}$ then | $z$ is $C_1$ |
| ... | | | |
| $\Re_m$: | if | $x_1$ is $A_{m1}$ and ... and $x_n$ is $A_{mn}$ then | $z$ is $C_m$ |
| Input: | | $x_1$ is $\bar{y}_1$ and ... and $x_n$ is $\bar{y}_n$ | |
| Output: | | | $z_0$ |

where $A_{ij} \in \mathcal{F}(U_j)$ is a value of linguistic variable $x_j$ defined in the universe of discourse $U_j \subset \mathbb{R}$, and $C_i \in \mathcal{F}(W)$ is a value of linguistic variable $z$

defined in the universe $W \subset \mathbb{R}$ for $i = 1, \dots, m$ and $j = 1, \dots, n$. We also suppose that $W$ is bounded and each $C_i$ has strictly monotone (increasing or decreasing) membership function on $W$. The procedure for obtaining the crisp output, $z_0$, from the crisp input vector $y = \{y_1, \dots, y_n\}$ and fuzzy rule-base $\Re = \{\Re_1, \dots, \Re_m\}$ consists of the following three steps:

- We find the firing level of the $i$-th rule as

$$\alpha_i = T(A_{i1}(y_1), \dots, A_{in}(y_n)), \ i = 1, \dots, m, \tag{5.29}$$

  where $T$ usually is the minimum or the product t-norm.
- We determine the (crisp) output of the $i$-th rule, denoted by $z_i$, from the equation $\alpha_i = C_i(z_i)$, that is,

$$z_i = C_i^{-1}(\alpha_i), \ i = 1, \dots, m,$$

  where the inverse of $C_i$ is well-defined because of its strict monotonicity.
- The overall system output is defined as the weighted average of the individual outputs, where associated weights are the firing levels. That is,

$$z_0 = \frac{\alpha_1 z_1 + \cdots + \alpha_m z_m}{\alpha_1 + \cdots + \alpha_m} = \frac{\alpha_1 C_1^{-1}(\alpha_1) + \cdots + \alpha_m C_m^{-1}(\alpha_m)}{\alpha_1 + \cdots + \alpha_m}$$

  i.e. $z_0$ is computed by the discrete Center-of-Gravity method.

If $W = \mathbb{R}$ then all linguistic values of $x_1, \dots, x_n$ also should have strictly monotone membership functions on $\mathbb{R}$ (that is, $0 < A_{ij}(x) < 1$ for all $x \in \mathbb{R}$), because $C_i^{-1}(1)$ and $C_i^{-1}(0)$ do not exist. In this case $A_{ij}$ and $C_i$ usually have sigmoid membership functions of the form

$$\text{big}(t) = \frac{1}{1 + \exp(-b(t - c))}, \quad \text{small}(t) = \frac{1}{1 + \exp(b'(t - c'))}$$

where $b, b' > 0$ and $c, c' > 0$. Let $f\colon \mathbb{R}^n \to \mathbb{R}$ be a function and let $X \subset \mathbb{R}^n$.

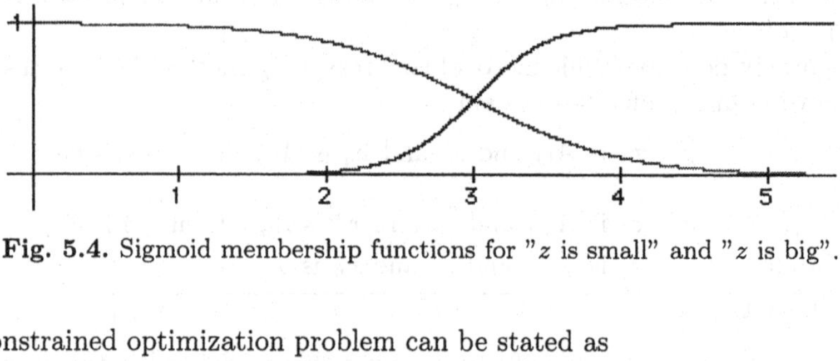


**Fig. 5.4.** Sigmoid membership functions for "$z$ is small" and "$z$ is big".

A constrained optimization problem can be stated as

$$\min f(x); \text{ subject to } x \in X.$$

In many practical cases the function $f$ is not known exactly. In this Section we consider the following fuzzy optimization problem

$$\min f(x);\ \text{subject to}\ \{\Re_1(x), \dots, \Re_m(x) \mid x \in X\}, \tag{5.30}$$

where $x_1, \dots, x_n$ are linguistic variables, $X \subset \mathbb{R}^n$ is a (crisp or fuzzy) set of constrains on the domain of $x_1, \dots, x_n$, and the only available knowledge about the values of $f$ is given as a block fuzzy if-then rules of the form

$$\Re_i(x) : \text{if } x_1 \text{ is } A_{i1} \text{ and } \dots \text{and } x_n \text{ is } A_{in} \text{ then } f(x) \text{ is } C_i,$$

here $A_{ij}$ are fuzzy numbers (with continuous membership function) representing the linguistic values of $x_i$ defined in the universe of discourse $U_j \subset \mathbb{R}$; and $C_i$, $i = 1, \dots, m$, are linguistic values (with strictly monotone and continuous membership functions) of the objective function $f$ defined in the universe $W \subset \mathbb{R}$. To find a fair solution to the fuzzy optimization problem (5.30) we first determine the crisp value of the objective function $f$ at $y \in X$ from the fuzzy rule-base $\Re$ using Tsukamoto's fuzzy reasoning method as

$$f(y) := \frac{\alpha_1 C_1^{-1}(\alpha_1) + \dots + \alpha_m C_m^{-1}(\alpha_m)}{\alpha_1 + \dots + \alpha_m}$$

where the firing levels,

$$\alpha_i = T(A_{i1}(y_1), \dots, A_{in}(y_n)),$$

for $i = 1, \dots, m$, are computed according to (5.29). To determine the firing level of the rules, we suggest the use of the product t-norm (to have a smooth output function).

In this manner our constrained optimization problem (5.30) turns into the following crisp (usually nonlinear) mathematical programmimg problem

$$\min f(y);\ \text{subject to}\ y \in X.$$

The same principle is applied to constrained maximization problems

$$\max f(x);\ \text{subject to}\ \{\Re_1(x), \dots \Re_m(x) \mid x \in X\}. \tag{5.31}$$

*Note 5.2.1.* If $X$ is a fuzzy set in $U_1 \times \dots \times U_n \subset \mathbb{R}^n$ with membership function $\mu_X$ (e.g. given by soft constraints as in [344]) and $W = [0, 1]$ then following Bellman and Zadeh [7] we define the fuzzy solution to problem (5.31) as

$$D(y) = \min\{\mu_X(y), f(y)\},$$

for $y \in U_1 \times \dots \times U_n$, and an optimal (or maximizing) solution, $y^*$, is determined from the relationship

$$D(y^*) = \sup_{y \in U_1 \times \dots \times U_n} D(y). \tag{5.32}$$

**Example 5.2.1** *Consider the optimization problem*

$$\min f(x); \ \{x_1 + x_2 = 1/2, \ 0 \leq x_1, x_2 \leq 1\}, \tag{5.33}$$

*and $f(x)$ is given linguistically as*

$$\Re_1 : \textit{if } x_1 \textit{ is small and } x_2 \textit{ is small then } f(x) \textit{ is small},$$
$$\Re_2 : \textit{if } x_1 \textit{ is small and } x_2 \textit{ is big then } f(x) \textit{ is big},$$

*and the universe of discourse for the linguistic values of $f$ is also the unit interval* $[0, 1]$.

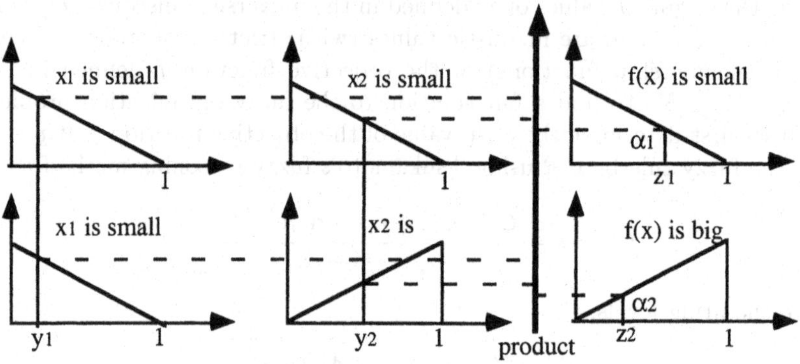


**Fig. 5.5.** Illustration of Example (5.33).

*We will compute the firing levels of the rules by the product t-norm. Let the membership functions in the rule-base $\Re$ be defined by (1.44) and let $[y_1, y_2] \in [0, 1] \times [0, 1]$ be an input vector to the fuzzy system. Then the firing leveles of the rules are*

$$\alpha_1 = (1 - y_1)(1 - y_2),$$
$$\alpha_2 = (1 - y_1)y_2,$$

*It is clear that if $y_1 = 1$ then no rule applies because $\alpha_1 = \alpha_2 = 0$. So we can exclude the value $y_1 = 1$ from the set of feasible solutions. The individual rule outputs are*

$$z_1 = 1 - (1 - y_1)(1 - y_2), \quad z_2 = (1 - y_1)y_2,$$

*and, therefore, the overall system output, interpreted as the crisp value of $f$ at $y$, is*

$$f(y) := \frac{(1 - y_1)(1 - y_2)(1 - (1 - y_1)(1 - y_2)) + (1 - y_1)y_2(1 - y_1)y_2}{(1 - y_1)(1 - y_2) + (1 - y_1)y_2} =$$

$$y_1 + y_2 - 2y_1y_2$$

*Thus our original fuzzy problem*

$$\min f(x); \textit{ subject to } \{\Re_1(x), \Re_2(x) \mid x \in X\},$$

*turns into the following crisp nonlinear mathematical programming problem*

$$(y_1 + y_2 - 2y_1y_2) \to \min$$

$$y_1 + y_2 = 1/2,$$

$$0 \le y_1 < 1,\ 0 \le y_2 \le 1.$$

*which has the optimal solution*

$$y_1^* = y_2^* = 1/4$$

*and its optimal value is*

$$f(y^*) = 3/8.$$

*It is clear that if there were no other constraints on the crisp values of* $x_1$ *and* $x_2$ *then the optimal solution to (5.33) would be* $y_1^* = y_2^* = 0$ *with* $f(y^*) = 0$.

*Note 5.2.2.* This example clearly shows that we can not just choose the rule with the smallest consequence part (the first first rule) and fire it with the maximal firing level ($\alpha_1 = 1$) at $y^* \in [0, 1]$, and take $y^* = (0, 0)$ as an optimal solution to (5.30).

The rules represent our knowledge-base for the fuzzy optimization problem. The fuzzy partitions for lingusitic variables will not ususally satisfy $\varepsilon$-completeness, normality and convexity. In many cases we have only a few (and contradictory) rules. Therefore, we can not make any preselection procedure to remove the rules which *do not play any role* in the optimization problem. All rules should be considered when we derive the crisp values of the objective function. We have chosen Tsukamoto's fuzzy reasoning scheme, because the individual rule outputs are crisp numbers, and therefore, the functional relationship between the input vector $y$ and the system output $f(y)$ can be relatively easily identified (the only thing we have to do is to perform inversion operations).

Consider the problem

$$\max_X f(x) \tag{5.34}$$

where $X$ is a fuzzy susbset of the unit interval with membership function

$$\mu_X(y) = \frac{1}{1+y},\ y \in [0, 1],$$

and the fuzzy rules are

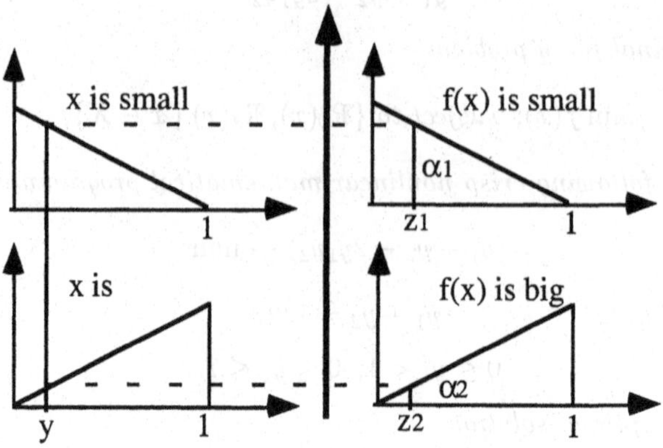


**Fig. 5.6.** Illustration of Example (5.34).

$$\Re_1 : \text{if } x \text{ is } small \text{ then } f(x) \text{ is } small,$$
$$\Re_2 : \text{if } x \text{ is } big \text{ then } f(x) \text{ is } big,$$

Let $y \in [0, 1]$ be an input to the fuzzy system $\{\Re_1, \Re_2\}$. Then the firing leveles of the rules are

$$\alpha_1 = 1 - y,$$
$$\alpha_2 = y.$$

the individual rule outputs are computed by

$$z_1 = (1 - y)y,$$
$$z_2 = y^2,$$

and, therefore, the overall system output is

$$f(y) = (1 - y)y + y^2 = y.$$

Then according to (5.32) our original fuzzy problem (5.34) turns into the following crisp biobjective mathematical programming problem

$$\max \min\{y, \frac{1}{1+y}\}; \text{ subject to } y \in [0, 1],$$

which has the optimal solution

$$y^* = \frac{\sqrt{5} - 1}{2}$$

and its optimal value is $f(y^*) = y^*$.

Consider the following one-dimensional problem

$$\max f(x); \text{ subject to } \{\Re_1(x), \dots, \Re_{K+1}(x) \mid x \in X\}, \tag{5.35}$$

where $U = W = [0, 1]$,

$$\Re_i(x) : \text{if } x \text{ is } A_i \text{ then } f(x) \text{ is } C_i.$$

and $A_i$ is defined by equations (1.41, 1.42, 1.43), the linguistic values of $f$ are selected from (1.45, 1.46), $i = 1, \dots, K+1$. It is clear that exactly two rules fire with nonzero degree for any input $y \in [0, 1]$. Namely, if

$$y \in I_k := \left[\frac{k-1}{K}, \frac{k}{K}\right],$$

then $\Re_k$ and $\Re_{k+1}$ are applicable, and therefore we get

$$f(y) = (k - Ky)C_k^{-1}(k - Ky) + (Ky - k + 1)C_{k+1}^{-1}(Ky - k + 1)$$

for any $k \in \{1, \dots, K\}$. In this way the fuzzy maximization problem (5.35) turns into $K$ independent maximization problem

$$\max_{k=1,\dots,K} \{\max_{X \cap I_k} (k - Ky)C_k^{-1}(k - Ky) + (Ky - k + 1)C_{k+1}^{-1}(Ky - k + 1)\}$$

If $x \in \mathbb{R}^n$, with $n \geq 2$ then a similar reasoning holds, with the difference that we use the same fuzzy partition for all the lingusitic variables, $x_1, \dots, x_n$, and the number of applicable rules grows to $2^n$.

It should be noted that we can refine the fuzzy rule-base by introducing new lingusitic variables modeling the linguistic dependencies between the variables and the objectives [26, 30, 109].

## 5.3 Multiobjective optimization with lingusitic variables

The principles presented above can be extended to multiple objective optimization problems under fuzzy if-then rules [49]. Namely, consider the following statement of multiple objective optimization problem

$$\max/\min \{f_1(x), \dots, f_K(x)\}; \quad \text{subject to } \{\Re_1(x), \dots, \Re_m(x) \mid x \in X\}, \tag{5.36}$$

where $x_1, \dots, x_n$ are linguistic variables, and

$$\Re_i(x) : \text{if } x_1 \text{ is } A_{i1} \text{ and } \dots \text{ and } x_n \text{ is } A_{in} \text{ then } f_1(x) \text{ is } C_{i1} \text{ and } \dots \text{ and } f_K(x) \text{ is } C_{iK},$$

constitutes the only knowledge available about the values of $f_1, \dots, f_K$, and $A_{ij}$ and $C_{ik}$ are fuzzy numbers.

To find a fair solution to the fuzzy optimization problem (5.36) with continuous $A_{ij}$ and with strictly monotone and continuous $C_{ik}$, representing the linguistic values of $f_k$, we first determine the crisp value of the $k$-th objective function $f_k$ at $y \in \mathbb{R}^n$ from the fuzzy rule-base $\Re$ using Tsukamoto's fuzzy reasoning method as

$$f_k(y) := \frac{\alpha_1 C_{1k}^{-1}(\alpha_1) + \cdots + \alpha_m C_{mk}^{-1}(\alpha_m)}{\alpha_1 + \cdots + \alpha_m}$$

where

$$\alpha_i = T(A_{i1}(y_1), \dots, A_{in}(y_n))$$

denotes the firing level of the $i$-th rule, $\Re_i$ and $T$ is a t-norm. To determine the firing level of the rules, we suggest the use of the product t-norm (to have a smooth output function). In this manner the constrained optimization problem (5.36) turns into the crisp (usually nonlinear) multiobjective mathematical programmimg problem

$$\max/\min \{f_1(y), \dots, f_K(y)\}; \text{ subject to } y \in X. \tag{5.37}$$

**Example 5.3.1** *Consider the optimization problem*

$$\max \{f_1(x), f_2(x)\}; \; \{x_1 + x_2 = 3/4, \; 0 \le x_1, x_2 \le 1\}, \tag{5.38}$$

*where $f_1(x)$ and $f_2(x)$ are given linguistically by*

$\Re_1(x)$ : *if $x_1$ is small and $x_2$ is small then $f_1(x)$ is small and $f_2(x)$ is big,*
$\Re_2(x)$ : *if $x_1$ is small and $x_2$ is big then $f_1(x)$ is big and $f_2(x)$ is small,*

*and the universe of discourse for the linguistic values of $f_1$ and $f_2$ is also the unit interval $[0,1]$. We will compute the firing levels of the rules by the product t-norm. Let the membership functions in the rule-base $\Re = \{\Re_1, \Re_2\}$ be defined by*

$$\text{small}(t) = 1 - t, \quad \text{big}(t) = t.$$

*Let $0 \le y_1, y_2 \le 1$ be an input to the fuzzy system. Then the firing leveles of the rules are*

$$\alpha_1 = (1 - y_1)(1 - y_2),$$
$$\alpha_2 = (1 - y_1)y_2.$$

*It is clear that if $y_1 = 1$ then no rule applies because $\alpha_1 = \alpha_2 = 0$. So we can exclude the value $y_1 = 1$ from the set of feasible solutions. The individual rule outputs are*

$$z_{11} = 1 - (1 - y_1)(1 - y_2),$$
$$z_{21} = (1 - y_1)y_2,$$
$$z_{12} = (1 - y_1)(1 - y_2),$$
$$z_{22} = 1 - (1 - y_1)y_2,$$

*and, therefore, the overall system outputs are*

$$f_1(y) = \frac{(1 - y_1)(1 - y_2)(1 - (1 - y_1)(1 - y_2)) + (1 - y_1)y_2(1 - y_1)y_2}{(1 - y_1)(1 - y_2) + (1 - y_1)y_2}$$
$$= y_1 + y_2 - 2y_1y_2,$$

*and*

$$f_2(y) = \frac{(1 - y_1)(1 - y_2)(1 - y_1)(1 - y_2) + (1 - y_1)y_2(1 - (1 - y_1)y_2)}{(1 - y_1)(1 - y_2) + (1 - y_1)y_2}$$
$$= 1 - (y_1 + y_2 - 2y_1y_2).$$

*Modeling the anding of the objective functions by the minimum t-norm our original fuzzy problem (5.38) turns into the following crisp nonlinear mathematical programming problem*

$$\max \min\{y_1 + y_2 - 2y_1y_2, 1 - (y_1 + y_2 - 2y_1y_2)\}$$

$$\text{subject to } \{y_1 + y_2 = 3/4, 0 \leq y_1 < 1,\ 0 \leq y_2 \leq 1\}.$$

*which has the following optimal solutions*

$$y^* = \begin{pmatrix} y_1^* \\ y_2^* \end{pmatrix} = \begin{pmatrix} 1/2 \\ 1/4 \end{pmatrix},$$

*and*

$$\begin{pmatrix} 1/4 \\ 1/2 \end{pmatrix},$$

*from symmetricity, and its optimal value is*

$$(f_1(y^*), f_2(y^*)) = (1/2, 1/2).$$

*Note 5.3.1.* We can introduce trade-offs among the objectives function by using an OWA-operator in (5.37). However, as Yager has pointed out in [324], constrained OWA-aggregations are not easy to solve, because the usually lead to a mixed integer mathematical programming problem of very big dimension.

## 5.4 Interdependent multiple criteria decision making

Decision making with interdependent multiple criteria is normal in standard business decision making; in mcdm theory the standard assumption is to assume that the criteria are independent, which makes optimal mcdm solutions less useful than they could be. Following Carlsson and Fullér [30] in this Section we describe a method for both dealing with and making use of the interdependence of multiple criteria.

Interdependence is a fairly obvious concept: consider a decision problem, in which we have to find a $x^* \in X$ such that three different criteria $c_1$, $c_2$ and $c_3$ all are satisfied, when $c_1$ and $c_2$ are *supportive* of each others, $c_2$ and $c_3$ are *conflicting*, and $c_1$ and $c_3$ again are *supportive* of each others (with respect to some directions). Unless it is obvious, the choice of an optimal decision alternative will become a very complex process with an increasing number of criteria.

There has been a growing interest and activity in the area of multiple criteria decision making (MCDM), especially in the last 20 years. Modeling and optimization methods have been developed in both crisp and fuzzy environments. The overwhelming majority of approaches for finding best compromise solutions to MCDM problems do not make use of the interdependences among the objectives. However, as has been pointed out by Carlsson [25], in modeling real world problems (especially in management sciences) we often encounter MCDM problems with interdependent objectives.

In this Section we introduce measures of interdependences between the objectives, in order to provide for a better understanding of the decision problem, and to find effective and more correct solutions to MCDM problems.

P.L. Yu explains that we have habitual ways of thinking, acting, judging and responding, which when taken together form our habitual domain (HD) [331]. This domain is very nicely illustrated with the following example ([331] p 560):

> A retiring chairman wanted to select a successor from two finalists ($A$ and $B$). The chairman invited $A$ and $B$ to his farm, and gave each finalist an equally good horse. He pointed out the course of the race and the rules saying, "From this point whoever's horse is slower reaching the final point will be the new chairman". This rule of horse racing was outside the habitual ways of thinking of $A$ and $B$. Both of them were puzzled and did not know what to do. After a few minutes, $A$ all of a sudden got a great idea. he jumped out of the constraint of his HD. He quickly mounted $B$'s horse and rode as fast as possible, leaving his own horse behind. When $B$ realized what was going on, it was too late. $A$ became the new chairman.

Part of the HD of multiple criteria decision making is the intuitive assumption that all criteria are independent; this was initially introduced as a safeguard to get a feasible solution to a multiple criteria problem, as there were no means available to deal with interdependence. Then, gradually, conflicts were introduced as we came to realize that multiple goals or objectives almost by necessity represent conflicting interests [343, 317]. Here we will "jump out of the constraints" of the HD of MCDM and leave out the assumption of independent criteria.

The existence of the HD is a partial explanation of why MCDM is not an explicit part of managerial decision making, although it is always claimed that it is implicitly pursued by all economic agents under most circumstances [343]. By not allowing interdependence multiple criteria problems are simplified beyond recognition and the solutions reached by the traditional algorithms have only marginal interest. Zeleny also points to other circumstances [343] which have reduced the visibility and usefulness of MCDM: (i) time pressure reduces the number of criteria to be considered; (ii) the more complete and precise the problem definition, the less criteria are needed; (iii) autonomous decision makers are bound to use more criteria than those being controlled by a strict hierarchical decision system; (iv) isolation from the perturbations of changing environment reduces the need for multiple criteria; (v) the more complete, comprehensive and integrated knowledge of the problem the more criteria will be used - but partial, limited and non-integrated knowledge will significantly reduce the number of criteria; and (vi) cultures and organisations focused on central planning and collective decision making rely on aggregation and the reduction of criteria in order to reach consensus. When we combine these circumstances with the HD we get a most challenging field of research: to make MCDM both more realistic and more relevant to the decision makers of the business world. We believe that this can be done both by introducing interdependence and by developing MCDM-based decision support systems; here we will pursue the first task.

A typical approach to solving multiple criteria decision problems is the SIMOLP procedure introduced by Reeves and Franz [276]; we have the following muliobjective linear programming formulation,

$$\max\{\langle c^1, x\rangle = z_1\}$$

$$\max\{\langle c^2, x\rangle = z_2\}$$

$$\dots$$

$$\max\{\langle c^k, x\rangle = z_k\}$$

$$\text{subject to } x \in X = \{x \in \mathbb{R}^n \mid Ax = b, x \geq 0,\ b \in \mathbb{R}^m\}$$

for which the optimal solution is found in the following sequence [276]:

(i) optimize each objective function individually over the feasible region; solve the $k$ single objective linear programming problems and obtain $k$ efficient points $x^i$, $i = 1, \dots, k$ and the $k$ nondominated criterion vectors $z^i$ ; define these vectors in both the decision and the criteria space as $E^* = \{x^i,\ i = 1, \dots, k\}$; $N^* = \{z^i,\ i = 1, \dots, k\}$;

(ii) have the decision maker (DM) review the $k$ elements of $N^*$; if the DM finds a preferred element, the procedure terminates; if none of the elements is preferred, set $i = k$ and continue with the next step;

(iii) set $i = i+1$; form the hyperplane $z_i$ which passes through the $k$ elements of $N^*$; solve the following LP problem,

$$\max_{x \in X} z_i$$

to obtain the efficient point $x^i$ and the nondominated vector $z^i$.

(iv) if $z^i$ is not a member of $N^*$ and if $z^i$ is preferred to at least one element in $N^*$, then replace this element with $z^i$ and return to step iii.

(v) if $z^i$ is a member of $N^*$ or if the DM does not prefer $z^i$ to any element of $N^*$, have the DM select the most preferred element of $N^*$ and stop;

As can be sen from this procedure the DM should have a *dilemma*: he is expected to be able to formulate his preferences regarding the objectives, but he cannot have much more than an intuitive grasp of the trade-offs he is probably doing among the objectives. This is taken care of with a convenient assumption: the DM is taken to be a fully informed, rational decision maker who relies on some underlying utility function as a basis for his preferences.

It is well known that there does not exist any concept of *optimal solution* universally accepted and valid for any multiobjective problem [342]. Delgado et al [79] provided a unified framework to use fuzzy sets and possibility theory in multicriteria decision and multiobjective programming. Felix [108] presented a novel theory for multiple attribute decision making based on fuzzy relations between objectives, in which the interactive structure of objectives is inferred and represented explicitely. Carlsson [25] used the fuzzy Pareto optimal set of nondominated alternatives as a basis for an OWA-type operator [317] for finding a best compromise solution to MCDM problems with interdependent criteria.

We provide a new method for finding a compromise solution to MCDM problems by using explicitely the interdependences among the objectives and combining the results of [24, 25, 79, 108, 345]. First we define interdependences beween the objectives of a decision problem defined in terms of multiple objectives. Consider the following problem

$$\max_{x \in X} \{f_1(x), \ldots, f_k(x)\} \tag{5.39}$$

where $f_i \colon \mathbb{R}^n \to \mathbb{R}$ are objective functions, $x \in \mathbb{R}^n$ is the decision variable, and $X$ is a subset of $\mathbb{R}^n$ without any additional conditions for the moment.

An $x^* \in X$ is said to be efficient for (5.39) iff there exists no $x^{**} \in X$ such that $f_i(x^{**}) \geq f_i(x^*)$ for all $i$ with strict inequality for at least one $i$.

**Definition 5.4.1** *Let $f_i$ and $f_j$ be two objective functions of (5.39). We say that*

*(i) $f_i$ supports $f_j$ on $X$ (denoted by $f_i \uparrow f_j$) if $f_i(x') \geq f_i(x)$ entails $f_j(x') \geq f_j(x)$, for all $x', x \in X$;*

*(ii) $f_i$ is in conflict with $f_j$ on $X$ (denoted by $f_i \downarrow f_j$) if $f_i(x') \geq f_i(x)$ entails $f_j(x') \leq f_j(x)$, for all $x', x \in X$;*

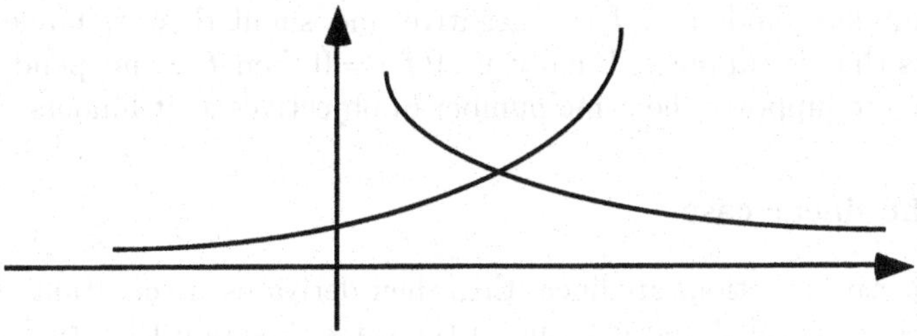

**Fig. 5.7.** A typical example of conflict on $\mathbb{R}$.

*(iii)* $f_i$ *and* $f_j$ *are independent on* $X$*, otherwise.*

If $X = \mathbb{R}^n$ then we say that $f_i$ supports (or is in conflict with) $f_j$ *globally*.

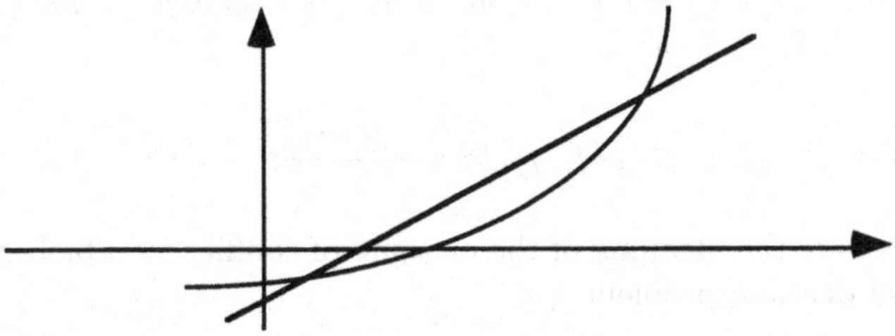

**Fig. 5.8.** Supportive functions on $\mathbb{R}$.

If the objective functions are differentiable on $X$ then we have

$$f_i \uparrow f_j \text{ on } X \iff \partial_e f_i(x)\partial_e f_j(x) \geq 0 \text{ for all } e \in \mathbb{R}^n \text{ and } x \in X,$$
$$f_i \downarrow f_j \text{ on } X \iff \partial_e f_i(x)\partial_e f_j(x) \leq 0 \text{ for all } e \in \mathbb{R}^n \text{ and } x \in X,$$

where $\partial_e f_i(x)$ denotes the derivative of $f_i$ with respect to the direction $e \in \mathbb{R}^n$ at $x \in \mathbb{R}^n$. If for a given direction $e \in \mathbb{R}^n$,

$$\partial_e f_i(x)\partial_e f_j(x) \geq 0 \quad [\partial_e f_i(x)\partial_e f_j(x) \leq 0]$$

holds for all $x \in X$ then we say that $f_i$ supports $f_j$ [$f_i$ is in conflict with $f_j$] with respect to the direction $e$ on $X$. Let $f_i$ be an objective function of (5.39). Then we define the grade of interdependency, denoted by $\Delta(f_i)$, of $f_i$ as

$$\Delta(f_i) = \sum_{f_i \uparrow f_j, i \neq j} 1 - \sum_{f_i \downarrow f_j} 1, \quad i = 1, \dots, k. \tag{5.40}$$

If $\Delta(f_i)$ is positive and large then $f_i$ supports a majority of the objectives, if $\Delta(f_i)$ is negative and large then $f_i$ is in conflict with a majority of the objectives, if $\Delta(f_i)$ is positive and small then $f_i$ supports more objectives than it hinders, and if $\Delta(f_i)$ is negative and small then $f_i$ hinders more objectives than it supports. Finally, if $\Delta(f_i) = 0$ then $f_i$ is independent from the others or supports the same number of objectives as it hinders.

### 5.4.1 The linear case

If the objective functions are linear then their derivates are constant. So if two objectives are parallel and growing in the same direction then they support each others, otherwise we can globally measure only the conflict between them. Consider the following problem with multiple objectives

$$\max_{x \in X} \{f_1(x), \dots, f_k(x)\} \tag{5.41}$$

where $f_i(x) = \langle c_i, x \rangle = c_{i1}x_1 + \cdots + c_{in}x_n$ and $||c_i|| = 1,\ i = 1, \dots, k$.

**Definition 5.4.2** *Let $f_i(x) = \langle c_i, x \rangle$ and $f_j(x) = \langle c_j, x \rangle$ be two objective functions of (5.41). Then the measure of conflict between $f_i$ and $f_j$, denoted by $\kappa(f_i, f_j)$, is defined by*

$$\kappa(f_i, f_j) = \frac{1 - \langle c_i, c_j \rangle}{2}.$$

We illustrate the meaning of the measure of conflict by a biobjective two-dimensional decision problem

$$\max_{x \in X} \{\alpha(x), \beta(x)\},$$

where $\alpha(x) = \langle \mathbf{n}, x \rangle$ and $\beta(x) = \langle \mathbf{m}, x \rangle$.

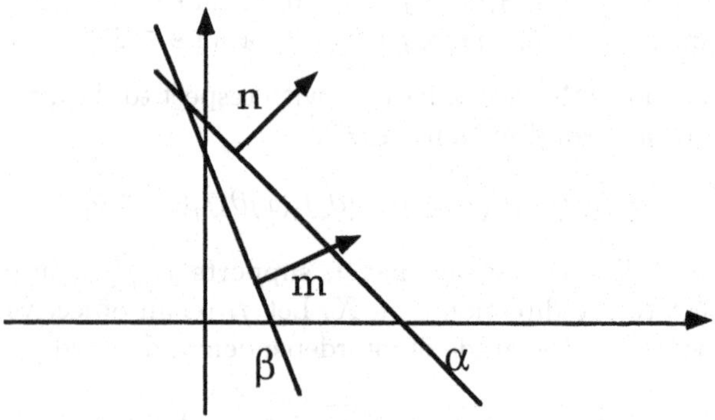


**Fig. 5.9.** The measure of conflict between $\alpha$ and $\beta$ is $|\mathbf{n}||\mathbf{m}| \cos(\mathbf{n}, \mathbf{m})$.

The bigger the angle between the lines $\alpha$ and $\beta$ the bigger the degree of conflict between them.

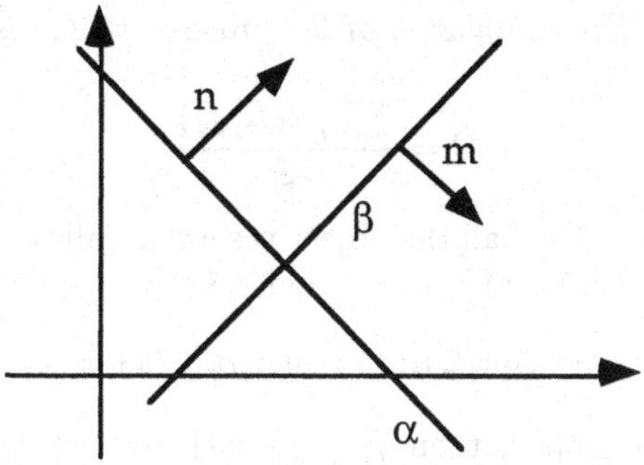


**Fig. 5.10.** $\kappa(\alpha, \beta) = 1/2$ - the case of perpendicular objectives.

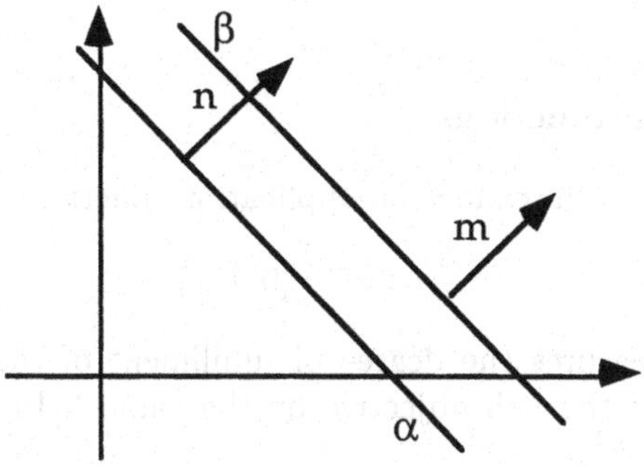


**Fig. 5.11.** $\kappa(\alpha, \beta) = 0$ - the case of parallel objectives.

If $\kappa(\alpha, \beta) = 1/2$ and the set of feasible solutions is a convex polyhedron in $\mathbb{R}^n$ then $\alpha$ and $\beta$ attend their independent maximum at neighbour vertexes of $X$.

If $\kappa(\alpha, \beta) = 0$ and the set of feasible solutions is a convex polyhedron subset of $\mathbb{R}^n$ then $\alpha$ and $\beta$ attend their independent maximum at the same vertex of $X$.

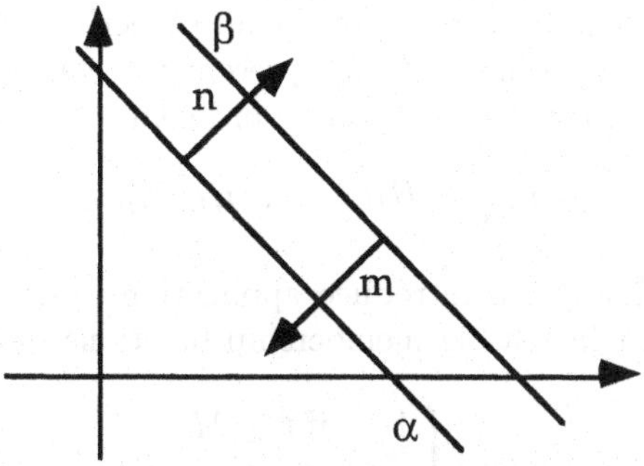


**Fig. 5.12.** $\kappa(\alpha, \beta) = 1$ - the case of opposite objectives.

**Definition 5.4.3** *The complexity of the problem (5.41) is defined as*

$$\Omega = \frac{\sum_{i,j}^{k} \kappa(f_i, f_j)}{2}.$$

It is clear that $\Omega = 0$ iff all the objectives are parallel, i.e. we have a single objective problem. Let $f_i(x) = \langle c_i, x\rangle$ and $f_j(x) = \langle c_j, x\rangle$ with $c_i \neq c_j$. If

$$\operatorname{sign} c_{ir} = \operatorname{sign} \partial_r f_i(x) = \operatorname{sign} \partial_r f_j(x) = \operatorname{sign} c_{jr},$$

for some basic direction $r$, then $f_i \uparrow f_j$ with respect to direction $r$. This information can be useful in the construction of a scalarizing function, when we search for a nondominated solution being closest to an ideal point in a given metric.

### 5.4.2 Application functions

Following [345, 79] we introduce an application function

$$h_i\colon \mathbb{R} \to [0,1]$$

such that $h_i(t)$ measures the degree of fulfillment of the decision maker's requirements about the $i$-th objective by the value $t$. In other words, with the notation of

$$H_i(x) = h_i(f(x)),$$

$H_i(x)$ may be considered as the degree of membership of $x$ in the fuzzy set "good solutions" for the $i$-th objective. Then a "good compromise solution" to (5.39) may be defined as an $x \in X$ being "as good as possible" for the whole set of objectives. Taking into consideration the nature of $H_i$, $i = 1, \dots k$, it is quite reasonable to look for such a kind of solution by means of the following auxiliary problem

$$\max_{x\in X} \{H_1(x), \dots, H_k(x)\} \tag{5.42}$$

As $\max\{H_1(x), \dots, H_k(x)\}$ may be interpreted as a synthetical notation of a conjuction statement (maximize jointly all objectives) and $H_i(x) \in [0,1]$, it is reasonable to use a t-norm $T$ to represent the connective AND. In this way (5.42) turns into the single-objective problem

$$\max_{x\in X} T(H_1(x), \dots, H_k(x)).$$

There exist several ways to introduce application functions [197]. Usually, the authors consider increasing membership functions (the bigger is better) of the form

$$h_i(t) = \begin{cases} 1 & \text{if } t \geq M_i \\ v_i(t) & \text{if } m_i \leq t \leq M_i \\ 0 & \text{if } t \leq m_i \end{cases} \tag{5.43}$$

where

$$m_i := \min\{f_i(x) \mid x \in X\},$$

is the independent mimimum and

$$M_i := \max\{f_i(x) \mid x \in X\},$$

is the independent maximum of the $i$-th criterion. As it has been stated before, our idea is to use explicitely the interdependences in the solution method. To do so, first we define $H_i$ by

$$H_i(x) = \begin{cases} 1 & \text{if } f_i(x) \geq M_i \\ 1 - \dfrac{M_i - f_i(x)}{M_i - m_i} & \text{if } m_i \leq f_i(x) \leq M_i \\ 0 & \text{if } f_i(x) \leq m_i \end{cases}$$

i.e. all membership functions are defined to be linear.

Then from (5.40) we compute $\Delta(f_i)$ for $i = 1, \dots, k$, and we change the shapes of $H_i$ according to the value of $\Delta(f_i)$ as follows

- If $\Delta(f_i) = 0$ then we do not change the shape.
- If $\Delta(f_i) > 0$ then we use a concave membership function defined as

$$H_i(x, \Delta(f_i)) = \begin{cases} 1 & \text{if } f_i(x) \geq M_i \\ \tau_2(x) & \text{if } m_i \leq f_i(x) \leq M_i \\ 0 & \text{if } f_i(x) \leq m_i \end{cases}$$

where

$$\tau_2(x) = \left(1 - \frac{M_i - f_i(x)}{M_i - m_i}\right)^{\dfrac{1}{\Delta(f_i) + 1}}$$

- If $\Delta(f_i) < 0$ then we use a convex membership function defined as

$$H_i(x, \Delta(f_i)) = \begin{cases} 1 & \text{if } f_i(x) \geq M_i \\ \tau_3(x) & \text{if } m_i \leq f_i(x) \leq M_i \\ 0 & \text{if } f_i(x) \leq m_i \end{cases}$$

where

$$\tau_3(x) = \left(1 - \frac{M_i - f_i(x)}{M_i - m_i}\right)^{|\Delta(f_i)|+1}$$

Then we solve the following auxiliary problem

$$\max_{x \in X} T(H_1(x, \Delta(f_1)), \dots, H_k(x, \Delta(f_k))) \tag{5.44}$$

Let us suppose that we have a decision problem with many ($k \geq 7$) objective functions. It is clear (due to the interdependences between the objectives), that we find optimal compromise solutions rather closer to the values of independent minima than maxima.

The basic idea of introducing this type of shape functions can be explained then as follows: if we manage to increase the value of the $i$-th objective having a large positive $\Delta(f_i)$ then it entails the growth of the majority of criteria (because it supports the majority of the objectives), so we are getting essentially closer to the optimal value of the scalarizing function (because the losses on the other objectives are not so big, due to their definition).

One of the most important questions is the efficiency of the obtained compromise solutions. Delgado et al obtained the following result [79]:

**Theorem 5.4.1** *[79] Let $x^*$ be an optimal solution to*

$$\max_{x \in X} T(H_1(x), \ldots, H_k(x)) \tag{5.45}$$

*where $T$ is a t-norm, $H_i(x) = h_i(f_i(x))$ and $h_i$ is an application function of the form (5.43), $i = 1, \ldots, k$. If $h_i$ is strictly increasing on $[m_i, M_i]$, $i = 1, \ldots, k$ then $x^*$ is efficient for the problem*

$$\max_{x \in X} \{f_1(x), \ldots, f_k(x)\} \tag{5.46}$$

*if either (i) $x^*$ is unique; (ii) $T$ is strict and $0 < H_i(x^*) < 1$, $i = 1, \ldots, k$.*

It is easy to see that our application functions are strictly increasing on $[m_i, M_i]$, and, therefore any optimal solution $x^*$ to the auxiliary problem (5.44) is an efficient solution to (5.46) if either (i) $x^*$ is unique; (ii) T is strict and $0 < H_i(x^*) < 1$, $i = 1, \ldots, k$.

The choice of a particular t-norm depends upon several factors such as the nature of the problem, the environment or decision maker's knowledge representation model. Minimum and product t-norms are primarily used in literature to solve (5.46) through (5.45). The associated problems are,

$$\min \{H_1(x, \Delta(f_1)), \ldots, H_k(x, \Delta(f_k))\} \to \max; \text{ subject to } x \in X,$$

and

$$H_1(x, \Delta(f_1)) \times \cdots \times H_k(x, \Delta(f_k)) \to \max; \text{ subject to } x \in X,$$

respectively. We prefer to use the Łukasiewicz t-norm, $T_L$, in (5.44), because it contains the sum of the particular application functions, which is increasing rapidly if we manage to improve the value of an objective function supporting the majority of the objectives.

Then we get the following auxiliary problem

$$\max_{x \in X} \max \left\{ \sum_{i=1}^{k} H_i(x, \Delta(f_i)) - k + 1, 0 \right\} \tag{5.47}$$

The Łukasiewicz t-norm is not strict, so an optimal solution $x^*$ to (5.47) is efficient for (5.46) iff $x^*$ is the only optimal solution to (5.47).

**Example 5.4.1** *We illustrate the proposed method by an 5-objective one dimensional decision problem. Consider the problem*

$$\max_{x \in X} \{f_1(x), \dots, f_5(x)\}, \tag{5.48}$$

*with objective functions*

$$\begin{aligned} f_1(x) &= x, \\ f_2(x) &= (x+1)^2 - 1, \\ f_3(x) &= 2x + 1, \\ f_4(x) &= x^4 - 1, \\ f_5(x) &= -3x + 1, \end{aligned}$$

*and $X = [0, 2]$. It is easy to check that we have the following interdependences*

$$f_1 \uparrow f_2,\ f_2 \uparrow f_3,\ f_3 \uparrow f_4,\ f_4 \downarrow f_5$$

*Then the grades of interdependences are*

$$\Delta(f_1) = \Delta(f_2) = \Delta(f_3) = \Delta(f_4) = 3,\ \ \Delta(f_5) = -4,$$

*and we get*

$$\begin{aligned} H_1(x, \Delta(f_1)) = H_3(x, \Delta(f_3)) &= \left[\frac{x}{2}\right]^{1/4}, \\ H_2(x, \Delta(f_2)) &= \left[\frac{x(x+2)}{8}\right]^{1/4}, \\ H_4(x, \Delta(f_4)) &= \frac{x}{2}, \\ H_5(x, \Delta(f_5)) &= \left[1 - \frac{x}{2}\right]^5. \end{aligned}$$

*And if the product t-norm is chosen to represent the decision maker's preferences, we get the following single objective MP*

$$\left(\frac{1}{2}\right)^{1/4} \left(\frac{x}{2}\right)^{7/4} \left(\frac{x}{2}+1\right)^{1/4} \left(1 - \frac{x}{2}\right)^5 \to \max$$

$$\text{subject to } 0 \le x \le 2.$$

*This problem has a unique solution*

$$x^* = \frac{-19 + \sqrt{1145}}{28} \approx 0.53$$

*which is a nondominated solution to the problem (5.48) with the values of the objective functions*

$$(0.53, 1.34, 2.06, -0.92, -0.59).$$

*Note 5.4.1.* We think that the traditional assumption used in MCDM-modelling - that the criteria should be independent - is rather an unfortunate one. In some of the MOLP-methods there are pairwise trade offs among conflicting objectives, but further interdependences among the objectives are not recognized. It makes the model unrealistic and its recommendations rather abstract: a decision maker who accepts an optimal solution from the model cannot be sure that he has made the correct trade offs among the objectives. There is another type of interdependence which should be recognized: some of the objectives might *support* each others, which should be exploited in a problem solving method. Zeleny recognized these possibilities [343] when he pointed out the fallacy with using weights independent from criterion performance, but he did not take this insight further. In this Section we have presented a method for explicitly using interdependence among the criteria of a multiple criteria problem. We have shown that it will give a well-defined solution and we have illustrated the technique with a simple numerical example.

## 5.5 MOP with interdependent objectives

We consider multiple objective programming (MOP) problems with additive interdependences, i.e. when the states of some chosen objective are attained through *supportive* or *inhibitory* feed-backs from several other objectives. MOP problems with independent objectives (i.e. when the cause-effect relations between the decision variables and the objectives are completely known) will be treated as special cases of the MOP in which we have interdependent objectives. We illustrate our ideas by a simple three-objective and a real-life seven-objective problem.

In their classical text *Theory of Games and Economic Behavior* John von Neumann and Oskar Morgenstern (1947) described the problem with *interdependence*; in their outline of a social exchange economy they discussed the case of two or more persons exchanging goods with each others ([261], page 11):

> ... then the results for each one will depend in general not merely upon his own actions but on those of others as well. Thus each participant attempts to maximize a function ... of which he does not control all variables. This is certainly no maximum problem, but a

> peculiar and disconcerting mixture of several conflicting maximum problems. Every participant is guided by another principle and neither determines all variables which affects his interest.
> This kind of problem is nowhere dealt with in classical mathematics. We emphasize at the risk of being pedantic that this is no conditional maximum problem, no problem of the calculus of variations, of functional analysis, etc. It arises in full clarity, even in the most "elementary" situations, e.g., when all variables can assume only a finite number of values.

The interdependence is part of the economic theory and all market economies, but in most modelling approaches in multiple criteria decision making there seems to be an implicit assumption that objectives should be independent. This appears to be the case, if not earlier than at least at the moment when we have to select some optimal compromise among the set of nondominated decision alternatives. Milan Zeleny [342] - and many others - recognizes one part of the interdependence (page 1),

> Multiple and conflicting objectives, for example, "minimize cost" and "maximize the quality of service" are the real stuff of the decision maker's or manager's daily concerns. Such problems are more complicated than the convenient assumptions of economics indicate. Improving achievement with respect to one objective can be accomplished only at the expense of another.

but not the other part: objectives could support each others.

Situations with multiple interdependent objectives are not only derived from some axiomatic framework as logical conclusions, or built as illustrations of complex decision problems in classical text books, there are real life situations which, if we ponder them systematically, reveal themselves to have interdependent objectives.

A well-known negotiation problem is the *Buyer/Seller* dilemma [273], in which it is unclear for both parties at which price they are going to settle when they start the negotiation process:

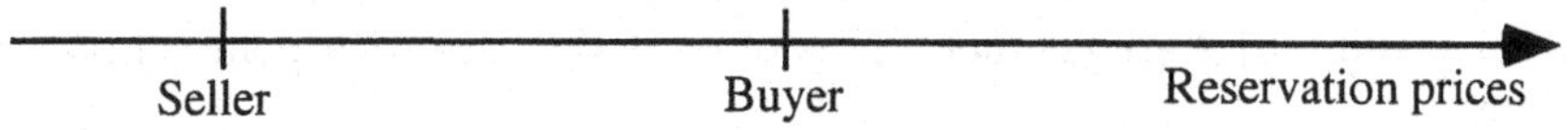


**Fig. 5.13.** Buyer/Seller negotiation problem.

Their objectives are clearly conflicting: the Buyer wants the price to be as low as possible; the Seller tries to keep the price as high as possible. There are two points, the reservation prices, beyond which the negotiations break down. The Buyer will not discuss a price higher than the (Buyer)-point; the

Seller will find a price lower than the (Seller)-point insulting. If both parties compromise they can eventually settle on a price somewhere at the mid-point of the interval. The problem becomes interesting and challenging when none of the parties can be sure of the other party's reservation price, but the setup is simple in the sense that the objectives are conflicting, and the problem can be solved with standard methods.

Let us now assume that there is a third party, the *Government*, involved and that the Government reacts to the negotiation process by working out consequences of both the reservation prices and the offers made during the negotiations. Let us also assume that the Government wants to intervent in the process in order to promote its own objectives.

In this way the negotiation problem becomes much more complex as there are a number of new objectives involved over which the primary parties have no control. The Buyer and the Seller influence two different objectives of the

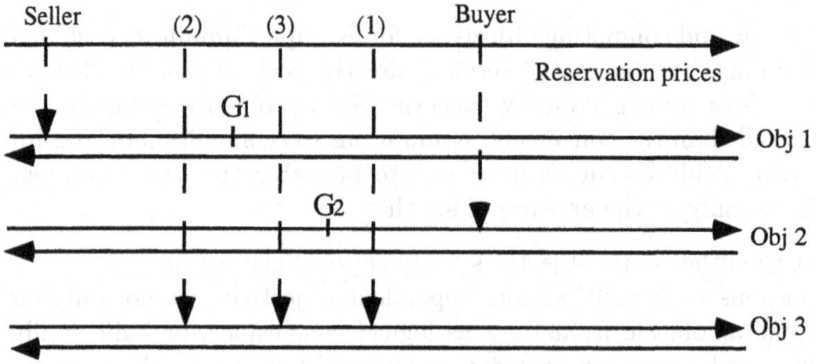


**Fig. 5.14.** A modified Buyer/seller negotiation problem.

Government respectively (Obj 1 and Obj 2):

- a low Seller reservation price will support Obj 1, but a high Seller reservation price will be in conflict with Obj 1 after some point G1 ;
- a high Buyer reservation price will support Obj 2, but a low Buyer reservation price will be in conflict with Obj 2 after some point G2 ,
- Obj 1 and Obj 2 are conflicting (as often is the case with political objectives).

The negotiation process ((1), (2), (3)) influences Obj 3 of the Government:

- short steps and a small interval both support the attainment of Obj 3, but
- large, oscillating steps and a large interval are hinders for the attainment.

There are a number of cases of labor market negotiations in which these types of interdependences are present. Because Obj 1-3 are influenced by the Buyer-Seller negotiations the Government can not remain passive, but will influence the objectives of the primary negotiators. Then we get a set of decision problems for all parties involved, in which we have multiple interdependent objectives; these problems are not easy to cope with and to resolve. In some labor market negotiations in the spring 1996 the Finnish government managed to both define such levels of its own objectives and to push the reservation prices of the primary negotiators to levels which were unattainable. When the government finally agreed to face-saving compromises the country was 12 hours from a general strike.

We will in the following explore the consequences of allowing objectives to be interdependent.

## 5.6 Additive linear interdependences

Objective functions of a multiple objective programming problem are usually considered to be independent from each other, i.e. they depend only on the decision variable $x$. A typical statement of an MOP with independent objective functions is

$$\max_{x \in X} \{f_1(x), \ldots, f_k(x)\} \tag{5.49}$$

where $f_i$ is the $i$-th objective function, $x$ is the decision variable, and $X$ is a subset, usually defined by functional inequalities. Throughout this Section we will assume that the objective functions are normalized, i.e. $f_i(x) \in [0, 1]$ for each $x \in X$.

However, as has been shown in some earlier work by by Carlsson and Fullér [26, 30], and Felix [109], there are management issues and negotiation problems, in which one often encounters the necessity to formulate MOP models with interdependent objective functions, in such a way that the objective functions are determined not only by the decision variables but also by one or more other objective functions.

*Typically, in complex, real-life problems, there are some unidentified factors which effect the values of the objective functions. We do not know them or can not control them; i.e. they have an impact we can not control. The only thing we can observe is the values of the objective functions at certain points. And from this information and from our knowledge about the problem we may be able to formulate the impacts of unknown factors (through the observed values of the objectives).*

First we state the multiobjective decision problem with independent objectives and then adjust our model to reality by introducing interdependences among the objectives. Interdependences among the objectives exist whenever the computed value of an objective function is not equal to its observed value. We claim that the real values of an objective function can be identified by the help of feed-backs from the values of other objective functions.

Suppose now that the objectives of (5.49) are interdependent, and the value of an objective function is determined by a *linear combination* of the values of other objectives functions. That is

$$f_i'(x) = f_i(x) + \sum_{j=1,\ j\neq i}^{k} \alpha_{ij} f_j(x),\ 1 \le i \le k \tag{5.50}$$

or, in matrix format

$$\begin{pmatrix} f_1'(x) \\ f_2'(x) \\ \vdots \\ f_k'(x) \end{pmatrix} = \begin{pmatrix} 1 & \alpha_{12} & \ldots & \alpha_{1k} \\ \alpha_{21} & 1 & \ldots & \alpha_{2k} \\ \vdots & \vdots & \vdots & \vdots \\ \alpha_{k1} & \alpha_{k2} & \ldots & 1 \end{pmatrix} \begin{pmatrix} f_1(x) \\ f_2(x) \\ \vdots \\ f_k(x) \end{pmatrix},$$

where $\alpha_{ij}$ is a real numbers denoting the grade of interdependency between $f_i$ and $f_j$.

If $\alpha_{ij} > 0$ then we say that $f_i$ is supported by $f_j$; if $\alpha_{ij} < 0$ then we say that $f_i$ is hindered by $f_j$; if $\alpha_{ij} = 0$ then we say that $f_i$ is independent from $f_j$ (or the states of $f_j$ are irrelevant to the states of $f_i$). The matrix of interdependences, $(\alpha_{ij})$, denoted by $I(f_1, \ldots, f_k)$, and defined by

$$I(f_1, \ldots, f_k) = \begin{pmatrix} 1 & \alpha_{12} & \ldots & \alpha_{1k} \\ \alpha_{21} & 1 & \ldots & \alpha_{2k} \\ \vdots & \vdots & \vdots & \vdots \\ \alpha_{k1} & \alpha_{k2} & \ldots & 1 \end{pmatrix}$$

is called the interdependency matrix of (5.49).

In such cases, i.e. when the feed-backs from the objectives are directly proportional to their independent values, then we say that the objectives are *linearly* interdependent. It is clear that if $\alpha_{ij} = 0,\ \forall i \neq j$, i.e.

$$I(f_1, \ldots, f_k) = \begin{pmatrix} 1 & 0 & \ldots & 0 \\ 0 & 1 & \ldots & 0 \\ \vdots & \vdots & \vdots & \vdots \\ 0 & 0 & \ldots & 1 \end{pmatrix}$$

then we have an MOP problem with independent objective functions.

The grade of interdependency, denoted by $\Delta(f_i)$, of an objective function $f_i$ is defined by (5.40)

$$\Delta(f_i) = \sum_{i\neq j} \mathrm{sign}(\alpha_{ji}) = \sum_{\substack{\alpha_{ji}>0,\\ i\neq j}} 1 - \sum_{\alpha_{ji}<0} 1$$

i.e. $\Delta(f_i)$ is nothing else that the number of objectives supported by $f_i$ minus the number of objectives hindered by $f_i$, $i = 1, \ldots, k$.

Taking into consideration the linear interdependences among the objective functions (5.50), (5.49) turns into the following problem (which is treated as an independent MOP)

$$\max_{x \in X} \{f'_1(x), \dots, f'_k(x)\} \tag{5.51}$$

It is clear that the solution-sets of (5.49) and (5.51) are usually not identical.

A typical case of interdependence is the following (almost) real world situation. We want to buy a house for which we have defined the following three objectives

- $f_1$: the house should be non-expensive
- $f_2$: as we do not have the necessary skills, the house should not require much maintenance or repair work
- $f_3$: the house should be more than 10 year old so that the garden is fully grown and we need not look at struggling bushes and flowers

We have the following interdependences:

- $f_1$ is supported by both $f_2$ and $f_3$ as in certain regions it is possible to find 10 year old houses which (for the moment) do not require much repair and maintenance work, and which are non-expensive.
- $f_2$ can be conflicting with $f_3$ for some houses as the need for maintenance and repair work increases with the age of the house; thus $f_3$ is also conflicting with $f_2$.
- $f_3$ is supporting $f_1$ for some houses; if the garden is well planned it could increase the price, in which case $f_3$ would be in partial conflict with $f_1$; if the neighbourhood is completed and no newbuilding takes place, prices could rise and $f_3$ be in conflict with $f_1$.

To explain the issue more exactly, consider a three-objective problem with linearly interdependent objective functions

$$\max_{x \in X} \{f_1(x), f_2(x), f_3(x)\} \tag{5.52}$$

Taking into consideration that the objectives are linearly interdependent, the interdependent values of the objectives can be expressed by

$$\begin{aligned} f'_1(x) &= f_1(x) + \alpha_{12} f_2(x) + \alpha_{13} f_3(x), \\ f'_2(x) &= f_2(x) + \alpha_{21} f_1(x) + \alpha_{23} f_3(x), \\ f'_3(x) &= f_3(x) + \alpha_{31} f_1(x) + \alpha_{32} f_2(x). \end{aligned}$$

That is

$$\begin{pmatrix} f'_1(x) \\ f'_2(x) \\ f'_3(x) \end{pmatrix} = \begin{pmatrix} 1 & \alpha_{12} & \alpha_{13} \\ \alpha_{21} & 1 & \alpha_{23} \\ \alpha_{31} & \alpha_{32} & 1 \end{pmatrix} \begin{pmatrix} f_1(x) \\ f_2(x) \\ f_3(x) \end{pmatrix}.$$

For example, depending on the values of $\alpha_{ij}$ we can have the following simple linear interdependences among the objectives of (5.52)

- if $\alpha_{12} = 0$ then we say that $f_1$ is independent from $f_2$;
- if $\alpha_{12} > 0$ then we say that $f_2$ unilaterally supports $f_1$;
- if if $\alpha_{12} < 0$ then we say that $f_2$ hinders $f_1$;
- if $\alpha_{12} > 0$ and $\alpha_{21} > 0$ then we say that $f_1$ and $f_2$ mutually support each others;
- if $\alpha_{12} < 0$ and $\alpha_{21} < 0$ then we say that $f_1$ and $f_2$ are conflicting;
- if $\alpha_{12} + \alpha_{21} = 0$ then we say that $f_1$ are $f_2$ are in a trade-off relation.

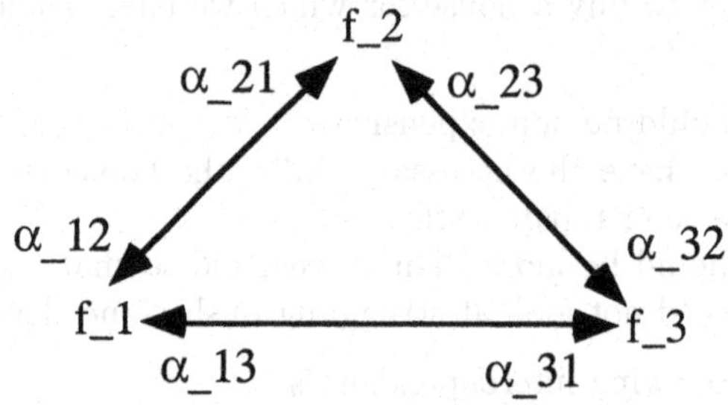


**Fig. 5.15.** A three-objective interdependent problem with linear feed-backs.

It is clear, for example, that if $f_2$ unilaterally supports $f_1$ then the larger the improvement $f_2$ (supporting objective function) the more significant is its contribution to $f_1$ (supported objective function).

To illustrate our ideas consider the following simple decision problem.

$$\max\{x, 1 - x\}; \text{ subject to } x \in [0, 1]. \tag{5.53}$$

Choosing the minimum-norm to aggregate the values of objective functions this problem has a unique solution $x^* = 1/2$ and the optimal values of the objective functions are $(0.500, 0.500)$.

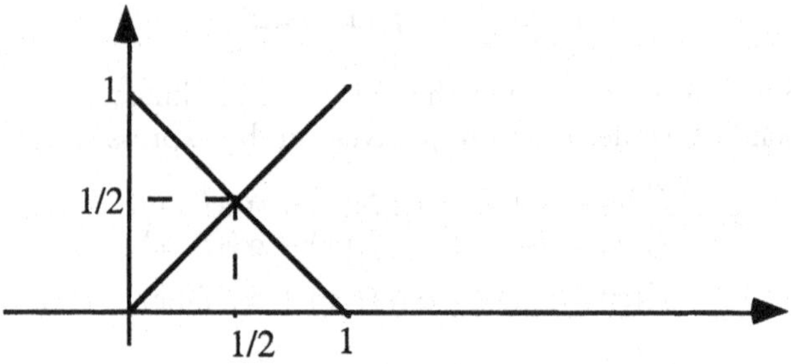


**Fig. 5.16.** Independent problem.

Suppose that for example $f_1$ is unilaterally supported by $f_2$ on the whole decision space $[0, 1]$ and the degree of support is given by

$$f_1'(x) = f_1(x) + 1/2f_2(x) = x + 1/2(1-x) = 1/2 + x/2$$

Then (5.53) turns into the following problem

$$\max\{1/2 + x/2, 1 - x\}; \text{ subject to } x \in [0, 1].$$

Choosing the minimum-norm to aggregate the values of objective functions this problem has a unique solution $x^* = 1/3$ and the optimal values of the objective functions are $(0.667, 0.667)$.

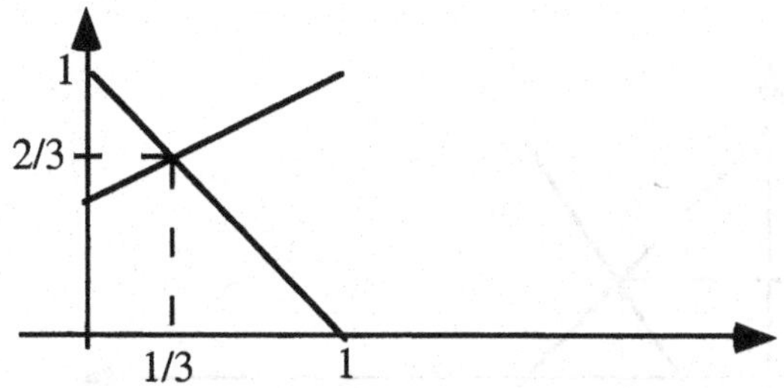


**Fig. 5.17.** Unilateral support.

Suppose now that $f_1$ and $f_2$ support each other mutually, i.e. the better the value of $f_1$ the more significant is its support to $f_2$ and *vica versa.* The degrees of supports are given by

$$f_1'(x) = f_1(x) + 1/2f_2(x) = x + 1/2(1-x) = 1/2(1+x),$$

$$f_2'(x) = f_2(x) + 1/2f_1(x) = (1-x) + 1/2x = 1 - x/2.$$

In this case our interdependent problem turns into

$$\max\{1/2(1+x), 1 - x/2\}; \text{ subject to } x \in [0, 1].$$

Choosing the minimum-norm to aggregate the values of objective functions this problem has a unique solution $x^* = 1/2$ and the optimal values of the objective functions are $(0.750, 0.750)$. Suppose now that $f_2$ hinders $f_1$, i.e. the better the value of $f_2$ the more significant is its negative feed-back to $f_1$. The degree of hindering is

$$f'(x) = f_1(x) - 1/2(1-x) = x - 1/2 + 1/2x = 3/2x - 1/2.$$

So our interdependent problem turns into

$$\max\{3/2x - 1/2, 1 - x\}; \text{ subject to } x \in [0, 1].$$

Choosing the minimum-norm to aggregate the values of objective functions this problem has a unique solution $x^* = 3/5$ and the optimal values of the

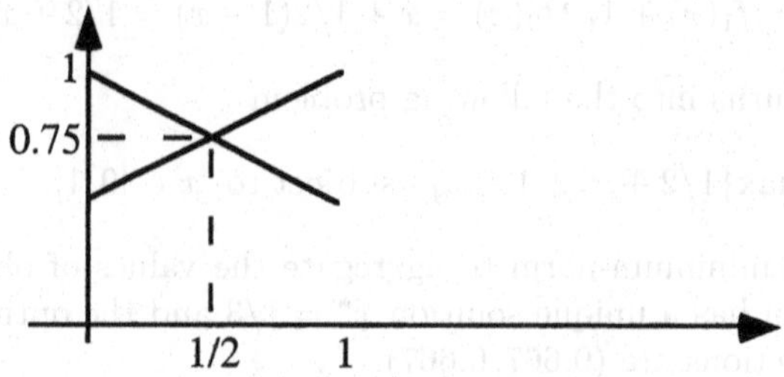


**Fig. 5.18.** Mutual support.

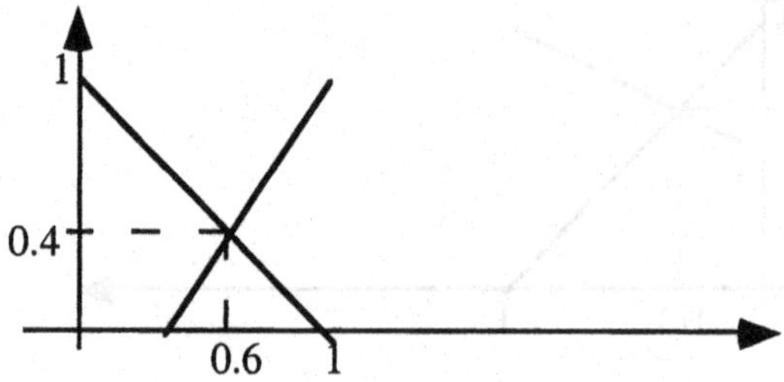


**Fig. 5.19.** Hindering.

objective functions are (0.400, 0.400). Suppose now that $f_2$ hinders $f_1$, but $f_1$ supports $f_2$

$$f_1'(x) = f_1(x) - 1/2f_2(x) = x - 1/2(1-x) = 3/2x - 1/2,$$

$$f_2'(x) = f_2(x) + 1/2f_1(x) = (1-x) + 1/2x = 1 - x/2.$$

So our interdependent problem turns into

$$\max\{3/2x - 1/2, 1 - x/2\}; \text{ subject to } x \in [0,1].$$

Choosing the minimum-norm to aggregate the values of objective functions

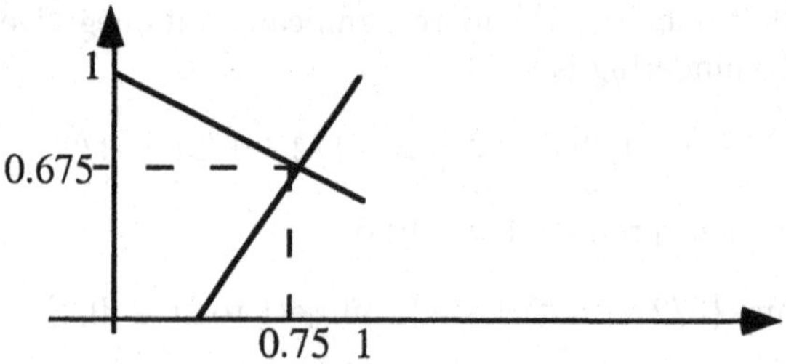


**Fig. 5.20.** Hindering and support.

this problem has a unique solution $x^* = 3/4$ and the optimal values of the objective functions are $(0.625, 0.625)$. These findings can be summarized as follows:

| case | solution | optimal values |
|---|---|---|
| independent objectives | 0.5 | (0.500, 0.500) |
| $f_1$ is supported by $f_2$ | 0.333 | (0.667, 0.667) |
| mutual support | 0.5 | (0.750, 0.750) |
| $f_2$ hinders $f_1$ | 0.6 | (0.400, 0.400) |
| $f_2$ hinders $f_1$ and $f_1$ supports $f_2$ | 0.75 | (0.625, 0.625) |

**Table 5.1.** Cases and solutions.

## 5.7 Additive nonlinear interdependences

Suppose now that the objectives of (5.49) are interdependent, and the value of an objective function is determined by an *additive combination* of the feed-backs of other objectives functions

$$f_i'(x) = f_i(x) + \sum_{j=1,\ j\neq i}^{k} \alpha_{ij}[f_j(x)],\ 1 \leq i \leq k \tag{5.54}$$

or, in matrix format

$$\begin{pmatrix} f_1'(x) \\ f_2'(x) \\ \vdots \\ f_k'(x) \end{pmatrix} = \begin{pmatrix} id & \alpha_{12} & \dots & \alpha_{1k} \\ \alpha_{21} & id & \dots & \alpha_{2k} \\ \vdots & \vdots & \vdots & \vdots \\ \alpha_{k1} & \alpha_{k2} & \dots & id \end{pmatrix} \circ \begin{pmatrix} f_1(x) \\ f_2(x) \\ \vdots \\ f_k(x) \end{pmatrix}$$

where $\alpha_{ij}\colon [0,1] \to [0,1]$ is a - usually nonlinear - function defining the value of feed-back from $f_j$ to $f_i$, $id(z) = z$ denotes the identity function on $[0,1]$ and $\circ$ denotes the composition operator.

If $\alpha_{ij}(z) > 0, \forall z$ we say that $f_i$ is supported by $f_j$; if $\alpha_{ij}(z) < 0, \forall t$ then we say that $f_i$ is hindered by $f_j$; if $\alpha_{ij}(z) = 0, \forall z$ then we say that $f_i$ is independent from $f_j$. If $\alpha_{ij}(z_1) > 0$ and $\alpha_{ij}(z_2) < 0$ for some $z_1$ and $z_2$, then $f_i$ is supported by $f_j$ if the value of $f_j$ is equal to $z_1$ and $f_i$ is hindered by $f_j$ if the value of $f_j$ is equal to $z_2$.

Consider again a three-objective problem

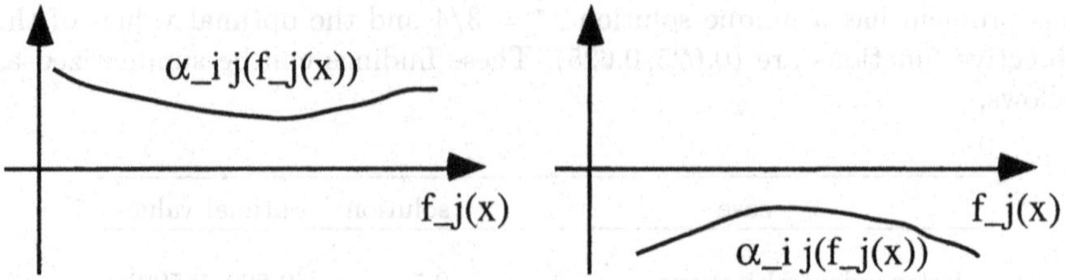


**Fig. 5.21.** Nonlinear unilateral support and hindering.

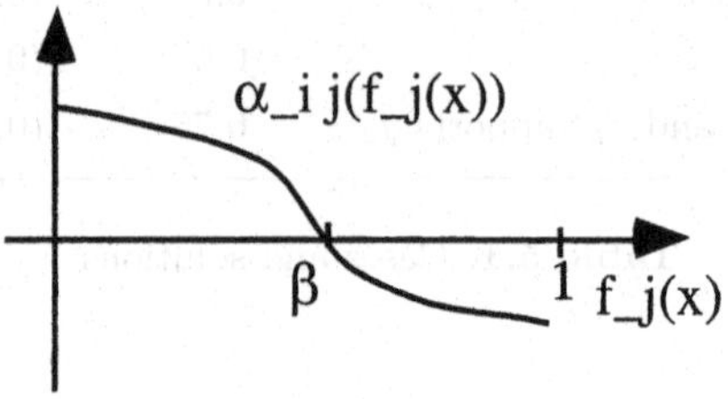


**Fig. 5.22.** $f_j$ supports $f_i$ if $f_j(x) \leq \beta$ and $f_j$ hinders $f_i$ if $f_j(x) \geq \beta$.

$$\max_{x \in X} \{f_1(x), f_2(x), f_3(x)\}$$

with nonlinear interdependences. Taking into consideration that the objectives are interdependent, the interdependent values of the objectives can be expressed by

$$f_1'(x) = f_1(x) + \alpha_{12}[f_2(x)] + \alpha_{13}[f_3(x)],$$
$$f_2'(x) = f_2(x) + \alpha_{21}[f_1(x)] + \alpha_{23}[f_3(x)],$$
$$f_3'(x) = f_3(x) + \alpha_{31}[f_1(x)] + \alpha_{32}[f_2(x)].$$

That is

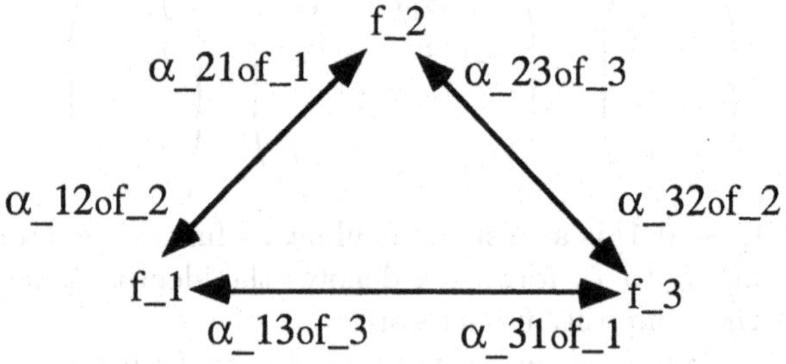


**Fig. 5.23.** A three-objective interdependent problem with nonlinear feed-backs.

$$\begin{pmatrix} f_1'(x) \\ f_2'(x) \\ f_3'(x) \end{pmatrix} = \begin{pmatrix} id & \alpha_{12} & \alpha_{13} \\ \alpha_{21} & id & \alpha_{23} \\ \alpha_{31} & \alpha_{32} & id \end{pmatrix} \circ \begin{pmatrix} f_1(x) \\ f_2(x) \\ f_3(x) \end{pmatrix}$$

For example, depending on the values of the correlation functions $\alpha_{12}$ and $\alpha_{21}$ we can have the following simple interdependences among the objectives of (5.52)

- if $\alpha_{12}(z) = 0, \forall z$ then we say that $f_1$ is independent from $f_2$;
- if $\alpha_{12}(z) > 0, \forall z$ then we say that $f_2$ unilaterally supports $f_1$;
- if if $\alpha_{12}(z) < 0, \forall z$ then we say that $f_2$ hinders $f_1$;
- if $\alpha_{12}(z) > 0$ and $\alpha_{21}(z), \forall z > 0$ then we say that $f_1$ and $f_2$ mutually support each others;
- if $\alpha_{12}(z) < 0$ and $\alpha_{21}(z) < 0$ for each $z$ then we say that $f_1$ and $f_2$ are conflicting;
- if $\alpha_{12}(z)+\alpha_{21}(z) = 0$ for each $z$ then we say that $f_1$ are $f_2$ are in a trade-off relation;

However, despite of the linear case, we can have here more complex relationships between two objective functions, e.g.

- if for some $\beta \in [0, 1]$

$$\alpha_{12}(z) = \begin{cases} \text{positive if } 0 \leq z \leq \beta \\ \text{negative if } \beta \leq z \leq 1 \end{cases}$$

  then $f_2$ unilaterally supports $f_1$ if $f_2(x) \leq \beta$ and $f_2$ hinders $f_1$ if $f_2(x) \geq \beta$.
- if for some $\beta, \gamma \in [0, 1]$

$$\alpha_{12}(z) = \begin{cases} \text{positive if } 0 \leq z \leq \beta \\ 0 \qquad\quad\ \text{if } \beta \leq z \leq \gamma \\ \text{negative if } \gamma \leq z \leq 1 \end{cases}$$

  then $f_2$ unilaterally supports $f_1$ if $f_2(x) \leq \beta$, $f_2$ does not affect $f_1$ if $\beta \leq f_2(x) \leq \gamma$ and then $f_2$ hinders $f_1$ if $f_2(x) \geq \gamma$.

## 5.8 Compound interdependences

Let us now more consider the case with compound interdependences in multiple objective programming, which is - so far - the most general case.

Assume again that the objectives of (5.49) are interdependent, and the value of an objective function is determined by an *additive combination* of the feed-backs from other objectives functions

$$f_i'(x) = \sum_{j=1}^{k} \alpha_{ij}[f_1(x), \dots, f_k(x)],\ 1 \leq i \leq k \tag{5.55}$$

where $\alpha_{ij} \colon [0, 1]^k \to [0, 1]$ is a - usually nonlinear - function defining the value of feed-back from $f_j$ to $f_i$. We note that $\alpha_{ij}$ depends not only on the value of $f_j$, but on the values of other objectives as well (this is why we call it compound interdependence [36]). Let us again consider the three-objective problem with nonlinear interdependences

$$\max_{x \in X} \{f_1(x), f_2(x), f_3(x)\}.$$

With the assumptions of (5.55) the interdependent values of the objectives can be expressed by

$$f_1'(x) = \alpha_{11}[f_1(x), f_2(x), f_3(x)] + \alpha_{12}[f_1(x), f_2(x), f_3(x)] + \alpha_{13}[f_1(x), f_2(x), f_3(x)],$$

$$f_2'(x) = \alpha_{22}[f_1(x), f_2(x), f_3(x)] + \alpha_{21}[f_1(x), f_2(x), f_3(x)] + \alpha_{23}[f_1(x), f_2(x), f_3(x)],$$

$$f_3'(x) = \alpha_{33}[f_1(x), f_2(x), f_3(x)] + \alpha_{31}[f_1(x), f_2(x), f_3(x)] + \alpha_{32}[f_1(x), f_2(x), f_3(x)].$$

Here we can have more complicated interrelations between $f_1$ and $f_2$, because the feedback from $f_2$ to $f_1$ can depend not only on the value of $f_2$, but also on the values of $f_1$ (self feed-back) and $f_3$. Unfortunately, in real life cases we usually have compound interdependences.

We have considerd only additive interdependences and time independent feed-backs. It should be noted, however, that in negotiation processes the feed-backs from other objectives are always time-dependent.

Time-dependent additive linear interdependences in MOP (5.49) can be defined as follows

$$f_i'(x) = f_i(x) + \sum_{\substack{j=1,\\ j \neq i}}^{k} \alpha_{ij}(t) f_j(x), \ 1 \le i \le k,$$

where $\alpha_{ij}(t)$ denotes the dynamical grade of interdependency between functions $f_i$ and $f_j$ at time $t$.

Interdependence among criteria used in decision making is part of the classical economic theory even if most of the modelling efforts in the theory for multiple criteria decision making has been aimed at (the simplified effort of) finding optimal solutions for cases where the criteria are multiple but independent.

Decision making with interdependent objectives is not an easy task. However, with the methods proposed in this Section we are able to at least start dealing with interdependence. If the exact values of the objective functions can be measured (at least partially, or in some points), then from this information and some (incomplete or preliminary) model we may be able to approximate the effects of other objective functions, and of the set of decision variables we have found to be appropriate for the problem. In this way we will be able to deal with more complex decision problems in a more appropriate way.

In this Section we have tried to tackle interdependence head-on, i.e. we have deliberately formulated decision problems with interdependent criteria and found ways to deal with the "anomalies" thus created.

In the next Chapter we will demonstrate, with a fairly extensive case, called Nordic Paper Inc, that the situations we first described as just principles do have justifications in real world decision problems. It turned out that the introduction of interdependences creates complications for solving the decision problem, and there are no handy tools available for dealing with more complex patterns of interdependence. We can have the case, in fact, that problem solving strategies deciding the attainment of some subset of objectives will effectively cancel out all possibilities of attaining some other subset of objectives.

Allowing for additive, interdependent criteria appears to open up a new category of decision problems.

## 5.9 Biobjective interdependent decision problems

Let us now illustrate how the solution of a biobjective decision problem changes under interdependent objectives. A biobjective independent decision problem in a (normalized) criterion space can be defined as follows

$$\max\{f_1, f_2\}; \text{ subject to } 0 \leq f_1, f_2 \leq 1. \tag{5.56}$$

As $f_1$ and $f_2$ take their values independently of each others, we can first maximize $f_1$ subject to $f_1 \in [0, 1]$ then $f_2$ subject to $f_2 \in [0, 1]$ and take the (feasible) *ideal point*, $(1, 1)$, as the unique solution to problem (5.56). A typical two-dimensional independent problem is

$$\max\{x_1, x_2\}; \text{ subject to } 0 \leq x_1, x_2 \leq 1,$$

that is, $f_1(x_1, x_2) = x_1$ and $f_2(x_1, x_2) = x_2$.

More often than not, the ideal point is not feasible, that is, we can not improve one objective without giving away something of the other one. If we happen to know the exact values of the objectives in all conceivable cases then a good compromise solution can be defined as a Pareto-optimal solution satisfying some additional requirements specified by the decision maker [76, 222].

Suppose that the interdependent values $f_1'$ and $f_2'$ of $f_1$ and $f_2$, respectively, are observed to satisfy the following equations

$$f_1' = f_1 + \alpha_{12} f_2, \quad f_2' = f_2 + \alpha_{21} f_1$$

The following two theorems characterize the behavior of max-min compromise solutions of biobjective linearly interdependent decision problems with conflicting and supporting objective functions.

**Theorem 5.9.1** *If* $f_1' = f_1 - \alpha f_2$ *and* $f_2' = f_2 - \alpha f_1$, *i.e.,* $f_1$ *hinders* $f_2$ *globally and* $f_2$ *hinders* $f_1$ *globally with the same degree of hindering* $0 \leq \alpha \leq 1$ *then*

$$\max \min\{f_1', f_2'\} \leq (1-\alpha) \max \min\{f_1, f_2\};$$

$$\text{subject to } 0 \leq f_1, f_2 \leq 1.$$

*Proof.* Suppose $f_1 \leq f_2$. Then

$$f_1' = f_1 - \alpha f_2 \leq f_2' = f_2 - \alpha f_1 \Rightarrow \min\{f_1', f_2'\} = f_1'$$

and

$$\begin{aligned}(1-\alpha) \max \min\{f_1, f_2\} &= (1-\alpha) f_1 \\ &\geq f_1 - \alpha f_2 = f_1',\end{aligned}$$

That is,

$$\begin{aligned}(1-\alpha) \min\{f_1, f_2\} &\geq \min\{f_1 - \alpha f_2, f_2 - \alpha f_1\} \\ &= \min\{f_1', f_2'\}.\end{aligned}$$

Similar reasoning holds for the case $f_1 \geq f_2$.

In other words, Theorem (5.9.1) shows an upper bound for the max-min compromise solution, which can be interpreted as 'the bigger the conflict between the objective functions the less are the criteria satisfactions'. For example, in the extremal case, $\alpha = 1$ we end up with totally opposite objective functions

$$f_1' = f_1 - f_2, \quad f_2' = f_2 - f_1,$$

and, therefore, we get

$$\begin{aligned}\max \min\{f_1', f_2'\} &= \max \min\{f_1 - f_2, f_2 - f_1\} \\ &\leq (1-\alpha) \max \min\{f_1, f_2\} = 0.\end{aligned}$$

On the other hand, if $\alpha = 0$ then the objective functions remain independent, that is,

$$\begin{aligned}\max \min\{f_1', f_2'\} &\leq (1-\alpha) \max \min\{f_1, f_2\} \\ &= \max \min\{f_1, f_2\}.\end{aligned}$$

**Theorem 5.9.2** *If* $f_1$ *supports* $f_2$ *globally with the degree* $\alpha \geq 1$ *then*

$$\max \min\{f_1', f_2'\} = \max f_1;$$

$$\text{subject to } 0 \leq f_1, 0 \leq f_2.$$

*Proof.* From $\alpha \geq 1$ we get

$$f_1 \leq f_2 + \alpha f_1$$

and therefore,

$$\max \min\{f_1, f_2 + \alpha f_1\} = \max f_1,$$

which ends the proof.

Theorem 5.9.2 demonstrates that if one objective supports the other one globally with a degree of support bigger than one, then the independent maximum of the supporting objective gives the max-min compromise solution to the interdependent problem. In other words, in the case of unilateral support, it is enough to maximize the supporting objective function to reach a max-min compromise solution.

It should be noted that Theorem 5.9.2 remains valid for non-negative objective functions (that is, the constraints $f_1 \leq 1$ and $f_2 \leq 1$ can be omitted). If, however $f_1$ does satisfy the constraint $f_1 \leq 1$ then the ideal point $(1, 1)$ will be the unique max-min solution.

# 6. Applications in Management

## 6.1 Nordic Paper Inc.

We show an example to illustrate the interdependencies by a real-life problem.

Nordic Paper Inc. (NPI) is one of the more successful paper producers in Europe[1] and has gained a reputation among its competitors as a leader in quality, timely delivery to its customers, innovations in production technology and customer relationships of long duration. Still it does not have a dominating position in any of its customer segments, which is not even advisable in the European Common market, as there are always 2-5 competitors with sizeable market shares. NPI would, nevertheless, like to have a position which would be dominant against any chosen competitor when defined for all the markets in which NPI operates.

We will consider strategic decisions for the planning period 2001-2004.

Decisions will be made on how many tons of 6-9 different paper qualities should be produced for 3-4 customer segments in *Germany, France, UK, Benelux, Italy* and *Spain*. NPI is operating 9 paper mills which together cover all the qualities to be produced. Price/ton of paper qualities in different market segments are known and forecasts for the planning period are available. Capacities of the paper mills for different qualities are known and production costs/ton are also known and can be forecasted for the planning period. The operating result includes distribution costs from paper mills to the markets, and the distribution costs/ton are also known and can be forecasted for the planning period.

Decisions will also have to be made on how much more added capacity should be created through investments, when to carry out these investments and how to finance them. Investment decisions should consider target levels on productivity and competitive advantages to be gained through improvements in technology, as well as improvements in prices/ton and product qualities.

There are about 6 significant competitors in each market segment, with about the same (or poorer) production technology as the one operated by NPI. Competition is mainly on paper qualities, just-in-time deliveries, long-

[1] NPI is a fictional corporation, but the case is realistic and quite close to actual decisions made in the forest products industry.

term customer relationships and production technology; all the competitors try to avoid competing with prices. Competition is therefore complex: if NPI manages to gain some customers for some specific paper quality in Germany by taking these customers away from some competitor, the competitive game will not be fought in Germany, but the competitor will try to retaliate in (for instance) France by offering some superior paper quality at better prices to NPI customers; this offer will perhaps not happen immediately but over time, so that the game is played out over the strategic planning interval. NPI is looking for a long-term strategy to gain an overall dominance over its competitors in the European arena.

Decisions will have to be made on how to attain the best possible operating results over the planning period, how to avoid both surplus and negative cash flow, how to keep productivity at a high and stable level, and how to keep up with market share objectives introduced by shareholders, who believe that attaining dominating positions will increase share prices over time.

*There are several objectives which can be defined for the 2000-2003 strategic planning period.*

- Operating result [$f_1$]
  should either be as high as possible for the period or as close as possible to some acceptable level.
- Productivity [$f_2$],
  defined as output (in ton) / input factors, should either be as high as possible or as close as possible to yearly defined target levels.
- Available capacity [$f_3$]
  defined for all the available paper mills, should be used as much as possible, preferably at, or close to their operational limits.
- Market share [$f_4$]
  objectives for the various market segments should be attained as closely as possible.
- Competitive position [$f_5$]
  assessed as a relative strength to competitors in selected market segments, should be built up and consolidated over the planning period.
- Return on investments [$f_6$]
  should be as high as possible when new production technology is allocated to market segments with high and stable prices and growing demand.
- Financing [$f_7$]
  target levels should be attained as closely as possible when investment programs are decided and implemented; both surplus financial assets and needs for loans should be avoided.

There seems to be the following forms of interdependence among these objectives:

- $f_1$ and $f_4$ are in conflict, as increased market share is gained at the expense of operating result; if $f_5$ reaches a dominant level in a chosen market segment, then $f_4$ will support $f_1$; if $f_5$ reaches dominant levels in a sufficient number of market segments, then $f_4$ will support $f_1$ overall.

- $f_4$ supports $f_5$, as a high market share will form the basis for a strong competitive position; $f_5$ supports $f_4$ as a strong competitive position will form the basis for increasing market shares; there is a time lag between these objectives.
- $f_3$ supports $f_2$, as using most of the available capacity will increase productivity.
- $f_2$ supports $f_1$ as increasing productivity will improve operating results.
- $f_3$ is in conflict, partially, with $f_1$, as using all capacity will reduce prices and have a negative effect on operating result.
- $f_6$ is supporting $f_1$, $f_4$ and $f_5$, as increasing return on investment will improve operating result, market share and competitive position; $f_4$ and $f_5$ support $f_6$ as both objectives will improve return on investment; $f_6$ is in conflict with $f_3$ as increasing return on investment will increase capacity.
- $f_7$ supports $f_1$, as a good financial stability will improve the operating result.
- $f_5$ supports $f_2$, as a strong competitive position will improve productivity, because prices will be higher and demand will increase, which is using more of the production capacity.
- $f_4$ and $f_6$ are in conflict, as increasing market share is counterproductive to improving return on investment, which should focus on gaining positions only in market segments with high prices and stable growths.

### 6.1.1 Outline of a macro algorithm

Let $X$ be a set of possible strategic activities of relevance for the context in the sense that they are instrumental for attaining the objectives $f_1 - f_7$. Strategic activities are decisions and action programs identified as appropriate and undertaken in order to establish positions of sustainable competitive advantages over the strategic planning period. As the objectives are interdependent the strategic activities need to be chosen or designed in such a way that the interdependences can be exploited, i.e. we can make the attainment of the various objectives more and more effective. In the following we describe a macro algorithm for solving the NPI problem. There is a numerical case available on request (too extensive to be used here), which proved to have several alternate solutions.

Let X be composed of several context-specific strategic activities:

$$X \subset \{X_{MP}, X_{CP}, X_{PROD}, X_{INV}, X_{FIN}, X_{PROF}\},$$

where the context-specific activities are defined as follows:

- $X_{MP}$, market-oriented activities for demand, selling prices and market shares

- $X_{CP}$, activites used for building competitive positions
- $X_{PROD}$, production technology and productivity-improving activities
- $X_{INV}$, investment decisions
- $X_{FIN}$, financing of investments and operations
- $X_{PROF}$, activities aimed at enhancing and consolidating profitability

It is clear that these activities have some temporal interdependences; it is, for instance, normally the case that a market position will influence the corresponding competitive position with some delay - in some markets this can be 2-3 months, in other markets 6-12 months. In the interest of simplicity we will disregard these interdependences.

1.1 check through the database on markets, customers for an intuitive view on potential changes in demand, prices, sales;
1.2 work out $X_{MP}$ and list expected consequences on demand, selling prices and market shares;
1.3 work out consequences for $f_4$ and check if the objective will be attained during the planning period; if not got to 1.1, otherwise proceed;
1.4.1 work out the impact of $f_4$ on $f_1$; if $f_1$ is untenable, go to 1.2, otherwise proceed;
1.4.2 work out the impact of $f_4$ on $f_5$, and the impact of $f_5$ on $f_4$; if $f_5$ is tenable, proceed, otherwise go to 1.2;
1.4.3 work out the impact of $f_4$ on $f_6$; if $f_6$ is tenable, proceed, otherwise go to 1.2;
1.4.4 work out the impact of $f_6$ on $f_4$; if $f_4$ is tenable, proceed, otherwise go to 1.2;
1.4.5 if 1.4.1-1.4.4 have iterated $n$ times, then stop;
2.1 check through the database on markets, customers for intuitive view on the positions of key competitors;
2.2 work out $X_{CP}$ and list expected consequences on overall status on critical success fac-tors and competitive positions;
2.3 work out consequences for $f_5$ and check if the objective will be attained during the planning period; if not got to 2.1, otherwise proceed;
2.4.1 work out the impact of $f_5$ on $f_4$ and $f_1$; if $f_1$, $f_4$ are untenable, go to 2.2, otherwise proceed;
2.4.2 work out the impact of $f_4$ on $f_5$, and the impact of $f_5$ on $f_4$; if $f_4$ is tenable, proceed, otherwise go to 2.2;
2.4.3 work out the impact of $f_5$ on $f_6$; if $f_6$ is tenable, proceed, otherwise go to 2.2;
2.4.4 work out the impact of $f_5$ on $f_2$; if $f_2$ is tenable, proceed, otherwise go to 2.2;
2.4.5 if 2.4.1-2.4.4 have iterated $n$ times, then stop;
3.1 check through the database on markets, customers for an intuitive view on potential changes in product demand, quality constraints, requirements on technology;

3.2 work out $X_{PROD}$ and list expected consequences on the production program, required selling prices and market shares;
3.3 work out consequences for $f_2$ and check if the objective will be attained during the planning period; if not got to 3.1, otherwise proceed;
3.4.1 work out the impact of $f_3$ on $f_2$; if $f_2$ is tenable, proceed, otherwise go to 3.1;
3.4.2 work out the impact of $f_2$ on $f_1$; if $f_1$ is tenable, proceed, otherwise go to 3.2;
3.4.3 work out the impact of $f_5$ on $f_2$; if $f_2$ is tenable, proceed, otherwise go to 3.2;
3.4.4 if 3.4.1-3.4.3 have iterated $n$ times, then stop;
4.1 check through $X_{MP}$, $X_{CP}$, $X_{PROD}$;
4.2 work out $X_{INV}$ and list expected consequences on productivity, competitive position and market position;
4.3 work out consequences for $f_6$ and check if the objective will be attained during the planning period; if not got to 4.1, otherwise proceed;
4.4.1 work out the impact of $f_6$ on $f_1$, $f_4$ and $f_5$; if all of them are tenable, proceed; otherwise go to 4.2;
4.4.2 work out the impact of $f_4$ and $f_5$ on $f_6$; if $f_6$ is tenable, proceed, otherwise go to 4.2;
4.4.3 work out the impact of $f_6$ on $f_3$; if $f_3$ is tenable, proceed, otherwise go to 4.2;
4.4.4 if 4.4.1-4.4.3 have iterated $n$ times, then stop;
5.1 check through $X_{MP}$, $X_{CP}$, $X_{PROD}$, $X_{INV}$;
5.2 work out $X_{FIN}$ and list expected consequences on profitability and cash flow;
5.3 work out consequences for $f_7$ and check if the objective will be attained during the planning period; if not got to 5.1, otherwise proceed;
5.4.1 work out the impact of $f_7$ on $f_1$; if $f_1$ is tenable, proceed, otherwise go to 5.2;
5.4.2 if 5.4.1 has iterated $n$ times, then stop;
6.1 check through $X_{MP}$, $X_{CP}$, $X_{PROD}$, $X_{INV}$;
6.2 work out $X_{PROF}$ and list expected consequences on profitability, capital structure, cash flow and key ratios;
6.3 work out consequences for $f_1$ and check if the objective will be attained during the planning period; if not got to 6.1 (or possibly 1.1), otherwise proceed;
6.4.1 work out the impact of $f_1$ on $f_4$; if $f_4$ is untenable, go to 6.2, otherwise proceed;
6.4.2 work out the impact of $f_5$ on $f_4$, and the impact of $f_4$ on $f_1$; if $f_4$ is tenable, proceed, otherwise go to 6.2;
6.4.3 work out the impact of $f_2$ on $f_1$; if $f_1$ is tenable, proceed, otherwise go to 6.2;

6.4.4 work out the impact of $f_3$ on $f_1$; if $f_4$ is untenable, go to 6.2, otherwise proceed;
6.4.5 work out the impact of $f_6$ on $f_1$; if $f_1$ is tenable, proceed, otherwise go to 6.2;
6.4.6 work out the impact of $f_7$ on $f_1$; if $f_1$ is tenable, proceed, otherwise go to 6.2;
6.4.7 if 6.4.1-6.4.6 have iterated $n$ times, then stop;

There are second and third degree interdependences between the objectives, and there are degrees to the interdependences; all with an impact on the design of the set of strategic activities:

$$X \subset \{X_{MP}, X_{CP}, X_{PROD}, X_{INV}, X_{FIN}, X_{PROF}\}.$$

These will not be worked out here, as this illustration is sufficient to show the inherent complexity. There are 4-5 different numerical solutions to the NPI case, which can be obtained from the authors.

*Note 6.1.1.* Here we have considered only additive interdependences and time independent feed-backs. It should be noted, however, that in negotiation processes the feed-backs from other objectives are always time-dependent. Time-dependent additive linear interdependences in MOP (5.49) can be defined as follows

$$f_i'(x) = f_i(x) + \sum_{j=1,\ j\neq i}^{k} \alpha_{ij}(t) f_j(x),\ 1 \le i \le k,$$

where $\alpha_{ij}(t)$ denotes the dynamical grade of interdependency between $f_i$ and $f_j$ at time $t$.

## 6.2 A fuzzy approach to real option valuation

*Financial options* are known from the financial world where they represent the right to buy or sell a financial value (mostly a stock) for a predetermined price (the exercise price), without having the obligation to do so. *Real options* in option thinking are based on the same principals as financial options. In real options, the options involve *real* assets as opposed to financial ones. To have a *real option* means to have the possibility for a certain period to either choose for or against something, without binding oneself up front. Real options are valued (as financial options), which is quite different with from discounted cashflow investment approaches.

The *real option rule* is that one should invest today only if the net present value is high enough to compensate for giving up the value of the option to wait. Because the option to invest loses its value when the investment is irreversibly made, this loss is an opportunity cost of investing. However, the pure (probabilistic) *real option rule* characterizes the present value of expected cash flows and the expected costs by a single number, which is not realistic in many cases. In this paper we consider the *real option rule* in a more realistic setting, namely, when the present values of expected cash flows and expected costs are estimated by trapezoidal fuzzy numbers.

### 6.2.1 Probabilistic real option valuation

Options are known from the financial world where they represent the right to buy or sell a financial value, mostly a stock, for a predetermined price (the exercise price), without having the obligation to do so. The actual selling or buying of the underlying value for the predetermined price is called exercising your option. One would only exercise the option if the underlying value is higher than the exercise price in case of a call option (the right to buy) or lower than the exercise prise in the case of a put option (the right to sell).

In 1973 Black and Scholes [8] made a major breakthrough by deriving a differential equation that must be satisfied by the price of any derivative security dependent on a non-dividend paying stock. For risk-neutral investors the *Black-Scholes pricing formula* for a call option is

$$C_0 = S_0 N(d_1) - X e^{-rT} N(d_2),$$

where

$$d_1 = \frac{\ln(S_0/X) + (r + \sigma^2/2)T}{\sigma\sqrt{T}}, \quad d_2 = d_1 - \sigma\sqrt{T},$$

and where

| | | |
|---|---|---|
| $C_0$ | = | current call option value |
| $S_0$ | = | current stock price |
| $N(d)$ | = | the probability that a random draw from a standard normal distribution will be less than $d$. |
| $X$ | = | exercise price |
| $r$ | = | the annualized continuously compounded rate on a safe asset with the same maturity as the expiration of the option, |
| $T$ | = | time to maturity of option, in years |
| $\sigma$ | = | standard deviation |

In 1973 Merton [248] extended the Black-Scholes option pricing formula to dividends-paying stocks as

$$C_0 = S_0 e^{-\delta T} N(d_1) - X e^{-rT} N(d_2) \tag{6.1}$$

where,

$$d_1 = \frac{\ln(S_0/X) + (r - \delta + \sigma^2/2)T}{\sigma\sqrt{T}}, \quad d_2 = d_1 - \sigma\sqrt{T}$$

where $\delta$ denotes the dividends payed out during the life-time of the option.

*Real options* in option thinking are based on the same principals as financial options. In real options, the options involve "real" assets as opposed to financial ones. To have a "real option" means to have the possibility for a certain period to either choose for or against something, without binding oneself up front. For example, owning a power plant gives a utility the opportunity, but not the obligation, to produce electricity at some later date.

Real options can be valued using the analogue option theories that have been developed for financial options, which is quite different with from traditional discounted cashflow investment approaches. In traditional investment approaches investments activities or projects are often seen as *now or never* and the main question is whether to go ahead with an investment *yes or no.*

Formulated in this way it is very hard to make a decision when there is uncertainty about the exact outcome of the investment. To help with these tough decisions valuation methods as *Net Present Value* (NPV) or *Discounted Cash Flow* (DCF) have been developed. And since these methods ignore the value of flexibility and discount heavily for external uncertainty involved, many interesting and innovative activities and projects are cancelled because of the uncertainties.

However, only a few projects are now or never. Often it is possible to delay, modify or split up the project in strategic components which generate important learning effects (and therefore reduce uncertainty). And in those cases option thinking can help. The new rule, derived from option pricing theory (6.1), is that you should invest today only if the net present value is high enough to compensate for giving up the value of the option to wait. Because the option to invest loses its value when the investment is irreversibly made, this loss is an opportunity cost of investing. Following Leslie and Michaels [234] we will compute the value of a real option by

$$\mathrm{ROV} = S_0 e^{-\delta T} N(d_1) - X e^{-rT} N(d_2)$$

where,

$$d_1 = \frac{\ln(S_0/X) + (r - \delta + \sigma^2/2)T}{\sigma\sqrt{T}}, \quad d_2 = d_1 - \sigma\sqrt{T}$$

and where

| | | |
|---|---|---|
| ROV | = | current real option value |
| $S_0$ | = | present value of expected cash flows |
| $N(d)$ | = | the probability that a random draw from a standard normal distribution will be less than $d$. |
| $X$ | = | (nominal) value of fixed costs |
| $r$ | = | the annualized continuously compounded rate on a safe asset |
| $T$ | = | time to maturity of option, in years |
| $\sigma$ | = | uncertainty of expected cash flows |
| $\delta$ | = | value lost over the duration of the option |

We illustrate the principial difference between the traditional (passive) NPV decision rule and the (active) real option approach by an example quoted from [234]:

> ...another oil company has the opportunity to acquire a five-year licence on block. When developed, the block is expected to yield 50 million barrels of oil. The current price of a barell of oil from this field is $10 and the present value of the development costs is $600 million. Thus the NPV of the project opportunity is
>
> $$50 \text{ million} \times \$10 - \$600 \text{ million} = -\$100 \text{ million}.$$
>
> Faced with this valuation, the company would obviously pass up the opportunity. But what would option valuation make of the same case? To begin with, such a valuation would recognize the importance of uncertainty, which the NPV analysis effectively assumes away. There are two major sources of uncertainty affecting the value of the block: the quantity of the price of the oil. ...Assume for the sake of argument that these two sources of uncertainty jointly result in a 30 percent standard deviation ($\sigma$) around the growth rate of the value of operating cash inflows. Holding the option also obliges one to incur the annual fixed costs of keeping the reserve active - let us say, $15 million. This represents a dividend-like payout of three percent (i.e. 15/500) of the value of the assets.
> We already know that the duration of the option, $T$, is five years and the risk-free rate, $r$, is 5 percent, leading us to estimate option value at
>
> $$\begin{aligned} \text{ROV} &= 500 \times e^{-0.03\times 5} \times 0.58 - 600 \times e^{-0.05\times 5} \times 0.32 \\ &= \$251 \ \ \text{million - } \$151 \ \ \text{million} = \$100 \ \ \text{million}. \end{aligned}$$

It should be noted that the fact that real options are like financial options does not mean that they are the same. Real options are concerned about strategic decisions of a company, where degrees of freedom are limited to the capabilities of the company. In these strategic decisions different s takeholders play a role, especially if the resources needed for an investment are significant and thereby the continuity of the company is at stake. Real options therefore, always need to be seen in the larger context of the company, whereas financial options can be used freely and independently.

### 6.2.2 A hybrid approach to real option valuation

Usually, the present value of expected cash flows can not be be characterized by a single number. We can, however, estimate the present value of expected cash flows by using a trapezoidal possibility distribution of the form

$$S_0 = (s_1, s_2, \alpha, \beta)$$

i.e. the most possible values of the present value of expected cash flows lie in the interval $[s_1, s_2]$ (which is the core of the trapezoidal fuzzy number $S_0$), and $(s_2 + \beta)$ is the upward potential and $(s_1 - \alpha)$ is the downward potential for the present value of expected cash flows.

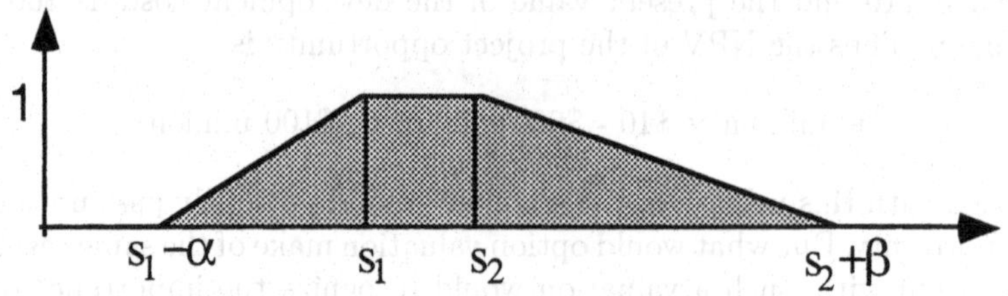


**Fig. 6.1.** The possibility distribution of present values of expected cash flow.

In a similar manner we can estimate the expected costs by using a trapezoidal possibility distribution of the form

$$X = (x_1, x_2, \alpha', \beta'),$$

i.e. the most possible values of expected cost lie in the interval $[x_1, x_2]$ (which is the core of the trapezoidal fuzzy number $X$), and $(x_2 + \beta')$ is the upward potential and $(x_1 - \alpha')$ is the downward potential for expected costs.

In these circumstances we suggest the use of the following formula for computing fuzzy real option values

$$\text{FROV} = S_0 e^{-\delta T} N(d_1) - X e^{-rT} N(d_2), \tag{6.2}$$

where,

$$d_1 = \frac{\ln(E(S_0)/E(X)) + (r - \delta + \sigma^2/2)T}{\sigma\sqrt{T}}, \quad d_2 = d_1 - \sigma\sqrt{T}.$$

$E(S_0)$ denotes the possibilistic mean value of the present value of expected cash flows, $E(X)$ stands for the the possibilistic mean value of expected costs and $\sigma := \sigma(S_0)$ is the possibilistic variance of the present value expected cash flows.

Using formulas (1.6, 1.7) for arithmetic operations on trapezoidal fuzzy numbers we find

$$\begin{aligned}\text{FROV} = (s_1, s_2, \alpha, \beta)e^{-\delta T}N(d_1) - (x_1, x_2, \alpha', \beta')e^{-rT}N(d_2) = \\ (s_1 e^{-\delta T}N(d_1) - x_2 e^{-rT}N(d_2), s_2 e^{-\delta T}N(d_1) - x_1 e^{-rT}N(d_2), \\ \alpha e^{-\delta T}N(d_1) + \beta' e^{-rT}N(d_2), \beta e^{-\delta T}N(d_1) + \alpha' e^{-rT}N(d_2)).\end{aligned} \tag{6.3}$$

**Example 6.2.1** *Suppose we want to find a fuzzy real option value under the following assumptions,*

$$S_0 = (\$400 \text{ million}, \$600 \text{ million}, \$150 \text{ million}, \$150 \text{ million}),$$

$r = 5\%$ *per year,* $T = 5$ *years,* $\delta = 0.03$ *per year and*

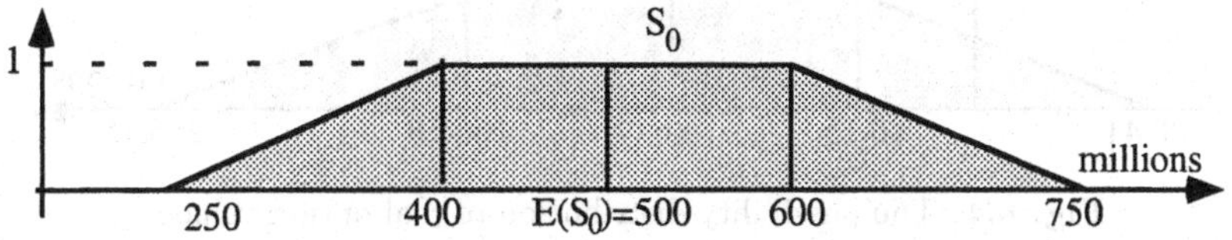


**Fig. 6.2.** The possibility distribution of expected cash flows.

$$X = (\$550 \text{ million}, \$650 \text{ million}, \$50 \text{ million}, \$50 \text{ million}),$$

*First calculate*

$$\sigma(S_0) = \sqrt{\frac{(s_2 - s_1)^2}{4} + \frac{(s_2 - s_1)(\alpha + \beta)}{6} + \frac{(\alpha + \beta)^2}{24}} = \$154.11 \text{ million},$$

*i.e.* $\sigma(S_0) = 30.8\%$,

$$E(S_0) = \frac{s_1 + s_2}{2} + \frac{\beta - \alpha}{6} = \$500 \text{ million},$$

*and*

$$E(X) = \frac{x_1 + x_2}{2} + \frac{\beta' - \alpha'}{6} = \$600 \text{ million},$$

*furthermore,*

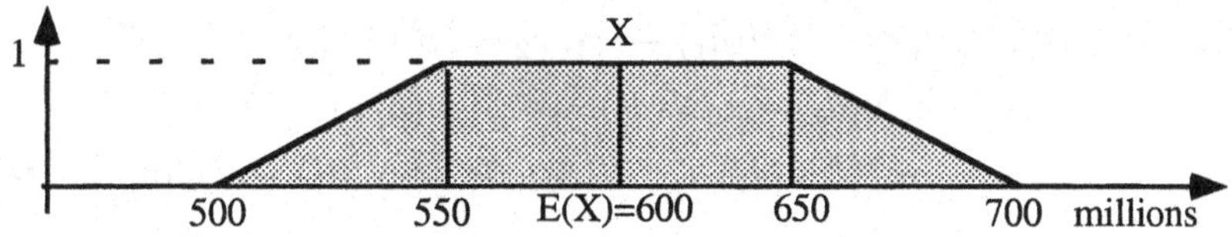


**Fig. 6.3.** The possibility distribution of expected costs.

$$N(d_1) = N\left(\frac{\ln(600/500) + (0.05 - 0.03 + 0.308^2/2) \times 5}{0.308 \times \sqrt{5}}\right) = 0.589,$$

$$N(d_2) = 0.321.$$

*Thus, from (6.2) we get that the fuzzy value of the real option is*

$$\text{FROV} = (\$40.15 \text{ million}, \$166.58 \text{ million}, \$88.56 \text{ million}, \$88.56 \text{ million}).$$

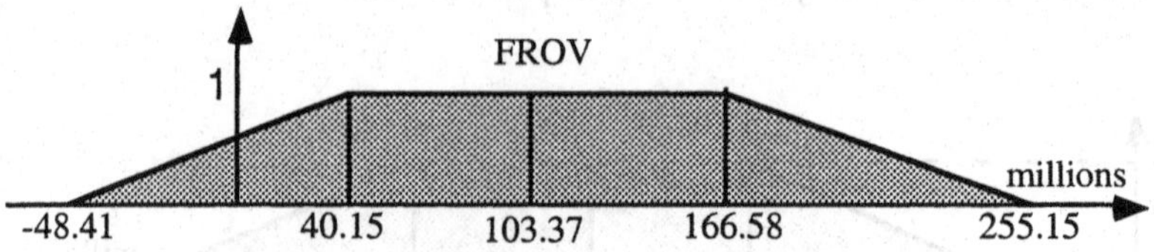


**Fig. 6.4.** The possibility distribution of real option values.

*The expected value of FROV is \$103.37 million and its most possible values are bracketed by the interval*

$$[\$40.15 \text{ million}, \$166.58 \text{ million}]$$

*the downward potential (i.e. the maximal possible loss) is \$48.41* million, *and the upward potential (i.e. the maximal possible gain) is \$255.15* million.

Suppose now that $X_0 = (x_1, x_2, \alpha', \beta')$ denotes the *present value* of expected costs. Then the equation for fuzzy real option value (6.2) can be written in the following form

$$\text{FROV} = S_0 e^{-\delta T} N(d_1) - X_0 N(d_2)$$

where,

$$d_1 = \frac{\ln(E(S_0)/E(X_0)) + (r - \delta + \sigma^2/2)T}{\sigma\sqrt{T}}, \quad d_2 = d_1 - \sigma\sqrt{T}$$

In this case we get

$$\begin{aligned} \text{FROV} &= (s_1, s_2, \alpha, \beta) e^{-\delta T} N(d_1) - (x_1, x_2, \alpha', \beta') N(d_2) \\ &= (s_1 e^{-\delta T} N(d_1) - x_2 N(d_2), s_2 e^{-\delta T} N(d_1) - x_1 N(d_2), \\ &\qquad \alpha e^{-\delta T} N(d_1) + \beta' N(d_2), \beta e^{-\delta T} N(d_1) + \alpha' N(d_2)). \quad (6.4) \end{aligned}$$

**Example 6.2.2** *Suppose we want to find a fuzzy real option value under the following assumptions,*

$$S_0 = (\$400 \text{ million}, \$600 \text{ million}, \$150 \text{ million}, \$150 \text{ million}),$$

$r = 5\%$ *per year,* $T = 5$ *years,* $\delta = 0.03$ *per year and*

$$X_0 = (\$550 \text{ million}, \$650 \text{ million}, \$50 \text{ million}, \$50 \text{ million}),$$

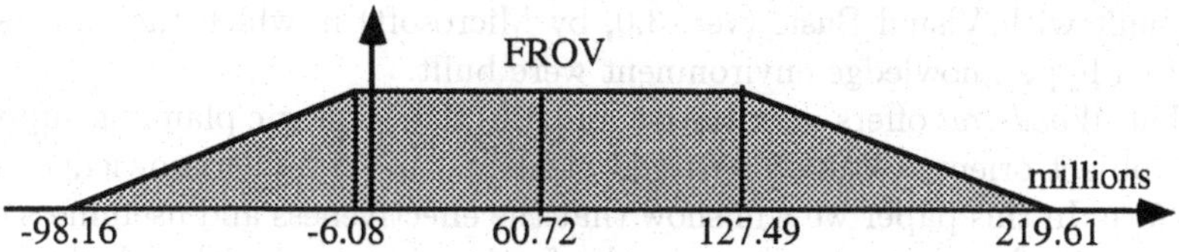


**Fig. 6.5.** The possibility distribution of real option values.

*Then from (6.4) we get that the fuzzy value of the real option is*

$$\text{FROV} = (-\$6.08 \text{ million}, \$127.49 \text{ million}, \$92.12 \text{ million}, \$92.12 \text{ million}).$$

*The expected value of FROV is \$60.72 million and its most possible values are bracketed by the interval*

$$[-\$6.08 \text{ million}, \$127.49 \text{ million}]$$

*the downward potential (i.e. the maximal possible loss) is \$98.16* million, *and the upward potential (i.e. the maximal possible gain) is \$219.61* million.

In this Section we have considered the *real option rule* for capital investment decisions in a more realistic setting, namely, when the present values of expected cash flows and expected costs are estimated by trapezoidal fuzzy numbers.

## 6.3 The Woodstrat project

*Strategic Management* is defined as a system of action programs which form sustainable competitive advantages for a corporation, its divisions and its business units in a strategic planning period.

A research team of the IAMSR institute has developed a support system for strategic management, called the *Woodstrat*, in two major Finnish forest industry corporations in 1992-96. The system is modular and is built around the actual business logic of strategic management in the two corporations, i.e. the main modules cover the *market position*, the *competitive position*, the *productivity position* and the *profitability* and *financing positions* . The innovation in *Woodstrat* is that these modules are linked together in a hyperknowledge fashion, i.e. when a strong market position is built in some market segment it will have an immediate impact on profitability through links running from key assumptions on expected developments to the projected income statement. There are similar links making the competitive position interact with the market position, and the productivity position interact with both the market and the competitive positions, and with the profitability and financing positions. The basis for this is rather unusual: the *Woodstrat* system was built with Visual Basic (ver. 3.0, by Microsoft) in which the objects to create a hyperknowledge environment were built.

The *Woodstrat* offers an intuitive and effective strategic planning support with object-oriented expert systems elements and a hyperknowledge user interface. In this paper we will show that the effectiveness and usefulness of a hyperknowledge support system can be further advanced with links built on fuzzy logic and inference mechanisms developed from approximate reasoning.

### 6.3.1 Fuzzy hyperknowledge support systems

In the *Woodstrat* project we developed and implemented a support systems technology for strategic management in two major Finnish forest industry corporations in 1992-96. The development work was done interactively with the SBU management teams and involved more than 60 managers in 14 strategic business units (SBUs). The first version in 1992 was done with a Lisp-based expert system shell, which rather quickly proved to be too inflexible and conceptually too poor for interactive planning. As the shell also had some technical problems it was followed in 1993 with a full-scale prototype system in Windows/PC ToolBook (which has been described as a "hyperknowledge environment") which was implemented and tested in both corporations; the most recent version, finished and implemented during Spring 1994, is built with Windows/Visual Basic, in which all the expert systems and hyperknowledge features of both the Lisp and Toolbook versions have been constructed as objects, with their elements designed to jointly perform the hyperknowledge functions. Progress reports on the system have been reported in [29, 304, 305] and [306].

In terms of technology, the *Woodstrat* is a hybrid of an object-oriented expert system and a hyperknowledge system. It is built with Visual Basic (version 3.0) in which the expert and hyperknowledge properties of the previous prototypes in Lisp and Toolbook were reconstructed. As it is a Windows software we could fully exploit the graphical user interface (GUI) technology; we have used the multiple document interface (MDI), the object linking and embedding (OLE), dynamic data exchange (DDE) and the effective graphics routines of Windows; we made the system user supportable and intuitive by calling procedures in dynamic-link libraries (DLL). The system is run on portable PCs that allows the user to allocate time with the system out of office. The end result was that the *Woodstrat* is actually and actively run by SBU managers, it is extensively used as a support system in strategic management and the users are actively improving the system while they use it.

As we needed a basic understanding of strategic management for our work with the managers we constructed the following conceptual skeleton:

*strategic management* is the process through which a company for a chosen planning period (i) defines its operational context, (ii) outlines and decides upon its strategic goals and long-term objectives, (iii) explores and decides upon its strengths, weaknesses, opportunities and threats, (iv) formulates its sustainable competitive advantages and (v) develops a program of actions, which exploit its compettive advantages and ensure profitability, financial balance, adaptability to sudden changes and a sound development of its capital structure.

It is quite easy to verify that this formulation is consistent with most definitions given by various authors (cf [3, 75, 255, 254]).

A definite drawback and limitation for a systematic validation of the *Woodstrat*, and the strategy formation processes we believe have taken place, have been the ongoing controversies in the field in the last few years [3, 253, 254].

The *first issue* is that much of the information and knowledge used by senior managers in strategic management, but also in top-level planning and decision making, is such that numerical precision and relevance tend to become conflicting considerations [23]. Nevertheless, Ansoff [3] shows that systematic planning with an adequate, empirical database and advanced modeling tools will give us better business results. On the other hand, there is Goguen's observation [153]: *imprecision* is the basis for richer, more meaningful and better information.

The *second* issue is the shifting dominance between various schools of thought in strategic management [255], which is an obstacle for systematic research in the field as there seems to be no consensus on what constitutes valid results.

Ansoff, who is the founder of one of the schools, has developed a *prescriptive* approach (he shows how strategic management should be done) which relies on a well-validated foundation of empirical research; a synthesis of this work was published as an applied theory of strategic behavior [3], and has been further developed into both a repeatedly tested and validated strategic success hypothesis and a practical procedure for strategic diagnosis; this latter extension was developed into an interactive computer software for strategy formulation.

Mintzberg may represent the opposing view. Ansoff [3] describes this view (which may not seem fair, but he is corroborated in Mintzberg [255]) as aimed at an implicit strategy formation, which amounts to strategy and capabilities being allowed to evolve organically, through trial and error, and thus without any explicit strategy formulation. This *emergent strategy* approach relies on the interaction of people in an organization to eventually come up with a joint strategy; Mintzberg [254] describes strategy formation as an interplay of environment, leadership and bureaucracy; emergent strategies ("not intended but realized") are different from deliberate ("intended and realized") and from unrealized ("intended but not realized") strategies. The Mintzberg approach is *descriptive* (he reports on how strategic management is done in organizations), but his empirical base seems fairly limited for the taxonomy and the generalizing conclusions he offers [3].

The *third* issue is that Mintzberg declares strategic planning a fallacy (cf [255]), which cannot fail to provoke discussions about the validity of more systematic approaches - like using support systems in strategic management. His arguments are structured around what he calls the basic assumptions behind strategic planning (cf [255], pp. 221-225):

- *assumptions of formalization* - the strategy making process can be programmed by the use of systems;
- *assumptions of detachment* - thought must be detached from action, strategy from operations, ostensible thinkers from real doers, and, therefore, "strategists" from the objects of their strategies;
- *assumption of quantification* - the strategy making process is driven by "hard data", comprising quantitative aggregates of the detailed "facts" about the organization and its environment;
- *assumption of predetermination* - because the context for strategy making is stable, or at least predictable, the process itself as well as its consequence (strategies) can be predetermined;

Mintzbergs conclusion on strategic planning is damning and elegant (cf [255], page 321): "Because analysis is not synthesis, strategic planning is not strategy formation".

Here it is sufficient to point out that *Woodstrat* was built and implemented without any need for the assumptions:

(i) *re formalization*: the strategy making process is supported, not programmed;
(ii) *re detachment*: the strategies are formulated by the SBU managers themselves;
(iii) *re quantification*: the system is built around both hard facts and qualitative assessments, and
(iv) *re predetermination*: the systems design is aimed at a dynamic, complex environment in which teams of SBU managers jointly form their strategies. This despite the fact that Wood- strat basically is an analytical tool.

The reason for this is the *hyperknowledge* approach we have used in *Woodstrat*; the theory behind it is a fairly recent one (cf [62, 231, 149]). Chang et al ([62], page 30) introduced it as a cognitive metaphor,

> ...we might conceive of an ideal DSS as a knowledge-rich environment in which a decision maker is immersed. In this environment, the decision maker is allowed to contact and manipulate knowledge embodied in any of a wide range of interrelated concepts. The decision maker is able to navigate spontaneously through the DSS's concepts in either a direct or associative fashion, pausing at a concept currently in focus to interact with it or an image of it. The type of interaction that is possible depends on the nature of the concept

or its image. A decision support environment ideally is an extension of the user's private cognitive world, pushing back cognitive limits on knowledge representation. Its knowledge processing capabilities augment the user's mental skills, overcoming cognitive limits on the speed and capacity of strictly human knowledge processing.

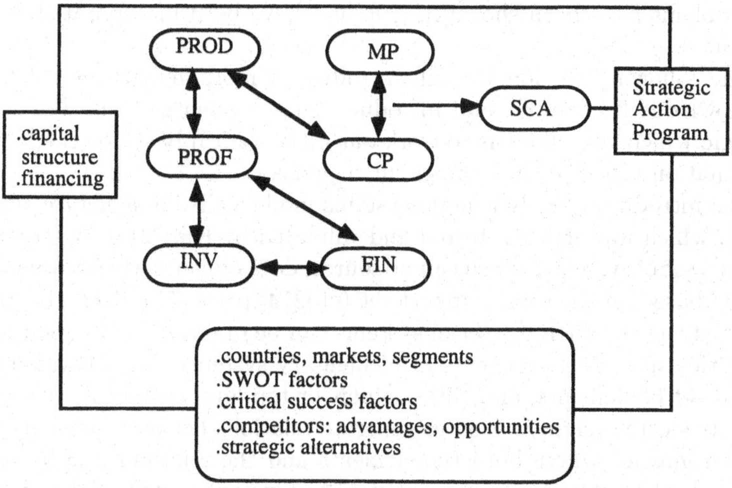


**Fig. 6.6.** Essential elements of the strategy building process.

In our work with the *Woodstrat* this metaphor was conceived of as a system of sets of concepts (cf fig.6.6): (i) to formulate visions of sustainable competitive advantages in terms of MP, CP, INV, FIN, PROD and PROF; (ii) to outline and define the operational context in terms of countries, markets, SWOT-factors and competitors, (iii) to formulate and define strategic action programs for the SBUs and co-ordinate them with corporate programs, and, (iv) to evaluate the consequences of strategic action programs in terms of profitability, capital structure and financing.

In the *Woodstrat* the SBU manager works in a hyperknowledge environment: he can start with any module (MP, for instance) and then work out the interdependencies and interactions of this module with all or any of the others (CP, INV, FIN, PROD and PROF); he can do benchmarking with external data or with the knowledge base of competitors, success factors and strategic alternatives and work out the implications in the modules; there is a MEMO- function to allow him to record and evaluate any insights he may want to interact on with his colleagues.

There are some useful characteristics of a hyperknowledge environment (cf [62]): (i) the user can navigate through and work with diverse concepts; (ii) concepts can be different epistemologically, (iii) concepts can be organized in cognitive maps, (iv) the concepts can be made interrelated and interdependent, (v) relations can be structured or dynamic, and (vi) relations can change with or adapt to the context.

There are also a couple of problems with hyperknowledge (cf [231]): (vii) it has turned out to be too informal and unstructured for handling complex problems, and (viii) users get lost in a conceptually over-rich environment, i.e. they lose touch with the task they try to accomplish. Some ways to handle these problems have been shown in [29], and have been incorporated in the *Woodstrat.*

In the following section we will introduce a more general model for a hyperknowledge framework, and introduce some elements of fuzzy sets and fuzzy logic which will allow us to work out a theoretical basis for the knowledge formation processes in strategic management.

Let us introduce a fairly general systems model called a *structure system* [214, 22], which was created, tested and validated by Klir [213]. A structure system is a set of systems, which can be source, data or generative systems but should be based on the same support set (cf [214] page 177); it can be given a specific structure; then the set of systems can be organized (hierarchically) in categories such as (i) elements or elementary systems, (ii) subsystems or organized set of elements, and (iii) a super- or top level system.

The structure system is used to generate relations between elements and their environment, where both the elements and the relations can be given some chosen characteristics and functions. A structure system is defined by,

$$\Upsilon_{3n} = \langle E, e_\Theta, \Gamma_N, f_N, C \rangle$$

where E is a finite, nonempty set of identifiers of elements; $e_\Theta$ is the environment; $\Gamma_N$ is a nonemptive set of neutral generative systems; $f_N$: E $\longrightarrow$ $\Gamma_N$ is a function which identifies a particular generative system for each element; $C$ is a matrix of couplings between all parts of the elements as well as between individual elements and the environment.

When it is adapted to the strategic management context we have designed here the structure system should be built around the following elements and given the following properties,

$$\Upsilon_{SM} = \langle \mathbf{MP}, \mathbf{CP}, \mathbf{INV}, \mathbf{FIN}, \mathbf{PROD}, \mathbf{PROF}, \Gamma_H, \Gamma_T, \Gamma_L \rangle$$

where **MP, CP, INV, FIN, PROD,** and **PROF** are finite, nonempty sets of identifiers of elements which are necessary and sufficient representations of the concepts we need to form market and competitive positions, investments, productivity and financing. Some of the elements are based on empirical facts and can be interpreted as standard sets; some elements need a qualitative representation and should then be interpreted with fuzzy sets [333]. The context is formed by the concepts

$$\langle \mathbf{MP}, \mathbf{CP}, \mathbf{INV}, \mathbf{FIN}, \mathbf{PROD}, \mathbf{PROF} \rangle$$

and the generative systems, which are identified with particular elements or subsystems. The systems constructs $\Gamma_H$, $\Gamma_H$ and $\Gamma_L$ are generative systems, of which $\Gamma_H$ organizes the elements of the concepts hierarchically; $\Gamma_H$ arranges elements and subsystems in temporal sequences, which creates chains of cause-effect relationships; with $\Gamma_L$ elements and subsystems are linked with some logical properties. Then we have,

$$\Upsilon_H = \langle \mathbf{MP}, \mathbf{CP}, \mathbf{INV}, \mathbf{FIN}, \mathbf{PROD}, \mathbf{PROF}, \Gamma_H \rangle \quad (6.5)$$

$$\Upsilon_T = \langle \mathbf{MP}_H, \mathbf{CP}_H, \mathbf{INV}_H, \mathbf{FIN}_H, \mathbf{PROD}_H, \mathbf{PROF}_H, \Gamma_T \rangle \quad (6.6)$$

$$\Upsilon_L = \langle \mathbf{MP}_{H,T}, \mathbf{CP}_{H,T}, \mathbf{INV}_{H,T}, \mathbf{FIN}_{H,T}, \mathbf{PROD}_{H,T}, \mathbf{PROF}_{H,T}, \Gamma_L \rangle \quad (6.7)$$

Let us now assume that $\Gamma_{L1}$ is used to link (in some sense) proper $\mathrm{MP}_{H,T}$ action programs to some observed $\mathrm{CP}_{H,T}$ events,

$$\Upsilon_{MP,CP} = \langle \mathbf{MP}_{H,T}, \mathbf{CP}_{H,T}, \Gamma_{L1} \rangle \quad (6.8)$$

and that $\Gamma_{L2}$ correspondingly can be used to link proper $\mathrm{MP}_{H,T}$ action programs to some observed both $\mathrm{CP}_{H,T}$ and $\mathrm{PROD}_{H,T}$ events ,

$$\Upsilon_{MP,CP,PRO} = \langle \mathbf{MP}_{H,T}, \mathbf{CP}_{H,T}, \mathbf{PROD}_{H,T}, \Gamma_{L2} \rangle \quad (6.9)$$

These constructs can be extended to cover all combinations of concepts, but (6.8) and (6.9) are sufficient to illustrate the principles.

The generative systems $\Gamma_{L1}$ and $\Gamma_{L2}$ are normally rather general and non-structured when designed to operate on standard sets; in some cases they are random and the resulting structure systems should be tested for consistency and usefulness (cf [164]). If we need to further define "proper" - as can be expected - some simple form of $\langle if \ldots then \rangle$ - connectives will do; we could have, for instance:

$$\langle \text{ if [some } \mathbf{CP}_{H,T} \text{and some } \mathbf{PROF}_{H,T}$$

$$\text{event] then [some } \mathbf{MP}_{H,T} \text{ action program]} \rangle$$

It has been shown (cf [22] ) that structure systems similar to (6.9) can serve as a basis for very operational applications, such as mathematical programming models with both single and multiple objective functions.

This is, of course, not quite enough as a knowledge base for strategic management; with the structure systems, as we now have constructed them, we are able to describe possible programs of action to build market and competitive positions, etc. with conceptual elements organized hierarchically and temporally (with 6.5 and 6.6); we can describe logical connectives between the elements (with 6.7); we can define logical links between action programs and observed events (with 6.8) with temporal and hierarchical reference points, and we can extend this description to all the concepts we have in the structure system (with 6.9 and extensions). This is normally sufficient for building and implementing a support system if we have some good software tool available.

The elements forming the sets and the generative systems are normally constructed as numerical sets. We need a better conceptual framework in order to get more substance in the structure system $\Upsilon_{SM}$ - one way to expand beyond the numerical sets is to introduce fuzzy sets and develop the system to include verbal concepts [333]. We should also use some more advanced form of logical links to be able to move beyond descriptions and to create a basis for explanations, conclusions and predictions.

A possible solution is to redefine the structure systems with the help of hyperknowledge-functions, which are built around linguistic organizers (quantifiers) and fuzzy logic.

Let us find out what this could be: *hyperknowledge* is formed as a system of sets of interlinked concepts [62], much in the same way as hypertext is built with interlinked text strings [263]; then hyperknowledge-functions would be constructs which link concepts/systems of concepts in some predetermined or wanted way. As we want them to retain the structure of structure systems, they should also "add" some hierarchical and temporal organization to the concepts, and should provide us with some logical links of the type defined in (6.8 and 6.9). Then we could have the following type of constructs:

$$\Psi_{SM} = \langle \mathbf{MP,CP,\ INV,\ FIN,\ PROD,\ PROF}, \Phi_H, \Phi_T, \Phi_L \rangle \tag{6.10}$$

where the generative systems $\Phi_H$, $\Phi_T$, $\Phi_L$ are linguistic organizers/quantifiers based on fuzzy sets [333]; this allows us to build the concepts both on empirical facts and qualitative assessments, to represent them with either mathematical models or linguistic variables, and to use them in a verbal, more descriptive and understandable form.

Much in the same way as we could use generative systems in (6.5)-(6.7), we can also use fuzzy set theory-based generative systems to build the structures of (6.10). The systems $\Phi_H$, $\Phi_T$ are used to organize action programs hierarchically and in time; the system $\Phi_H$ can be represented as "aggregation / disaggregation", which then will result in a hierarchical structure of more general vs. more detailed concepts; correspondingly, the system $\Phi_T$ will show interdependence in time between action programs and/or events in the operational context (cf (6.11)-(6.13)):

$$\Psi_H = \langle \mathbf{MP,CP,\ INV,\ FIN,\ PROD,\ PROF}, \Phi_H \rangle \tag{6.11}$$

$$\Psi_T = \langle \mathbf{MP}_H, \mathbf{CP}_H, \mathbf{INV}_H, \mathbf{FIN}_H, \mathbf{PROD}_H, \mathbf{PROF}_H, \Phi_T \rangle \tag{6.12}$$

$$\Psi_L = \langle \mathbf{MP}_{H,T}, \mathbf{CP}_{H,T}, \mathbf{INV}_{H,T}, \mathbf{FIN}_{H,T}, \mathbf{PROD}_{H,T}, \mathbf{PROF}_{H,T}, \Phi_L \rangle \tag{6.13}$$

With fuzzy set representations of the concepts we can now get more detailed systems constructs:

$$\mathbf{MP}_{H,T} = f_1[\text{volume, price, market share, competitive position}] \quad (6.14)$$

where,

$$\begin{aligned}
\text{volume} &= f_{11}\ [\text{market growth, demand, macro factors; } \textit{data}] \\
\text{price} &= f_{12}\ [\text{market growth, price hist., demand, macro fact.; } \textit{data}] \\
\text{market share} &= f_{13}\ [\text{market growth, competitors, CSFs; } \textit{assessments}] \\
\text{comp. pos.} &= f_{14}\ [\text{CSFs, competitors, strategies; } \textit{assessments}] \\
f_1 &= f_{11} \wedge f_{12} \wedge f_{13} \wedge f_{14},
\end{aligned}$$

and each $f_{ij}$ is an operator forming fuzzy sets of the type introduced by Zadeh [333]; the combination of the operators is carried out with fuzzy combination operators.

$$\mathbf{CP}_{H,T} = f_2[\text{market growth, CSFs, competitors, market position}] \quad (6.15)$$

where,

$$\begin{aligned}
\text{market growth} &= f_{21}\ [\text{customers, demand, macro factors; } \textit{data}] \\
\text{CSFs} &= f_{22}\ [\text{techn., logistics, customer knowl.; } \textit{data, assessments}] \\
\text{competitors} &= f_{23}\ [\text{technology, logistics, CSFs; } \textit{data, assessments}] \\
\text{market posit.} &= f_{24}\ [\text{volume, price, market share; } \textit{data}] \\
f_2 &= f_{21} \wedge f_{22} \wedge f_{23} \wedge f_{24},
\end{aligned}$$

and the quality of the assessments is dependent on the knowledge we can get about the competition.

$$\mathbf{INV}_{H,T} = f_3[\text{technology, CSFs, product mix, market position}] \quad (6.16)$$

where,

$$\begin{aligned}
\text{technology} &= f_{31}\ [\text{customer demand, competitors, productivity; } \textit{data}] \\
\text{CSFs} &= f_{32}\ [\text{techn., logistics, customer knowl.; } \textit{data, assessments}] \\
\text{product mix} &= f_{33}\ [\text{customer demand, competitors, CSFs; } \textit{assessments}] \\
\text{market position} &= f_{34}\ [\text{volume, price, market share; } \textit{data}]] \\
f_3 &= f_{31} \wedge f_{32} \wedge f_{33} \wedge f_{34},
\end{aligned}$$

and the knowledge about customers and the competition can be obtained from benchmarking studies in the market.

$$\mathbf{PROD}_{H,T} = f_4[\text{factors, technology, investments, product mix}] \quad (6.17)$$

where,

$$\begin{aligned}
\text{factors} &= f_{41}\ [\text{factor productivity, techn., investments; } \textit{data, assess.}]\\
\text{technology} &= f_{42}\ [\text{volume, price, competitors, productivity; } \textit{data, assess.}]\\
\text{investments} &= f_{43}\ [\text{technology, product mix, volume, price; } \textit{data, assess.}]\\
\text{product mix} &= f_{44}\ [\text{customer demand, CSFs, competitors; } \textit{assess.}]\\
f_4 &= f_{41} \wedge f_{42} \wedge f_{43} \wedge f_{44},
\end{aligned}$$

and the measuring of productivity, in principle, is well-defined and straightforward; in practice it has turned out to be complex and inconsistent, as there is much controversy on which factors to include and how to estimate relations between the factors and a productivity measure.

Analogously with (6.8)-(6.9) we need some logical connectors to build the structure system; let us now work through the logical generative systems $\Phi_{L1}$ and $\Phi_{L2}$,

$$\Psi_{MP,CP} = \langle \mathbf{MP}_{H,T}, \mathbf{CP}_{H,T}, \Phi_{L1} \rangle \qquad (6.18)$$

$$\Psi_{MP,CP,PROD} = \langle \mathbf{MP}_{H,T}, \mathbf{CP}_{H,T}, \mathbf{PROD}_{H,T}, \Phi_{L2} \rangle \qquad (6.19)$$

which are built around fuzzy logic and linguistic quantifiers ([201, 338, 340]).

It turns out that a number of practical constructs for our present purposes have been introduced in fuzzy logic (cf [338]): *generalized modus ponens* [GMP, GMPT]

$$\begin{array}{l} x \text{ is } A \rightarrow y \text{ is } B \\ x \text{ is } A' \\ \hline \\ y \text{ is } B' \end{array} \qquad \begin{array}{l} (x \text{ is } A \rightarrow y \text{ is } B) \text{ is } \tau_1 \\ (x \text{ is } A) \text{ is } \tau_2 \\ \hline \\ y \text{ is } B' \end{array}$$

where the reasoning scheme with truth values allows the conclusion [$y$ is $B'$] only with some classification. Magrez and Smets [238] have developed operational versions of the GMP scheme, and they show that this operationalisation can be done with fuzzy versions of some classical implication rules: *S-rules* and *R-rules.*

As we then have a variety of implications we can use, and as it is shown in [341] that it is possible to use an "imprecise" modus ponens scheme, we could then use it on (6.14)-(6.17) to carry out necessary assessments from imprecise data and knowledge. We need, however, to add to the set of instruments a couple of more fuzzy logic constructs (cf Zadeh, [341]): *the projection rule* [PR], *the compositional rule* [CR], *the extension principle* [EP] which we now could use in various combinations to build the structure system; the generative systems $\Phi_{L1}$ and $\Phi_{L2}$ could, for instance, be designed in the following way:

$$\Phi_{L1}[\text{GMPT}]:$$

$$\begin{array}{l} [\text{a } \mathbf{CP}_{H,T} \text{ event occurs} \rightarrow \text{an } \mathbf{MP}_{H,T} \text{ action program is proper}] \text{ is } \tau_1 \\ [\text{a strong } \mathbf{CP}_{H,T} \text{ event (competitor) occurs}] \text{ is } \tau_2 \\ \hline \\ \text{a strong } \mathbf{MP}_{H,T} \text{ action program is proper} \end{array}$$

$\Phi_{L2}$[EP, GMPT, PR, CR] :

.a price reduction is a competitor event

---

.a strong price reduction is a $\mathbf{CP}_{H,T}$ event

[a $\mathbf{CP}_{H,T}$ event (competitor) occurs $\rightarrow$ action program is proper] is $\tau_1$
[a strong $\mathbf{CP}_{H,T}$ event (competitor) occurs] is $\tau_1$

---

a strong $\mathbf{MP}_{H,T}$ action program is proper

.a strong ($\mathbf{MP}_{H,T}$, $\mathbf{CP}_{H,T}$) is mostly unprofitable

---

.$\mathbf{MP}_{H,T}$ is mostly unprofitable

or,

.a strong ($\mathbf{MP}_{H,T}$, $\mathbf{CP}_{PH,T}$ ) is mostly unprofitable
.$\mathbf{CP}_{H,T}$ is moderate

---

.$\mathbf{MP}_{H,T}$ is moderate mostly unprofitable

The generative systems $\Phi_{L1}$ and $\Phi_{L2}$ can be further developed to serve as structure systems for the elements of (6.14)-(6.17); let us now consider the following modification of $\Phi_{L2}$[EP, GMPT, PR, CR]:

$$\mathbf{MP}_{H,T} = \Phi_{\mathbf{MP}} \text{ [volume, price, market share, competitive position]} \quad (6.20)$$

where,

$$\begin{aligned}
\text{volume} &= \phi_1 \text{ [market growth, demand, macro factors; } \textit{data}] \\
\text{price} &= \phi_2 \text{ [market growth, price hist., demand, macro fact.; } \textit{data}] \\
\text{market share} &= \phi_3 \text{ [market growth, competitors, CSFs; } \textit{assessments}] \\
\text{compet. pos.} &= \phi_4 \text{ [CSFs, competitors, strategies, } \textit{assessments}] \\
\Phi_{\mathbf{MP}} &= \phi_1 \circ \phi_2 \circ \phi_3 \circ \phi_3 .
\end{aligned}$$

It is shown in [22] that the generative systems constructs become simpler and more easily validated when we move down to the detailed, elementary systems level and as the membership functions of the fuzzy sets get anchored in empirical data. Now we can reformulate (6.14)-(6.17) in terms of the fuzzy logic generative systems (the constructs are only indicated):

$$\mathbf{MP}_{H,T} \leftarrow \Phi_{\mathbf{MP}}\{\phi_{1\mathbf{MP}} \circ \phi_{2\mathbf{MP}} \circ \phi_{3\mathbf{MP}} \circ \phi_{4\mathbf{MP}}\} \quad (6.21)$$
$$\mathbf{CP}_{H,T} \leftarrow \Phi_{\mathbf{CP}}\{\phi_{1\mathbf{CP}} \circ \phi_{2\mathbf{CP}} \circ \phi_{3\mathbf{CP}} \circ \phi_{4\mathbf{CP}}\} \quad (6.22)$$
$$\mathbf{INV}_{H,T} \leftarrow \Phi_{\mathbf{INV}}\{\phi_{1\mathbf{INV}} \circ \phi_{2\mathbf{INV}} \circ \phi_{3\mathbf{INV}} \circ \phi_{4\mathbf{INV}}\} \quad (6.23)$$
$$\mathbf{PROD}_{H,T} \leftarrow \Phi_{\mathbf{PROD}}\{\phi_{1\mathbf{PROD}} \circ \phi_{2\mathbf{PROD}} \circ \phi_{3\mathbf{PROD}} \circ \phi_{4\mathbf{PROD}}\} \quad (6.24)$$

With these constructs it is now easy to build the interdependencies we have included in the definitions of the various modules (cf (6.14)-(6.17)):

$$\mathbf{MP}_{H,T} \leftarrow \Phi_{\mathbf{MP}} \wedge \Phi_{\mathbf{CP}} \tag{6.25}$$
$$\mathbf{CP}_{H,T} \leftarrow \Phi_{\mathbf{CP}} \wedge \Phi_{\mathbf{MP}} \wedge \Phi_{\mathbf{PROD}} \tag{6.26}$$
$$\mathbf{INV}_{H,T} \leftarrow \Phi_{\mathbf{INV}} \wedge \Phi_{\mathbf{MP}} \tag{6.27}$$
$$\mathbf{PROD}_{H,T} \leftarrow \Phi_{\mathbf{PROD}} \wedge \Phi_{\mathbf{INV}} \tag{6.28}$$

where the combinations are built with fuzzy connective operators. Then, finally, it is also possible to construct the concepts of the highest level with the same generative systems:

$$\text{PROF} \leftarrow \Phi_{\mathbf{MP}} \wedge \Phi_{\mathbf{CES}} \wedge \Phi_{\mathbf{PROD}} \tag{6.29}$$
$$\text{CAP STR} \leftarrow \Phi_{\mathbf{PROD}} \wedge \Phi_{\mathbf{INV}}$$
$$\text{SUST COMP ADV} \leftarrow \Phi_{\mathbf{MP}} \wedge \Phi_{\mathbf{CP}} \wedge \Phi_{\mathbf{CES}} \wedge \Phi_{\mathbf{INV}} \wedge \Phi_{\mathbf{PROD}}$$

In (6.25)-(6.29) we have now re-created the loose systems structure we had in fig. 6.6; with the fuzzy logic constructs, and with the concepts defined by fuzzy sets, we will in a support system eventually be able to re-create the following reasoning scheme:

i. there is *some* evidence that A is becoming a cost leader in segment S;
ii. *usually* differentiation is a *good* counter strategy for cost leadership;
iii. then differentiation is a proper strategy;
iv. there is *significant* evidence that differentiation works *properly* to eliminate cost leadership benefits;
v. differentiation is a *very proper* strategy is *probable*;
vi. with a proper strategy we will get a dominating competitive position;
vii. then it is *very probable* that we get a *dominating* competitive position;

Now it is tempting to briefly return to our initial discussion of strategic management and Mintzberg's belief that *"because analysis is not synthesis, strategic planning is not strategy formation"*.

The knowledge based support system we constructed, both as the *Woodstrat* and as the fuzzy logic-based system in (6.11)-(6.29), is basically a system of analytical models which have been developed from empirical market, competitor and production data; this system has been enhanced with mathematical and logical links to analytical models, which cover investments, financing, profitability and capital structure; the overall structure - which was given hyperknowledge features with added mathematical and logical links - supports synthesis along a number of dimensions (the following is a sample):

(i) effects of critical success factors on market positions (country/market/segment);
(ii) effects of macroeconomic factors on volume and price developments in markets (country/market/segment);

(iii) effects of competitors and their critical success factors on market positions (country/market/segment);
(iv) effects of productivity on competitive positions (country/market/segment);
(v) effects of investments on productivity;
(vi) effects of productivity on profitability;
(vii) effects of product mix on profitability, market position and competitive position;
(viii) effects of customer reactions (in benchmarking tests) on market and competitive positions;
(ix) effects of product mix, market and competitive positions on long term cash flow and capital structure;
(x) effects of strategic investments (new markets, new products, new production technology, new distribution networks, strategic alliances, etc.) on market and competitive positions, profitability, productivity, long term cash flows and capital structure;

When the hyperknowledge links are built around fuzzy logic constructs the support system is enhanced with the possibility to combine analytical models with qualitative assessments; a consequence of this is that the assumptions Mintzberg listed as fundamental to strategic planning are not necessary, and the support system moves closer (or even very close) to the context of the SBU managers.

As we have seen, analysis becomes synthesis (and a synthesis can be traced to its analytical elements), strategies are being formed in the synthesis (as described by the examples in (i. - x.) above) and the support produced with the system is both analytically consistent and relevant in substance for strategic management. Hence, Mintzberg is wrong.

### 6.3.2 Cognitive maps for hyperknowledge representation

*Cognitive maps* were introduced by Axelrod [2] to represent crisp cause-effect relationships which are perceived to exist among the elements of a given environment. *Fuzzy cognitive maps* (FCM) are fuzzy signed directed graphs with feedbacks, and they model the world as a collection of concepts and causal relations between concepts [223].

When addressing strategic issues cognitive maps are used as action-oriented representations of the context the managers are discussing. They are built to show and simulate the interaction and interdependences of multiple belief systems as these are described by the participants - by necessity, these belief systems are qualitative and will change with the context and the organizations in which they are developed. They represent a way to make sure, that the intuitive belief that strategic issues should have consequences and implications, that every strategy is either constrained or enhanced by a network of other strategies, can be adequately described and supported.

For simplicity, in this Section we illustrate the strategy building process by the following fuzzy cognitive map with six states (sse Fig. 6.7) The causal

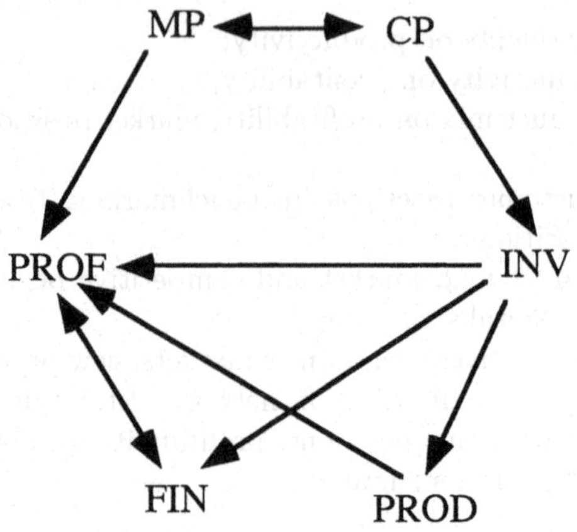


**Fig. 6.7.** Essential elements of the strategy building process.

connections between the states MP (Market position), CP (Competitive position), PROF (Profitability), FIN (Financing position), PROD (Productivity position) and INV (Investments) are derived from the opinions of managers' of different Strategic Business Units.

It should be noted that the cause-effect relationships among the elements of the strategy building process may be defined otherwise (you may want to add other elements or delete some of these, or you may draw other arrows or rules or swap their signs or weight them in some new way).

### 6.3.3 Adaptive FCM for strategy formation

It is relatively easy to create cause-effect relationships among the elements of the strategy building process, however it is time-consuming and difficult to fine-tune them. Neural nets give a shortcut to tuning fuzzy cognitive maps. The trick is to let the fuzzy causal edges change as if they were synapses (weights) in a neural net. Each arrow in Fig. 6.8 defines a fuzzy rule. We weight these rules or arrows with a number from the interval $[-1, 1]$, or alternatively we could use *word weights* like *little*, or *somewhat*, or *more or less.* The states or nodes are fuzzy too. Each state can fire to some degree from 0% to 100%. In the crisp case the nodes of the network are *on* or *off.* In a real FCM the nodes are fuzzy and fire more as more causal juice flows into them.

Adaptive fuzzy cognitive maps can learn the weights from historical data. Once the FCM is trained it lets us play what-if games (e.g. *What if demand goes up and prices remain stable? - i.e. we improve our MP*) and can predict the future.

In the following we describe a learning mechanism for the FCM of the strategy building process, and illustrate the effectiveness of the map by a simple training set. Fig. 6.8 shows the structure of the FCM of the strategy building process. Inputs of states are computed as the weighted sum of the

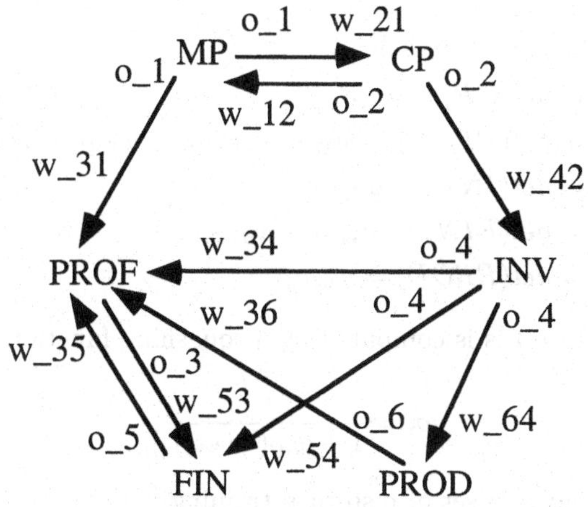


**Fig. 6.8.** Adaptive fuzzy cognitive map for the strategy formation process.

outputs of its causing states

$$\text{net} = Wo,$$

where $W$ denotes the matrix of weights, $o$ is the vector of computed outputs, and *net* is the vector of inputs to the states. In our case the weight matrix is given by

$$W = \begin{pmatrix} 0 & w_{12} & 0 & 0 & 0 & 0 \\ w_{21} & 0 & 0 & 0 & 0 & 0 \\ w_{31} & 0 & 0 & w_{34} & w_{35} & w_{36} \\ 0 & w_{42} & 0 & 0 & 0 & 0 \\ 0 & 0 & w_{53} & w_{54} & 0 & 0 \\ 0 & 0 & 0 & w_{64} & 0 & 0 \end{pmatrix}$$

where the zero elements denote no causal link between the states, and

$$\text{net} = \begin{bmatrix} \text{net}_1 \\ \text{net}_2 \\ \text{net}_3 \\ \text{net}_4 \\ \text{net}_5 \\ \text{net}_6 \end{bmatrix} = \begin{bmatrix} net(MP) \\ net(CP) \\ net(PROF) \\ net(INV) \\ net(FIN) \\ net(PROD) \end{bmatrix}$$

and

$$o = \begin{bmatrix} o_1 \\ o_2 \\ o_3 \\ o_4 \\ o_5 \\ o_6 \end{bmatrix} = \begin{bmatrix} o(MP) \\ o(CP) \\ o(PROF) \\ o(INV) \\ o(FIN) \\ o(PROD) \end{bmatrix}$$

That is,

$$\begin{aligned} \text{net}_1 &= net(MP) = w_{12}o_2, \\ \text{net}_2 &= net(CP) = w_{21}o_1, \\ \text{net}_3 &= net(PROF) = w_{31}o_1 + w_{34}o_4 + w_{35}o_5 + w_{36}o_6, \\ \text{net}_4 &= net(INV) = w_{42}o_2, \\ \text{net}_5 &= net(FIN) = w_{54}o_4 + w_{53}o_3, \\ \text{net}_6 &= net(PROD) = w_{64}o_4 \end{aligned}$$

The output of state $i$ is is computed by a squashing function

$$o_i = \frac{1}{1 + \exp(-\text{net}_i)}.$$

Suppose we are given a set of historical training data

$$(MP(t), CP(t), PROF(t), INV(t), FIN(t), PROD(t))$$

where $t = 1, \ldots, K$. Here $MP(t)$ is the observed value of the market position, $CP(t)$ is the value of the competitive position at time $t$, and so on. Using an error correction learning procedure we find the weights by minimizing the overall error

$$E(W) = \frac{1}{2}\sum_{t=1}^{K} \Big\{ (MP(t) - o_1(t))^2 + (CP(t) - o_2(t))^2$$

$$+(PROF(t) - o_3(t))^2 + (INV(t) - o_4(t))^2$$

$$+(FIN(t) - o_5(t))^2 + (PROD(t) - o_6(t))^2 \Big\},$$

where $o_i(t)$, the computed value of the $i$-th state at time $t$, is determined as

$$o_i(t) = \frac{1}{1 + \exp\left[-\text{net}_i(t-1)\right]} = \frac{1}{1 + \exp\left[-\sum_j w_{ij} o_j(t-1)\right]}$$

where $j$ is a causing state for state $i$. The weights are initialized at small random values. The rule for changing the weights of the states is derived from gradient descent method.

Consider a simple training set of historical data shown in Table 6.1. The observed values of the states are measured from the interval $[1, 5]$, where 1 stands for *weak*, 2 stands for *rather weak*, 3 stands for *medium*, 4 stands for *rather strong* and 5 stands for *strong*, intermediate values are denoted by $\{1.5, 2.5, 3.5, 4.5\}$.

For example, at reference time 7 we have a medium market position, weak-rather weak competitive position, rather strong profitability, strong investments, weak financing and rather strong productivity position. After the training we get the following weight matrix

$$W = \begin{pmatrix} 0 & 0.65 & 0 & 0 & 0 & 0 \\ 0.46 & 0 & 0 & 0 & 0 & 0 \\ 0.54 & 0 & 0 & 0.33 & 0.14 & -0.05 \\ 0 & 0.23 & 0 & 0 & 0 & 0 \\ 0 & 0 & -0.18 & 0.31 & 0 & 0 \\ 0 & 0 & 0 & 0.27 & 0 & 0 \end{pmatrix}.$$

Our findings can be interpreted as the market and competitive positions are the driving forces for the overall profitability position.

| | MP | CP | PROF | INV | FIN | PROD |
|---|---|---|---|---|---|---|
| 1. | 3 | 3 | 3 | 3 | 3 | 3 |
| 2. | 4 | 3.5 | 3.5 | 3 | 4 | 3 |
| 3. | 4 | 4 | 3.5 | 4 | 5 | 3.5 |
| 4. | 3 | 4 | 3.5 | 4 | 4 | 3.5 |
| 5. | 3 | 3.5 | 4 | 4 | 3 | 4 |
| 6. | 2 | 3 | 4 | 4 | 2 | 4 |
| 7. | 3 | 2.5 | 4 | 5 | 1 | 4 |
| 8. | 3 | 3 | 4 | 5 | 2 | 3.5 |
| 9. | 4 | 3 | 4 | 5 | 3 | 3.5 |
| 10. | 3 | 3.5 | 4 | 5 | 4 | 3 |

**Table 6.1.** A training set.

The *Woodstrat* is a *support system* for strategy formation. The links between the logical elements of the system follow an intuitive, internal logic which has gradually emerged through interactive work with the SBU-managers. This has created the foundations for a quick and effective user acceptance.

*Woodstrat* is used for strategy formation, which was seen in the use of the various modules (the actual use was traced through the Memos):

1. the database of *external data* served as an instrument to establish reference points for growth and price estimates;

2. the *Market Position (MP)* module served both analysis and synthesis; it was first used to build estimates of price and volume developments for specific product groups in specific market segments; then it was used to get a feeling for the expected development in a product group or in a country; then the estimates were reiterated until some acceptable levels were reached;
3. *The Competitive Position (CP)* module was used for similar analysis/ synthesis iterations in the same countries, product groups and market segments; now the iterations were in terms of critical success factors; reference points for these were established with analogous iterations of the critical success factors for three key competitors; the results were used to establish relative competitive positions; these positions were then used to establish a new set of reference points for the estimates of price and volume developments;
4. the MP and CP modules are then used to determine the net sales and variable costs of the income statement in the *PROF* module; when worked out with a complete set of variable and fixed costs the resulting profit is either satisfactory or non-satisfactory; in the latter case it triggers reiterations of the MP and CP modules; if satisfactory it is further evaluated in terms of capital structure, the use of funds and key ratios; on a number of reference points reiterations can be triggered;
5. the CP determines the need for investments; the corresponding module triggers the financing of these investments; reiterations are triggered by reference points in the income statement, the capital structure, the use of funds and key ratios;
6. the MP and the PROF modules update and trigger the determination of the productivity index in the PROD module; reference points induce reiterations of investments and of the MP and CP modules.

There are a number of minor processes also included in the system, but the major processes shown in (1) - (6) represent the strategy formation process.

The extensions of *Woodstrat* to a fuzzy hyperknowledge support system shown here will have the effect to (i) support approximate reasoning schemes in linking the MP, CP, PROD, PROF, INV and FIN elements of strategic management; (ii) approximate reasoning gives us conclusions from imprecise premises; (iii) fuzzy sets and fuzzy logic support a synthesis of quantitative and qualitative concepts, which develops strategic planning to a strategy formation process.

## 6.4 Soft computing methods for reducing the bullwhip effect

In this Section consider a series of companies in a supply chain, each of which orders from its immediate upstream collaborators. Usually, the retailer's order do not coincide with the actual retail sales. The *bullwhip effect* refers to the phenomenon where orders to the supplier tend to have larger variance than sales to the buyer (i.e. demand distortion), and the distortion propagates upstream in an amplified form (i.e. variance amplification). We show that if the members of the supply chain share information with intelligent support technology, and agree on better and better fuzzy estimates (as time advances) on future sales for the upcoming period, then the bullwhip effect can be significantly reduced.

The *Bullwhip Effect* has been the focus of theoretical work on and off during the last 20 years. However, the first papers reporting research findings in a more systematic fashion [232] have been published only recently. The effect was first identified in the 1980'es through the simulation experiment, *The Beer Game*, which demonstrated the effects of distorted information in the supply chain (which is one of the causes of the bullwhip effect).

A number of examples has been published which demonstrate the bullwhip effect, e.g. the Pampers case: (i) P & G has over the years been successful producers and sellers of Pampers, and they have seen that babies are reliable and steady consumers; (ii) the retailers in the region, however, show fluctuating sales, although the demand should be easy to estimate as soon as the number of babies in the region is known; (iii) P & G found out that the orders they received from distributors showed a strong variability, in fact much stronger than could be explained by the fluctuating sales of the retailers; finally, (iv) when P & G studied their own orders to 3M for raw material they found these to be wildly fluctuating, actually much more than could be explained by the orders from the distributors. Systematic studies of these fluctuations with the help of inventory models revealed the bullwhip effect.

The context we have chosen for this study is the forest products industry and the markets for fine paper products. The chain is thus a business-to-business supply chain, and we will show that the bullwhip effect is as dominant as in the business-to-consumer supply chain.

The key driver appears to be that the variability of the estimates or the forecasts of the demand for the paper products seems to amplify as the orders move up the supply chain from the printing houses, through the distributors and wholesalers to the producer of the paaper mills.

We found out that the bullwhip effect will have a number of negative effects in the paper products industry, and that it will cause significant inefficiencies:

1. <u>Excessive inventory investments</u> throughout the supply chain as printing houses, distributors, wholesalers, logistics operators and paper mills need to safeguard themselves against the variations.
2. <u>Poor customer service</u> as some part of the supply chain runs out of products due to the variability and insufficient means for coping with the variations.
3. <u>Lost revenues</u> due to shortages, which have been caused by the variations.

4. The productivity of invested capital in operations becomes substandard as revenues are lost.
5. Decision-makers react to the fluctuations in demand and make investment decisions or change capacity plans to meet peak demands. These decisions are probably misguided, as peak demands may be eliminated by reorganizations of the supply chain.
6. Demand variations cause variations in the logistics chain, which again cause fluctuations in the planned use of transportation capacity. This will again produce sub-optimal transportation schemes and increase transportation costs.
7. Demand fluctuations caused by the bullwhip effect may cause missed production schedules, which actually are completely unnecessary, as there are no real changes in the demand, only inefficiencies in the supply chain.

In two recent studies [232, 233], three more reasons have been identified to cause the bullwhip effect besides the demand forecasts: these include (i) order batching, (ii) price fluctuations and (iii) rationing and shortage gaming.

The *order batching* will appear in two different forms: (i) periodic ordering and (ii) push ordering. In the first case there is a number of reasons for building batches of individual orders. The costs for frequent order processing may be high, which will force customers into periodic ordering; this will in most cases destroy customer demand patterns. There are material requirement planning systems in use, which are run periodically and thus will cause that orders are placed periodically. Logistics operators often favor full truck load (FTL) batches and will determine their tariffs accordingly. These reasons for periodic ordering are quite rational, and will, when acted upon, amplify variability and contribute to the bullwhip effect. Push ordering occurs, as the sales people employed by the paper mills try to meet their end-of-quarter or end-of-year bonus plans. The effect of this is to amplify the variability with orders from customers overlapping end-of-quarter and beginning-of-quarter months, to destroy connections with the actual demand patterns of customers and to contribute to the bullwhip effect [232].

The paper mills initiate and control the *price fluctuations* for various reasons. Customers are driven to buy in larger quantities by attractive offers on quantity discounts, or price discounts. Their behavior is quite rational: to make the optimal use of opportunities when prices shift between high and low. The problem introduced by this behavior is that buying patterns will not reflect consumption patterns anymore, customers buy in quantities which do not reflect their needs. This will amplify the bullwhip effect. The consequences are that the paper mills (rightfully) suffer: manufacturing is on overtime during campaigns, premium transportation rates are paid during peak seasons and paper mills suffer damages in overflowing storage spaces [232].

The *rationing* and *shortage gaming* occurs when demand exceeds supply. If the paper mills once have met shortages with a rationing of customer deliveries, the customers will start to exaggerate their real needs when there is a fear that supply will not cover demand. The shortage of DRAM chips and the following strong fluctuations in demand was a historic case of the rationing and shortage game. The bullwhip effect will amplify even further if customers are allowed to cancel orders when their real demand is satisfied. The gaming leaves little information on real demand and will confuse the demand patterns of customers [232, 233]. On the other hand, there have not been any cases of shortage of production capacity of the paper products in the last decade; there is normally excess capacity. Thus we have excluded this possible cause from further study.

It is a fact that these four causes of the bullwhip effect may be hard to monitor, and even harder to control in the forest products industry. We should also be aware of the fact that the four causes may interact, and act in concert, and that the resulting combined effects are not clearly understood, neither in theory nor in practice. It is also probably the case that the four causes are dependent on the supply chain's infrastructure and on the strategies used by the various actors.

The factors driving the bullwhip effect appear to form a hyper-complex, i.e. a system where factors show complex interactive patterns. The theoretical challenges posed by a hyper-complex merit study, even if significant economic consequences would not have been involved. The costs incurred by the consequences of the bullwhip effect (estimated at 200-300 MFIM annually for a 300 kton paper mill) offer a few more reasons for carrying out serious work on the mechanisms driving the bullwhip.

Thus, we have built a theory to explain at least some of the factors and their interactions, and we have created a support system to come to terms with them and to find effective means to either reduce or eliminate the bullwhip effect.

With a little simplification there appears to be three possible approaches to counteract the bullwhip effect:

1. Find some means to share information from downstream the supply chain with all the preceding actors.
2. Build channel alignment with the help of some co-ordination of pricing, transportation, inventory planning and ownership - when this is not made illegal by anti-trust legislation.
3. Improve operational efficiency by reducing cost and by improving on lead times.

The first approach can probably be focused on finding some good information technology to accomplish the information sharing, as this can be shown to be beneficial for all the actors operating in the supply chain. We should probably implement some internet-based support technology for intelligent sharing of validated demand data.

The second approach can first be focused on some non-controversial element, such as the co-ordination of transportation or inventory planning, and then the alignment can be widened to explore possible interactions with other elements.

The third approach is probably straight-forward: find operational inefficiencies, then find ways to reduce costs and to improve on lead times, and thus explore if these solutions can be generalised for more actors in the supply chain.

The most effective - and the most challenging - effort will be to find ways to combine elements of all three approaches and to find synergistic programs to eliminate the bullwhip effect, which will have the added benefit of being very resource-effective.

### 6.4.1 The bullwhip effect, some additional details

In 1998-99 we carried out a research program on the bullwhip effect with two major fine paper producers. The project, known as EM-S Bullwhip, worked with actual data and in interaction with senior decision makers. The two corporate members of the EM-S Bullwhip consortium had observed the bullwhip effects in their own markets and in their own supply chains for fine paper products. They also readily agreed that the bullwhip effect is causing problems and significant costs, and that any good theory or model, which could give some insight into dealing with the bullwhip effect, would be a worthwhile effort in terms of both time and resources.

Besides the generic reasons we introduced in the previous section, there are a few practical reasons why we get the bullwhip effect in the fine paper markets.

The first reason is to be found in the structure of the market (see Fig.6.9). The paper mills do not deal directly with their end-customers, the printing houses, but fine paper products are distributed through wholesalers, merchants and retailers. The paper mills may (i) own some of the operators in the market supply chain, (ii) they may share some of them with competitors or (iii) the operators may be completely independent and bound to play the market game with the paper producers. The operators in the market supply chain do not willingly share their customer and market data, information and knowledge with the paper mills.

Thus, the paper producers do not get *neither precise nor updated information* on the real customer demand, but get it in a filtered and/or manipulated way from the market supply chain operators. Market data is collected and summarized by independent data providers, and market forecasts are produced by professional forest products consultants and market study agencies, but it still appears that these macro level studies and forecasts do not apply exactly to the markets of a single paper producer. The market information needed for individual operations still needs to come from the individual market, and this information is not available to paper mills.

The second, more practical, reason for the bullwhip effect to occur is found earlier in the supply chain. The demand and price fluctuations of the pulp

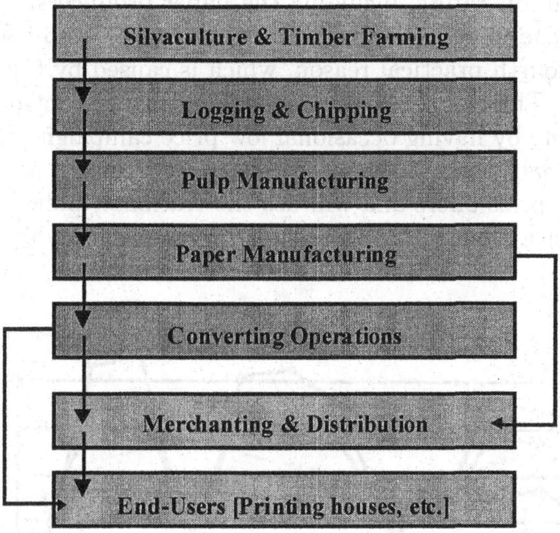


**Fig. 6.9.** The supply chain of the market for fine paper products.

markets dominate also the demand and price patterns of the paper products markets, even to such an extent, that the customers for paper products anticipate the expectations on changes in the pulp markets and act accordingly. If pulp prices decline, or are expected to decline, demand for paper products will decline, or stop in anticipation of price reductions. Then, eventually, prices will in fact go down as the demand has disappeared and the paper producers get nervous. The initial reason for fluctuations in the pulp market may be purely speculative, or may have no reason at all. Thus, the construction of any reasonable, explanatory cause-effect relationships to find out the market mechanisms that drive the bullwhip may be futile. If we want to draw an even more complex picture we could include the interplay of the operators in the market supply chain: their anticipations of the reactions of the other operators and their individual, rational (possibly even optimal) strategies to decide how to operate. This is a later task, to work out a *composite bullwhip effect* among the market supply chain operators, as we cannot deal with this more complex aspect here.

The third practical reason for the bullwhip effect is specialized form of order batching. The logistics systems for paper products favor shiploads of paper products, the building of inventories in the supply chain to meet demand fluctuations and push ordering to meet end-of-quarter or end-of-year financial needs. The logistics operators are quite often independent of both the paper mills and the wholesalers and/or retailers, which will make them want to operate with optimal programs in order to meet their financial goals. Thus they decide their own tariffs in such a way that their operations are effective and profitable, which will - in turn - affect the decisions of the market supply chain operators, including the paper producers. The adjustment to proper shipload or FTL batches will drive the bullwhip effect.

There is a fourth practical reason, which is caused by the paper producers themselves. There are attempts at influencing or controlling the paper products markets by having occasional low price campaigns or special offers. The market supply chain operators react by speculating in the timing and the level of low price offers and will use the (rational) policy of buying only at low prices for a while. This normally triggers the bullwhip effect.

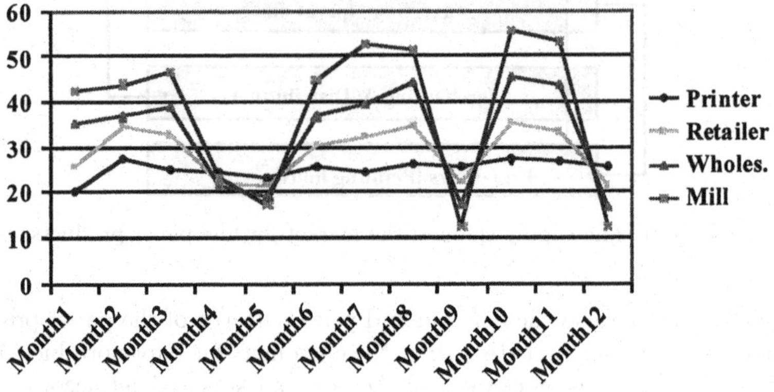


**Fig. 6.10.** The bullwhip effect in the fine paper products market.

The bullwhip effect may be illustrated as in Fig.6.10. The variations shown in Fig.6.10 are simplifications, but the following patterns appear: (i) the printer (an end-customer) orders once per quarter according to the real market demand he has or is estimating; (ii) the dealer meets this demand and anticipates that the printer may need more (or less) than he orders; the dealer acts somewhat later than his customer; (iii) the paper mill reacts to the dealer's orders in the same fashion and somewhat later than the dealer. The resulting overall effect is the bullwhip effect.

In the following section, we will present the standard theory for explaining the bullwhip and for coming to terms with it.

### 6.4.2 Explanations for the bullwhip effect: standard results

Lee et al [232, 233] focus their study on the demand information flow and worked out a theoretical framework for studying the effects of systematic information distortion as information works its way through the supply chain. They simplify the context for their theoretical work by defining an idealised situation. They start with a multiple period inventory system, which is operated under a periodic review policy. They include the following assumptions:

(i) past demands are not used for forecasting, (ii) re-supply is infinite with a fixed lead time, (iii) there is no fixed order cost, and (iv) purchase cost of the product is stationary over time. If the demand is stationary, the standard optimal result for this type of inventory system is to order up to $S$, where $S$ is a constant. The optimal order quantity in each period is exactly equal to the demand of the previous period, which means that orders and demand have the same variance (and there is no bullwhip effect).

This idealized situation is useful as a starting point, as is gives a good basis for working out the consequences of distortion of information in terms of the variance, which is the indicator of the bullwhip effect. By relaxing the assumptions (i)-(iv), one at a time, it is possible to produce the bullwhip effect.

### 6.4.3 Demand signal processing

Let us focus on the retailer-wholesaler relationship in the fine paper products market (the framework applies also to a wholesaler-distributor or distributor-producer relationship). Now we consider a multiple period inventory model where demand is non-stationary over time and demand forecasts are updated from observed demand.

Lets assume that the retailer gets a much higher demand in one period. This will be interpreted as a signal for higher demand in the future, the demand forecasts for future periods get adjusted, and the retailer reacts by placing a larger order with the wholesaler. As the demand is non-stationary, the optimal policy of ordering up to $S$ also gets non-stationary. A further consequence is that the variance of the orders grows, which is starting the bullwhip effect. If the lead-time between ordering point and the point of delivery is long, uncertainty increases and the retailer adds a "safety margin" to $S$, which will further increase the variance - and add to the bullwhip effect.

Lee et al simplify the context even further by focusing on a single-item, multiple period inventory, in order to be able to work out the exact bullwhip model.

The timing of the events is as follows: At the beginning of period $t$, a decision to order a quantity $z_t$ is made. This time point is called the "decision point" for period $t$. Next the goods ordered $\nu$ periods ago arrive. Lastly, demand is realized, and the available inventory is used to meet the demand. Excess demand is backlogged. Let $S_t$ denote the amount in stock plus on order (including those in transit) after decision $z_t$ has been made for period $t$. Lee at al [232] assume that the retailer faces serially correlated demands which follow the process

$$D_t = d + \rho D_{t-1} + u_t$$

where $D_t$ is the demand in period $t$, $\rho$ is a constant satisfying $-1 < \rho < 1$, and $u_t$ is independent and identically normally distibuted with zero mean and variance $\sigma^2$. Here $\sigma^2$ is assumed to be significantly smaller than $d$, so that the probability of a negative demand is very small. The existence of $d$, which is some constant, basic demand, is doubtful; in the forest products markets a producer cannot expect to have any "granted demand". The use of $d$ is technical, to avoid negative demand, which will destroy the model, and it does not appear in the optimal order quantity. After formulating the cost minimization problem Lee et al proved the following theorem,

**Theorem 6.4.1** [232] *In the above setting, we have:*

1. *If $0 < \rho < 1$, the variance of retails orders is strictly larger than that of retail sales; that is,*
$$\mathrm{Var}(z_1) > \mathrm{Var}(D_0)$$
2. *If $0 < \rho < 1$, the larger the replenishment lead time, the larger the variance of orders; i.e.* $\mathrm{Var}(z_1)$ *is strictly increasing in $\nu$.*

This theorem has been proved using the relationships

$$z_1^* = S_1 - S_0 + D_0 = \frac{\rho(1-\rho^{\nu+1})}{1-\rho}(D_0 - D_{-1}) + D_0 \tag{6.30}$$

and

$$\mathrm{Var}(z_1^*) = \mathrm{Var}(D_0) + \frac{2\rho(1-\rho^{\nu+1})(1-\rho^{\nu+2})}{(1+\rho)(1-\rho)^2} > \mathrm{Var}(D_0)$$

where $z_1^*$ denotes the optimal amount of order. Which collapses into

$$\mathrm{Var}(z_1^*) = \mathrm{Var}(D_0) + 2\rho$$

for $\nu = 0$.

The optimal order quantity is an optimal ordering policy, which sheds some new light on the bullwhip effect. The effect gets started by rational decision making, i.e. by decision makers doing the best they can. In other words, there is no hope to avoid the bullwhip effect by changing the ordering policy, as it is difficult to motivate people to act in an irrational way. Other means will be necessary.

It appears obvious that the paper mill could counteract the bullwhip effect by forming an alliance with either the retailers or the end-customers. The paper mill could, for instance, provide them with forecasting tools and build a network in order to continuously update market demand forecasts. This is, however, not allowed by the wholesalers.

### 6.4.4 Order batching

In order to study this cause for the bullwhip effect we need to change the context. Consider an inventory system with periodic reviews and full backlogging at a retailer. Let us assume that the demand is stationary, in which case the optimal order policy is to order up to $S$, which is equal to the previous review cycle's demand in every review cycle. Let us further assume that we have n retailers, all of which use a periodic review system with a review cycle of $r$ periods, and that each retailer faces a demand pattern with mean m and variance $\sigma^2$.

Let us then focus on the wholesaler. From his perspective he has $n$ retailers acting together through (i) random ordering, (ii) (positively) correlated ordering and (iii) balanced ordering, and it is evident that the use of his production capacity will be affected by the ordering patterns of the retailers. If all the retailers need to get their deliveries at exactly the same time, his delivery will run differently as compared to deliveries taking place uniformly in the order/production/delivery cycle.

Lee et al [232] show that with random ordering, each retailer appears with an order randomly during the cycle, the demand variance as seen by the wholesaler is the same as the demand variance seen by the retailer, if the review cycle $r = 1$. If the review cycle is longer, the wholesaler's demand variance will always be larger and the bullwhip effect gets initiated.

In the case of (positively) correlated ordering, we have an extreme situation, that all retailers order at exactly the same instance of the review cycle $r$. Lee et al [232] show that the resulting variance is much larger than the variance for random ordering. This is quite understandable, as the wholesaler will have ordering peaks on (for instance) one day and nothing during the rest of the review cycle. If ordering and delivery policies are negotiated with retailers, a wholesaler should take care to avoid a situation where the retailers find it beneficial to use positively correlated ordering, as it for sure will drive the bullwhip effect.

The ideal case is one in which the retailers order in a way, which is evenly distributed in the review cycle $r$. In order for this to happen, the wholesaler needs a co-ordination scheme in which the retailers are organized in groups. Then all retailers in the same group order in a designated period within the review cycle $r$, and no other group orders in the same period.

Lee et al [232] show that this scheme gives the wholesaler the smallest variance. This is reasonable, because the wholesaler can use his resources evenly during the review cycle and can estimate the order quantities to come in from each group.

Thus, different ordering patterns generate different variances in the review period. *Correlated ordering* with all orders appearing at the same instance shows the largest variance. *Balanced ordering* with all orders perfectly coordinated shows the lowest variance, and the *random ordering* falls in between the two other patterns. In all cases Lee et al was able to prove, that the variance experienced by the wholesaler was larger than the variance of any chosen retailer, which shows that the bullwhip effect is present with all three ordering patterns.

The ordering pattern models can be extended to a three-layer supply chain: retailer, wholesaler and producer, in which case we get combinations of ordering patterns as the wholesaler would not necessarily use the same ordering pattern as his retailers. The variance the producer experiences will in most cases be larger than the variance seen by the wholesaler. Rational decision making will force the wholesaler to replicate and amplify the variance he is getting from the retailers with his producer.

There is an ideal case, in which the bullwhip effect can be eliminated. If the wholesaler can get his retailers to form one single group for the review cycle, and then can persuade them to agree on their total orders $m$ (as well as agreeing among themselves. how to share this total amount) then there will be no bullwhip effect. Such a case is a bit hard to find in the forest products markets, as the EU would not look kindly on attempts of this kind to limit competition.

### 6.4.5 Price variations

Let us change context one more time. We will assume that a retailer faces an independent demand $\Phi(\cdot)$ for each period (but identically distributed for all periods). The wholesaler, the only source for the retailer, alternates between two prices $c^L$ and $c^H$ over time. The retailer perceives that the alternating is random with probabilities $q$ and $(1-q)$ for $c^L$ and $c^H$ respectively.

Lee et al [232] show that the optimal ordering policy for the retailer is to determine two ordering levels, $S^L$ for $c^L$ and $S^H$ for $c^H$. Then, as the price is low order as much as possible (i.e. $S^L$) and as the price is high order as little as possible (i.e. $S^H$) or nothing at all. It is clear that this will drive the bullwhip effect, as it is an optimal policy for the retailer to allow the orders to fluctuate with the price variations. It can be shown that even anticipated price variations will introduce the bullwhip effect as it is an optimal policy to adapt orders to anticipated price variations.

If we extend the price variations to more layers of the supply chain and include the producer, it is clear that the price variations reflected by the wholesaler have their origins with the producer. It would be an extreme, speculative case if the wholesaler could generate price variations on his own. Thus, the producer will face an optimal ordering policy from the wholesaler and find out that he gets orders only when he is offering the low price $c^L$. The variance faced by the wholesaler gets amplified as it is passed to the producer and the bullwhip effect seen by the producer is much stronger.

Inversely, it is possible to argue that if the producer refrains from price variations, and declares this policy publicly, then the bullwhip effect could be significantly reduced as the retailers would not allow the wholesalers to introduce any significant price variations. In the forest products market this would be possible but for the price variations forced by the strongly varying pulp prices, which seem to follow a logic of their own and which appears to be very difficult to forecast.

As the optimal, crisp ordering policy drives the bullwhip effect we decided to try a policy in which orders are imprecise. This means that orders can be intervals, and we will allow the actors in the supply chain to make their orders more precise as the (time) point of delivery gets closer. We can work out such a policy by replacing the crisp orders by fuzzy numbers.

In the following we will carry this out only for the demand signal processing case. It should be noted, however, that the proposed procedure can be applied also to the price variations module and - with some more modeling efforts - to the cases with the rationing game and order batching. These enhanced models will be worked out in some forthcoming papers.

### 6.4.6 A fuzzy approach to demand signal processing

Let us consider equation (6.30) with trapezoidal fuzzy numbers

$$z_1^* = S_1 - S_0 + D_0 = \frac{\rho(1-\rho^{\nu+1})}{1-\rho}(D_0 - D_{-1}) + D_0. \tag{6.31}$$

Then from Theorem 1.13.3 we get

$$\begin{aligned}\mathrm{Var}(z_1^*) = &\left[\frac{\rho(1-\rho^{\nu+1})}{1-\rho}\right]^2 \mathrm{Var}(D_0 - D_1) + \mathrm{Var}(D_0)\\ &+ 2\left|\frac{\rho(1-\rho^{\nu+1})}{1-\rho}\right| \mathrm{Cov}(D_0 - D_{-1}, D_0) > \mathrm{Var}(D_0).\end{aligned}$$

so the simple adaptation of the probabilistic model (i.e. the replacement of probabilistic distributions by possibilistic ones) does not reduce the bullwhip effect.

We will show, however that by including better and better estimates of future sales in period one, $D_1$, we can reduce the variance of $z_1$ by replacing the old rule for ordering (6.31) with an adjusted rule. Suppose now that a sequence of $D_{1,i}$, $i = 1, 2, \dots$ can be derived such that

$$H(D_1, D_{1,i}) \le H(D_1, D_{1,j}) \text{ if i} \ge \text{j},$$

i.e. $D_{1,i}$ is a better estimation of $D_1$ than $D_{1,j}$ if $i \ge j$. We can reduce the variance of $z_1$ by replacing the old rule for ordering (6.31) with the adjusted rule

$$z_{1,i} = \left[\frac{\rho(1-\rho^{\nu+1})}{1-\rho}(D_0 - D_{-1}) + D_0\right] \cap D_{1,i}.$$

Really, from Theorem 1.13.4 and from

$$z_{1,i} = \left[\frac{\rho(1-\rho^{\nu+1})}{1-\rho}(D_0 - D_{-1}) + D_0\right] \cap D_{1,i} \subset z_1^*, \tag{6.32}$$

we get

$$\mathrm{Var}(z_{1,i}) < \mathrm{Var}(z_1^*),$$

which means that the variance of the suggested optimal order, $z_{1,i}$, is getting smaller and smaller as $D_{1,i}$ is getting sharper and sharper. The crisp value of the optimal order is defined as the most typical value of $z_{1,i}$, that is, its expected value, $E(z_{1,i})$.

It can be seen that, similarly to the probabilistic case, $\mathrm{Var}(z_{1,i})$ is a strictly increasing function of the replenishment lead time $\nu$. However if $\nu = 0$ then equation (6.32) reads

$$z_{1,i} = [\rho(D_0 - D_{-1}) + D_0] \cap D_{1,i},$$

and, furthermore, if $\rho$ tends to zero then

$$\lim_{i\to\infty} \mathrm{Var}(z_{1,i}) = \mathrm{Var}(D_0 \cap D_1),$$

that is, the bullwhip effect can be completely eliminated.

### 6.4.7 A fuzzy logic controller to demand signal processing

If the participants of the supply chain do not share information, or they do not agree on the value of $D_1$ then we can apply a neural fuzzy system that uses an error correction learning procedure to predict $z_1$. This system should include historical data, and a supervisor who is in the position to derive some initial linguistic rules from past situations which would have reduced the bullwhip effect.

A typical fuzzy logic controller (FLC) describes the relationship between the change of the control $\Delta u(t) = u(t) - u(t-1)$ on the one hand, and the error $e(t)$ (the difference between the desired and computed system output) and its change

$$\Delta e(t) = e(t) - e(t-1).$$

on the other hand. The actual output of the controller $u(t)$ is obtained from the previous value of control $u(t-1)$ that is updated by $\Delta u(t)$. This type of controller was suggested originally by Mamdani and Assilian in 1975 and is called the *Mamdani-type* FLC [240].

A prototype rule-base of a simple FLC, which is realized with three linguistic values {*negative, zero, positive*} is listed in the following

| | | |
|---|---|---|
| $\Re_1$: | If $e$ is "positive" and $\Delta e$ is "near zero" | then $\Delta u$ is "positive" |
| $\Re_2$: | If $e$ is "negative" and $\Delta e$ is "near zero" | then $\Delta u$ is "negative" |
| $\Re_3$: | If $e$ is "near zero" and $\Delta e$ is "near zero" | then $\Delta u$ is "near zero" |
| $\Re_4$: | If $e$ is "near zero" and $\Delta e$ is "positive" | then $\Delta u$ is "positive" |
| $\Re_5$: | If $e$ is "near zero" and $\Delta e$ is "negative" | then $\Delta u$ is "negative" |

Or in tabular form

| $\Delta e(t) \mid e(t) \rightarrow$ <br> $\downarrow$ | N | ZE | P |
|---|---|---|---|
| N | N | N | ZE |
| ZE | N | ZE | P |
| P | ZE | P | P |

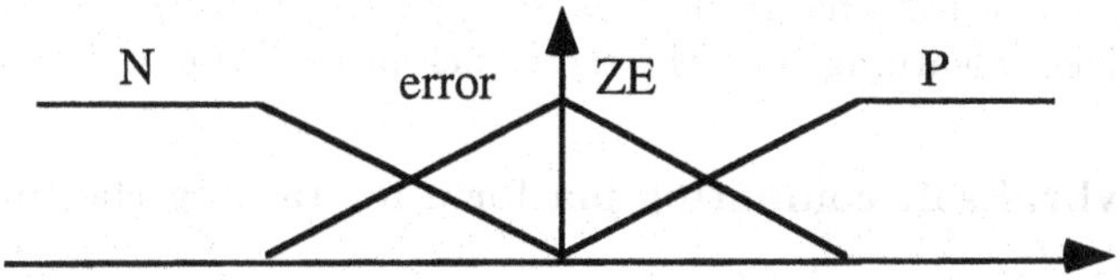


**Fig. 6.11.** Initial membership functions for the *error*.

To reduce the bullwhip effect we suggest the use of a fuzzy logic controller. Demand realizations $D_{t-1}$ and $D_{t-2}$ denote the volumes of retail sales in periods $t-1$ and $t-2$, respectively. We use a FLC to determine the change in *order*, denoted by $\Delta z_1$, in order to reduce the bullwhip effect, that is, the variance of $z_1$. We shall derive $z_1$ from $D_0$, $D_{-1}$ (sales data in the last two periods) and from the last order $z_0$ as

$$z_1 = z_0 + \Delta z_1$$

where the crisp value of $\Delta z_1$ is derived from the rule base $\{\Re_1, \dots, \Re_5\}$, where $e = D_0 - z_0$ is the difference between the past realized demand (sales), $D_0$ and order $z_0$, and the change of error

$$\Delta e := e - e_{-1} = (D_0 - z_0) - (D_{-1} - z_{-1})$$

is the change between $(D_0 - z_0)$ and $(D_{-1} - z_{-1})$.

To improve the performance (approximation ability) we can include more historical data $D_{t-3}$, $D_{t-4} \dots$, in the antecedent part of the rules. The problem is that the fuzzy system itself can not learn the membership function of $\Delta z_1$, so we could include a neural network to approximate the crisp value of $z_1$, which is the most typical value of $z_0 + \Delta z_1$.

It is here, that the supervisor should provide crisp historical learning patterns for the concrete problem, for example,

$$\{5, 30, 20\}$$

which tells us that if at some past situations $(D_{k-2} - z_{k-2})$ was 5 and $(D_{k-1} - z_{k-1})$ was 30 then then the value of $z_k$ should have been $(z_{k-1} + 20)$ in order to reduce the bullwhip effect.

The meaning of this pattern can be interpreted as: if the preceding chain member ordered a little bit less than he sold in period $(k-2)$ and much less in period $(k-1)$ then his order for period $k$ should have been enlarged by 20 in order to reduce the bullwhip effect (otherwise - at a later time - the order from this member would unexpectedly jump in order to meet his customers' demand - and that is the bullwhip effect).

Then the output of the neural fuzzy numbers is computed as the most typical value of the fuzzy system, and the system parameters (i.e. the shape functions of the error, change in error and change in order) are learned by the generalized $\delta$ learning rule (the error back propagation algorithm).

### 6.4.8 A hybrid soft computing platform for taming the bullwhip effect

Having understood the core elements of the bullwhip effect and the mechanisms, which drive it, the next challenge is to create instruments to deal with it. Our first step was to build a platform for experimenting with the drivers of the bullwhip effect and for testing our understanding of how to reduce or eliminate the effect.

This platform is one in the series of hyperknowledge platforms, which have been developed by IAMSR in the last 6-7 years. The platform shown in fig. 6.12 is a prototype, which was built mainly to validate and to verify the theory we have developed for coping with the bullwhip effect - a more advanced platform is forthcoming, as the work with finding new ways to tame the bullwhip effect continues in other industries than the fine paper products.

The platform is built in Java 2.0 and it was designed to operate over the Internet or through a corporate intranet. This makes it possible for a user to work with the bullwhip effect as (i) part of a corporate strategic planning session, as (ii) part of a negotiation program with retailers and/or wholesalers, as (iii) part of finding better ECR solutions when dealing with end customers, as (iv) support for negotiating with transport companies and logistics subcontractors, and as (v) a basis for finding new solutions when organizing the supply chain for the end customers. In the future, we believe that some parts of the platform could be operated with mobile, WAP-like devices.

The platform includes the following elements (cf. fig. 6.12): The platform is operated on a secure server, which was built at IAMSR in order to include some non-standard safety features.

There are four models operated on the platform: (i) *DSP* for demand signal processing, (ii) *Rationing Game* for handling the optimal strategies as demand exceeds supply and the deliveries have to be rationed, (iii) *Order Batching* for working out optimal delivery schemes when there are constraints like *full shipload*, and (iv) *Price Variations* for working out the best pricing policies when the paper mill wants to shift between low and high prices.

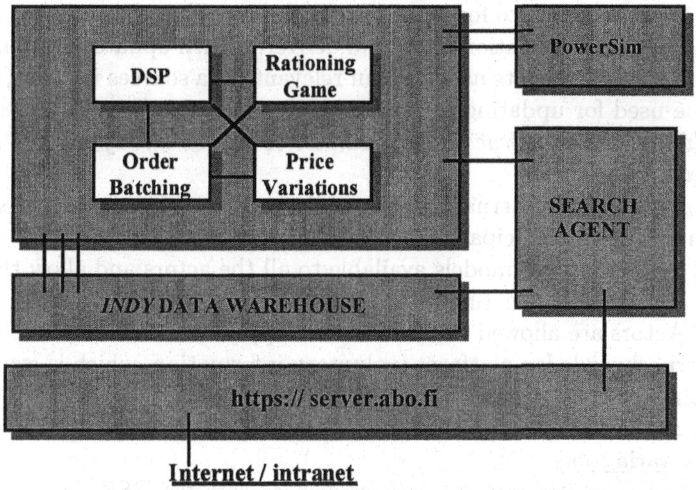


**Fig. 6.12.** A soft computing platform.

The hyperknowledge features allow the models to be in-terconnected, which means that the effects of the DSP can be taken as input when working out either Order Batching or Price Variations effects. Thus, models can be operated either individually or as cause-effect chains.

Data for the models is collected with search agents, which operate on either databases in the corporate intranet or on data sources in the Internet. Also the search agents have been designed, built in Java and implemented for corporate partners by IAMSR as part of a series of research programs. The agents can be used to feed the models directly or to organize the data as input formats (e.g. as spreadsheets) tailored to the models and stored in a data warehouse. The INDY application used for the platform is a spreadsheet-oriented data warehouse with intelligent support for import and export of data.

As part of the experimental platform we have also included support for the PowerSim package, which makes it possible to carry out *systems dynamics*-type simulations of possible action programs as these change and adapt to changing data.

After experimenting with the platform we summarized our findings in the following *macro-algorithm for taming the bullwhip effect*:

1. Demand Signal Processing.
   1.1 *Information on true demand can be shared throughout the supply chain.*
   1.1.1 Establish a secure Internet portal for the supply chain actors.
   1.1.2 Make forecasting tools available and request that all actors use them.

1.1.3 Post and update forecasts of actual demand.
1.1.4 Support negotiations of actual deliveries with updates of changes in demand; search agents used to scan relevant data sources for data, which can be used for updating forecasts.
1.2 *Information on true demand cannot be shared throughout the supply chain.*
1.2.1 Establish an internal ordering policy and negotiate for all the supply chain actors to participate.
1.2.2 Make the DSP models available to all the actors and allow them to work out optimal ordering policies.
1.2.3 Actors are allowed to monitor the supply chain inventories through the hyperknowledge platform (voluntary information, which is evaluated against optimal inventory policies).
1.2.4 Actors can elect to use the DSP models or not.

2. Price variations.
2.1 *Start from the ordering policies derived with the DSP.*
2.1.1 Find and negotiate a stable pricing policy for all the actors; implement this and eliminate the bullwhip effect.
2.2 *A stable pricing policy cannot be agreed upon (there may be, for instance, significant changes in the pulp prices.*
2.2.1 Use the fuzzy numbers model to determine good price intervals.
2.2.2 Make the Price Variations models available to all the actors and allow them to work out optimal ordering policies.
2.2.3 Actors are allowed to monitor the supply chain inventories through the hyperknowledge platform (voluntary information, which is evaluated against optimal inventory policies).
2.2.4 Actors can elect to use the Price Variations models or not.

3. Order Batching.
3.1 Start from the ordering policies derived with the DSP.
3.2 The paper mill will negotiate optimal production batches with the whole-salers (and retailers and end-customers if possible; normally the wholesalers do not give access to the parts of the supply chain they control) and reacts to demand variations with an AR scheme of the type discussed above.
3.3 If the negotiations are not possible due to partisan interests, each actor will decide on the order batching individually.
3.3.1 The Order Batching model is an AR scheme, which allows each actor to find a flexible scheme for order batching.
3.3.2 Make the Order Batching models available to all the actors and allow them to work out optimal ordering policies.
3.3.3 Actors are allowed to monitor the supply chain inventories through the hyperknowledge platform (voluntary information, which is evaluated against optimal inventory policies).
3.3.4 Actors can elect to use the Order Batching models or not.

4. Rationing Game.
   4.1 For the last decade rationing has not been necessary in the fine paper markets, as there is a stable overcapacity available due to excessive investments in (very) large paper mills.
   4.2 The Nash equilibrium model with fuzzy numbers is a challenge still to be faced.

All steps of the macro algorithm can and should be supported with the hyperknowledge platform, which will help to coordinate and work out action programs. The programs will either reduce or eliminate the bullwhip effect.

The compound effects of multiple bullwhip effects are complex and represent topics for future research.

In summary, the macro algorithm offers some first possibilities to come to terms with the bullwhip effect, which appears to be made worse with the use of stochastic models. The random factors used by Lee at al [232] actually increase the variance (and the bullwhip effect) as the optimal solutions offered incorporate random factors and crisp policies - and this will produce a 'bang-bang' effect of shifting between optimally small and large orders.

**Summary 6.4.1** *The results reached in the EM-S Bullwhip project are mainly theoretical results, which also was the goal and the aim for the research program. Nevertheless, many of the results we have found in working with both the standard Lee et al model and with the new EM-S Bullwhip model have practical implications. Even if we propose them as "ways to handle the bullwhip effect for paper mills", it should be clear that significant validation and verification work remains to be done before this statement will be fully true. The validation and verification process requires access to specific data on real market operations, preferably on the paper mill level.*

*As a tool for the verification and validation process, we built a prototype of a decision support system in which we have implemented causal models, which describe the four bullwhip-driving factors. The system is a platform for testing different policy solutions with the bullwhip models, for collecting data from different data sources with intelligent agents, which also update the models, and for running simulations of the processes involved with the PowerSim software package.*

*Nevertheless, quite some work is needed for re-engineering the logistics chain and getting its operators to agree on sharing information. This is essential, as we can hope to eliminate the bullwhip effect only to some degree if we have to keep estimating the activities of the supply chain operators.*

*If this negotiating process gets complex and time-consuming, a business unit can still work with the bullwhip effect internally by following up on its demand and sales patterns, and by trying to find ways to neutralize the most violent variations. For this purpose, the mathematical results we have found will be most useful. This work can be combined with running experiments with different solutions with the help of the PowerSim models.*

# 7. Future Trends in Fuzzy Reasoning and Decision Making

In the quest to develop faster and more advanced, intelligent support systems the introduction of software agents a few years ago has opened new possibilities to build and implement useful support systems. The reason for wanting more advanced and intelligent systems is simple: we want to be able to cope with complex and fast changing business contexts.

In this chapter we will introduce some software agents we have built and implemented and then show how fuzzy reasoning schemes can be included in the agent constructs in order to enhance their functionality.

## 7.1 Software agents and agent-based systems

Let us start with a short review of software agents and their functionality.

The field of agents is rich and diverse, yet fragmented. The word "agent" is nowadays so widely used that it is best described as an umbrella term for a heterogeneous body of research and development. Different communities refer to it in different ways and it bears multiple names and forms in different contexts as it comes in many physical guises: *robots, daemons, knowbots, softbots, taskbots, userbots, personal agents, personal assistants* and so on (cf. [190], [210] [265]). To get a general picture of the agent world, Franklin and Graesser's [114] agent tree is very helpful (it is reproduced here in a simplified form):

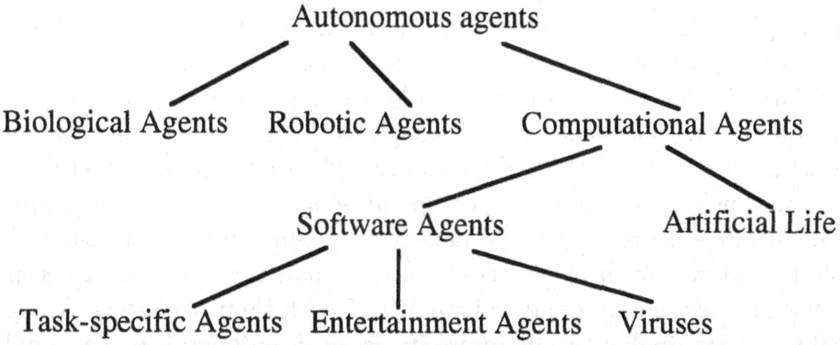


The type of agents of concern to us is software agents. Similarly, there seems to be almost as many definitions of software agents as researchers since no two developers appear to share exactly the same opinion on what constitutes a software agent (cf. [190]). Nevertheless, the automation of work and the automation of computer using are central to the idea of software agents. Kay [206] described software agents as soft robots living and doing its business within the computer's world. Cheong [66] described software agents as primarily human-delegated software entities that can perform a variety of tasks for their human masters. Maes [237] described a software agent as its user's personal digital assistant, that provides personalised assistance in a specialised task. According to Jennings and Wooldridge (cf. [191], [190]) most agent researchers would find themselves in broad agreement with the following key principals in the definition of software agents and agent based systems:

> Software agents are computational programs or entities situated in computing environment and assisting users with computer based tasks. They act to accomplish specialized tasks on behalf of users and act towards reaching certain user-specified or automatically generated goals with a certain degree of autonomy and flexibility (cf. [154], [190], [237], [313]). Agent-based systems refer to systems in which the key abstraction used, either in conceptualisation, design, or implementation, is that of an agent (cf. [190]).

The key attributes emphasised here are (i) situatedness, (ii) autonomy and (iii) flexibility. *Situatedness* means that an agent receives sensory input from its environment and that it can perform actions which change the environment in certain way. *Autonomy* means that the system is able to take initiative, to solve problems without direct intervention or constant guidance from a user or other agents, and it has control over its own action and internal state. To be *flexible* means that the system is *responsive, adaptive or robust*, which again requires that it perceives the environment and responds in a timely fashion to changes which occur in it, and takes account of changing user needs and a changing task environment. In this way, an agent system comes to know about the user's preferences and can tailor interactions and actions to reflect them. Finally, an agent system can be made *proactive*. Then it not simply acts in response to the environment, but it is also able to exhibit opportunistic, goal-oriented behaviour and to take the initiative where appropriate. It does not wait to be told what to do next, rather it makes suggestions to the user (cf. [191], [190], [265], [313]).

In addition to this, other often mentioned important properties of software agents include *sociability or co-operative ability, mobility, learning ability*, and *intelligence* (cf. [265]). When deemed appropriate, an agent should be able to interact with other agents or a human user in order to complete their own problem solving and to help others with their activities. An agent's capability to personalise or customise its assistance depends on its capability of adaptation and learning ability. Agents can play different types of roles and accomplish different tasks and responsibilities. Depending on their role definitions, different agents tend to differ in their co-operation ability, intelligence, mobility and autonomy. For example, an agent that supplies decision support functionality acts autonomously and proactively to gather information and make recommendations. The human user of the agent will, nevertheless, make the final decision. In contrast, an agent may also assume a completely autonomous role and take responsibility for the whole process of problem solving. Not all agents can exhibit smart problem solving behaviour, some do and are limited by the current state of the art in related fields. In some cases the individual agents of a system may not be that intelligent at all, but in combination and co-operation they lead to the intelligence and smartness of an agent-system (cf. [164]).

The very first idea of the agent approach suggests the delegation of tasks and responsibility. Such an approach allows users to move away from computing details while focusing on more conceptual constructs. It reduces complexity and increases efficiency and the delegation of functions supports user mobility (cf. [101, 102], [237]). Agents can be used to solve new types of problems and to build new applications that were previously too complicated to build. The agent concept makes it natural, easier and advantageous to conceptualise problem domains of a complex nature. If a problem domain is particularly complex, large, open-ended or unpredictable (the structure is capable of dynamic changing, e.g. the Internet), then the agent approach presents a good alternative solution (cf. [190], [272]).

For the same reason, software agents also offer an alternative solution to improve the efficiency of software development. As is widely known, the most powerful tool for handling complexity in software development is modularity and abstraction. Software agents present a natural metaphor and powerful tool for making systems modular and offer a better means for conceptualising, designing and implementing applications. In many cases, real-world entities and their interactions can be directly mapped into problem solving agents with their own resources and expertise (cf. [190], [272]).

The abstraction at the user level enables agent systems to marry underlying system complexity with a high level of user friendliness. They encapsulate hardware or software changes inside themselves without making users aware of them, users are only aware of the functionality or service changes. In fact, software agents are establishing a new paradigm for human-computer interaction that is less like the traditional master-slave relationship and more like a partnership (cf. [190], [272]). The dominant, standard interface of computer applications has been direct manipulation (see-and-point interfaces), which means that a program will only do something that a user explicitly tells it to do. It is a one-way interaction; it requires software objects to be visible and it constantly informs the user about the kind of things he can act upon. For many of the user tasks direct manipulation is a distinct improvement over command-line interfaces. However, many of its advantages begin to fade as tasks grow in scale or complexity. There are often times, when sequences of actions could be better automated than directly performed by the user in simple, tedious steps. It would be desirable to have programs that in certain circumstances could take the initiative, rather than wait for the user to tell exactly what they want (cf. [12], [191]). Software agents bring about an indirect interfacing approach (ask-and-delegate).

In summary, agent systems differ from and complement traditional systems mainly in four aspects. *First*, traditional systems are *functional*, which means that they work simply by taking some input, computing a function of it and giving this result as output. They do not interact directly with any environment. They receive information but not via sensors, rather through a user acting as a middleman. In the same way they do not act on any environment, rather they give feedback information or advice to a third party (cf. [191]). They usually remain dormant until specifically called by user instructions. On the other hand, agent systems - as reactive systems - maintain an ongoing interaction with the environment and can act on the environment (cf. [168]). Because of this, agent systems can work in both real time processing (user initiated) and in batch processing (a scheduled time or conditioned time). Agents are always "alive" and ready for action, and they do not rely on users' explicit actions to be activated. They work in the background, serve around-the-clock, and perform automatic actions at the user-level of abstraction (cf. [237] [247]).

*Second*, traditional systems always depend on users to explore and use them. They show ubiquity, which means that users typically have to describe each step that needs to be performed to solve a problem, down to the smallest level of detail (cf. [191]). With agent systems users need only specify a high-level goal instead of issuing explicit instructions, and can leave the 'how' and 'when' decisions to the agents. Agent systems make it possible for the programs to work independently of the users' presence and instructions, and to deliver only customised user-wanted information and service (cf. [190], [237], [247]). As Negroponte [260] claimed, the future of computing will be 100rather than manipulating computers.

*Third*, the agent approach adds diversity and competitive value to existing systems. Applications with agent functionality possess competitive advantage to those without it. Agents make it easier to supply customised computing products and services than conventional systems. They provide products that are easier to use, bypass intermediaries between products/services and customers (users), eliminate delay in the process and free up human resources (time, cognitive efforts) for other work.

*Fourth*, agent wrappers can be built around legacy systems to enable them to inter-operate with other systems (cf. [190]).

In addition to the individual agent features we have just worked through there is some work done on creating a class of *collaborative agents*, which will have both individual features and features they get through the collaboration (cf. Nwana and Ndumu [266]). Collaborative agents emphasise autonomy and co-operation with other agents in order to perform tasks for their users in open and time-constrained multi-agent environments. The may have some (limited parametric) learning properties and they may have to "negotiate" in order to reach mutually acceptable agreements.

The motives for building a collaborative agent system include: (i) solving problems that may be too large for a centralised single agent, (ii) allowing for the interconnecting and interoperation of existing legacy systems (e.g. decision support systems, conventional software systems, etc.), and (iii) providing solutions to inherently distributed problems, such as drawing on distributed data sources or distributed sensor networks.

The PLEIADES project developed collaborative agents for organisational decision making over the "info-sphere", which actually was a collection of Internet-based heterogeneous resources. The PLEIADES has two layers of abstraction: (i) contains task-specific collaborative agents, and (ii) information-specific collaborative agents. Task-specific agents (TA) perform a particular task for their users, e.g. arranging appointments and meetings with other task agents, and they co-operate with each other within layer (i) in order to resolve conflicts and integrate information. The TAs request information from information-specific agents (IA) on layer (ii) in order to carry out their tasks. The IAs may collaborate with one another, within their own layer, in order to fulfill the request from the TAs. The sources of the information delivered are the many databases (DBs) in the info-sphere. Ultimately, the TAs proposes a solution to the user. The TAs has a model of the task domain and knowledge of how to perform tasks, as well as a model of the capabilities of other TAs or IAs. The IAs possesses knowledge of various information sources and how to access them, and a model of the capabilities of other IAs.

Individually, an agent was built as a planning module in the PLEIADES, which is linked to a local facts and beliefs database. It also has a local scheduler, a co-ordination module and an execution monitor. We will use some of these ideas for the SA.

At BT Laboratories two prototype, collaborative agent systems have been developed: ADEPT for business process reengineering, and MII for decentralised management and control of consumer electronics.

The world of collaborative agents is being extended to the multi-agent (MA) systems. The MA systems are gaining in acceptance especially for Internet applications such as electronic commerce, virtual enterprises, (shared) scientific computing, intelligent manufacturing, home automation, component-based software construction and power distribution management. The MA systems allow sets of agents with differing capabilities to interact to solve problems, they allow for scalability, they permit us to reuse software modules, they handle software evolution and they promote open systems.

There are a number of applications available in the market, which illustrate how these systems are designed, built and implemented (cf. Communications of the ACM, March 1999, for a series of articles on MA systems; this special section was edited by Anupam Joshi and Munindar P. Singh).

The ISES project in Sweden uses MA systems over an electric power grid to create networked smart homes, in which an MA system of smart appliances can work in conjunction with utility agents to balance load, to save energy and to provide safety. An interesting added feature is that ISES appliances not only obtain power from the electric grid, but also use it as an integrated Internet connection.

Another project called SciAgents has developed an MA system to support networked scientific computing. Here the MA system allows scientists to view networked hardware and software resources as a single *virtual metacomputer.* This has been described for many years already in a number of projects but only the arrival of the MA technology has made it feasible in practice to build affordable virtual metacomptuers. Collaborating agents locate, combine and invoke the resources needed to solve given (often complex) problems.

The GAMS system is an example of a tool system available for virtual computing. The GAMS is a virtual mathematical software repository system with access to thousands of software modules, it promotes easy access and encourages software reuse in distributed computing environments. The GAMS has a seven level, tree structured taxonomy of mathematical and software problems, which offers an effective interface for a user to home in on appropriate modules for the problem to be solved. For example, the problem class I refers to modules catering to differential and integral equations, I2 indexes modules about PDEs, I2b caters to elliptic boundary value problems, I2b1 refers to the linear kind of these problems, and so on. This taxonomy indexes problem-solving modules from software packages maintained at four software repositories on the Internet (cf. [11] for details).

Virtual enterprises build on MA systems, which monitor and control business and manufacturing processes. In this context the problem of coherence has become visible, i.e. how different activities in a distributed system consisting of heterogeneous and autonomous parts relate to each other. In this sense, working on coherence is moving beyond interoperating as it considers the global structure of different activities, not just the exchange of data among them. The DARPA and the Lycos systems represent approaches to deal with coherence, and similar tasks have been pursued in studies of human-agent interaction and in games to mimic real-life markets.

For MA systems to succeed, a systematic collaboration of agents is necessary. This, again, requires that the agents have been designed and built in such a way that the internal cognitive structure of the agents is conducive to collaboration. If this is the case, then there is basis for building MA systems with some learning and planning capabilities. As we found out previously, the learning and planning capabilities reside in the interaction of agents and probably not with the individual agents

What should be noted, is that agent systems are not universal solutions to all problems. It is not especially advantageous in many applications to employ agent technology and conventional approaches can be far more appropriate. Agents are an alternative approach for abstraction with which to understand and manage complexity and with which to conceptualise, design and implement complex software systems. Atomic problem solving components within an agent system still have to be able to perform the necessary domain tasks, which tends to be limited by the techniques that are currently available. Tasks that are beyond the scope of automation using non-agent techniques will not necessarily be made possible simply by adapting an agent approach. It is important to exploit related technology when implementing software agents (cf. [190]).

Software agents are making inroads in the DSS technology. Hess et al (cf. [168]) works out principles for including software agents in the model management system of a DSS to enable automated planning and meta-planning. They promise that this will generate the next generation of DSS tools and that they will give greatly expanded support for a decision-maker. They use the approach to build and implement a product-pricing DSS for a manufacturing firm.

Software agents are a technology with many unknown ramifications. For example, agents sent out to a computing environment could come back laden with virus. Agents can intrude people's privacy by carrying out research on personal information without pre-announcement. When tasks are delegated to agents, users need to gain confidence in the systems that work on their behalf and this process can take time. During this period the agent systems must strike a balance between continually seeking guidance while unnecessarily distracting the user, and never seeking guidance in which it may exceed its authority (cf. [190], [300]). These are a few issues, which call for careful consideration in the design of support systems.

## 7.2 Intelligence and software agents

Software agents (SA) are not intelligent in the human sense, but they can be used to produce intelligent solutions to problems. Statistics, decision theory and operations research all provide methodologies that are similarly motivated and have been used extensively to build decision support models for problems that can be described mathematically. In the same sense, an agent can be described as a set of decision rules, which are used to select and activate instructions from a set of instructions. Agents are used to help model users to reach intelligent solutions in semi- or ill-structured problems. In the present context agents would be used for model-based scenarios and industry foresight (which are semi- and ill-structured tasks) and models for forecasting (which is a well-structured task).

To specify the intelligence provided by a particular analytic decision tool, software (including agents), models and even a theory, Dahr and Stein [74] introduced the term *intelligence density* (ID), which is a heuristic measure. Think of it as the amount of useful "decision support information" that a decision-maker gets from using the output from a decision tool (or a software, a model, or by pondering a theory) for a certain amount of time. The amount of ID for a support is a function of how quickly the support user can get to the essence of the underlying data from the output produced by the support. The ID for a model used for forecasting is higher than the ID produced with heuristic judgement tools; the ID for an agent & model(s) combination used for a scenario or industry foresight, is higher than the unsupported use of a model.

The main objective for using agents in decision support systems is to quickly get at the essence of what we want to achieve with a support system. Translated to the present context this means that the SA should help a user to quickly get at the core of model-based scenarios and foresight reports in order to flesh out the description of a strategic context. The faster the systems user is able to accomplish his task when supported by the SA, the higher the ID of the SA.

Conceptually ID can be viewed as the ratio of the units of "conclusion capacity" gained (hard, if not impossible, to measure) to the number of time units spent (easily measured) by the user of the support system (with the SA). Even if the ID is hard to measure, it can be assessed with some rough categories, such as "low, rather low, medium, rather high, high". One way to find these assessments is (through experiments) to find out how much faster a user is able to build a scenario (of equal quality) with or without the SA. If the time used with the SA support is 3 min, and the time used without the SA support is 30 min, then the ID of SA-supported work is 10 times the ID of scenario work without the SA support.

Plainly gaining access to and getting the data on trends or breaking point events is by itself not very useful, and does not constitute a high ID. From a user's perspective, however, it is more worthwhile to have the SA get the data than to spend time collecting it. In this sense, the SA-supported operations constitute a higher ID.

The first step in establishing a higher ID is to condense the data. A SA, which is locating data from several data sources, knows how to query them, and then "cleans" the data, is classified with a higher ID than a SA, which picks up pre-specified data from a single data source.

"Cleaning" the data involves three steps: (i) scrubbing the data, means cleaning up inconsistent or conflicting data; (ii) integrating the data, means combining and consolidating data from several data sources, and (iii) transforming the data, means building compound or aggregate data items from individual data items (also from different sources). A SA, which is cleaning the data in this sense, is classified with a higher ID than a SA, which is only locating and querying data sources.

The next level of ID boosting involves discovery, which is a model-based endeavour to find similarities and differences. If a conceptual or theoretical framework is specified through a model, data may be used to test and probe if the insight formulated by the theory and the concepts can be correct or valid. Agents can in some cases use models for this purpose; in the actual context, the user should make the discoveries with the help of the models and the SA should support the process of discovery.

The highest level of ID boosting is learning, which so far - with some exceptions - is regarded as a human capability. The context in which we can have learning agents is normally well and highly structured, which is not the case for the description of new telecom services.

So far, we have looked at ID as a characteristic of one agent but the picture is more complex than this: multi-agent systems are becoming more and more popular, and the ID can be defined and used also for the interplay of agents in a multiagent system. As we will see in section 4, the SA is designed as a multiagent environment.

Multiagent (MA) systems are gaining in acceptance especially for Internet applications such as electronic commerce, virtual enterprises, (shared) scientific computing, intelligent manufacturing, home automation, component-based software construction and power distribution management. The MA systems allow sets of agents with differing capabilities to interact to solve problems, they allow for scalability, they permit us to reuse software modules, they handle software evolution and they promote open systems.

There are a number of applications available in the market, which offer us a basis for describing an MA-ID.

The ISES project in Sweden uses MA systems over an electric power grid to create networked smart homes, in which an MA system of smart appliances can work in conjunction with utility agents to balance load, to save energy and to provide safety. An interesting added feature is that ISES appliances not only obtain power from the electric grid, but also use it as an integrated Internet connection.

Another project called SciAgents has developed an MA system to support networked scientific computing. Here the MA system allows scientists to view networked hardware and software resources as a single *virtual metacomputer.* This has been described for many years already in a number of projects but only the arrival of the MA technology has made it feasible in practice to build affordable virtual metacomptuers. Collaborating agents locate, combine and invoke the resources needed to solve given (often complex) problems.

NTT in Japan has developed MA communities called *socialware.* This is described as an infrastructure, which will support virtual communities (neighborhoods, offices, organisations and so on) that exist in cyberspace and will allow them to interact in a shared virtual space.

Virtual enterprises build on MA systems, which monitor and control business and manufacturing processes. In this context the problem of coherence has become visible, i.e. how different activities in a distributed system consisting of heterogeneous and autonomous parts relate to each other. In this sense, working on coherence is moving beyond interoperating as it considers the global structure of different activities, not just the exchange of data among them. The DARPA and the Lycos systems represent approaches to deal with coherence, and similar tasks have been pursued in studies of human-agent interaction and in games to mimic real-life markets.

For MA systems to succeed, a systematic collaboration of agents is necessary. This, again, requires that the agents have been designed and built in such a way that the internal cognitive structure of the agents is conducive to collaboration. If this is the case, then there is basis for building MA systems with some learning and planning capabilities. As we found out previously, the learning and planning capabilities reside in the interaction of agents and probably not with the individual agents (cf. Communications of the ACM, March 1999, for a series of articles on MA systems; this special section was edited by Anupam Joshi and Munindar P. Singh).

Intuitively the ID for an MA system should be higher than the ID for a single agent, as the simple sum of individual IDs is greater than the ID for one agent. However, if we can master the *coherence* there is a chance for a joint ID, which is greater than the sum of the individual IDs in an MA system. This synergy effect comes from the characteristics of the MA system that agents jointly can perform a task, which is impossible for any individual agent. Thus, we should be aware of the fact that the agent ID is measured in different ways if we work on the individual agent ID or on the agent ID as part of an MA system.

## 7.3 Scenario agents

Model-based scenarios and scenario planning can be of two kinds: open world scenarios and model-based scenarios. In the former case model-based scenarios are built with support from a decision support system and used both for independent scenario planning and as a basis and input for the dcecision models (as the scenario material is stored in the DSS database). In the latter case, the decision scenarios are built to drive models and (i) input data is produced to model standards and/or (ii) is combined with model outputs to be used as input to other models (and should thus follow model standards).

The scenario agent (ScA) should thus support both the construction of open world model-based scenarios and the application of scenarios to decision models.

The tasks involved in the construction of open world (OW) model-based scenarios can be sketched out as follows.

1. Define the scope of the OW scenario, i.e. the context, the players, the time framework, the empirical objects (e.g. services, countries, etc.) and the variables to be covered.
2. Collect information on possible future developments of all the elements of the OW scenario in the chosen time framework. This information can be found in the DSS database itself or in external data sources. Some subsets of the data stored in the DSS database have been generated as output from decision models, and provisions should be made to run (and rerun) the models as part of the OW scenario construction process.
3. Form scenario statements in formats supported by the DSS system. These should include (i) verbal story building with empirical data in numerical and graphical form, (ii) rule-based approximate reasoning schemes supported with empirical material in numerical or graphical form, and (iii) data for parameters and variables produced according to the decision model standards.
4. Group the scenario statements to form meaningful scenario storylines and define each storyline as a "Scenario for ...". The model-based scenarios should be stored for easy distribution through email or through secure Internet services. They should have links to primary data sources for immediate updates with significant changes and they should be linked with I21 models to allow for (e.g.) quick evaluations and sensitivity analyses of the consequences of new data.

The model-based scenarios can be of two types: (i) a subset of OW model-based scenarios, which possibly have been refocused, have been made more specific and/or been simplified; (ii) decision scenarios produced to run models (single models or a system of models) as part of a strategy to sketch out future developments of the context, the players, the time framework, the empirical objects (e.g. services, countries, etc.) and the variables to be covered.

The second type of decision scenarios represents projections of an understanding of the strategic context and the business based on the knowledge we have on the past and the present. The first type of scenarios will, relative to this, have more futuristic elements and may be more difficult to adjust to the model standards.

The tasks involved in the construction of scenarios can be sketched out as follows.

1. Select a decision model together with the necessary input data and run the model with that input data, producing the decision model output. This is the "standard application" of the model.
2. Select a scenario, i.e. a set of scenario statements. These could include (i) data for parameters and variables produced according to decision model standards. They could also include (ii) verbal stories with empirical data in numerical and graphical form, in which case support should be provided for extracting input for the models. Finally, the scenario could

have the form of (iii) rule-based approximate reasoning schemes supported with empirical material in numerical or graphical form, and support should be provided to extract fuzzy numbers and to reformat them according to model standards.

3. Verify the applicability of the scenario for decision models (either single models or a system of models). This is a process with several steps: (i) cleaning the input data for the models (which include scrubbing, integrating and transforming the data), which makes sure that it fits the model standard; (ii) checking that input data is within critical parameter limits; (iii) checking that input data fits predefined model constraints, and (iv) checking that necessary and sufficient model elements get specified through the scenario.
4. Change the decision model structure by including additional decision variables, which are worked out in the scenario (but not in the original decision model, which is an exceptional case). In this case, support should be provided to find out what variables have no counterpart in the used model(s).
5. Re-run the - now possibly changed - decision model(s) using the scenario data as input. The changed model is thus run not with collected empirical data, but with assumed future data. The scenario-supported results are hypothetical, they cannot be validated but they allow systematic comparisons with the present state of the world as described with the system of decision models.

The construction of OW scenarios, and the application of model-based scenarios to decision models, is part of a process to build an industry foresight for chosen parts of the strategic context and the business we want to understand. An essential part of the foresight-building process is to handle large amounts of basically inconsistent data in a systematic and effective way. This allows a DSS user to quickly scan and use data from many (tens, hundreds of) data sources and to summarize findings and insights in a form, which can be used in the verbal storyline part of both OW and model-based scenarios. The SA should have support facilities for the foresight-building process.

Neither OW scenarios nor model-based scenarios should be one-off constructs. Scenarios, when found relevant and useful should be used repeatedly as a basis for rational reactions to a changing environment. Thus, the SA should support evaluations of sudden developments, breaking news and significant changes to allow for fast and relevant reactions to them.

A popular requirement on all support tools for scenario building, scenario planning and foresight processes is a capacity to react to and evaluate so-called weak signals, which will allow a DSS user to plan for the future ahead of the competition. Thus, the ScA should support the detection and evaluation of weak signals.

### 7.3.1 The scenario agent: basic functionality

The basic functionality of the ScA can be outlined as an extension of what we have planned to accomplish with OW and model based scenarios. This outline should be seen as a first basic understanding of what are relevant support functions, which we will give more depth and substance later on. We have identified 7 groups of basic support functions we have found to be necessary and sufficient for the ScA.

We discussed the need for building OW scenarios, i.e. scenarios not built for running decision models but as a support for building an industry foresight. We noted that the material produced, and stored in the DSS database, should be adapted to the actual business world in such a way that it could be used as a basis for building and using decision models. Thus, we want the ScA to:

**1. Help and support when building OW model-based scenarios**

The other part of the ScA support should be focused on building support for the creation and application of model-based scenarios. We noted that this could be either and adapted and focused subset of the OW model-based scenarios, or that it could be model-based scenarios, which are produced to run decision models (single models or a system of models). Thus we want:

**2. Help and support functions for scenario builders**

The building and application of both OW and model-based scenarios need to rely on the use of multiple data sources. We have envisioned the use of tens or hundreds of data sources, and as the human mind has difficulties to systematically screen even less than 10 data sources, the ScA support should include a searching, scanning and reporting functionality. The OW scenarios rely more on external data sources than the model-based scenarios; both should use all data available in the DSS database as effectively as possible. Thus, we want the ScA to support:

**3. The screening of data sources in the Internet, intranet and the DSS database**

The building of scenarios are not one-off operations, but they should be used as a basis for continuous screening, follow up and assessment of changes in the environment. This should be an active acquisition of data on significant events and relationships, which are either covered by the decision models or identified as critical by consensus or private knowledge. Data, which has been cleaned and condensed as information, should not be given as indpendent observations, but should be linked to the data sources from which it has been acquired. Thus, the ScA should provide the service of:

**4. Linking new information to existing or new data sources**

Besides having the active linking support functionality, the ScA should also support a passive monitoring functionality, which allows the DSS user to spot changes of interest to him/her. This functionality is one way to detect the "weak signals". Thus, the ScA should have (an):

**5. Automatic ticker for the monitoring of data sources**

The OW scenarios require some good support functionality for accessing and combining a multitude of data sources, for cleaning and condensing data and for building summaries for future use. The model-based scenarios require both a linking of multiple data sources and linking of decision models to systems, as well as combining outputs from models with data from external data sources. In both cases, a hyperknowledge platform will give the necessary conceptual linking of decision model elements to make sure that we get consistent, valid and logically coherent results as a basis for assessments of the telecom markets. The ScA should give:

**6. Hyperknowledge support for different categories of scenario builders**

If approximate reasoning (AR) schemes are used in the OW and model-based scenarios, the ScA will need a generic functionality to operate with fuzzy logic reasoning schemes and with fuzzy numbers. The AR schemes are the only remedies for spotty, incomplete, imprecise or corrupted data as they can be used to overcome or approximate missing data elements. The DSS will have a number of data sources and will thus have to cope with problems with data of unequal quality. Thus, the ScA should provide support for working with data, which - until it is worked over with the AR schemes - will not satisfy model standards. The ScA should have:

**7. Approximate reasoning schemes**

In the next three sections we will work through some material on scenarios, forecasting and foresight in order to build the basis for a more detailed study of the structure and functionality of scenario agents.

## 7.4 Scenarios and scenario planning: key features

Model-based scenarios and scenario planning have been around for a while. The "numbers planning" approach developed in the 1950s by Harvard and McKinsey evolved into the Boston Consulting Group "growth share" matrix of the 1970s. Another strand was Hermann Kahn's work at RAND Corporation, and later at Hudson Institute, which actually gave birth to the concept "scenario" (he had borrowed the word from Hollywood, as the alternative "screenplay" was found not enough dignified). Kahn pioneered a technique called "future-now" thinking, aiming in the use of detailed analysis plus imagination to be able to produce a report as it might be written by people living in the furture. Kahn soon got competition from Stanford University, which founded its own think-tank in 1947 and called it Stanford Research Institute

(SRI). The SRI offered long-range planning for business incorporating operations research, economics and political strategy, which in the 1970s had developed into "softer" modelling approaches, such as the SRI "changing images of man". This was a result of the SRI futures group abandoning a straight modelling approach and starting to combine numeric forecasts with literature searches on utopias and dystopias to create plausible model-based scenarios for the US to the year 2000 (this was done in 1968-70).

The GE scenario approach has been widely quoted as a benchmark approach for scenario planning, and it has been widely used by GE itself for a couple of decades. The overall structure can be described as follows:

1. Prepare background. Assess overall environmental factors for the industrial sector under investigation, such as demographic & lifestyle factors, general business & economic factors, legislative & regulatory factors, and scientific & technological factors.
2. Select critical indicators. Identify the industry's key indicators (trends). Identify potential future events, which may have an impact on the key trends (from various data sources). Use Delphi panel, whose expert opinions are credible in evaluating the industry's future.
3. Establish past behaviour for each indicator. Establish the historical performance for each indicator. Enter these data into a database for the trend impact analysis program. Analyse reasons for past behaviour of each trend: demographic & social, economic, political & legislative, technological.
4. Verify potential future events. Interrogate Delphi panel to evaluate past trends, to assess potential impact of future events, to assess probability of future events, and to forecast future values. Specify and document assumptions for forecast. Specify and document rationale for projected values.
5. Forecast each indicator. Carry out trend impact analysis (TIA) and cross impact analysis (CIA). Operate the TIA and CIA programs on data from various sources. Combine with Delphi output to establish the range of future values. Produce forecast results from the combined analyses.
6. Write model-based scenarios.

The GE approach has been replaced by more technology supported methods, but the basic ideas are sound and still hold relevance for efforts to gain some insight in possible future developments of an industry or some market.

In the 1980s the use of model-based scenarios decreased from the peak of interest in the 1970s. There were several reasons for this: the threat of the oil price shock had decreased, corporate staffs were reduced in the recessions in the early 1980s and the over-simplistic use of the technique - with a confusion between forecasts and model-based scenarios - gave scenario planning a bad name. There were massive corporate planning systems in use in the early 1980s, they were built with scenario planning as a key component, and they failed to predict the recessions of the early 1980s. There were large US corporations using the BCG matrix, which suffered bad losses because they were losing market shares to Japanese and European competitors. The planning techniques made it impossible for them to foresee this development and they were unprepared for the changes. Instead of finding faults with the management, it is easier to blame a bad planning technique.

Changes were needed and Michael Porter emerged on the scene. He considered model-based scenarios to be important tools for understanding and so getting ahead of trends, and he recommended building alternative model-based scenarios as a form of sensitivity analysis. He described model-based scenarios as "*an internally consistent view of what the future might turn out to be - not a forecast, but one possible future outcome*".

The 1990s represent a resurgence of interest in scenario planning as a part of the new emphasis on sources of value and growth in corporations. The approach has now changed from the "massive planning systems" of the early 1980s to focus on business value, market attractiveness, competitive advantages, economic value added, etc.

Companies that have used scenario thinking claim a number of results including (cf. [277]):

1. The insurance company *Erste Allgemeine Versicherung* spotted the results of political changes in the former Eastern Europe and was able to establish themselves early in these countries.
2. The consumer goods company Electrolux has been able to see the opportunity for new businesses, e.g. service business based on re-using consumer products.
3. The wiring and cable supplier KRONE was able to develop 200 new product ideas.
4. Pacific Gas and Electricity was able to dispel assumptions about the "Official Future" and to cause it to work to reduce energy consumption.
5. The UK National Health Service was able to provide a way for a very dispersed, large and disparate organisation to think through new relationships, internally and to customers.

ICL reports on developing a number of model-based scenarios in the 1990s for its business focus in the IT industry (cf. [159]), and found out that a working scenario developing process has the following phases: (i) identify focal issue or decision, (ii) key forces in the local environment, (iii) driving forces, (iv) rank by importance and uncertainty, (v) selecting the scenario logics, (vi) fleshing out the model-based scenarios, (vii) working out implications, (viii) selection of leading indicators and signposts. The ICL approach appears to be a more or less state-of-the-art approach for scenario building.

Patrick van der Duin and co-authors [241] report on work with socio-cultural consumer model-based scenarios to make it possible to reflect on information and telecommunication behavior of the residential user in 2015.

This work, which was very successful in involving also senior managers, operated with simple taxonomies to make it possible to discuss about consumer behavior well in the future. The study shows that simplicity, when it is combined with a profound market insight and a professional approach to represent essential relationships, is the best way to make the use of model-based scenarios to work. The suggestive names of typical customers (Ordered Otto, Virtual Victoria, Associative Alex and Ruthless Ruth) and the carefully prepared frameworks for the scenario discussion, initiated animated discussions and got much approval among senior managers. One of the advantages of this type of scenario planning and discussion appears to be the creation of a common mindset, something which would be a good objective also for the use of the I21 platform. Patrick and his co-authors, however, have some cautionary remarks. Not all participants were able to make the intellectual leap to 2015, their future world did not differ much from the present. The main result seems to be educational, the work with consumer model-based scenarios appeared not to have any systematic effects on the long range thinking. Nevertheless, when we plan the work with the Decision support system we should bear in mind the setup of the KPN experiments and try to emulate them as far as possible - they represent one approach which works.

Kees van der Heijden [159] points to the role of scenario thinking as "providing laboratories in which different models of the future environment can be tested". As this is - in some sense - similar to what we want to accomplish with the Imagine 21 system, an adaptation of his five uses for model-based scenarios has been outlined below.

1. Use model-based scenarios for sensitivity analysis or for risk assessments, i.e. find out under what circumstances a described new service will work/not work.
2. Evaluation of services, when the basic development model is based on forecasts, against possible other outcomes when other forecasts are used.
3. Use model-based scenarios to describe market penetration processes for services, when available knowledge (and sufficient data) makes it possible to use explanative or predictive models.
4. Use a range of model-based scenarios to describe market penetration processes for services, when available knowledge (with insufficient data) is spotty, incomplete or uncertain, and makes it not worthwhile to build precise models.
5. Use model-based scenarios to demonstrate reasoning, to test and train planners, to improve communication and understanding, to find key indicators to monitor and control, etc.

As can be found from these observations, model-based scenarios and scenario planning offer a number of methods and ideas, which are useful for our present purposes. This material is used as a background for designing the basic user support, which is to be built into the scenario agent.

## 7.5 Forecasting

Spiros Makridakis [239] has written extensively on forecasting and the management uses of forecasts. We will summarise some of his points on forecasting in the following. Makridakis identifies three principal uses of forecasting: (i) satisfying curiosity, (ii) improving decision making and (iii) generating consensus. In this context, we are mostly concerned with the latter two uses, even if all of us will have to admit to a ceratin degree of curiosity on the shape and forms of new telecom services.

The accuracy of forecasts will be determined by how much patterns and relationships change and by how much people (inluding a company itself and its competitors) can influence future events.

*Patterns or relationships might change over time.* A critical assumption for accurate forecasting (as well as for modelling in general) is that patterns or relationships, once identified and measured, remain constant. Weather forecasters can predict tomorrow's weather rather accurately when weather patterns do not change. However, they do not know when or how they will change. Weather forecasters have access to advanced mathematical models, they use superfast computers, they have specialised satellites and they have sophisticated weather stations, but still wheather forecasts have not increased significantly in precision over the last thirty years. This is simply because changes in weather patterns cannot be predicted. Although weather patterns can be better tracked and more accurately predicted if they do not change, inaccuracies inevitably develop when they do change. In the business context, patterns and relationships change much more, and much more often than the weather.

*People can influence future events.* In a business context, predictions can become self-fulfilling or self-defeating prophecies, nullifying the forecasts. An attractive opportunity for investment might bring significant losses, if several competitors arrive at the same forecast. The fact that the forecasts themselves can influence future events and change their course, complicates the task of forecasting. It is no longer sufficient to predict accurately what is going to happen - managers must also forecast what competitors will do in response to such predictions. Because people can change the course of future events, the task of forecasting becomes much more difficult. This is different from weather forecasting.

There are some additional factors, which affect the possibility to produce accurate forecasts.

*The time horizon of forecasting.* The longer the time horizon of the forecast, the greater the chance that established patterns and relationships will change, or that competitors will be able to react to predicted events or the predictions themselves, which will invalidate the forecasts.

*Technology change.* The higher the rate of technology change will be in a given industry, the greater the chance that established patterns and relationships will change and the greater the chance that competitors will be able to influence the industry through technological innovations. An excellent example is high-tech industries, where forecasting is almost impossible as firms strive to create the future according to their own conceptions.

*Barriers to entry.* The lighter the barriers to entry into a market, the more inaccurate the forecasting as new competitors (both domestic and foreign) can drastically change established patterns and relationships in their quest to gain competitive advantages.

*Dissemination of information.* The faster the dissemination of information, the less useful the value of forecasting as everyone will have the same information and can arrive at similar predictions. In such a case it becomes impossible to gain advantages from accurate forecasting, which means that accurate forecasts are not necessarily useful. On the other hand, those making accurate forecasts will most of the time have a competitive advantage over those who operate without any forecasting. The growth in mainframes and microcomputers was correctly predicted, but few gains resulted as many companies that used the accurate forecasts went bankrupt.

*Elasticity of demand.* The more elastic the demand the less accurate the forecasts. Thus, demand for necessities can be predicted with a higher degree of accuracy than for nonnecessities.

Consumer versus industrial products. Forecasts for consumer products are more accurate than those made for industrial products. Industrial products are sold to a few customers, who are well informed and can receive offers of bargain terms from competitors. Thus, they will change suppliers quickly and in unpredictable ways, which makes forecasts inaccurate.

*Short-term predictions.* In the short term, forecasting can benefit by extrapolating the inertia (momentum) that exists in the economic and business context. Seasonality can also be predicted fairly well. Empirical evidence has shown that seasonality does not change much. Thus, once computed it can be projected together with the momentum of the series being forecast, with a high degree of accuracy. The momentum in series and their seasonality constitute the two greatest advanatages that can be gained by using formal forecasting methods. The larger the number of customers or items involved, the smaller the effect of random forces and the higher the reliability of forecasting. Short-term forecasting and the estimation of uncertainty are technically feasible and can be employed on a routine basis to provide improved customer satisfaction, better production and service scheduling. In these cases, overwhelming empirical evidence shows concrete benefits from using simple statistical methods instead of using judgment to make the forecasts and to estimate uncertainty.

*Medium-term predictions.* The usual length of a medium-term forecast is about 2 years, which makes forecasting relatively easy when patterns and relationships do not change. Economic cycles can and do change established patterns and relationships, and we are not yet able to accurately predict the timing and depth of recessions or the start and strength of booms. This makes medium-term forecasting hazardous, as recessions and booms can start any time during a planning horizon of up to 2 years. In addition, the uncertainty in forecasting becomes greater and less easy to measure or deal with, because the differences between forecasts and actual results can be substantial, especially in cyclical industries. Because recessions and booms cannot be predicted, it becomes necessary over the medium term to monitor for possible recessions or booms. Although monitoring is not forecasting, it helps managers not to be taken completely by surprise. In practical terms, it makes little sense to attempt to forecast recessions or booms.

*Long-term predictions.* Long-term forecasts are needed mostly for capital expansion plans, selecting R&D projects, launching new products and formulating long-term goals and strategies. The critical element in long-term forecasting appears to be the prevailing trends. A challenge is to determine when and how such trends might change, and how societal and consumer attitudes will differ in the future. The chances that there will be changes in long-term trends caused by new products, new services, new competitive structures, new forms of organisation and other novelties are great, making the task of forecasting difficult but also of critical importance. Makridakis divides the long term into three types: emerging, distant and faraway.

In the emerging long term (2-5 years), most changes requiring consideration have already started. It therefore becomes a question of figuring out their effects on the market and what can be done to deal with such changes. When moving to the distant and faraway long term, the accuracy of specific forecasts will decrease drastically, as many things can happen to change established patterns and relationships. The purpose of forecasting in such cases is to provide general directions and to identify major opportunities as well as dangers ahead.

The foremost challenge is to predict technological innovations and how they will affect the markets. New technologies can drastically change established demand, societal attitudes, costs, distribution channels and the competitive structure of an industry. A major purpose of such long-term forecasting is to help planners form a consensus about the future and start considering ways of adapting new technologies once they become economically profitable. Distant and faraway long-term forecasts cannot be specific and will always be highly uncertain.

Kees van der Heijden [159] agrees with Makridakis on some key points, put wants to stress the shortcomings of forecasting. He points out that a forecast is an efficient way of describing the future, but it is also impoverished, as it is a summary. The efficiency of forecasting comes from reducing rich information into a simple form (such as the data for decision making algorithms) in which it can be passed on for operational purposes. Model-based scenarios have much more information, they are richer because they give the whole cause and effect story, culminating in an understanding of why things happen. Forecasts can be tested after the event, model-based scenarios cannot be proven or disproved. There is no claim that a particular scenario will materialise as such, and they are not supposed to be used on that basis. Therefore, model-based scenarios cannot be tested against what will happen, as that information is simply not available when they are needed and can have no bearing on conclusions to be drawn from a scenario.

In the words of van der Heijden, *forecasting and scenario planning have very different purposes*, which in a specific context can be complementary. Forecasting is useful in the short term, where things are reasonably predictable and uncertainty is relatively small compared to our ability to predict. In the long term, where very little is predictable with any grade of certainty planning is not a useful activity. It is in the intermediate future, where uncertainty and predictability are both significant that scenario planning makes its contribution (which is in line with Makridakis' discussion).

## 7.6 Industry foresight

*Industry foresight* is different from forecasting in the sense that there is not much use for time series analysis and mathematical modelling. The reason for this is that the scope of a foresight lies 5 years ahead (in some cases even 10-15 years), which is equivalent with the Makkridakis emerging long term. Another reason is that we look for changing trends, or the emergence of new trends, and that the knowledge and the data we have available from past observations are not necessarily relevant or valid. In order to support the building of industry foresight we need new and different tools, and it appears that there also is a need for new theory (cf. [29], [41], [34]).

The UK Foresight programme[1] is specified much along these lines. It is to develop visions of the future, i.e. looking at possible future needs, opportunities and threats, and deciding what should be done now to make sure that we are ready for the upcoming new challenges. If we paraphrase the problem formulation used for the programme for our present context, it would be something along the following lines:

It appears that the underlying task is to find a logical basis for industry foresight in the existing and potential markets for new telecom services in business-to-business communication, which includes two separate subtasks: (i) to find theoretical frameworks which can explain the scope and substance of this industry foresight, and (ii) to find methods and models for describing, explaining and predicting the development of key components causing changing trends or the emergence of new trends. This is, of course, an easy statement but a hard program to carry out.

The program carries with it a third task: (iii) to find good solutions with information systems technology to help users work with methods and models to create, to maintain, to modify and adapt, and to update reliable, good

[1] Cf. http://193.82.159,123/documents

quality foresights. The IT solutions this requires should help the users access data sources and should support their work in such a way that they are more productive and effective when working on foresight reports. We will discuss this task in more detail in section 3.4 and we will describe how search agents can be used for this purpose.

A standard reference for work on industry foresight (and strategic planning issues) is the Hamel-Prahalad book *Competing for the Future* (cf. [158]). Although a number of points made in the book can and should be debated, it is a good reference as a theoretical framework for industry foresight (cf. subtask (i)). Hamel and Prahalad identify the key needs to be satisfied with industry foresight methods as answers to the following three questions:

- What new types of customer benefits should we seek to provide in 5, 10 or 15 years?
- What new competencies will we need to build (or acquire) in order to offer those benefits to customers?
- How should we reconfigure the customer interface over the next several years?

If a company fails to develop (and then to understand and use) a good industry foresight, it will have some potentially disastrous consequences. There are a number of (sad) cases in a number of industries; here we will quote only two cases.

IBM could not fully exploit the market created by the PC, which became a market standard; instead IBM gave a good start to companies like Intel and Microsoft, and later Compaq and Dell, which now are destroying the basis for IBM's erstwhile core business. IBM is implementing a new strategy built around its e-Business concept, which may become an effective counter-move to the producers of PC-based systems.

The Japanese car industry focused on quality, cycle time and flexibility - and spent 20 years to develop a sharp competitive edge in these factors. Now its competitors are on their way to spend an additional 20 years to catch up to a market formed by Japanese performance standards, which by the time they eventually catch up will be significantly different.

Hamel and Prahalad formulate some reasonable ideas on how to develop *industry foresight*, and we will build upon some of them here as there are some empirical cases to show that they work.

- We need to understand the key elements of intellectual leadership in an industry before we can hope to gain market leadership; thus, the work with industry foresight should be aimed at finding key elements of intellectual leadership.
- In order to build sustainable competitive positions we must either be able to see opportunities, or to exploit opportunities others have seen; thus, focus work on industry foresight on finding market opportunities.

- As a way to build sustainable market positions, we can try acquisitions or "grass-root intrapreneurship". Still these approaches will not compensate for intellectual laziness and failures to see and comprehend the core competencies of the business. Thus, focus work on industry foresight to find changes in core competencies, which may significantly change sustainable market positions.
- A way to understand how competitors operate is to follow up on how core competencies are exploited through new venture divisions, incubator projects and alliances with other companies with some specific, better foresights on supporting activities. Thus, focus work on industry foresight to follow up on competitor activities in this respect.

This list of four key focal points is not exhaustive but is a good starting point to find the activities we need to support.

Hamel and Prahalad also offer some practical issues, which can be used as hints of what to look for when building an industry foresight:

- Find material, which can help to enlarge the opportunity horizon.
- Develop methods and collect data to find the white spaces in the market.
- Find ways to work from functionality thinking, do not collect material only on current products.
- Search for material, which will help to challenge price-performance assumptions.
- Find material, which can support you in a day-long debate on the following question: what are the forces already at work in this industry that have the potential to profoundly transform industry structure?
- Develop methods to collect data, which can help you to speculate on issues like: what is the impact of virtual reality on marketing means and methods?
- We need to find material to trace future trends in the intersection of changes in technology, lifestyles, regulation, demographics and geopolitics - products like the Nokia communicator can probably best be understood if the scope is wide enough.
- If we can find material to describe prevailing trends, we should also find ways to collect material for working out a contrary approach.
- If enough data and knowledge can be collected to trace and describe customer needs, we should look for ways to move beyond that and find out about unexplored opportunities.

Besides these more general and theoretical issues, there are very practical problems involved in working out the industry foresight. We should work out a reasonable scheme for how to find relevant data sources and to use them in the analysis. We need to design a support system for the users of these data sources, and we need to build user interfaces which will make it possible for them to use the system. We should remember to train the users so that they will be able to use and understand the knowledge, which is made available, and we should find ways to facilitate communication among the users and thus support the exchange of tacit knowledge (cf. [29],[41]) for a detailed discussion).

In the UK Foresight programme the foresight process is formulated in much more specific terms:

- What could the future be like?
- What does this mean for me/us/the company?
- What should we do next?
- Then what?

The Foresight programme when used in a corporate setting is envisioned to produce a number of benefits: (i) reduced risks and better rates of return for shareholders, (ii) new opportunities, (iii) more effective management and (iv) better strategic planning. This may well be the case, but experience shows that the instruments we use to work with the data to produce foresight visions and model-based scenarios will have a significant impact on the quality of the foresight.

## 7.7 The scenario agent

The inherent attributes of software agents make them useful for a number of information management tasks. Agents also have potentially many uses in executive support, for example, automated e-mail handling, meeting scheduling, web browsing, Internet news detecting and alert, external information gathering and filtering. In problems of automatically gathering, filtering and searching for information, the software agent approach represents one of the most popularly exploited solutions. In the environmental scanning activity of senior managers, the agent approach presents a novel way to supply information and to help conduct information acquisition.

The ScA will in fact be a multi-agent system, which is built as a group of collaborative agents. The group will have a layered structure and the individual agents of the group will be either TAs or Ias (cf. section 7.3). The ScA will be a reactive system, which maintains an ongoing interaction with the environment and can react to it. The ScA will be designed to deliver customised user-wanted data (information, knowledge), and the ScA will be to some extent used as a wrapper around decision models.

The overall design of the ScA follows two major design principles: (i) support for *open world* (OW) scenarios, and (ii) support for model-based scenario building. In the former case scenarios are built with support from the DSS and used both for independent scenario planning and as a basis and input for the decision models (as the scenario material is stored in the DSS database). In the latter case, the model-based scenarios are built to drive decision models and (i) input data is produced to decision model standards and/or (ii) is combined with decision model outputs to be used as input to other decision models (and should thus follow decision model standards).

### 7.7.1 Support for OW scenarios

When we build the ScA to support the building and the use of OW scenarios for an industry foresight of the strategic context the main emphasis will be on (i) collecting data from identified data sources (in the DSS database, on Internet or on an intranet), (ii) cleaning and condensing the data as information, (iii) combining data from different types of data sources, (iv) supporting the use of data sources which have been built and used manually, (v) supporting the use of database or data warehouse depositories, and (vi) supporting the extraction and editing of data (information, knowledge) for the verbal storyline of an OW scenario. The ScA for OW scenarios is a search agent, which also supports data insertion in a database/data warehouse, the handling of a database/data warehouse and the editing and writing of OW scenario reports.

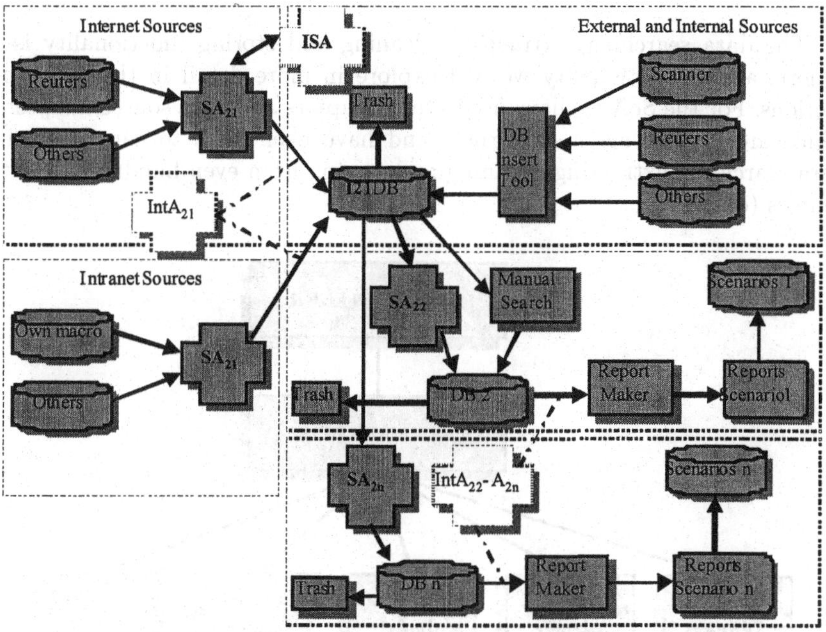


**Fig. 7.1.** Layout of the SCA for support of OW scenarios.

The functionality of this part of the system can be summarised as follows:

- ScA21.
  - Collects data from different sources on the Internet and from various intranet sources.
  - Can work with Internet sources that are password protected (Reuters);
  - Analyses the data based on its content; handles text and numerical data;
  - Stores interesting data in a data warehouse application (built with DSS database);

- Retrieves only new and changed data;
- Builds meta-data on retrieved data to follow up on retrieval;
- Scans different data sources and sites frequently for new data;
- Represents an effective use of data sources, which in fact is faster than human users;

• ScA22 - ScA2n.
- Analyses and collects data on selected topics based on user-defined profiles;
- Sorts the data based on date, content and profiles;
- Sorted data, which is related, is stored together in DB2 - DBn;

• Report Maker.
- Allows the user to select data from profile-defined folders;
- Selected data can be edited and ScAved as reports;
- Edited data can be traced to the unmodified (original) data if needed;

The data searching, extracting, cleaning and storing functionality is a generic agent functionality we will explore in more detail in the following sections. For the ScA we have used event adapters and data source adapters, which are generic agent constructs and have been built to carry out the data searching, extracting, cleaning and storing from even hundreds of data sources (cf. fig.7.2):

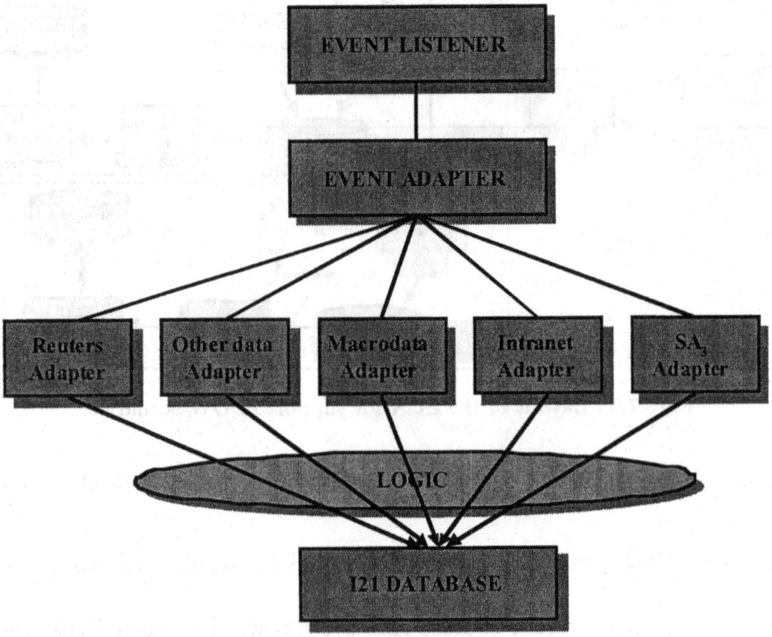


**Fig. 7.2.** The event listener-adapter functionality for ScA21.

The search agent system ScA21 - ScA22 - ScA2n is an extended and enhanced version of a scanning agent system, which has been built in Java and implemented in the Windows NT 4.0. The data warehouse application was implemented in Oracle 8.0 and was supported with INDY, an intelligent data warehouse supporting application built in Java. INDY was designed to generate meta-data for retrieved data, to help users to decide categories for retrieved data and to insert scanned articles and pictures. INDY operates an intelligent layer for data access and manages dynamic data storage in the data warehouse.

Tests with the scanning agent system showed that it retrieves data very fast and efficiently from selected data sources and that both the storing and retrieval of data can be made very fast and time saving for the user. Repeated tests with the system have shown that the quality of material retrieved improved as the search profiles became more focused and better defined. The definition of search profiles and the selection of data in the subsequent use of agents is reserved for the user. So far, no attempt has been made at making the agents adaptive, or at giving them learning capabilities, as scenarios and industry foresight still needs to be much better understood - there are simply no well-defined routines to implement for the agents.

One of the basic ideas was to use Internet extensively as a data source for the scanning agent system. Comparisons we made in several case studies with the scanning system quickly showed that the quality of the data retrieved was not very good, the insights, which could be collected, were not very profound and repetitions of the same material from different data sources were frequent. A series of experiments with the Reuters Business Briefing, showed that the quality of data was much better. In later tests with scanning agents on other commercial data sources the same pattern was repeated: there are significant differences in quality between public data sources on the Internet and the commercial data sources which can be accessed through Internet services. This should be noted and acted upon when data sources for the OW scenarios are selected and used.

### 7.7.2 Support for model-based scenarios

As the ScA supports the building and use of model-based scenarios, there is a more focused use of data sources than for the OW scenarios. The primary data source is the DSS database from which the ScA should collect data to generate the scenarios for driving decision models. The DSS database holds primary data for the DSS or (if the OW scenarios have been run first) scenario data from different data sources. A third possibility is that the DSS user wants to add data of his own (using e.g. the INDY tool) to use for the model-based scenarios. The support offered by the ScA is more focused, but it is basically the same as for the OW scenario: (i) collecting data from identified data sources (in the DSS database, on Internet or on an intranet), (ii) cleaning and condensing the data as information, (iii) combining data from different types of data sources, (iv) supporting the use of data sources which have been built and used manually, (v) supporting the use of database or data warehouse depositories, and (vi) supporting the extraction and editing of data (information, knowledge) for the verbal storyline of a model-based scenario.

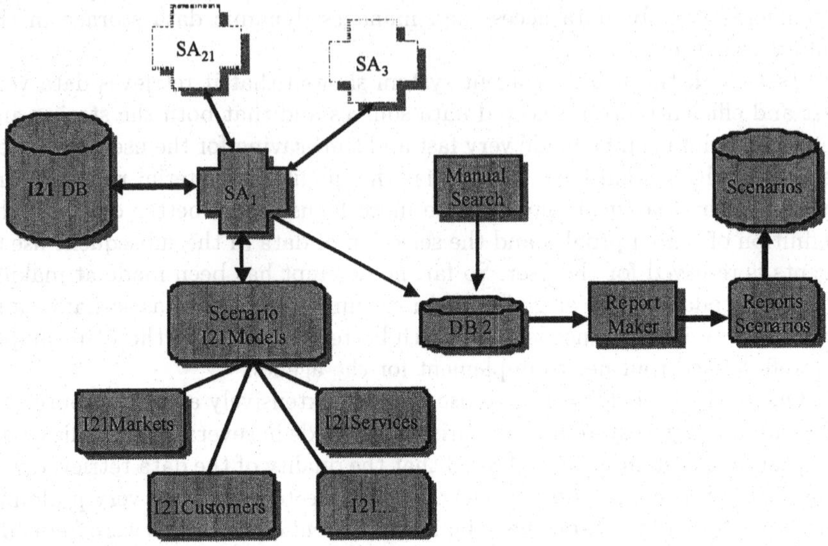


**Fig. 7.3.** Layout of the ScA for model-based scenarios.

The ScA for model-based scenarios is a database/data warehouse handling agent, which inputs data into decision models, run them, stores the result in the DSS database (or in a data warehouse application) and supports the writing of scenario reports.

The functionality of the system can be summarised as follows:

- <u>ScA1.</u>
  - Activated through data-generated events, events connected to time or user-generated events;
  - Works as an information customiser, i.e. it collects, scrubs, integrates and transforms data for the scenario-building models from the DSS;
  - Provides help desk support;
  - Offers level of support (novice, intermediate, experienced, advanced); depending on the choice, the support can be either an off-line help function or an autonomous information customiser and help desk;
  - Applies the event listener-event adapter-specific adapters logic;

- Runs decision models with data elements of the DSS database, stores intermediate results in DB2, runs a Report Maker (which support the user in making a scenario) and stores scenarios.

Part of the ScA1 features should be the event listener-adapter features shown in the previous section, which are generic and can be reused for the ScA1. The selected adapters are now built to follow the input from the collaborative agents (cf. fig. 7.4):

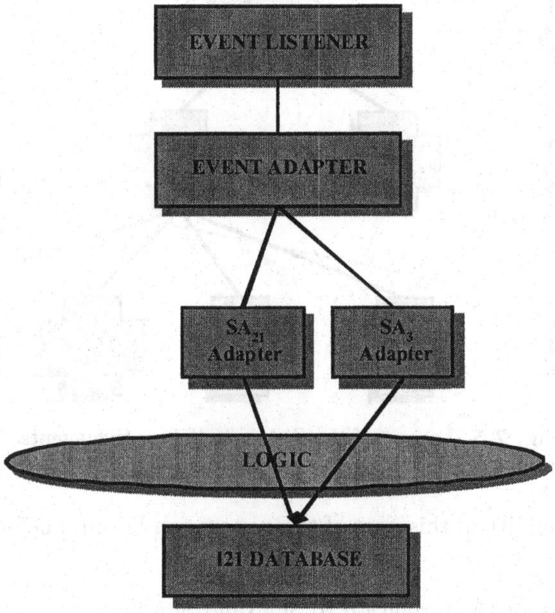


**Fig. 7.4.** The event listener-adapter functionality for ScA1.

In addition to the individual agent features we have just worked through there is some work done on creating a class of *collaborative agents*, which will have both individual features and features they get through the collaboration (cf. Nwana and Ndumu [266]). Collaborative agents emphasise autonomy and co-operation with other agents in order to perform tasks for their users in open and time-constrained multi-agent environments. They may have some (limited parametric) learning properties and they may have to "negotiate" in order to reach mutually acceptable agreements.

The motives for building a collaborative agent system include: (i) solving problems that may be too large for a centralised single agent, (ii) allowing for the interconnecting and interoperation of existing legacy systems (e.g. decision support systems, conventional software systems, etc.), and (iii) providing solutions to inherently distributed problems, such as drawing on distributed data sources or distributed sensor networks.

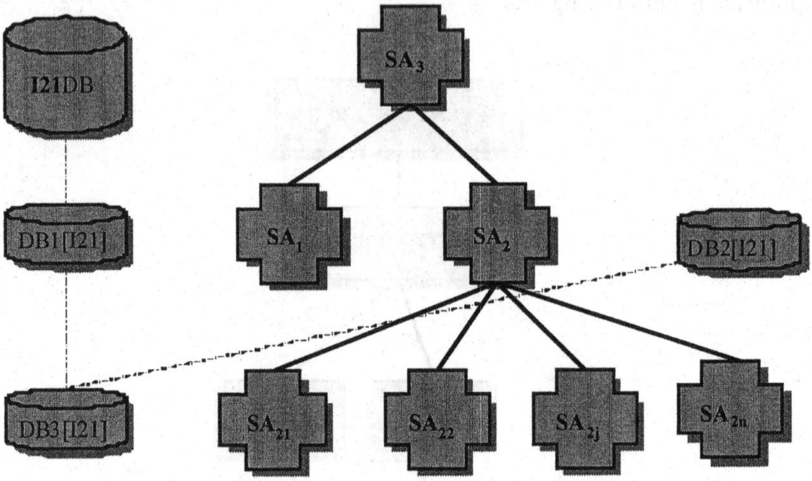


**Fig. 7.5.** Layout of the ScA as collaborative agents.

The functionality of this part of the system can be summarised as follows:

- ScA3.
  - Operates as an IA in relation to ScA1and ScA2.
  - ScA2 operates as an IA in relation to ScA21 - ScA2n.
  - All the ScA21 - ScA2n are designed as TAs.

The world of collaborative agents is being extended to the multi-agent (MA) systems, which allow sets of agents with differing capabilities to interact to solve problems, they allow for scalability, they permit us to reuse software modules, they handle software evolution and they promote open systems.

The ISES project in Sweden uses MA systems over an electric power grid to create networked smart homes, in which an MA system of smart appliances can work in conjunction with utility agents to balance load, to save energy and to provide safety. The ISES project is an example of agents with differing capabilities. We could use some of these results for the ScA.

The GAMS system is an example of a tool system available for virtual computing. Collaborating agents locate, combine and invoke the resources needed to solve given (often complex) problems. The GAMS is a virtual mathematical software repository system with access to thousands of software modules, it promotes easy access and encourages software reuse in distributed computing environments. The GAMS system is an example of interacting agents, which solve problems; the GAMS is a good example of how to reuse software modules. The GAMS has some similarities to the approach we have called model-based scenarios and we should try to apply the GAMS solutions.

Virtual enterprises build on MA systems, which monitor and control business and manufacturing processes. In this context the problem of coherence has become visible, i.e. how different activities in a distributed system consisting of heterogeneous and autonomous parts relate to each other. In this sense, working on coherence is moving beyond interoperating as it considers the global structure of different activities, not just the exchange of data among them. The DARPA and the Lycos systems represent approaches to deal with coherence, and similar tasks have been pursued in studies of human-agent interaction and in games to mimic real-life markets. We will have to find ways to deal with the coherence problems, especially for the model-based scenarios. For MA systems to succeed, a systematic collaboration of agents is necessary. This, again, requires that the agents have been designed and built in such a way that the internal cognitive structure of the agents is conducive to collaboration. If this is the case, then there is basis for building MA systems with some learning and planning capabilities. As we found out previously, the learning and planning capabilities reside in the interaction of agents and probably not with the individual agents.

The SCA, in its various forms of ScA1, ScA2, and ScA3, should be an MA system of collaborative agents, which (i) interact to produce OW and model-based scenarios, (ii) allow scalability, and (iii) are built by reusing software modules - which should follow a software evolution strategy.

### 7.7.3 Support for scenario building and foresight

The support we need from the ScA is an extension of what we have planned to accomplish with OW and model-based scenarios. We discussed and motivated the need for building OW scenarios, i.e. scenarios which support the building of an industry foresight for the strategic context and the business environment. We noted that the material produced, and stored in the DSS database, should be adapted to the business world we want to understand in such a way that it could be used as a basis for building and using decision models. Let us then summarise the ScA functionality we have introduced and motivated with material from a number of sources.

**Help and support when building OW scenarios.**
The ScA2 layout in fig.7.1 shows how the building of OW scenarios can be accomplished.

**Help and support functions for model-based scenario builders.**
The other part of the ScA support should be focused on building support for the creation and application of model based scenarios. We noted that this

could be either an adapted and focused subset of the OW scenarios, or that it could be scenarios, which are produced to run decision models (single models or a system of models). The ScA1 layout in fig.7.3 shows the agent support for building model based scenarios.

**The screening of data sources in the Internet, intranet and the DSS database.**

The building and application of both OW and model based scenarios need to rely on the use of multiple data sources. We have envisioned the use of tens or hundreds of data sources, and as the human mind has difficulties to systematically screen even less than 10 data sources, the ScA support should include a searching, scanning and reporting functionality. The OW scenarios rely more on external data sources than the I21 scenarios. Both should use all data available in the DSS database as effectively as possible. The ScA21 and ScA2 agents perform the screening of data sources in the Internet, the intranet and in the DSS database.

**Linking new information to existing or new data sources.**

Scenarios are not one-off operations, but they should be used as a basis for continuous screening, follow up and assessment of changes in the business environment. This should be an active acquisition of data on significant events and relationships, which are either covered by the decision models or identified as critical by consensus or private knowledge. Data, which has been cleaned and condensed as information, should not be given as independent observations, but should be linked to the data sources from which it has been acquired. This is part of both the ScA22 - ScA2n and the ScA1 functionality.

**Automatic ticker for the monitoring of data sources.**

Besides having the active linking support functionality, the ScA should also support a passive monitoring functionality, which allows the DSS user to spot changes of interest to him/her. This functionality is one way to detect the "weak signals". The ScA21 agent feeds and operates a ticker, which can be turned on or off and can be run in - for instance - a screen saver mode.

**Hyperknowledge support for different categories of scenario builders.**

The OW scenarios require a good support functionality for accessing and combining a multitude of data sources, for cleaning and condensing data and for building summaries for future use. The model based scenarios require both a linking of multiple data sources and linking of Decision models to systems, as well as combining outputs from Decision models with data from external data sources. In both cases, a hyperknowledge platform will give the necessary conceptual linking of decision model elements to make sure that we get consistent, valid and logically coherent results as a basis for assessments of a strategic business context. The information agent ScA3 provides hyperknowledge support in relation to the task agents ScA1 and ScA2. The MA system will be operated on a hyperknowledge platform.

**Approximate reasoning schemes**

If approximate reasoning (AR) schemes are used in the OW and model based scenarios, the ScA will need a generic functionality to operate with fuzzy logic reasoning schemes and with fuzzy numbers. The AR schemes are the only remedies for spotty, incomplete, imprecise or corrupted data as they can be used to overcome or approximate missing data elements. The decision support system will have a number of data sources and will thus have to cope with problems with data of unequal quality. Thus, the ScA should provide support for working with data, which - until it is worked over with the AR schemes - will not satisfy Decision model standards.

## 7.8 Interpretation agent

Our basic proposal is to use interpretation agents (IntA:s) in tandem with the scenario agents, as this is the area of application, in which a DSS user is working with the most material of the greatest diversity. At the same time, building and working with scenarios is time-consuming and an interpretation agent would potentially be very productive in supporting DSS users at these tasks.

The ScA was designed to support both the construction of open world (OW) scenarios and the application of scenarios to decision models. Then the IntA should basically be designed to (i) interpret data, which is being used as input to OW scenarios, (ii) interpret the output data from OW scenarios, (iii) interpret input data for model based scenarios (and decision models), and (iv) interpret output data from model based scenarios (and models) as a basis for using it in decision models.

From the use with model based scenarios follows, that an interpretation agent should be designed and built in such a way that it can be used to interpret both input and output data to and from decision models. Here we will have a choice of aiming at a generic agent design, which would be useful for most decision models, or aiming at a flexible design, which can be adapted to the use of specific decision models.

Finally, an interpretation agent could (and should) be used to quickly make sense of data stored in a data warehouse. This need would often be in preparation for work with OW scenarios, when a DSS user needs to decide if the necessary data can be found from the data warehouse, or if time and resources should be spent on collecting primary data, or secondary data from other sources. A similar point can be made also for model based scenarios and decision models, but the data need is in most cases already specified for these applications, and we know from the meta-data what we have available in the DSS database.

### 7.8.1 The interpretation agent: basic functionality

The basic functionality of the IntA can be outlined on the basis of what we have planned to accomplish with OW and model based scenarios, with the use of decision models and with the making sense of data collected in a data warehouse. This outline should be seen as a first basic understanding of what are relevant support functions, which we will give more depth and further on. We have identified 4 groups of basic support functions we need to plan for implementation in the IntA.

Let us start with the most unstructured part first, the making sense of data collected in a data warehouse, and then progress to OW and model based scenarios, and finally to decision models. Thus, we want the IntA to:

**Help and support when making sense of large amounts of data.**

This involves a number of functions:

1.1 Periodically visiting the data warehouse, watching for new or recent data, tracking updates of key issue indicators and triggering signals to show significant changes.
1.2 Comparing and relating new data to existing data set, recognizing and selecting significant events, trends, and deviating signals.
1.3 Support the user in reasoning and explaining about the possible causes for the events and trends.
1.4 Support the user in identifying the major groups of issues and in assessing their impacts, in predicting the probability of occurrence and in formulating the development course and milestones.
1.5 Ranking the issues according to the perceived impacts and probability of occurrence and development. The ranking may be interactive and supportive of the user.
1.6 Generating summary reports of the interpretation results. The objectives here are (i) to ScAve time for the user, and (ii) to quickly focus work with the data on meaningful subsets of data. Let us then move to more specialized support functionalities.

**Help and support in identifying results worth further attention.**

This again involves a number of functions:

2.1 Specified input/output data to and from decision models is evaluated in relation to reference points or benchmarks, and is classified as normal or unusual; the latter category is singled out for further attention.
2.2 Specified input/output data used and worked out in model based scenarios is evaluated as plausible or implausible with the help of reference points or benchmarks; the latter category is singled out for more work and data collection.

2.3 Selected (but not necessarily specified) input/output data used and worked out in OW scenarios is evaluated in terms of plausible or implausible, and in terms of the categories (crisis, opportunities and threats) with the help of reference points and benchmarks (which may be imprecise); the categories being plausible and which are found to represent crisis, opportunities and threats are singled out for more work and a continued gathering of data from selected data sources.
2.4 Collected data in the data warehouse is evaluated against keywords, benchmarks and reference points (if numerical), and against subjective assessment criteria; data singled out as unusual will be the focus of a continued collection of data and further study. The objectives will now be to help the user (i) to focus his/her work on essentials, and (ii) to get a better understanding of the context, which may not be possible without the support of the IntA. Now we can take one more step towards a further specified functionality.

**Help and support in tracing potential cause-effect chains.**

This involves a number of functions; we will move from the most specific to the most open-ended:

3.1 When working with several decision models, the IntA should follow (and on request display) the input and output data used for and produced by the decision models. The patterns thus derived may indicate cause-effect relationships.
3.2 When working with I21 scenarios, the IntA should follow (and on request display) the sequence and combinations of Decision models used. The scenario patterns may show cause-effect relationships among the events built in the scenarios when displayed over time.
3.3 When working with OW scenarios, the IntA should keep trace of data variations in relation to reference points and benchmarks. When displayed over time, the scenario patterns may show underlying cause-effect relationships, or may indicate where further data gathering may reveal cause-effect relationships.
3.4 When working with sets of data in a data warehouse, cause-effect relationships are difficult to trace. If benchmarks or reference points can be established, variations in relation to these may be traced and displayed over time to suggest cause-effect relationships. The objective here is simply to help the user trace potential cause-effect relationships, which may be important if no relationships have been known before. Let us then take a final step towards a specified functionality.

**Help and support in finding similar results.**

This support function will contain one part:

4.1 When working with decision models and finding some specific results, we may want to know if these results already have been derived with some other decision model or have been collected from some data source. The IntA should use the output to initiate a search for similar results in the DSS database or in a data warehouse used as a basis for input data. The objectives here are (i) to avoid inconsistency by having similar results analysed and worked on in parallel, and (ii) to find similarities in time, and avoid double work.

**Sense-making and interpretation**

The idea to design, build and use interpretation agents is appealing and there appears to be not much to it at first sight. We would have an automatic device, which "looks at" data we retrieve from various data sources, which we produce with decision models and which we produce and use for both OW and model based scenarios. Then this automatic device "presents" us with an interpretation, which will give us a quick overview of the issues involved and will help us to make sense of the material. The overview is manageable, if not unproblematic, but the "making sense" is more demanding than what is apparent.

## 7.9 Coping with imprecision

Professor Lotfi Zadeh, the founder of the fuzzy logic paradigm, has neatly summarized the main issues in sense-making in an interview more than 10 years ago (cf [316]). In the following we will work through his main points and try to identify their implications for the interpretation agent. Let us start with the problem of summarization. Progress has been made on summarizing stereotypical stories by researchers at the Yale University (Roger Schank and co-workers). A good example of a stereotypic story is a report on an automobile accident: there is an indication of what kind of accident it was, when it occurred, where it occurred, the vehicles involved, whether there were injuries, the type of injuries, etc. A stereotypical story has a predetermined structure (in a sense similar to the structure we have assumed for model based scenarios). If we have a predetermined structure, then we can understand a story and summarize it.

Even at this moment, it is very difficult and often impossible to write a program to summarize a story, because tha ability to summarize is an acid test of the ability to understand, which in turn is a test of intelligence and competence. Suppose we asked a person not familiar with mathematics to summarize a paper in a mathematical journal. It would be impossible for him to summarize it, because he does not understand what the paper is about, what the results are, what the significance is, and so forth. The process of interpretation is quite similar to the process of summarization.

Another key to interpretation is the ability to arrive at assessments. We are good at making assessments of age just by looking at a person: all of us can see the distinctions between someone 70 years old and someone 5 years old; a 20 year old quickly makes distinctions between somebody 16 years old and 20 years old, which is harder for somebody 40 years old. Our points of reference for making assessments tend to shift with our own context. At this point, it is a tough challenge to write a computer program, which would be capable of making assessments of this kind. The key is that we cannot articulate too well the rules we employ subconsciously to assess a person's age.

Another key part of interpretation is reasoning. Agents are artificial intelligence (AI) constructs and follow the tradition built in AI over more than four decades. The conservative AI approach is built around first order logic (an example of first order logic is the classical scheme: "all men are mortal; Socrates is a man; therefore Socrates is mortal"). We got an opposition against this conservative approach, which claims that logic is of limited or no relevance to AI (Roger Schank (Yale University), Marvin Minsky (MIT)). They believe that first order logic is too limited to be able to deal effectively with the complexity of human cognitive processes. Instead of systematic, logical methods, this second camp relies on the use of ad hoc techniques and heuristic procedures.

Fuzzy logic and approximate reasoning is forming a third camp within AI. Zadeh maintains that we need logic in AI constructs (including agents), but the logic needed is not first-order logic but fuzzy logic, the logic, which underlies inexact or approximate reasoning. Most human reasoning is imprecise and much of it is what we might call common sense reasoning. First-order logic is much too precise and much too confining to serve as a good model for common sense reasoning.

In classical two-valued systems all classes are assumed to have sharply defined boundaries, which means that either an object is a member of a class or not. This is okay if we have classes with sharp boundaries, but most classes in the real world do not have sharp boundaries (think about user preferences in future mobile commerce markets). Classical two-valued logic is not designed to deal with properties that are a matter of degree. There is a generalization of two-valued logic called multi-valued logics. In a multi-valued logical system, a property can be present with a degree. In classical logic there are just two truth values: true/false, but in a multi-valued logic there are more than two truth values. There may be a finite or even an infinite number of degrees to which a property may be present; in a 3-valued system, for instance, something can be true, false or on the boundary; in an n-valued system we can have n types of truth values, and so on.

Even if the multi-valued systems were developed already in the 1920:es, they have not been used to any significant extent in linguistics, in psychology or in other fields where human cognition plays an important role. The reason is that they do not go far enough, that they do not yet allow us to fully capture the reasoning we need to work with human cognition. This is where fuzzy logic has become useful. In fuzzy logic, we can deal with fuzzy quantifiers, like most, few, many and several. Fuzzy quantifiers deal with enumeration, but they are fuzzy, as they do not give a precise count, but an imprecise or approximate count. In multi-valued logic, we have only two quantifiers all and some, whereas in fuzzy logic we have all the fuzzy quantifiers. In reality, there is actually an infinite number of fuzzy quantifiers, there is an infinite number of ways we can describe a count of objects in an approximate fashion.

Another key difference is that truth itself is allowed to be fuzzy, i.e. it is okay to say quite true or more or less true. We can also use fuzzy probabilities like not very likely, almost impossible or rarely. In this way, fuzzy logic builds a system, which is sufficiently flexible and expressive to serve as a natural framework for the semantics of natural languages. Furthermore, fuzzy logic can serve as a basis for reasoning with common sense knowledge, for pattern recognition, decision analysis, etc - application areas in which the underlying information is imprecise.

Even if fuzzy logic probably will not be the ultimate system for handling real world imprecision, it is far better suited for dealing with real-world problems than the traditional logical systems. The ability of the human mind to reason in fuzzy terms is actually a great advantage. Even if a huge amount of information is presented to the human senses in a given situation, somehow the human mind has the ability to discard most of this information and to concentrate only on the information that is task relevant. This ability of the human mind is connected with its ability to process fuzzy information. Unfortunately, there is an incompatibility between precision and complexity. As the complexity of a system increases, our ability to make precise and yet nontrivial assertions about its behaviour diminishes. For example, it is very difficult to prove a theorem about the behaviour of an economic system that is of relevance to real-world economics.

Time and again, it has been demonstrated that what actually happens in the realm of economics is very different from what the experts predicted. These predictions may be based on large-scale econometric models, sophisticated mathematics, powerful computers and advanced software, but the forecasts turn out to be wrong - very wrong. There are two reasons for this: (i) economic systems are very complex; (ii) human psychology plays an important role in the behaviour of these systems - the systems appear to adapt to the very process of being studied and modelled. Simply summarized: these are the issues we have to face as we want to build agent support for interpretations.

## 7.10 Interpretation in a business environment

Now we will shift context and look at interpretation, for a while, in the context of business information and the opportunities perceived by various authors as we do not have to worry too much about implementing the ideas.

Scanning and interpretation are intertwined processes. While scanning concerns mainly seeing and perceiving the environment, interpretation concerns meaning construction, impact analysis, and conceptual scheme assembling.

The aim of scanning is to capture what is going on in the environment and to recognize only those events that are relevant to our own business, as well as to classify the chaos of data into structures. Interpretation aims to understand the identified events, to bring meaning out of observations, to discover plausible relationships and structures (e.g. cause-impact maps), and to develop frames of reference or models for understanding (Daft and Weick, [73]).

Scanning is collecting data. Interpretation is translating the data into understanding. It is a sense-making process, in which people assign meanings to ongoing occurrences (Gioia and Chittipeddi, [150]).

More specifically, if we follow these ideas, the tasks of interpreting the business environment will include the following, rather simple and practical issues: Identifying *events and trends from data, recognizing them as meaningful issues, and formulating an issue-list.*

This list of tasks and issues is simple for a human information user to accept and judge. Most of the time experience and intuition will decide the choice of events and trends. If we want to build an AI construct to pursue the same activities, we will have to deal with a number of technical issues. In the following, we will try to make the operations needed a bit more precise and try to find out if they could be part of a support system for interpretation.

Judgement is made to determine the probability of occurrence, the likely time of occurrence and the significance of each issue in order to forecast their development in the long run. Judgement is needed to investigate the causes of events and trends, if we cannot build any good causal models. Judgement has to be used to examine the interdependencies and cross-impact relationships between issues if we cannot build any good model for interdependence. Then judgement would be used in order to see if the occurrence of any events has an influence on the occurrence of others, and to judge the strength of the impact (totally determined, partially determined, have a common determinant, totally unrelated). In order to be more precise, (i) if the occurrence of event A enhances or inhibits the probability of event B occurring, or (ii) if event A has no effect, or (iii) if event A is an essential prerequisite for event B to occur. There are some possibilities to build and/or support this type of judgement with approximate reasoning schemes.

Judgement can be applied again to assess the impacts of major groups of issues on business (represented by selection criteria or performance measures) and to categorize issues as crisis, threats, and opportunities.

Issues are also evaluated in terms of whether they are emergent, evolving, or urgent, controllable or uncontrollable, whether their impacts are positive or negative, and if they bring potential gain or loss.

The opportunity category implies a positive situation in which a gain is likely (holding possibilities for future gain) and over which the company has a fair amount of control. Opportunities suggest chances of new markets or some advantages to the company.

The threat category implies a negative situation in which a loss is likely (holding possibilities for future loss) and over which the company has relatively little control. Threats tend to hinder the performance of the business or to keep the company from implementing its strategy and achieving its objectives. Threats increase the risk associated with implementing a strategy, they increase the resources required to implement a set of strategies, or they suggest that one or more strategies may no longer be appropriate.

A crisis needs urgent handling. It has an immediate and important impact on business operations. Issues that have zero impacts tend to stabilize the company's current strategy and operations, and are regarded as unimportant (Schneider and Meyer, [290]).

When the issues have been evaluated, the next step is to rank and prioritise them and to formulate a strategic issue agenda. Issues are examined again in terms of the extent of their impacts on business (high, medium or low) and the probability of their occurrence. The issues are further ranked and prioritised in terms of their development (high, medium or low).

Issues that have a high impact and a high probability of occurrence have the highest priority for managerial attention. Issues that have a low impact on business and a low probability of occurrence have the lowest priority. Issues that have a high impact on business should be monitored closely and issues that have a low impact could be discarded.

When the issues have been ranked and prioritised, the final step is to *propose action/reaction strategies.* Issues that are *urgent* by nature and have a *high impact* need to be acted on immediately. Issues that have a *high impact* but are *emergent* by nature will be acted on later. *Unimportant* issues will call for no action.

There are three strategies for an interpreter, which usually can be employed for analysing and interpreting data for the program of (i) assessing the impact of major issues on business, (ii) ranking and prioritising them, and (iii) proposing action/reaction strategies:

1. Data-driven strategy. The interpreter performs a broad-based search and actively looks for interesting and important events, as well as patterns, in the environment data.

2. Goal-driven strategy. The interpreter develops hypothetic issues, seeks data support for the hypotheses, or, if a specific issue is known to exist, tries to find causes and reasons for the trends and events.
3. Mixed strategy: an integrated use of both data driven and goal driven strategies (Bayer and Harter, [6]). Again simply summarized: the interpretation agent could perhaps be built as an application and/or implementation of one of these three strategies. As we have seen in the preceding discussion, we need to solve a number of modelling and analysis problems on the way to making this agent a reality.

## 7.11 Mental models and cognitive maps

Mintzberg (cf [255]) has found that managers normally combine analysis and intuition in their management activities: facts are worked on with analytical tools and then conclusions and decisions are arrived at trough intuition and experience. Mintzberg describes their thinking processes as highly inferential and intuitive by nature. Managerial cognitive activities are characterised by cognitive simplification and selective perception, which are guided by knowledge, experience and judgement.

A mental model is the representation, at the conceptual level, of a cognitive structure, of beliefs and knowledge in the head. It is a mental map that describes an interconnected set of understandings and assumptions about the business elements and their relationships, as well as implicit views of what one's interests and concerns are, what is important, what demands action and what does not. Managers develop simplified mental models of reality using only a small part of the information available (identified as approximate rationality), combined with prior knowledge, experience and premises (Durand et al, [93]). Mental models may remain static during certain periods, if there are no changes in the business context, but there should be effective routines for adapting and changing them in tune with changes in time and in the business context.

Mental models describe and explain the way in which a manager makes sense of and explains the world around him, i.e. the way in which he interprets his context of decision making and action. In his interpretation process, mental models are employed to synthesize data, to make sense out of data and to perform well-learned behaviour patterns. They are the underlying assumptions that actually link environment to strategy, data items to issues. Mental models help the manager to understand the external environment, as new information is understood in this framework of existing mental beliefs and models. The key factors and links described and explained in the mental model affect the types of information used to evaluate impacts or to interpret the information. This is also one of the reasons why interpretation may produce a distorted reproduction of information as it is processed through already established mental constructs. A new understanding of the environment may in turn trigger a change in the existing mental models. How various issues are interpreted, and what the quality of the interpretation will be, always depends on the interpreter's knowledge, his experience, his mental models and his ability at creative thinking.

Cognitive maps have been worked out as the explicit descriptions and computing implementations of mental models. Cognitive maps consist of nodes generically called "concepts" about different aspects of the environment and the cause-and-effect relationships between these concepts. Cognitive maps give us a method for structuring multiple - and sometimes conflicting - aspects of argumentation. They represent a designed scheme for addressing both the substance of issues, and for working with the knowledge and expertise surrounding issues. Cognitive maps, finally, give us a tool for capturing the different views of issues and for helping managers to focus on important aspects of the issues. They appear to be appropriate intermediates between mental models and specific, operational rules of interpretation.

There are software packages available for an implementation and use of cognitive maps, which will support users in building and using mental models. They are, however, intended to be interactive and it is hard to see how they could be made automatic as part of an interpretation agent. The mental models appear, however, to be useful for an understanding of what elements need to be part of an interpretation process.

## 7.12 A preliminary description of an interpretation agent

In the following, we will quickly explore a possible outline for an Interpretation Agent, which is designed to work in the context of a data warehouse. This is a more structured context than the environments we have been addressing so far, but the description will serve to give us some points of reference on interpretation agent functionality and some hints at technical possibilities of implementation.

The interpretation agent aims to make sense out of collected environmental data, to identify meaningful issues from the data and to evaluate their strategic impacts (fig. 7.6).

The duties of an interpretation agent in the context of a data warehouse include:

1. Periodically visiting the data warehouse, watching for new information, tracking key issue indicators and alerting users to important developments.
2. Comparing and relating new information, recognizing and selecting significant events, trends, and deviating signals. Such signals may be truthful or may have errors, which is judged according to source features, signal characteristics (consistency, clarity) and conformity with others.

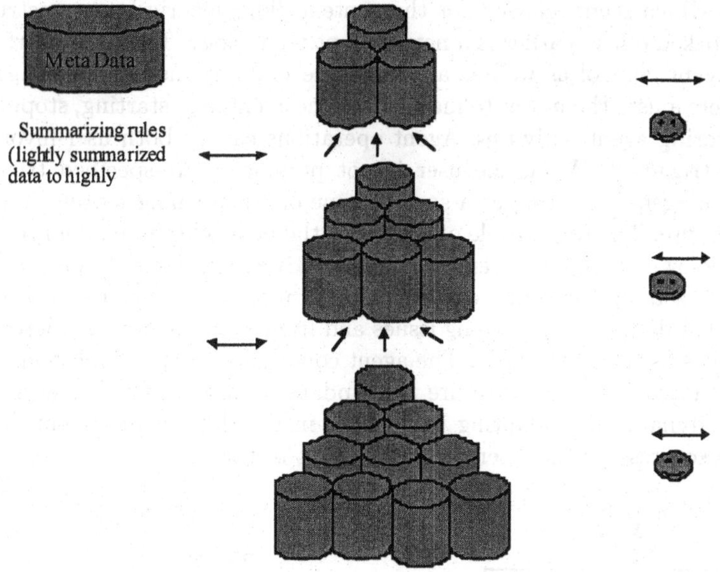


**Fig. 7.6.** Interpreting warehouse data

3. Reasoning and explaining about the possible causes for the events and trends, which is based on cognitive maps that affect the subject of the event. Another way is to use event-mapping techniques in order to form hypothesized issues or to examine interdependencies between issues. The final step will be to map event happenings onto trend lines.
4. Identifying the major groups of issues and assessing their impacts, predicting the probability of occurrence, the development course and milestones.
5. Ranking the issues according to the perceived impacts and probability of occurrence and development. Selecting and forming a key strategic issue list, on which issues with a high probability of development and a high impact should be brought to managerial attention and be monitored closely. Those issues with a low impact can be ignored, no matter whether there is a high probability of development or not.
6. Generate a summary report of the interpretation result; send notice to managers.

At our present state of thinking, most of the proposals listed above can be implemented, with the exception of the reasoning with cognitive maps described in step (3) and the identification of major issues and the assessing of their impact in step (4). These steps require input from the user of the agent, as there still is no good way to make this intellectual work automatic.

A very preliminary outline of the architecture for an interpretation agent is shown in fig. 7.6. This is only intended to give an overview of some possible principles, which seem relevant for the context. The generic IntA construct we have worked out in earlier is a newer agent technology. The user interface provides agent control as well as a user-profile building mechanisms. Agent control offers a user the power to manipulate the agent, e.g. starting, stopping and monitoring agent activities. Agent operations can be both user-invoked and event-triggered. When the user is not present, a pre-specified trigger activates an agent operation at a specific time or when changes occur in the data warehouse. The user profile offers a user the possibility to customize the agent to his own changing preferences, perspectives, and mental models.

The user sets up the context of interpretation for the agent. He also supplies his mental models concerning issues and frames of reference for perceiving the issues as cognitive maps. The agent could have template mechanisms to enable the user to easily acquire and update cognitive maps, or even be capable of dynamically adapting to changes in the data environment. The interface also presents the interpretation report to the user.

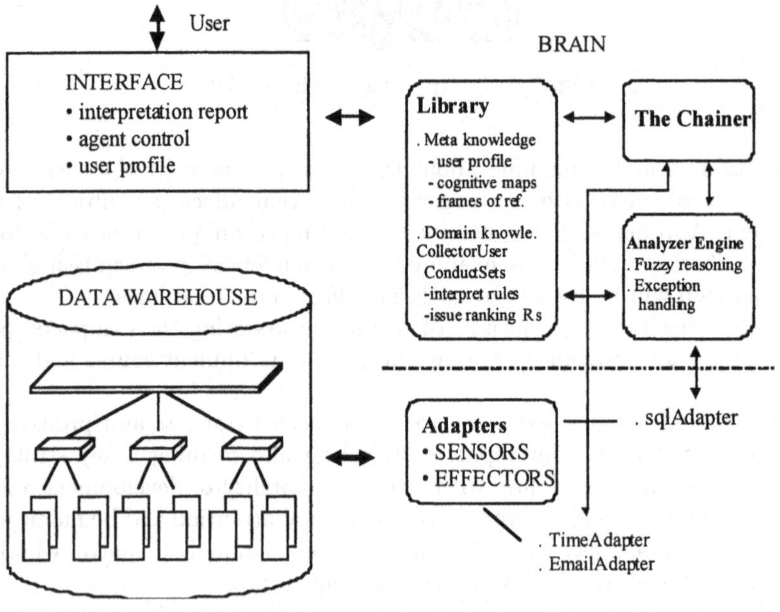


**Fig. 7.7.** The Interpretation Agent architecture.

For the interpretation agent to fulfil its responsibilities we need a number of adapters. In addition to the standard adapters (such as TimeAdapter, EmailAdapter, etc.) normally implemented, application-specific adapters need to be added. In this case, where we have a data warehouse, we will need a sqlAdapter. The sqlAdapter is responsible for opening a connection and querying the data warehouse, in order to track the issue indicators and to support issue discussions. It also creates and maintains a database for the client-side application.

The library will contain domain knowledge: interpreting rules supporting data and issue analysis and hypotheses about causes of potential events. It will also contain data about conduct sets - meta knowledge: user preferences, cognitive maps and frames of reference, surrounding issues and environmental subjects. These can be implemented in terms of predicates, sensors and effectors, which could be used in a rule set and a long-term fact set. At an even higher level, the library could store assumptions underlying cognitive maps and frames of reference. The decision as to what cognitive maps and interpreting rules the agent should use, could be based on values specified in rule atoms and could be modified through modifying profiles.

The chaining engine is a standard construct. The analyser engine needs to have reasoning mechanisms implementing multiple reasoning strategies: data-driven, goal-driven or mixed reasoning. There is no reason why approximate reasoning could not be implemented here.

In addition to this, exception handling needs to be considered. Generalized rules will be defeated when information is available to indicate that the agent is dealing with an exception to some rules. Users may reject part of the interpretation result given by the system. In such cases, the feedback from a user should be incorporated into the system as a means to revise the result. The user can also contribute to exception handling and could benefit from handling exceptions by constantly rethinking and updating his mental models.

At the client-side of the system (cf. Fig. 7.8 for a simple demo prototype), the user can easily get access to a summary report or to a strategic issue list (linking to supporting documents by clicking on active words in the list). A list of signal alerts, which are linked to specific issues, as well as all the new issues identified by the interpretation process are also provided. Using a multidimensional data model, the agent will be able to present the interpretation report in different styles (for example, key strategic issues by milestones, by impacts, by actions, by indicator signals, etc.) and to put the information into multiple perspectives.

With AddComments, the user can add comments to issues and signal alerts, which form his own perspectives. UserProfile helps the user to set up personal preferences and those issues that are of the most concern, and to create and update mental models as well as frames of reference. By attending to the captured signals and analyzed results, the user can modify cognitive maps to guide new interpretations. With AgentConfiguration, the user can define the interpretation context by describing company profiles, internal issues, business objectives and performance indicators.

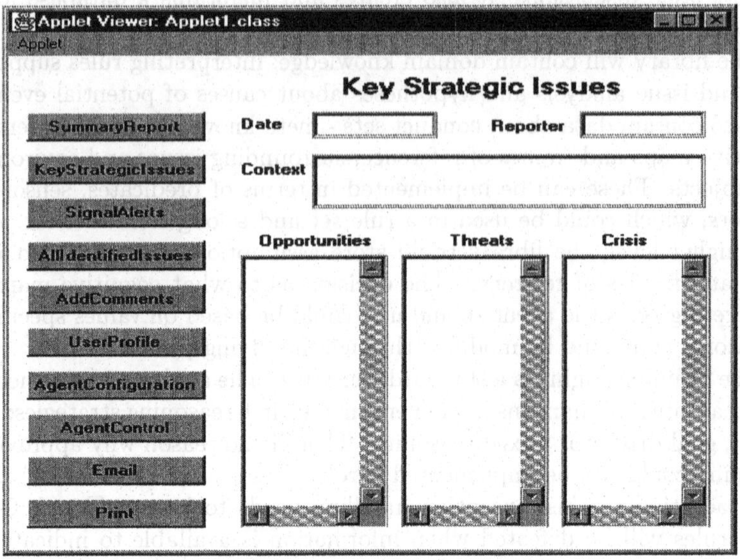


**Fig. 7.8.** Agent Client.

## 7.13 An interpretation agent: details

Agent technology is a fast growing area of information technology - new agent-based products, applications and services are being announced on an almost daily basis. The reason for the interest is that the metaphor of autonomous problem solving entities, which co-operate and co-ordinate to achieve their desired objectives is an intuitive and natural way to conceptualise many problems. Moreover, the conceptual framework and the methods developed within agent technology provide a powerful and useful set of structures and processes for designing and building complex software applications (cf. [9]).

The inherent attributes of software agents make them useful for a number of information management tasks: scanning data sources, retrieving and cleaning data, and (with the IntA) interpreting the data. Agents also have potentially many uses in executive support, for example, automated e-mail handling, meeting scheduling, web browsing, Internet news detecting and alert, external information gathering and filtering. In problems of automatically gathering, filtering and searching for information, the software agent approach represents one of the most popularly exploited solutions. In the environmental scanning activity of senior managers, the agent approach presents a novel way to supply information and to help conduct information acquisition. As we now add the functionality of the IntA to the gathering, filtering and searching for information we will add the possibilities to carry out several forms for interpretation of data.

We have envisioned that the IntA should be used in tandem with the scenario agent (ScA). As we already designed the ScA as a multi-agent system (MA), which is built as a group of collaborative agents, the combination IntA & ScA will be an MA. The group of IntA & ScA agents will have a layered structure, and the individual agents of the group will be either task agents (TAs) or information agents (IAs). The IntA & ScA will be a reactive system, which maintains an ongoing interaction with the environment and will react to it by collecting data and interpreting them. The MA will be designed to deliver customised user-wanted data (information, knowledge) with interpretations, and the MA will be to some extent used as a wrapper around decision models for which we need to provide interpretations of their outputs.

The overall design of the IntA & ScA follows four major design principles: (i) support for open world (OW) scenarios, (ii) support for scenario building, (iii) interpretation support for decision models, and (iv) interpretation support for data collected in a data warehouse.

In the first case scenarios are built with support from the DSS and used both for independent scenario planning and as a basis and input for the decision models (as the scenario material is stored in the DSS database). Interpretations should be produced to facilitate the scenario building process.

In the second case, the scenarios are built to drive decision models and (a) input data is produced to decision model standards and/or (b) is combined with decision model outputs to be used as input to other decision models (and should thus follow decision model standards). Interpretations should be produced to facilitate the choice of decision models, and in order to explain the scenario results produced with the models.

In the third case, interpretations support work with the input data to decision models and help to explain the results to recipients of reports.

In the fourth and final case the interpretation helps to quickly make sense of large sets of data collected in a data warehouse.

The model-based scenarios can be of two types. A subset of OW scenarios, which possibly have been refocused, have been made more specific and/or been simplified with the help of ScA support. Tailor-built scenarios, which have been produced to run decision models (single models or a system of models) as part of a strategy to sketch out future developments of a business context. The second type of scenarios represents projections of an understanding of key features of a business context based on the knowledge we have on the past and the present, and should be run with data from the DSS database. The first type of scenarios will - relative to this - have more futuristic elements and may be more difficult to adjust to the decision model standards as they will run with data generated for the OW scenarios. Consequently, there are differences in the interpretation tasks assigned to the IntA: in the first case "open categories" of elements and in the second case "decision model-specified categories".

The construction of OW scenarios, and the application of model-based scenarios to decision models, is part of the process to build an *industry foresight.* An essential part of the foresight-building process is to handle large amounts of inconsistent data in a systematic and effective way. The necessary support for that is to quickly scan and use data from many (tens, hundreds of) data sources, to interpret the data and to summarize findings and insights in a form, which can be used in the verbal storyline part of both OW and I21 scenarios. Interpretations add value to the data gathering and cleaning carried out by the ScA, and hence we may look at the IntA as a value-added service to the ScA. Neither OW nor model-based scenarios should be one-off constructs. Scenarios, when found relevant and useful, should be used repeatedly to support rational reactions to a changing environment. Then, for this the IntA & ScA should help evaluate and interpret sudden developments, breaking news and significant changes to the environment. Finally, the scenario building, scenario planning and the foresight processes should react to, evaluate and interpret so-called weak signals, which will allow a support systems user to plan for the future ahead of the competition. Thus, we need the IntA & ScA to support the detection and evaluation of weak signals.

### 7.13.1 Interpretation support for OW scenarios

When we build the IntA & ScA agents to support the building and the use of OW scenarios, the main emphasis will be on: (i) collecting data from identified data sources (in the DSS database, on Internet or on an intranet), (ii) cleaning and condensing the data as information, (iii) interpreting the data, which has been collected and condensed, (iv) combining data from different types of data sources, (v) supporting the use of data sources which have been built and used manually, (vi) supporting the use of database or data warehouse depositories, and (vii) supporting the extraction, editing and interpretation of data (information, knowledge) for the verbal storyline of an OW scenario. The ScA for OW scenarios is a *search agent*, which also supports data insertion in a database/data warehouse, the handling of a database/data warehouse and the editing and writing of OW scenario reports. The IntA for OW scenarios works with reference points and benchmarks to classify observations as crisis, *opportunities and threats.*

The functionality of this part of the system can be summarised as follows (the IntA parts are shown with italics):

- <u>IntA21 & ScA21.</u>
  - Collects data from different sources on the Internet and from various intranet sources.
  - Can work with Internet sources that are password protected (Reuters);
  - Analyses the data based on its content; handles text and numerical data;
  - *Interprets the data with the help of benchmarks and reference points stored in the DSS database, or which are given as input data by the user;*

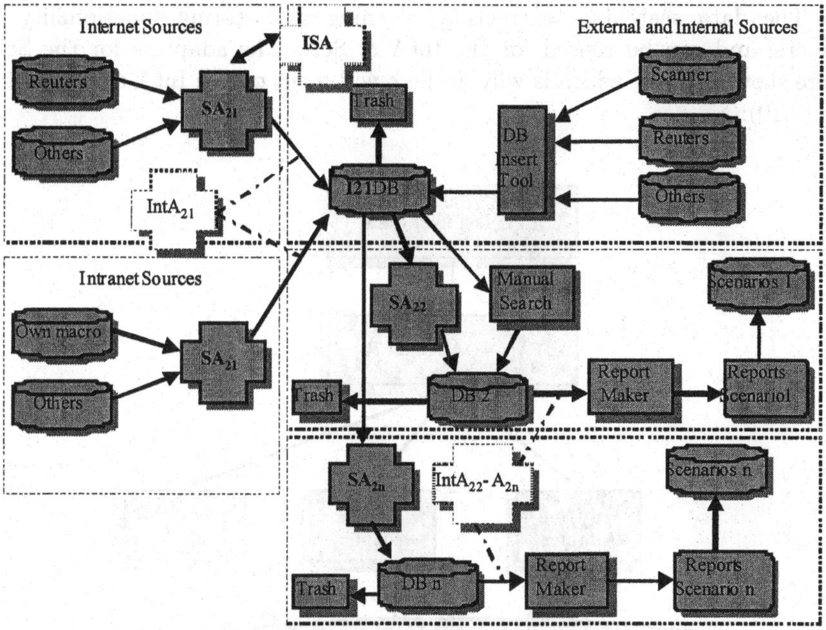


**Fig. 7.9.** A layout of the IntA & ScA for support of OW scenarios.

- Stores interesting data in a data warehouse application (built with DB and DB2 - DBn; all of them part of the DSS database);
- *Stores interpretations (linked to the data);*
- Retrieves only new and changed data;
- Builds meta-data on retrieved data to follow up on retrieval;
- scans different data sources and sites frequently for new data;
- Represents an effective use of data sources, which in fact is faster than human users;
- *Collaborates with IntA10 & ScA1 through coordination with the ISA;*

• <u>IntA22 & ScA22 - IntA2n & ScA2n.</u>
  - Analyses and collects data on selected topics based on user-defined profiles;
  - Sorts the data based on date, content and profiles;
  - *Interprets the data with the help of benchmarks and reference points stored in the DSS database;*
  - Sorted data which is related is stored together in DB2 - DBn;

• <u>Report Maker.</u>
  - Allows the user to select data from profile-defined folders;
  - *Interpretations can be retrieved with the data;*
  - Selected data can be edited and saved as reports;
  - Edited data can be traced to the unmodified (original) data if needed;

The data searching, extracting, cleaning and storing functionality is generic and can be reused for the IntA & ScA. The adapters for the ScA were shown earlier, which is why we here will focus on the IntA adapters (cf. fig. 7.10):

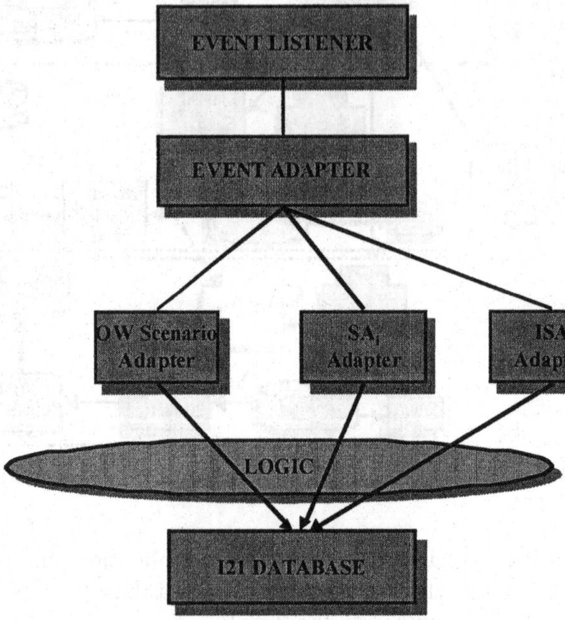


**Fig. 7.10.** The event listener-adapter functionality for the IntA2i.

The interpretation agents to be used for the OW scenario building support will have a generic basic layout and adaptive elements in order to fit them into their specific task environments (cf. IntA21 and IntA22 - IntA2n). In fig. 7.10 the OW Scenario Adapter refers to the series of adapters specified for various data sources for the ScA. The ScAi Adapter is designed for the interaction with the ScAi working in tandem with the IntAi, and the IScA Adapter for the co-ordination with the information agent co-ordinating the IntA & ScA pairs. The interpretation logic is covered by the LOGIC field, and will be described in more detail below.

One of the basic ideas we had with the design of the ScA was to use Internet extensively as a data source for the OW scenarios. In the last 2 years, we have carried out a series of studies with search agents on Internet data sources, and we have found that the quality of the data retrieved was not very good. The insights, which could be collected from publicly available data sources, were not very profound and repetitions of the same material from different data sources were frequent. We also carried out a series of experiments with the *Reuters Business Briefing* (as well as with other commercial data sources), which showed that the quality of data was much better. These observations have some relevance also for the design and use of the IntA: interpretation of inconsistent data (as can be found from public Internet data sources) is not a very worthwhile effort, the chances for success are much better when working with consistent data. This supports the use of either commercial Internet services for the building of OW scenarios or internal, evaluated and validated data sources.

### 7.13.2 Interpretation support for model-based scenarios

For the model-based scenarios, we have the ScA1 agent introduced above. For interpretation purposes the agent will be working with:

- IntA10, which is interpreting the data to be used as input to the decision models of the model-based scenarios;
- IntA11, which is interpreting the output from the model-based scenarios; the interpretations can then be stored with the output;
- IntA12, which provides one further interpretation after the scenario material has been enhanced with material from the manual search.

As the IntA1 & ScA1 supports the building and use of model-based scenarios, there is a more focused use of data sources than for the OW scenarios. The primary data source is the DSS database, which holds primary data for the DSS or (if the OW scenarios have been run first) scenario data from different data sources. A third possibility is that the DSS user wants to add data of his own (using e.g. the INDY tool) to use for the model-based scenarios.

The support offered by the IntA1 & ScA1 is more focused, but it is basically the same as for the OW scenario:

(i) collecting data from identified data sources (in the DSS database, on Internet or on an intranet),
(ii) cleaning and condensing the data as information,
(iii) interpreting the data, which has been collected and condensed,
(iv) combining data from different types of data sources,
(v) supporting the use of data sources which have been built and used manually,
(vi) supporting the use of database or data warehouse depositories, and
(vii) supporting the extraction, editing and interpretation of data (information, knowledge) for the verbal storyline of a model-based scenario.

The IntA1 & ScA1 for model-based scenarios is a database/data warehouse handling and data interpretation agent, which collects data, interprets selected parts of the data and inputs data into decision models, runs them, interprets the results, stores the result in the DSS database (or in a data warehouse application) and supports the writing of scenario reports.

The functionality of this part of the system can be summarised as follows (the IntA parts are shown with italics):

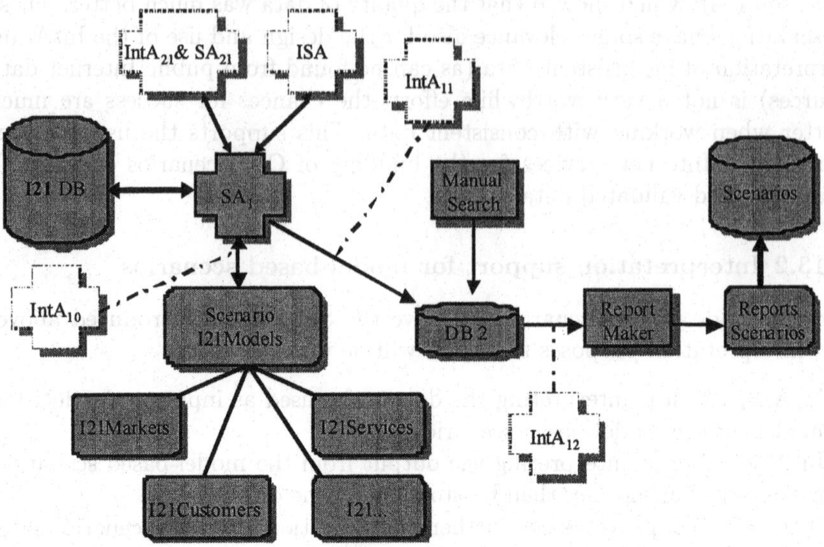


**Fig. 7.11.** A layout of the IntA1 & ScA1 for model-based scenarios.

- <u>IntA1 & ScA1.</u>
  - Activated through data-generated events, events connected to time or user-generated events;
  - Works as an information customizer, i.e. it collects, scrubs, integrates and transforms data for the decision (scenario-building) models from the DSS database;
  - *Interprets selected parts of the data through IntA10;*
  - Provides help desk support;
  - Offers level of support (novice, intermediate, experienced, advanced); depending on choice the support can be either an off-line help function or an autonomous information customizer and help desk;
  - Applies the event listener-event adapter-specific adapters logic of the ScA;
  - Runs Decision models with data elements of the DSS database,
  - *Interprets the scenario results with IntA11;*
  - Stores intermediate results in DB2 (part of the DSS database),
  - *Interprets the scenario results, after adding the results of the manual search, with IntA12;*
  - Runs a Report Maker (which support the user in making a scenario) and,
  - Stores scenarios in a DB (part of the DSS database).
  - Collaborates with IntA21 & ScA21 through co-ordination by the ISA;

Part of the IntA1 & ScA1 features should be the event listener-adapter features used for the ScA, which were generic and can be reused. The selected adapters are now built to follow the input from the collaborative agents ISA (cf. fig. 7.11) and to co-ordinate the interaction of the IntA1 with the ScA1.

In addition to the individual agent features we have just worked through there is some work done on creating a class of collaborative agents, which will have both individual features and features they get through the collaboration. Collaborative agents emphasise autonomy and co-operation with other agents in order to perform tasks for their users in open and time-constrained multi-agent environments. These features are relevant also for interpretation tasks, in which we may have agents to work out interpretations of selected parts of material from a data warehouse. This can also be done for specified parts of material produced with OW and model-based scenarios. Then the IntA should be able to combine these interpretations to some consistent scenarios through the collaboration. It is probably needless to state that the consistency will be manageable only through interaction with a knowledgable and experienced user. Also the IntA1 may have some (limited parametric) learning properties and they may have to "negotiate" in order to reach mutually acceptable agreements.

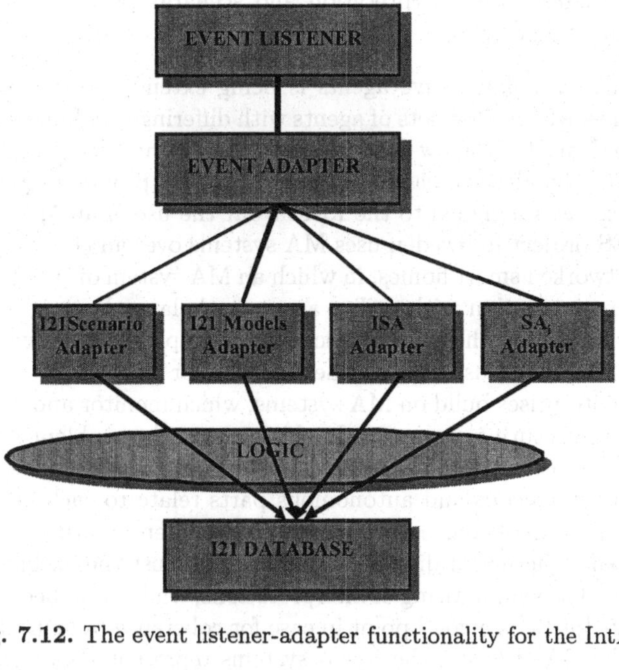


**Fig. 7.12.** The event listener-adapter functionality for the IntA1.

The motives for building collaborative agent systems include:

(i) solving problems that may be too large for a centralised single agent,
(ii) allowing for the interconnecting and interoperation of existing legacy systems (e.g. decision support systems, conventional software systems, etc.), and,
(iii) providing solutions to inherently distributed problems, such as drawing on distributed data sources or distributed sensor networks. With interpretation agents we may add one more motive:
(iv) interpretations can be run in parallel on carious parts of large data sets and then combined to form a quick and effective summary.

The functionality of this part of the system can be summarised as follows:

- <u>ISA</u>
  - Operates as an IA in relation to ScA1and ScA2.
  - IntA1 is context adapted to model-based scenarios and works in tandem with ScA1.
  - Each IntA2j is context adapted and is designed to work in tandem with a ScA2j .
  - ScA2 operates as an IA in relation to ScA21 - ScA2n.
  - All the ScA21 - ScA2n are designed as TAs.
  - All the IntA21 - IntA2n are designed as TAs.
  - Co-ordinates both interpretation and scenario agents, which requires multi-functionality.

The world of collaborative agents is being extended to the multi-agent (MA) systems, which allow sets of agents with differing capabilities to interact to solve problems, they allow for scalability, they permit us to reuse software modules, they handle software evolution and they promote open systems. The complex tasks assigned to the ISA favour the use of an MA approach.

The ISES project in Sweden uses MA systems over an electric power grid to create networked smart homes, in which an MA system of smart appliances can work in conjunction with utility agents to balance load, to save energy and to provide safety. The ISES project is an example of agents with differing capabilities. We could use some of these results for the ISA.

Virtual enterprises build on MA systems, which monitor and control business and manufacturing processes. In this context the problem of coherence has become visible, i.e. how different activities in a distributed system consisting of heterogeneous and autonomous parts relate to each other. In this sense, working on coherence is moving beyond interoperating as it considers the global structure of different activities, not just the exchange of data among them. The summarising of interpretations, which have been made with collaborative IntAs, is a good point in case for coherence (albeit a bit hard to achieve). The DARPA and the Lycos systems represent approaches to deal with coherence, and similar tasks have been pursued in studies of human-agent interaction and in games to mimic real-life markets. We will have to

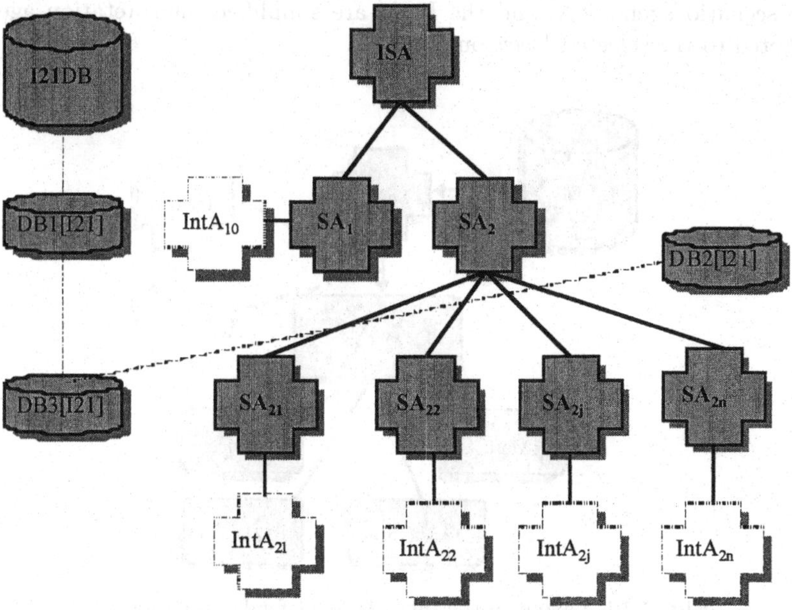


**Fig. 7.13.** Layout of the IntA & ScA as collaborative agents.

find ways to deal with the coherence problems, not only for the technical summaries but also for the semantic interpretations.

For MA systems of IntA & ScA pairs to succeed, a systematic collaboration of agents is necessary. This, again, requires that the agents have been designed and built in such a way that the internal cognitive structure of the agents is conducive to collaboration. If this is the case, then there is basis for building MA systems with some learning and planning capabilities. As we found out previously, the learning and planning capabilities reside in the interaction of agents and probably not with the individual agents.

The IntA, in its various forms of IntA10, IntA11, IntA12, IntA21 - IntA2n, should be an MA system of collaborative agents itself, which (i) interact to produce interpretations in support of OW and model-based scenarios, (ii) allow scalability from small to large data sets, and (iii) are built by reusing software modules - which should follow a software evolution strategy.

### 7.13.3 Interpretation support for decision models

Besides the use of the IntAj & ScAj pairs as interpretation support within an MA, the agent functionality also allows for simpler applications as interpretation support for selected decision models. In the following, we have outlined a construct in which agent pairs work with decision models as more or less stand-alone applications. The ScA1 is now the search agent part of the scenario agent ScA, and the IntAj are simplified interpretation agents adapted to the selected Decision models.

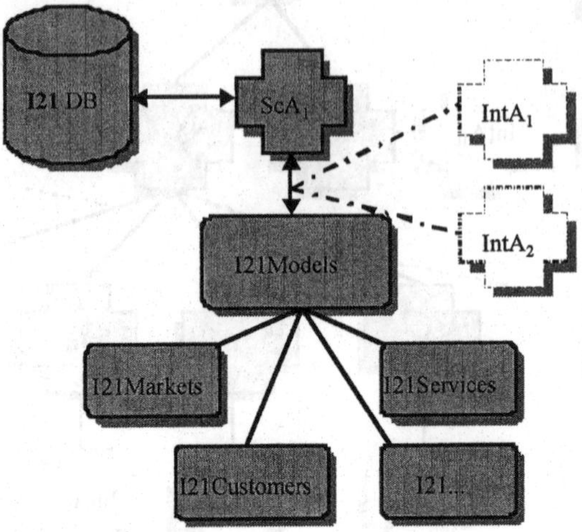


**Fig. 7.14.** Layout of the IntAj & ScA1 for Decision models.

The functionality of the support provided by the pairs of agents for Decision models can be summarised as follows (the IntA parts are shown with italics):

- IntAj & ScA1.
  - Activated through data-generated events, events connected to time or user-generated events;
  - Works as an information customiser, i.e. it collects, scrubs, integrates and transforms data for selected decision models from the DSS database;
  - *Interprets selected parts of the data through IntA1;*
  - Provides help desk support;
  - Offers level of support (novice, intermediate, experienced, advanced); depending on choice the support can be either an off-line help function or an autonomous information customiser and help desk;
  - Runs Decision models with data elements of the DSS database,
  - *Interprets the Decision model results with IntA2;*

Part of the IntAj & ScA1 features should be the event listener-adapter features used for the ScA, which were generic and can be reused. In this way, we can reuse all the software constructs we develop for the more advanced scenario and interpretation agent pairs. Let us the find out how the IntA functionality can be applied for one of the decision models. We have selected a generic model called Estimation of likely future market potential) as an example, and will in the following show how the IntA should be implemented in this context. The set of countries to be chosen is defined as a function of market potential and prices.

The IntA1 is used to interpret these data (cf. fig. 7.15) with linguistic categories (cf. the section onapproximate reasoning) such as ["small" - "great"] for market potential, and ["low - "high"] for prices. In this way, it is possible to classify countries according to similarities in terms of the analysed factors, and then to find groups and clusters of countries. This classification is one of the inputs for IntA2, which will use the grades of similarity, the classifications of sector-specific factors (which may be multiple attribute, linguistic classifications), the results of the regression analysis (which are interpreted in grades of significant/non-significant) and the model output on the market potential for the new service (which is interpreted in grades of [low, medium, high]).

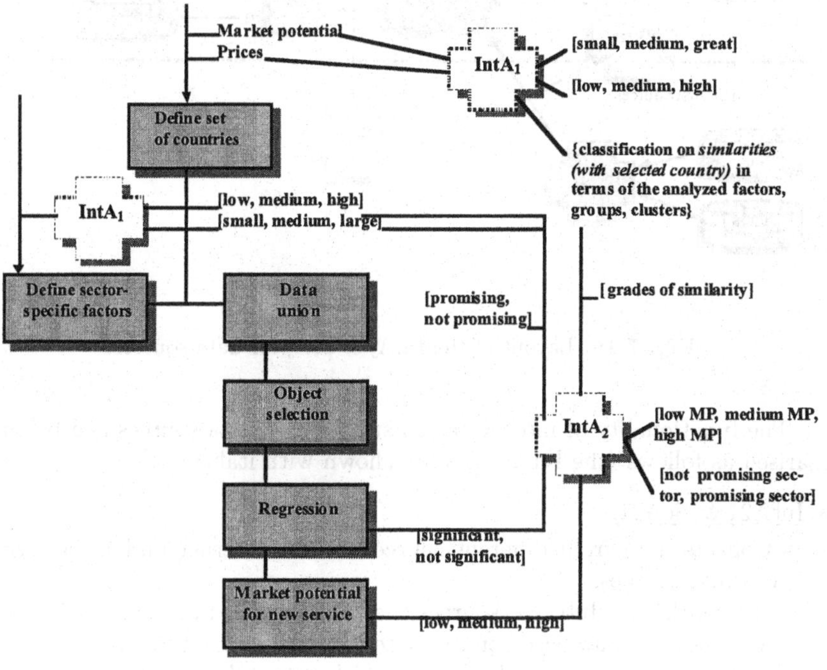


**Fig. 7.15.** The interpretation agents and a decision model

The output of IntA2 is a classification of the market potential for countries and sectors in terms of a combination of [low, medium, high] Market Potential and [promising, not promising] sectors.

### 7.13.4 Interpretation support for data sources

In a similar fashion as the interpretation agents for decision models, we may also use simplified versions of the scenario and interpretation agents to build interpretation support for the use of various data sources. Again we will use the search agent part of the scenario agent ScA and fit IntAs to them, which will be context adapted to selected data sources.

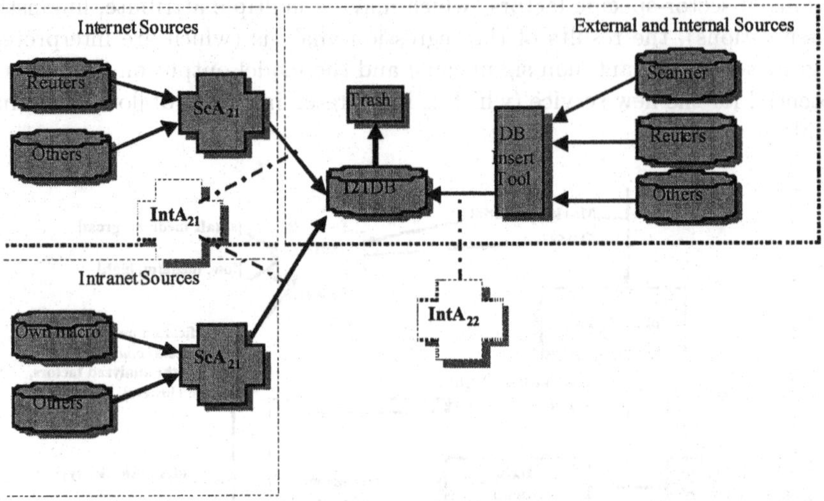


**Fig. 7.16.** Layout of the IntAj & ScAj for data sources.

The functionality of interpretation support for data sources can be summarised as follows (the IntA parts are shown with italics):

- <u>IntA21 & ScA21.</u>
  - Collects data from different sources on the Internet and from various intranet sources.
  - Can work with Internet sources that are password protected (Reuters);
  - Analyses the data based on its content; handles text and numerical data;
  - *Interprets the data with the help of benchmarks and reference points stored in the DSS database, or which are given as input data by the user;*
  - Stores interesting data in a data warehouse application;
  - *Stores interpretations (linked to the data);*
  - Retrieves only new and changed data;
  - Builds meta-data on retrieved data to follow up on retrieval;
  - Scans different data sources and sites frequently for new data;
  - Represents an effective use of data sources, which in fact is faster than human users;
- <u>IntA22.</u>

- *Interprets the data with the help of benchmarks and reference points stored in the DSS database;*
- *Sorted and interpreted data which is related is stored together in the DSS database;*

### 7.13.5 Generic interpretation of agent structures

It has probably become evident in the previous sections that the interpretation agents we have designed, have a common generic core in their designs. The interpretation agent IntA21, working in tandem with the search agent ScA21, will,

- collect data from different sources on the Internet, and from various intranet sources;
- analyse the data based on its content; handles text and numerical data;
- *interpret the data with the help of benchmarks and reference points stored in the DSS database, or which are given as input data by the user;*
- store interesting data in a data warehouse application;
- *store interpretations (linked to the data);*
- retrieve only new and changed data;
- build meta-data on retrieved data to follow up on retrieval;
- scan different data sources and sites frequently for new data;

This is actually the same functionality as that of IntA21, even if this agent works in the context of inserted, not scanned data. Furthermore, this is generically the same agent as the IntA21 in fig.7.9, even if the latter has some added functionality in order to deal with the collaborative environment. The interpretation agents IntA1 and IntA2 (cf. fig.7.14) have the same generic structure as the data they should work with is specified as input/output data for/from I21 models. The IntA10 and IntA11 agents of fig.7.11 will have the same generic structure unless the decision models used in model-based scenarios will have very diverse conceptual structures from the selection made for the decision models.

The *Logic* part of the agents can probably be built with the same fuzzy logic & approximate reasoning schemes for all interpretation agents, but the event adapters need to be tailored to the specific agent contexts: (i) OW scenarios, (ii) model-based scenarios, (iii) decision models, (iv) Internet, intranet and internal data sources, (v) collaborative agent environments and (vi) cooperative, ISA-controlled efforts. In this sense, the interpretation agents are partly generic and partly specific, context-adapted.

### 7.13.6 Approximate reasoning and sense-making

The use of fuzzy logic and fuzzy reasoning methods are becoming more and more popular in intelligent information systems, especially in hyperknowledge support systems, knowledge formation processes in knowledge-based systems, active decision support systems, medical support systems, robotics, financial analyses, control and pattern recognition.

As we outlined the basic functionality of the IntA we used *normal/unusual* and *plausible/unplausible* as descriptions of events and as labels to be attached to events, observations, results, etc. as part of the interpretation process. It should be clear that these labels are linguistic and imprecise, and that they cannot be found through any precise mathematical analysis, neither would we like them to be assigned by a user in a subjective fashion.

Previously we have made the case for the use of fuzzy sets and fuzzy logic if we want to be both imprecise and systematic when we interpret events and observations in a business context. It should be obvious, that future telecom services in business-to business communication is a context where we cannot be precise in observations or interpretations of data, information or knowledge.

### 7.13.7 Support for sense-making and interpretation

The basic functionality of the IntA can be outlined on the basis of what we have planned to accomplish with OW and model-based scenarios, with the use of decision models and with the making sense of data collected in a data warehouse. This outline should be seen as a first basic understanding of what are relevant support functions, We have identified 4 groups of basic support functions we need to plan for implementation in the IntA.

Let us start with the most unstructured part first, the making sense of data collected in a data warehouse, and then progress to OW and model-based scenarios, and finally to decision models. Thus, we want the IntA to:

**Help and support when making sense of large amounts of data.**

This involves a number of functions:

1. Periodically visiting the data warehouse, watching for new or recent data, tracking updates of key issue indicators and triggering signals to show significant changes.
2. Comparing and relating new data to existing data set, recognizing and selecting significant events, trends, and deviating signals.
3. Support the user in reasoning and explaining about the possible causes for the events and trends.
4. Support the user in identifying the major groups of issues and in assessing their impacts, in predicting the probability of occurrence and in formulating the development course and milestones.
5. Ranking the issues according to the perceived impacts and probability of occurrence and development. The ranking may be interactive and supportive of the user.

6. Generating summary reports of the interpretation results. The objectives here are (i) to save time for the user, and (ii) to quickly focus work with the data on meaningful subsets of data.

The agent pairs we have constructed provide this support:

- <u>IntA21 & ScA21.</u>
  - Collects data from different sources on the Internet and from various intranet sources.
  - Analyses the data based on its content; handles text and numerical data;
  - *Interprets the data with the help of benchmarks and reference points stored in the DSS database, or which are given as input data by the user;*
  - Stores interesting data in a data warehouse application;
  - *Stores interpretations (linked to the data);*
  - Retrieves only new and changed data;
  - Builds meta-data on retrieved data to follow up on retrieval;
  - Scans different data sources and sites frequently for new data;
  - *Collaborates with IntA10 & ScA1 through coordination with the ISA;*
- <u>IntA22 & ScA22 - IntA2n & ScA2n.</u>
  - Analyses and collects data on selected topics based on user-defined profiles;
  - Sorts the data based on date, content and profiles;
  - *Interprets the data with the help of benchmarks and reference points stored in the DSS database;*
  - Sorted data which is related is stored together in DB2 - DBn;
- <u>IntA1 & ScA1.</u>
  - Activated through data-generated events, events connected to time or user-generated events;
  - Works as an information customiser, i.e. it collects, scrubs, integrates and transforms data for the (scenario-building) models from the DSS database;
  - *Interprets selected parts of the data through IntA10;*
  - Provides help desk support;
  - Offers level of support (novice, intermediate, experienced, advanced); depending on choice the support can be either an off-line help function or an autonomous information customiser and help desk;
  - Applies the event listener-event adapter-specific adapters logic of the generic agent construct;
  - Runs decision models with data elements of the DSS database,
  - *Interprets the scenario results with IntA11;*
  - Stores intermediate results in DB2 (part of the DSS database),
  - *Interprets the scenario results, after adding the results of the manual search, with IntA12;*
  - Runs a Report Maker (which supports the user in making a scenario) and,

- Stores scenarios in a DB (part of the DSS database).
- Collaborates with IntA21 & ScA21 through co-ordination by the ISA;

Let us then move to more specialized support functionalities.

**Help and support in identifying results worth further attention.**

This again involves a number of functions:

1. Specified input/output data to and from decision models is evaluated in relation to reference points or benchmarks, and is classified as normal or unusual; the latter category is singled out for further attention.
2. Specified input/output data used and worked out in I21 scenarios is evaluated as plausible or implausible with the help of reference points or benchmarks; the latter category is singled out for more work and data collection.
3. Selected (but not necessarily specified) input/output data used and worked out in OW scenarios is evaluated in terms of plausible or implausible, and in terms of the categories (crisis, opportunities and threats) with the help of reference points and benchmarks (which may be imprecise); the categories being plausible and which are found to represent crisis, opportunities and threats are singled out for more work and a continued gathering of data from selected data sources.
4. Collected data in the data warehouse is evaluated against keywords, benchmarks and reference points (if numerical), and against subjective assessment criteria; data singled out as unusual will be the focus of a continued collection of data and further study.

The objectives will now be to help the user (i) to focus his/her work on essentials, and (ii) to get a better understanding of the context, which may not be possible without the support of the IntA.
The agent pairs we have constructed provide this support:

- <u>IntA22 & ScA22 - IntA2n & ScA2n.</u>
  - Analyses and collects data on selected topics based on user-defined profiles;
  - Sorts the data based on date, content and profiles;
  - *Interprets the data with the help of benchmarks and reference points stored in the DSS database;*
  - Sorted data which is related is stored together in DB2 - DBn;
  - Stores intermediate results in DB2,
  - *Interprets the scenario results, after adding the results of the manual search, with IntA12;*
  - Runs a Report Maker (which support the user in making a scenario) and,
  - Stores scenarios in a DB (part of the DSS database).

Now we can take one more step towards a further specified functionality.

**Help and support in tracing potential cause-effect chains.**

This involves a number of functions; we will move from the most specific to the most open-ended:

1. When working with several decision models, the IntA should follow (and on request display) the input and output data used for and produced by the decision models. The patterns thus derived may indicate cause-effect relationships.
2. When working with model-based scenarios, the IntA should follow (and on request display) the sequence and combinations of decision models used. The scenario patterns may show cause-effect relationships among the events built in the scenarios when displayed over time.
3. When working with OW scenarios, the IntA should keep trace of data variations in relation to reference points and benchmarks. When displayed over time, the scenario patterns may show underlying cause-effect relationships, or may indicate where further data gathering may reveal cause-effect relationships.
4. When working with sets of data in a data warehouse, cause-effect relationships are difficult to trace. If benchmarks or reference points can be established, variations in relation to these may be traced and displayed over time to suggest cause-effect relationships. The objective here is simply to help the user trace potential cause-effect relationships, which may be important if no relationships have been known before. The agent pairs we have constructed provide this support:

- <u>IntA1 & ScA1.</u>
  - Activated through data-generated events, events connected to time or user-generated events;
  - Works as an information customiszer, i.e. it collects, scrubs, integrates and transforms data for the (scenario-building) models from the DSS database;
  - *Interprets selected parts of the data through IntA10;*
  - Provides help desk support;
  - Offers level of support (novice, intermediate, experienced, advanced); depending on choice the support can be either an off-line help function or an autonomous information customiser and help desk;
  - Applies the event listener-event adapter-specific adapters logic of the ScA;
  - Runs Decision models with data elements of the DSS database,
  - *Interprets the scenario results with IntA11;*
  - Stores intermediate results in DB2,
  - *Interprets the scenario results, after adding the results of the manual search, with IntA12;*

- Runs a Report Maker (which supports the user in making a scenario) and,
- Stores scenarios in a DB (part of the DSS database).
- Collaborates with IntA21 & ScA21 through co-ordination by the ISA;

Let us then take a final step towards a specified functionality.

**Help and support in finding similar results.**

This support function will contain one part:

1. When working with decision models and finding some specific results, we may want to know if these results already have been derived with some other decision model or have been collected from some data source. The IntA should use the output to initiate a search for similar results in the DSS database or in a data warehouse used as a basis for input data. The objectives here are (i) to avoid inconsistency by having similar results analysed and worked on in parallel, and (ii) to find similarities in time, and avoid double work.

The agent pairs we have constructed provide this support:

- IntA21 & ScA21.
  - Collects data from different sources on the Internet and from various intranet sources.
  - Can work with Internet sources that are password protected (Reuters);
  - Analyses the data based on its content; handles text and numerical data;
  - *Interprets the data with the help of benchmarks and reference points stored in the DSS database, or which are given as input data by the user;*
  - Stores interesting data in a data warehouse application (built with DB and DB2 - DBn);
  - *Stores interpretations (linked to the data);*
  - Retrieves only new and changed data;
  - Builds meta-data on retrieved data to follow up on retrieval;
  - Scans different data sources and sites frequently for new data;
  - Represents an effective use of data sources, which in fact is faster than human users;
  - *Collaborates with IntA10 & ScA1 through coordination with the ISA;*
- IntA22 & ScA22 - IntA2n & ScA2n.
  - Analyses and collects data on selected topics based on user-defined profiles;
  - Sorts the data based on date, content and profiles;
  - *Interprets the data with the help of benchmarks and reference points stored in the DSS database;*
  - Sorted data which is related is stored together in DB2 - DBn.

# Bibliography


1. N.J. Abboud, M. Sakawa and M. Inuiguchi, A fuzzy programming approach to multiobjective multidimensional 0-1 knapsack problems, *Fuzzy Sets and Systems*, 86(1997) 1-14
2. R. Axelrod, *Structure of Decision: the Cognitive Maps of Political Elites* (Princeton University Press, Princeton, New Jersey, 1976).
3. H. I. Ansoff, Critique of Henry Mintzberg's The Design School: Reconsidering the Basic Premises of Strategic Managemen', *Strategic Management Journal*, 12(1991) 449-461.
4. B. De Baets and A. Markova, Addition of LR-fuzzy intervals based on a continuous t-norm, in: *Proceedings of IPMU'96 Conference*, (July 1-5, 1996, Granada, Spain), 1996 353-358.
5. B. De Baets and A. Marková-Stupňanová, Analytical expressions for addition of fuzzy intervals, *Fuzzy Sets and Systems*, 91(1997) 203-213.
6. J. Bayer and R.Harter, "Miner", "Manager" and "Researcher": Three Models of Analysis of Scanner Data, *International Journal of Research in Marketing*, 8(1991) 17-27.
7. R.E. Bellman and L.A. Zadeh, Decision-making in a fuzzy environment, *Management Sciences*, Ser. B 17(1970) 141-164.
8. F. Black and M. Scholes, The pricing of options and corporate liabilities, *Journal of Political Economy*, 81(1973) 637-659.
9. Z. Bodie, A. Kane and A.J. Marcus, *Investments* (Irwin, Times Mirror Higher Education Group, Boston, 1996).
10. S. Bodjanova, Approximation of fuzzy concepts in decision making, *Fuzzy Sets and Systems*, 85(1997) 23-29
11. R.F. Boisvert, S.E. Howe and D.K. Kahaner, The guide to the available mathematical software problem classification system, *Communications in Statistics, Simulation and Computation*, 20(1991) 811-842, (http://gams.nist.gov).
12. J. Bradshaw, Introduction to Software Agents, in: J. Bradshawed ed., *Software Agents*, (AAAI Press/The MIT Press, 1997) 3-46.
13. R.G. Brown, *Smoothing, Forecasting and Prediction of Discrete Time Series* (Prentice-Hall, Englewood Cliffs, 1963).
14. J.J.Buckley, Possibilistic linear programming with triangular fuzzy numbers, *Fuzzy sets and Systems*, 26(1988) 135-138.
15. J.J.Buckley, Solving possibilistic linear programming problems, *Fuzzy Sets and Systems*, 31(1989) 329-341.
16. J.J.Buckley, Multiobjective possibilistic linear programming, *Fuzzy Sets and Systems*, 35(1990) 23-28.
17. J.M. Cadenas and J.L. Verdegay, PROBO: an interactive system in fuzzy linear programming *Fuzzy Sets and Systems* 76(1995) 319-332.
18. E. Canestrelli and S. Giove, Optimizing a quadratic function with fuzzy linear coefficients, *Control and Cybernetics*, 20(1991) 25-36.

19. E. Canestrelli and S. Giove, Bidimensional approach to fuzzy linear goal programming, in: M. Delgado, J. Kacprzyk, J.L. Verdegay and M.A. Vila eds., *Fuzzy Optimization* (Physical Verlag, Heildelberg, 1994) 234-245.
20. E. Canestrelli, S. Giove and R. Fullér, Sensitivity analysis in possibilistic quadratic programming, *Fuzzy Sets and Systems*, 82(1996) 51-56.
21. B. Cao, New model with T-fuzzy variations in linear programming, *Fuzzy Sets and Systems*, 78(1996) 289-292.
22. C. Carlsson, Complex management problems and a systems concept: An adaptation and application of structure systems, in: R. Trappl, G. Klir and Pichler eds., *Progress in Cybernetics and Systems Research*, Vol. VIII, (Hemisphere Publ. Corp., Wahington 1982) 69-82.
23. C. Carlsson, Approximate reasoning through fuzzy MCDM-methods, *Operational Research'87*, (Elsevier, Amsterdam, 1988) 817-828.
24. C. Carlsson, On interdependent fuzzy multiple criteria, in: R. Trappl ed., *Cybernetics and Systems'90* (World Scientific, Singapore, 1990) 139-146.
25. C. Carlsson, On optimization with interdependent multiple criteria, in: R. Lowen and M. Roubens eds., *Fuzzy Logic: State of the Art*, Kluwer Academic Publishers, Dordrecht, 1992 415-422.
26. C. Carlsson and R. Fullér, Fuzzy if-then rules for modeling interdependencies in FMOP problems, in: *Proceedings of EUFIT'94 Conference*, September 20-23, 1994 Aachen, Germany (Verlag der Augustinus Buchhandlung, Aachen, 1994) 1504-1508.
27. C. Carlsson and R. Fullér, Interdependence in fuzzy multiple objective programming, *Fuzzy Sets and Systems*, 65(1994) 19-29.
28. C. Carlsson and R. Fullér, Fuzzy reasoning for solving fuzzy multiple objective linear programs, in: R.Trappl ed., *Cybernetics and Systems '94, Proceedings of the Twelfth European Meeting on Cybernetics and Systems Research* (World Scientific Publisher, London, 1994) 295-301.
29. C. Carlsson, Knowledge Formation in Strategic Management, *HICSS-27 Proceedings*, (IEEE Computer Society Press, Los Alamitos, 1994) 221-230.
30. C. Carlsson and R. Fullér, Multiple Criteria Decision Making: The Case for Interdependence, *Computers & Operations Research* 22(1995) 251-260.
31. C. Carlsson and R. Fullér, Active DSS and approximate reasoning, in: *Proceedings of EUFIT'95 Conference*, August 28-31, 1995, Aachen, Germany, Verlag Mainz, Aachen, 1995 1209-1215.
32. C. Carlsson and R. Fullér, On fuzzy screening system, in: *Proceedings of the Third European Congress on Intelligent Techniques and Soft Computing (EUFIT'95)*, August 28-31, 1995 Aachen, Germany, Verlag Mainz, Aachen, 1995 1261-1264.
33. C. Carlsson, Cognitive Maps and Hyperknowledge. A Blueprint for Active Decision Support Systems, in: *Cognitive Maps and Strategic Thinking*, C. Carlsson ed. May 1995, Åbo, Finland, (Meddelanden Från Ekonomisk-Statsvetenskapliga Fakulteten Vid Åbo Akademi, IAMSR, Ser. A:442) 27-59.
34. C. Carlsson and P. Walden, On Fuzzy Hyperknowledge Support Systems, in: *NGIT'95 Proceedings*, Tel Aviv, 1995.
35. C. Carlsson and R. Fullér, Fuzzy multiple criteria decision making: Recent developments, *Fuzzy Sets and Systems*, 78(1996) 139-153.
36. C. Carlsson and R. Fullér, Additive interdependences in MOP, in: M.Brännback and M.Kuula eds., *Proceedings of the First Finnish Noon-to-noon seminar on Decision Analysis*, Åbo, December 11-12, 1995, Meddelanden Från Ekonomisk-Statsvetenskapliga Fakulteten vid Åbo Akademi, Ser: A:459, Åbo Akademis tryckeri, Åbo, 1996 77-92.

37. C. Carlsson and R. Fullér, Compound interdependences in MOP, in: *Proceedings of the Fourth European Congress on Intelligent Techniques and Soft Computing (EUFIT'96)*, September 2-5, 1996, Aachen, Germany, Verlag Mainz, Aachen, 1996 1317-1322.
38. C. Carlsson and R. Fullér, Problem-solving with multiple interdependent criteria: Better solutions to complex problems, in: D.Ruan, P.D'hondt, P.Govaerts and E.E.Kerre eds., *Proceedings of the Second International FLINS Workshop on Intelligent Systems and Soft Computing for Nuclear Science and Industry*, September 25-27, 1996, Mol, Belgium, World Scientific Publisher, 1996 89-97.
39. C. Carlsson and R. Fullér, Adaptive Fuzzy Cognitive Maps for Hyperknowledge Representation in Strategy Formation Process, in: *Proceedings of International Panel Conference on Soft and Intelligent Computing*, Budapest, October 7-10, 1996, Technical University of Budapest, 1996 43-50.
40. C. Carlsson and R. Fullér, A neuro-fuzzy system for portfolio evaluation, in: R.Trappl ed., *Cybernetics and Systems '96, Proceedings of the Thirteenth European Meeting on Cybernetics and Systems Research*, Vienna, April 9-12, 1996, Austrian Society for Cybernetic Studies, Vienna, 1996 296-299.
41. C. Carlsson and P. Walden, Cognitive Maps and a Hyperknowledge Support System in Strategic Management, *Group Decision and Negotiation*, 6(1996), 7-36.
42. C. Carlsson, R. Fullér and S.Fullér, Possibility and necessity in weighted aggregation, in: R.R. Yager and J. Kacprzyk eds., *The ordered weighted averaging operators: Theory, Methodology, and Applications*, Kluwer Academic Publishers, Boston, 1997 18-28.
43. C. Carlsson, R. Fullér and S.Fullér, OWA operators for doctoral student selection problem, in: R.R. Yager and J. Kacprzyk eds., *The ordered weighted averaging operators: Theory, Methodology, and Applications*, Kluwer Academic Publishers, Boston, 1997 167-178.
44. C. Carlsson and R. Fullér, Problem solving with multiple interdependent criteria, in: J. Kacprzyk, H.Nurmi and M.Fedrizzi eds., *Consensus under Fuzziness*, The Kluwer International Series in Intelligent Technologies, Vol. 10, Kluwer Academic Publishers, Boston, 1997 231-246.
45. C. Carlsson and R. Fullér, OWA operators for decision support, in: *Proceedings of the Fifth European Congress on Intelligent Techniques and Soft Computing (EUFIT'97)*, September 8-11, 1997, Aachen, Germany, Verlag Mainz, Aachen, Vol. II, 1997 1539-1544.
46. C. Carlsson and R. Fullér, Soft computing techniques for portfolio evaluation, in: A. Zempléni ed., *Statistics at Universities: Its Impact for Society, Tempus (No. 9521) Workshop*, Budapest, May 22-23, 1997, Eötvös University Press, Budapest, Hungary, 1997 47-54.
47. C. Carlsson and R. Fullér, A novel approach to linguistic importance weighted aggregations, in: C. Carlsson and I.Eriksson eds., *Global & Multiple Criteria Optimization and Information Systems Quality*, Åbo Akademis tryckeri, Åbo, 1998 143-153.
48. C. Carlsson and R. Fullér, A new look at linguistic importance weighted aggregations, *Cybernetics and Systems '98, Proceedings of the Fourteenth European Meeting on Cybernetics and Systems Research*, Austrian Society for Cybernetic Studies, Vienna, 1998 169-174
49. C. Carlsson and R. Fullér, Multiobjective optimization with linguistic variables, in: *Proceedings of the Sixth European Congress on Intelligent Techniques and Soft Computing (EUFIT'98)*, Aachen, September 7-10, 1998, Verlag Mainz, Aachen, Vol. II, 1998 1038-1042.

50. C. Carlsson, R. Fullér and S. Giove, Optimization under fuzzy rule constraints, *The Belgian Journal of Operations Research, Statistics and Computer Science*, 38(1998) 17-24.
51. C. Carlsson and R. Fullér, Capital budgeting problems with fuzzy cash flows, *Mathware and Soft Computing*, 6(1999) 81-89.
52. C. Carlsson and R. Fullér, On interdependent biobjective decision problems, in: *Proceedings of the Seventh European Congress on Intelligent Techniques and Soft Computing (EUFIT'99)*, Aachen, September 13-16, 1999 Verlag Mainz, Aachen, 4 pages, (Proceedings on CD-Rom).
53. C. Carlsson and R. Fullér, On fuzzy capital budgeting problem, in: *Proceedings of the International ICSC Congress on Computational Intelligence Methods and Applications*, Rochester, New York, USA, June 22-25, 1999, ICSC Academic Press, [ISBN 3-906454-16-6], 1999 634-638.
54. C. Carlsson, R. Fullér and S. Giove, Optimization under fuzzy linguistic rule constraints, in: B.De Baets, J. Fodor and L. T. Kóczy eds., *Proceedings of the Fourth Meeting of the Euro Working Group on Fuzzy Sets and Second International Conference on Soft and Intelligent Computing (Eurofuse-SIC'99)*, Budapest, Hungary, 25-28 May 1999, Technical University of Budapest, 1999 184-187.
55. C. Carlsson and R. Fullér, Benchmarking in linguistic importance weighted aggregations, *Fuzzy Sets and Systems*, 114(2000) 35-41.
56. C. Carlsson and R. Fullér, Decision problems with interdependent objectives, *International Journal of Fuzzy Systems*, 2(2000) 98-107.
57. C. Carlsson and R. Fullér, Multiobjective linguistic optimization, *Fuzzy Sets and Systems*, 115(2000) 5-10.
58. C. Carlsson and R. Fullér, Optimization under fuzzy if-then rules, *Fuzzy Sets and Systems*, 119(2001) 11-120.
59. C. Carlsson and R. Fullér, On possibilistic mean value and variance of fuzzy numbers, *Fuzzy Sets and Systems*, 122(2001) 139-150.
60. C. Carlsson and P. Walden, Intelligent Support Systems - The Next Few DSS Steps. *Human Systems Management*, 19(2000) 135-147.
61. S. Chanas, Fuzzy Programming in Multiobjective Linear Programming – A Parametric Approach, *Fuzzy Sets and Systems*, 29(1989) 303-313.
62. A.-M. Chang, C.W. Holsapple and A.B. Whinston, Model Management Issues and Directions, *Decision Support Systems*, 9(1993) 19-37.
63. P. L. Chebyshev, On mean quantities, Mat. Sbornik, 2(1867); Complete Works, 2(1948).
64. S. J. Chen and C.L. Hwang, *Fuzzy Multiple Attribute decision-making, Methods and Applications*, Lecture Notes in Economics and Mathematical Systems, vol. 375 (Springer, Heildelberg, 1993).
65. S. Chen, Cognitive-map-based decision analysis based on NPN logics, *Fuzzy Sets and Systems*, 71(1995) 155-163
66. F.-C. Cheong, Internet Agents: Spiders, Wanderers, Brokers and Bots, New Riders Publishing, Indianapolis, 1996
67. R. T. Chi and E. Turban, Distributed Intelligent Executive Information Systems, *Decision Support Systems*, 14(1995) 117-130.
68. F. Chiclana, F. Herrera and E. Herrera-Viedma, Integrating three representation models in fuzzy multipurpose decision making based on fuzzy preference relations, *Fuzzy Sets and Systems*, 97(1998) 33-48.
69. C. Eden and J. Radford eds., *Tackling Strategic Problems. The Role of Group Support* (Sage Publications, London 1990).
70. E. Czogala, Multi-criteria decision-making by means of fuzzy and probabilistic sets, *Fuzzy Sets and Systems*, 36(1990) 235-244.

71. P. Czyźak and R. Słowiński, Possibilistic construction of fuzzy outranking relation for multiple-criteria ranking, *Fuzzy Sets and Systems*, 81(1996) 123-131.
72. Ruan Da, *A critical study of widely used fuzzy implication operators and their influence on the inference rules in fuzzy expert systems*, Ph.D. Thesis, State University of Ghent, 1990.
73. R.L. Daft and K.E.Weick, Towards a Model of Organizations as Interpretation Systems, *Academy of Management Review*, 9(1984) 284-295.
74. V. Dahr and R. Stein, Intelligent Decision Support Systems, (Prentice Hall, Upper Saddle River, NJ 1997).
75. G. Day, B. Weitz, and R. Wensley, eds., *The Interface of Marketing and Strategy*, (Jay Press Inc., Greenwich 1990).
76. M. Delgado, J.L.Verdegay and M.A.Vila, Solving the biobjective linear programming problem: A fuzzy approach, in: M.M.Gupta et al. eds., *Approximate Reasoning in Expert Systems*, North-Holland, Amsterdam, 1985 317-322.
77. M. Delgado, J.L. Verdegay and M.A. Villa, Imprecise costs in mathematical programming problems, *Control and Cybernetics* 16(1987) 114-121.
78. M. Delgado, J.L.Verdegay and M.A.Vila, A procedure for ranking fuzzy numbers using fuzzy relations, *Fuzzy Sets and Systems*, 26(1988) 49-62.
79. M. Delgado,J.L.Verdegay and M.A.Vila, A possibilistic approach for multiobjective programming problems. Efficiency of solutions, in: R.Słowinski and J.Teghem eds., *Stochastic versus Fuzzy Approaches to Multiobjective Mathematical Programming under Uncertainty*, Kluwer Academic Publisher, Dordrecht, 1990 229-248.
80. M. Delgado, F.Herrera, J.L.Verdegay and M.A.Vila, Post-optimality analysis on the membership functions of a fuzzy linear programming problem, *Fuzzy Sets and Systems*, 53(1993) 289-297.
81. M. Delgado and J. Kacprzyk and J.L. Verdegay and M.A. Vila eds., *Fuzzy Optimization. Recent Advances*, Physica-Verlag, 1994.
82. D.V.Deshpande, S.Zionts, Sensitivity analysis in multiply objective linear programming: Changes in the objective function matrix, Working paper no. 399(1979), State University of New York, USA.
83. J.Dombi, A general class of fuzzy operators, the De-Morgan class of fuzzy operators and fuziness measures induced by fuzzy operators, *Fuzzy Sets and Systems*, 8(1982) 149-163.
84. J.Dombi, Membership function as an evaluation, *Fuzzy Sets and Systems*, 35(1990) 1-21.
85. D. Dubois and H. Prade, Systems of linear fuzzy constraints, *Fuzzy Sets and Systems*, 3(1980) 37-48.
86. D. Dubois and H.Prade, Additions of interactive fuzzy numbers, *IEEE Transactions on Automatic Control*, 26(1981), 926-936.
87. D. Dubois and H. Prade, Criteria aggregation and ranking of alternatives in the framework of fuzzy set theory, *TIMS/Studies in the Management Sciences*, 20(1984) 209-240.
88. D. Dubois and H. Prade, A review of fuzzy set aggregation connectives, *Information Sciences*, 36(1985) 85-121.
89. D. Dubois and H. Prade, Weighted minimum and maximum operations in fuzzy sets theory, *Information Sciences*, 39(1986) 205-210.
90. D. Dubois and H. Prade, The mean value of a fuzzy number, *Fuzzy Sets and Systems* 24(1987) 279-300.
91. D. Dubois and H. Prade, *Possibility Theory* (Plenum Press, New York, 1988).
92. D. Dubois, H. Prade,and R.R. Yager, A Manifesto: Fuzzy Information Engineering, in: D. Dubois, H. Prade,and R.R. Yager eds., *Fuzzy Information Engineering: A Guided Tour of Applications*, Wiley, New York, 1997 1-8.

93. T.E. Durand, Mounoud, E. and B. Ramanantsoa, Uncovering Strategic Assumptions: Understanding Managers' Ability to Build Representations, *European Management Journal*, 14(1996) 389-397.
94. D. Dutta, J.R. Rao and R.N. Tiwari, Effect of tolerance in fuzzy linear fractional programming, *Fuzzy Sets and Systems*, 55(1993) 133-142.
95. P. Eklund, J. Forsström, A. Holm, M. Nyström, and G. Selén, Rule generation as an alternative to knowledge acquisition: A systems architecture for medical informatics, *Fuzzy Sets and Systems*, 66(1994) 195-205.
96. P. Eklund, Network size versus preprocessing, in: R.R. Yager and L.A. Zadeh eds., *Fuzzy Sets, Neural Networks and Soft Computing* (Van Nostrand, New York, 1994) 250-264.
97. P.Eklund, M.Fedrizzi and R. Fullér, Stability in multiobjective possibilistic linear programs with weakly noninteractive fuzzy number coefficients, in: M. Delgado, J. Kacprzyk, J.L.Verdegay and M.A.Vila eds., *Fuzzy Optimization: Recent Advances*, Studies Fuzziness, Vol. 2, Physica-Verlag, Heidelberg, 1994 246-252.
98. P. Eklund and J. Forsström, Computational intelligence for laboratory information systems, *Scand. J. Clin. Lab. Invest.*, 55 Suppl. 222 (1995) 75-82.
99. G. Elofson and B. Konsynski, Delegation Technologies: Environmental Scanning with Intelligent Agents, *Journal of Management Information Systems*, 8(1991) 37-62.
100. G. Elofson, P. M. Beranek and P. Thomas, An Intelligent Agent Community Approach to Knowledge Sharing, *Decision Support Systems*, 20(1997) 83-98.
101. O. Etzioni and D. Weld, Intelligent Agents on the Internet: Fact, Fiction and Forecast, *IEEE Expert*, August 1995.
102. O. Etzioni and D. Weld, A Softbot-Based Interface to the Internet, *Communications of the ACM*, 39(1996) 72-76.
103. M. Fedrizzi and L. Mich, Consensus reaching in group decisions using production rules, in: *Proceedings of Annual Conference of the Operational Research Society of Italy*, September 18-10, Riva del Garda. Italy, 1991 118-121.
104. M. Fedrizzi and R. Fullér, On stability in group decision support systems under fuzzy production rules, in: R.Trappl ed., *Proceedings of the Eleventh European Meeting on Cybernetics and Systems Research* (World Scientific Publisher, London, 1992) 471-478.
105. M. Fedrizzi and R. Fullér, Stability in possibilistic linear programming problems with continuous fuzzy number parameters, *Fuzzy Sets and Systems*, 47(1992) 187-191.
106. M. Fedrizzi, M, Fedrizzi and W. Ostasiewicz, Towards fuzzy modeling in economics, *Fuzzy Sets and Systems* (54)(1993) 259-268.
107. M. Fedrizzi, Fuzzy approach to modeling consensus in group decisions, in: *Proceedings of First Workshop on Fuzzy Set Theory and Real Applications*, Milano, May 10, 1993, Automazione e strumentazione, Supplement to November 1993 issue, 9-13.
108. R. Felix, Multiple attribute decision-making based on fuzzy relationships between objectives, in: *Proceedings of the 2nd International Conference on Fuzzy Logic and Neural Networks*, Iizuka Japan, July 17-22, 1992 805-808.
109. R. Felix, Relationships between goals in multiple attribute decision-making, *Fuzzy Sets and Systems*, 67(1994) 47-52.
110. R. Felix, Reasoning on relationships between goals and its industrial and business-oriented applications, in: *Proceedings of First International Workshop on Preferences and Decisions*, Trento, June 5-7, 1997, University of Trento, 1997 21-23.
111. D. Filev and R. R. Yager, On the issue of obtaining OWA operator weights, *Fuzzy Sets and Systems*, 94(1998) 157-169.

112. J.C. Fodor and M. Roubens, *Fuzzy Preference Modelling and Multicriteria Decision Aid* (Kluwer Academic Publisher, Dordrecht, 1994).
113. M.J. Frank, On the simultaneous associativity of $F(x,y)$ and $x+y-F(x,y)$, *Aequat. Math.*, 19(1979) 194-226.
114. S. Franklin and A. Graesser, Is It an Agent or just a Program? A Taxonomy for Autonomous Agents,in: *Proceedings of the Third International Workshop on Agent Theories, Architectures and Languages*, (Springer-Verlag, Heidelberg, 1996).
115. R. Fullér, On fuzzified linear programming problems, *Annales Univ. Sci. Budapest, Sectio Computatorica*, 9(1988) 115-120.
116. R. Fullér, On a special type of FLP, in: D. Greenspan and P. Rózsa eds., *Colloquia mathematica societatis János Bolyai 50. Numerical methods (Miskolc, 1986)*, North-Holland, Amsterdam-New York, 1988 511-520.
117. R. Fullér, On possibilistic linear systems, in: A. Iványi ed., *Proceedings of the 4-th Conference of Program Designers*, June 1-3, 1988 Budapest, Hungary, Eötvös Loránd University, 1988 255-260.
118. R. Fullér, On stability in fuzzy linear programming problems, *Fuzzy Sets and Systems*, 30(1989) 339-344.
119. R. Fullér, On T-sum of fuzzy numbers, *BUSEFAL*, 39(1989) 24-29.
120. R. Fullér, On stability in possibilistic linear equality systems with Lipschitzian fuzzy numbers, *Fuzzy Sets and Systems*, 34(1990) 347-353.
121. R.Fullér, On product-sum of triangular fuzzy numbers, *Fuzzy Sets and Systems*, 41(1991) 83-87.
122. R. Fullér and T. Keresztfalvi, On Generalization of Nguyen's theorem, *Fuzzy Sets and Systems*, 41(1991) 371–374.
123. R. Fullér, On Hamacher-sum of triangular fuzzy numbers, *Fuzzy Sets and Systems*, 42(1991) 205-212.
124. R. Fullér, Well-posed fuzzy extensions of ill-posed linear equality systems, *Fuzzy Systems and Mathematics*, 5(1991) 43-48.
125. R. Fullér, On the generalized method-of-case inference rule, *Annales Univ. Sci. Budapest, Sectio Computatorica*, 12(1991) 107-113.
126. R. Fullér and H.-J. Zimmermann, On Zadeh's compositional rule of inference, in: R.Lowen and M.Roubens eds., *Proceedings of the Fourth IFSA Congress, Volume: Artifical intelligence*, Brussels, 1991 41-44.
127. R. Fullér, On law of large numbers for L-R fuzzy numbers, in: R.Lowen and M.Roubens eds., *Proceedings of the Fourth IFSA Congress, Vol. Mathematics*, Brussels, 1991 74-77.
128. R. Fullér and B.Werners, The compositional rule of inference: introduction, theoretical considerations, and exact calculation formulas, *Working Paper, RWTH Aachen, institut für Wirtschaftswissenschaften*, No.1991/7.
129. R. Fullér and H.-J. Zimmermann, On computation of the compositional rule of inference under triangular norms, *Fuzzy Sets and Systems*, 51(1992) 267-275.
130. R. Fullér and T. Keresztfalvi, t-Norm-based addition of fuzzy intervals, *Fuzzy Sets and Systems*, 51(1992) 155-159.
131. R. Fullér and B. Werners, The compositional rule of inference with several relations, in: B.Riecan and M.Duchon eds., *Proceedings of the international Conference on Fuzzy Sets and its Applications*, Liptovsky Mikulás, Czecho-Slovakia, February 17-21, 1992 (Math. Inst. Slovak Academy of Sciences, Bratislava, 1992) 39–44.
132. R. Fullér, A law of large numbers for fuzzy numbers, *Fuzzy Sets and Systems*, 45(1992) 299-303.
133. R. Fullér and T.Keresztfalvi, A note on t-norm-based operations on fuzzy numbers, Supplement to *Kybernetika*, 28(1992) 45-49.

134. R. Fullér and H.-J. Zimmermann, On Zadeh's compositional rule of inference, In: R.Lowen and M.Roubens eds., *Fuzzy Logic: State of the Art*, Theory and Decision Library, Series D (Kluwer Academic Publisher, Dordrecht, 1993) 193-200.
135. R. Fullér and H.-J. Zimmermann, Fuzzy reasoning for solving fuzzy mathematical programming problems, *Fuzzy Sets and Systems*, 60(1993) 121-133.
136. R.Fullér and E.Triesch, A note on law of large numbers for fuzzy variables, *Fuzzy Sets and Systems*, 55(1993) 235-236.
137. R. Fullér and M.Fedrizzi, Stability in multiobjective possibilistic linear programs, *European Journal of Operational Research*, 74(1994) 179-187.
138. R. Fullér and S. Giove, A neuro-fuzzy approach to FMOLP problems, in: *Proceedings of CIFT'94*, June 1-3, 1994, Trento, Italy, University of Trento, 1994 97-101.
139. R. Fullér, L. Gaio, L. Mich and A. Zorat, OCA functions for consensus reaching in group decisions in fuzzy environment, in: *Proceedings of the 3rd International Conference on Fuzzy Logic, Neural Nets and Soft Computing*, Iizuka, Japan, August 1-7, 1994, Iizuka, Japan, 1994, Fuzzy Logic Systems institute, 1994 101-102.
140. R. Fullér, *Neural Fuzzy Systems*, Åbo Akademis tryckeri, Åbo, ESF Series A:443, 1995, 249 pages.
141. R. Fullér, Hyperknowledge representation: challenges and promises, in: P. Walden, M.Brännback, B.Back and H.Vanharanta eds., *The Art and Science of Decision-Making*, Åbo Akademi University Press, Åbo, 1996 61-89.
142. R. Fullér, OWA operators for decision making, in: C. Carlsson ed., *Exploring the Limits of Support Systems*, TUCS General Publications, No. 3, Turku Centre for Computer Science, Åbo, 1996 85-104.
143. R. Fullér, *An Introduction to Investment Management*, Åbo Akademis tryckeri, Åbo, ESF Series A:479, 1997, 136 pages.
144. R. Fullér, *Fuzzy Reasoning and Fuzzy Optimization*, TUCS General Publications, No. 9, Turku Centre for Computer Science, Åbo, 1998, 270 pages.
145. R. Fullér, *Introduction to Neuro-Fuzzy Systems*, Advances in Soft Computing Series, Springer-Verlag, Berlin/Heildelberg, 2000, 289 pages.
146. R. Fullér and P. Majlender, An analytic approach for obtaining maximal entropy OWA operator weights, *Fuzzy Sets and Systems*, 2001 (to appear).
147. T. Gal and K.Wolf, Stability in vector maximization - A survey,*European Journal of Operational Research*, 25(1986) 169-182.
148. O. Georgieva, Stability of quasilinear fuzzy system *Fuzzy Sets and Systems*, 73(1995) 249-258.
149. A. Gershman and E. Gottsman, Use of hypermedia for corporate knowledge dissemination, *HICSS-26 Proceedings*, (IEEE Computer Society Press, Los Alamitos, 1993) 411-420
150. D.A. Gioia and K.Chittipeddi, Sensemaking and Sensegiving in Strategic Change Initiation, *Strategic Management Journal*, 12(1991) 433-488.
151. V.I. Glushkov and A.N. Borisov, Analysis of fuzzy evidence in decision making models, in: Kacprzyk ed., *Optimization Models using Fuzzy Sets and Possibility Theory* (D. Reidel Publishing Co., Boston, 1987) 141-153.
152. R. Goetschel and W. Voxman, Elementary Fuzzy Calculus, *Fuzzy Sets and Systems*, 18(1986) 31-43.
153. M. Gougen, *On Fuzzy Robot Planning*, Memo No. 1 on AI, UCLA, Los Angeles, 1974.
154. S. Green L. Hurst, B. Nangle, P. Cunningham, F. Somers and R. Evans, Software Agents: A Review, (at: http://www.cs.tcd.ie/Brenda.Nangle/iag.html).

155. R. H. Guttman, A. G. Moukas and P. Maes, Agent Mediated Electronic Commerce: A Survey, (at: http://ecommerce.media.mit.edu), 1998.
156. H. Hamacher, H. Leberling and H.-J. Zimmermann, Sensitivity analysis in fuzzy linear programming, *Fuzzy Sets and Systems* 1(1978) 269-281.
157. H. Hamacher, Über logische Aggregationen nicht binär explizierter Entscheidung-kriterien (Rita G. Fischer Verlag, Frankfurt, 1978).
158. G. Hamel and C.K. Prahalad, *Competing for the Future* (Harvard Business School Press, Boston 1996).
159. K. vand der Heijden, *Scenarios. The Art of Strategic Conversation* (J. Wiley & Sons, Chichester 1996).
160. H. Hellendoorn, Closure properties of the compositional rule of inference, *Fuzzy Sets and Systems*, 35(1990) 163-183.
161. P. Henrici, *Discrete Variable Methods in Ordinary Differential Equations*, John Wiley & Sons, New York, 1962.
162. F. Herrera, E. Herrera-Viedma and J. L. Verdegay, Aggregating Linguistic Preferences: Properties of the LOWA Operator, in: *Proceedings of the 6th IFSA World Congress*, Sao Paulo (Brasil), Vol. II, 1995 153-157.
163. F. Herrera, E. Herrera-Viedma, J.L. Verdegay, Direct approach processes in group decision making using linguistic OWA operators, *Fuzzy Sets and Systems*, 79(1996) 175-190.
164. B. Hermans, Intelligent Software Agents on the Internet: An Inventory of Currently Offered Functionality in the Information Society and A Predication of (Near-) Future Developments, *Thesis of Tilberg University*, Tilberg, The Netherlands, July 1996
165. F. Herrera and E. Herrera-Viedma, Aggregation Operators for Linguistic Weighted Information, *IEEE Transactions on Systems, Man and Cybernetics - Part A: Systems and Humans*, (27)1997 646-656.
166. F. Herrera, E. Herrera-Viedma, J.L. Verdegay, Linguistic Measures Basedon Fuzzy Coincidence for Reaching Consensus in Group Decision Making, *International Journal of Approximate Reasoning*, 16(1997) 309-334.
167. E. Herrera and E. Herrera-Viedma, On the linguistic OWA operator and extensions, in: R.R.Yager and J.Kacprzyk eds., *The ordered weighted averaging operators: Theory, Methodology, and Applications*, Kluwer Academic Publishers, Boston, 1997 60-72.
168. T. J. Hess, Terry R. Rakes and Loren P. Rees, Using Automated Software Planning Agents to Extend the Model Management System in a Decision Support System, Decision Sciences Institute, in: *Proceedings of the 29th Annual Meeting of the Decision Sciences Institute*, Omnipress 1998 663-665.
169. D. Heyman and M. Sobel, *Stochastic Models in Operations Research*, vol. I, McGraw-Hill, New York, 1984.
170. D.H. Hong and S.Y.Hwang, On the convergence of $T$-sum of L-R fuzzy numbers, *Fuzzy Sets and Systems*, 63(1994) 175-180.
171. D.H. Hong, A note on product-sum of L-R fuzzy numbers, *Fuzzy Sets and Systems*, 66(1994) 381-382.
172. D.H. Hong and S.Y.Hwang, On the compositional rule of inference under triangular norms, *Fuzzy Sets and Systems*, 66(1994) 25-38.
173. D.H. Hong A note on the law of large numbers for fuzzy numbers, *Fuzzy Sets and Systems*, 64(1994) 59-61.
174. D.H. Hong A note on the law of large numbers for fuzzy numbers, *Fuzzy Sets and Systems*, 68(1994) 243.
175. D.H. Hong, A note on t-norm-based addition of fuzzy intervals, *Fuzzy Sets and Systems*, 75(1995) 73-76.

176. D.H. Hong and Y.M.Kim, A law of large numbers for fuzzy numbers in a Banach space, *Fuzzy Sets and Systems,* 77(1996) 349-354.
177. D.H. Hong and C. Hwang, Upper bound of T-sum of LR-fuzzy numbers, in: *Proceedings of IPMU'96 Conference* (July 1-5, 1996, Granada, Spain), 1996 343-346.
178. D.H. Hong, A convergence theorem for arrays of L-R fuzzy numbers, *Information Sciences*, 88(1996) 169-175.
179. D.H. Hong and S.Y.Hwang, The convergence of T-product of fuzzy numbers, *Fuzzy Sets and Systems*, 85(1997) 373-378.
180. D.H. Hong and C. Hwang, A T-sum bound of LR-fuzzy numbers, *Fuzzy Sets and Systems*, 91(1997) 239-252.
181. S. Horikowa, T. Furuhashi and Y. Uchikawa, On identification of structures in premises of a fuzzy model using a fuzzy neural network, in: *Proc. IEEE International Conference on Fuzzy Systems*, San Francisco, 1993 661-666.
182. C.L. Hwang and K. Yoon, *Multiple Attribute Decision Making - Methods and Applications, A State-of-the-Art Survey* (Springer-Verlag, New-York, 1981).
183. C.L. Hwang and M.J. Lin, *Group Decision Making Under Multiple Criteria* (Springer-Verlag, New-York, 1987).
184. S.Y.Hwang and D.H.Hong, The convergence of T-sum of fuzzy numbers on Banach spaces, *Applied Mathematics Letters* 10(1997) 129-134.
185. M.Inuiguchi, H.Ichihashi and H. Tanaka, Fuzzy Programming: A Survey of Recent Developments, in: Slowinski and Teghem eds., *Stochastic versus Fuzzy Approaches to Multiobjective Mathematical Programming under Uncertainty,* Kluwer Academic Publishers, Dordrecht 1990, pp 45-68
186. M. Inuiguchi, Fuzzy linear programming: what, why and how? *Tatra Mountains Math. Publ.*, 13(1997) 123-167.
187. M. Inuiguchi and T. Tanino, Portfolio selection under independent possibilistic information, *Fuzzy Sets and Systems,* **115**(2000) 83-92.
188. L.C.Jang and J.S.Kwon, A note on law of large numbers for fuzzy numbers in a Banach space, *Fuzzy Sets and Systems,* 98(1998) 77-81.
189. S.Jenei, Continuity in approximate reasoning, *Annales Univ. Sci. Budapest, Sect. Comp.*, 15(1995) 233-242.
190. N.R. Jennings, Katia Sycara and M. Wooldridge, A Roadmap of Agent Research and Development, *Autonomous Agents and Multi-Agent Systems,* 1(1998) 7-38.
191. N.R. Jennings and M. Wooldridge, Applications of Intelligent Agents, in: Nicholas R. Jennings and Michael J. Wooldridge eds., *Agent Technology Foundations, Applications, and Markets,* (Springer-Verlag, 1998).
192. B.Julien, An extension to possibilistic linear programming, *Fuzzy Sets and Systems,* 64(1994) 195-206.
193. J. Kacprzyk and R.R. Yager, "Softer" optimization and control models via fuzzy linguistic quantifiers, *Information Sciences,* 34(1984) 157-178.
194. J. Kacprzyk and R.R. Yager, *Management Decision Support Systems Using Fuzzy Sets and Possibility Theory,* Springer Verlag, Berlin 1985.
195. J. Kacprzyk, Group decision making with a fuzzy linguistic majority, *Fuzzy Sets and Systems,* 18(1986) 105-118.
196. J. Kacprzyk and S.A. Orlovski eds., *Optimization Models Using Fuzzy Sets and Possibility Theory* (D.Reidel, Boston,1987).
197. J. Kacprzyk and R.R. Yager, Using fuzzy logic with linguistic quantifiers in multiobjective decision-making and optimization: A step towards more human-consistent models, in: R.Slowinski and J.Teghem eds., *Stochastic versus Fuzzy Approaches to Multiobjective Mathematical Programming under Uncertainty,* Kluwer Academic Publishers, Dordrecht, 1990 331-350.

198. J. Kacprzyk and M. Fedrizzi, *Multiperson decision-making Using Fuzzy Sets and Possibility Theory* (Kluwer Academic Publisher, Dordrecht, 1990).
199. J. Kacprzyk and A.O. Esogbue, Fuzzy dynamic programming: Main developments and applications, *Fuzzy Sets and Systems*, 81(1996) 31-45.
200. J. Kacprzyk and R. R. Yager eds., *The ordered weighted averaging operators: Theory, Methodology, and Applications*, Kluwer Academic Publishers, Boston, 1997.
201. A. Kandel, *Fuzzy Mathematical Techniques with Applications* (Addison-Wesley, Reading, 1986).
202. J.A. Kahn, Inventories and the Volatility of Production, *American Economic Rev.*, 77(1987) 667-679.
203. O. Kaleva, Fuzzy differential equations, *Fuzzy Sets and Systems*, 24(1987) 301-317.
204. M.F.Kawaguchi and T.Da-te, A calculation method for solving fuzzy arithmetic equations with triangular norms, in: *Proceedings of Second IEEE international Conference on Fuzzy Systems*, 1993 470-476.
205. M.F.Kawaguchi and T.Da-te, Some algebraic properties of weakly non-interactive fuzzy numbers, *Fuzzy Sets and Systems*, 68(1994) 281-291.
206. A. Kay, Computer Software, *Scientific American*, 251(1984) 53-59.
207. O. Kaynak, I. J. Rudas, Soft computing methodologies and their fusion in mechatronic products, *Computing & Control Engineering Journal*, April 1995, 68-72.
208. O. Kaynak, L. A. Zadeh, B. Türksen, I. .J. Rudas eds., *Computational Intelligence: Soft Computing and Fuzzy-Neuro Integration with Applications*, Springer NATO ASI Series. Series F: Computer and Systems Sciences, Vol.192. 1998.
209. D. King and K. Jones, Competitive Intelligence, Software Robots and the Internet: The NewsAlert Prototype, *Proceedings of the HICSS'28 Conference* (IEEE Computer Society Press, Los Alamitos, CA, 1995) 624-631.
210. J. A. King, Intelligent Agents: Bring Good Things to Life, *AI Expert*, Feb. & Mar., 1995.
211. D. King and D.O'Leary, Intelligent Executive Information Systems, *IEEE Expert*, December 1996 30-35.
212. P. E. Klement and R. Mesiar, Triangular norms, *Tatra Mountains Mathematical Publications*, 13(1997) 169-193.
213. G.J. Klir and H. J. H. Uyttenhove, Computerized Methodology for Structure Modelling, *Annals of Systems Research*, 5(1976).
214. G. J. Klir, *Architecture of Systems Problem Solving* (Plenum Press, New York, 1989).
215. G.J. Klir and B.Yuan, Fuzzy Sets and Fuzzy Logic: Theory and Applications, Prentice Hall, 1995.
216. L.T. Kóczy, Approximate reasoning and control with sparse and/or inconsistent fuzzy rule bases, in: B. Reusch ed., *Fuzzy Logic Theorie and Praxis*, Springer, Berlin, 1993 42-65.
217. L.T. Kóczy and K. Hirota, Ordering, distance and Closeness of Fuzzy Sets, *Fuzzy Sets and Systems*, 59(1993) 281-293.
218. S. Korner, *Laws of Thought*, Encyclopedia of Philosophy, Vol. 4, (MacMillan, New York 1967) 414-417.
219. Jari Kortelainen, On relationship between modified sets, topological spaces and rough sets, *Fuzzy Sets and Systems*, 61(1994) 91-95.
220. Jari Kortelainen, Modifiers connect $L$-fuzzy sets to topological spaces, *Fuzzy Sets and Systems*, 89(1997) 267-273.

221. Jari Kortelainen, On the evaluation of compatibility with gradual rules in information systems: A topological approach, *Control and Cybernetics*, 28(1999) 121-131.
222. P. Korhonen and J. Karaivanova, An Algorithm for Projecting a Reference Direction onto the Nondominated Set of Given Points, International Institute for Applied Systems Analysis (IIASA), *Interim Report*, IR-98-011/March.
223. B. Kosko. Fuzzy cognitive maps. *International Journal of Man-Machine Studies*, 24(1986) 65–75.
224. M. Kovács, Fuzzification of ill-posed linear systems, in: D. Greenspan and P.Rózsa, Eds., Colloquia mathematica Societitas János Bolyai 50, Numerical Methods, North-Holland, Amsterdam, 1988, 521-532.
225. M. Kovács, F.P.Vasiljev and R. Fullér, On stability in fuzzified linear equality systems, *Proceedings of the Moscow State University*, Ser. 15, 1(1989), 5-9 (in Russian), translation in *Moscow Univ. Comput. Math. Cybernet.*, 1(1989), 4-9.
226. M. Kovács and R.Fullér, On fuzzy extended systems of linear equalities and inequalities, in: A.A.Tihonov and A.A. Samarskij eds., *Current Problems in Applied Mathematics*, Moscow State University, Moscow, [ISBN 5-211-00342-X], 1989 73-80 (in Russian).
227. M. Kovács, A stable embedding of ill-posed linear systems into fuzzy systems, *Fuzzy Sets and Systems*, 45(1992) 305–312.
228. R.Kruse, The strong law of large numbers for fuzzy random variables, *Information Sciences*, 28(1982) 233-241.
229. Y.J. Lai and C.L. Hwang, *Fuzzy Mathematical Programming, Methods and Applications*, Lecture Notes in Economics and Mathematical Systems, No. 394, Springer Verlag, Berlin 1992.
230. Y.-J. Lai and C.-L. Hwang, *Fuzzy Multiple Objective Decision Making: Methods and Applications*, Lecture Notes in Economics and Mathematical Systems, Vol. 404 (Springer-Verlag, New York, 1994).
231. D. B. Lange, Object-oriented hypermodeling of hypertext supported information systems, *HICSS-26 Proceedings*, (IEEE Computer Society Press, Los Alamitos, 1993) 380-389.
232. H.L. Lee, V. Padmanabhan and S. Whang, Information distortion in a supply chain: The bullwhip effect, *Management Science*, 43(1997) 546-558.
233. H.L. Lee, V. Padmanabhan and S. Whang, The Bullwhip Effect in Supply Chains, *Sloan Management Review*, Spring 1997 93-102.
234. K. J. Leslie and M. P. Michaels, The real power of real options, *The McKinsey Quarterly*, 3(1997) 5-22.
235. Hong Xing Li and Vincent C. Yen, *Fuzzy sets and fuzzy decision-making*, (CRC Press, Boca Raton, FL, 1995).
236. R. Lowen, *Fuzzy Set Theory*, Kluwer Academic Publisher, 1996.
237. P. Maes, Agents that Reduce Work and Information Overload, *Communications of the ACM*, 71(1994) 31-40.
238. P. Magrez and P. Smets, Fuzzy modus ponens: A new model suitable for applications, in: Knowledge-Based Systems, Dubois, Prade and Yager eds.,*Fuzzy Sets for Intelligent Systems*, (Morgan Kaufmann Publ, San Mateo, 1993).
239. Spyros G. Makridakis, *Forecasting, Planning and Strategy for the 21st Century* (Free Press, New York 1990).
240. E.H. Mamdani and S. Assilian, An experiment in linquistic synthesis with a fuzzy logic controller. *International Journal of Man-Machine Studies* 7(1975) 1-13.
241. E. Mante-Meijer, Patrick vand der Duin and Muriel Aveln, Fun with Scenarios, *Long Range Planning*, 31(1998) 628-637.

242. A. Marková, T-sum of L-R fuzzy numbers, *Fuzzy Sets and Systems*, 85(1997) 379-384.
243. H. Markowitz, Portfolio selection, *Journal of Finance*, **7**(1952) 77-91.
244. J. K. Mattila, On some logical points of fuzzy conditional decision making, *Fuzzy Sets and Systems*, 20(1986) 137-145.
245. J. K. Mattila, On modifier logic, in: L. A. Zadeh and J.Kacprzyk eds., *Fuzzy Logic for Management of Uncertainty*, Wiley, New-York, 1992.
246. J. K. Mattila, *Text Book of Fuzzy Logic*, (Art House, Helsinki, 1998).
247. S. McKie, Software Agents: Application Intelligence Goes Undercover, *DBMS Magazine*, 8(1995).
248. R. Merton, Theory of rational option pricing, *Bell Journal of Economics and Management Science*, 4(1973) 141-183.
249. R. Mesiar, A note to the T-sum of L-R fuzzy numbers, *Fuzzy Sets and Systems*, 79(1996) 259-261.
250. R. Mesiar, Shape preserving additions of fuzzy intervals, *Fuzzy Sets and Systems*, 86(1997) 73-78.
251. R. Mesiar, Triangular-norm-based addition of fuzzy intervals, *Fuzzy Sets and Systems*, 91(1997) 231-237.
252. L. Mich, M. Fedrizzi and L. Gaio, Approximate Reasoning in the Modelling of Consensus in Group Decisions, in: E.P. Klement and W. Slany eds., *Fuzzy Logic in Artifiacial intelligence*, Lectures Notes in Artifiacial intelligence, Vol. 695, Springer-Verlag, Berlin, 1993 91-102.
253. H. Mintzberg, Manager's Job: Folklore and fact, *Harvard Business Review*, July-August (1975).
254. H. Mintzberg, Patterns in strategy formation, *Management Science*, 24(1978) 934-948.
255. H. Mintzberg, *The Rise and Fall of Strategic Planning* (Prentice Hall, 1994).
256. M. Miyakoshi and M.Shimbo, A Strong Law of Large Numbers for Fuzzy Random Variables, *Fuzzy Sets and Systems*, 12(1984) 133-142.
257. M. Mizumoto, Method of fuzzy inference suitable for fuzzy control, *J. Soc. Instrument Control Engineering*, 58(1989) 959-963.
258. C.V. Negoita, The current interest in fuzzy optimization, *Fuzzy Sets and System*, 6(1981) 261-269.
259. C.V. Negoita, *Fuzzy Systems* (Abacus Press, Turnbridge-Wells, 1981).
260. N. Negroponte, Agents: From Direct Manipulation to Delegation, in: Jeffrey Bradshaw ed., *Software Agents* (AAAI Press/The MIT Press, 1997).
261. J. von Neumann and O. Morgenstern, *Theory of Games and Economic Behavior*, (Princeton University Press, Princeton 1947).
262. H.T. Nguyen, A note on the extension principle for fuzzy sets, *Journal of Mathematical Analysis and Applications*, 64(1978) 369-380.
263. J. Nielsen, *Hypertext & Hypermedia*, (Academic Press, San Diego, 1990).
264. H. Nurmi, Approaches to collective decision making with fuzzy preference relations, *Fuzzy Sets and Systems*, 6(1981) 249-259.
265. H.S. Nwana, Software Agents: An Overview, *Knowledge Engineering Review*, 11(1996), (also at: http://www.cs.umbc.edu/agents/introduction/ao).
266. H.S. Nwana and D.T. Ndumu, An Introduction to Agent Technology, in: Nwana and Azarmi eds., Software Agents and Soft Computing, (Springer-Verlag, Berlin 1997).
267. M. O'Hagan, Aggregating template or rule antecedents in real-time expert systems with fuzzy set logic, in: *Proc. 22nd Annual IEEE Asilomar Conf. Signals, Systems, Computers*, Pacific Grove, CA, 1988 81-689.
268. S.A. Orlovski, On formalization of a general fuzzy mathematical problem, *Fuzzy Sets and Systems*, 3(1980) 311-321.

269. S.A. Orlovski, Multiobjective Programming Problems with Fuzzy Parameters, *Control and Cybernetics*, 4(1984) 175-184.
270. S.A. Orlovski, Mathematical programming problems with fuzzy parameters, in: J. Kacprzyk ed., *Management Decision Support Systems Using Fuzzy Sets and Possibility Theory* (Springer Verlag, New York,1985) 136-145.
271. S.V. Ovchinnikov, Transitive fuzzy orderings of fuzzy numbers, *Fuzzy Sets and Systems*, 30(1989) 283-295.
272. H. V. D. Parunak, *Practical and Industrial Applications of Agent-Based Systems*, Industrial Technology Institute, 1998.
273. H. Raiffa, The Art and Science of Negotiation, Belknap/Harvard University Press, Cambridge, 1982.
274. M.B. Rao and A. Rashed, Some comments on fuzzy variables, *Fuzzy Sets and Systems*, 6(1981) 285-292.
275. J. Ramik and J.Rimanek, Inequality relation between fuzzy numbers and its use in fuzzy optimization, *Fuzzy Sets and Systems*, 16(1985) 123-138.
276. G.R. Reeves and L.S. Franz, A simplified interactive multiobjective linear programming procedure, *Compuetrs & Operations Research*, 12(1985) 589-601.
277. G. Ringland, *Scenario Planning. Managing for the Future*, (J. Wiley & Sons, Chichester 1998).
278. D. Rios Insua, Sensitivity Analysis in Multi-Objective Decision Making, Springer-Verlag, Berlin, 1990.
279. D. Rios Insua and S.French, A framework for sensitivity analysis in discrete multi-objective decision-making, *European Journal of Operational Research*, 54(1991) 176-190.
280. M. Rommelfanger and R. Hanuscheck and J. Wolf, Linear Programming with Fuzzy Objectives, *Fuzzy Sets and Systems*, 29(1989) 31-48.
281. H. Rommelfanger, *Fuzzy Decision Support-Systeme*, Springer-Verlag, Heidelberg, 1994 (Second Edition).
282. H. Rommelfanger, Fuzzy linear programming and applications, *European Journal of Operational Research*, 92(1996) 512-527.
283. M.Roubens and P.Vincke, *Preference Modeling*, Springer-Verlag, Berlin, 1985.
284. I. J Rudas and M. O. Kaynak, Minimum and maximum fuzziness generalized operators, *Fuzzy Sets and Systems*, 98(1998) 83-94.
285. I.J. Rudas, M.O. Kaynak, Entropy-Based Operations on Fuzzy Sets, *IEEE Transactions on Fuzzy Systems*, 6(1998) 33-40.
286. I. J. Rudas, O. Kaynak, New Types of Generalized Operations, in: O. Kaynak, L. A. Zadeh, B. Türksen and I. J. Rudas eds., *Computational Intelligence: Soft Computing and Fuzzy-Neuro Integration with Applications*, Springer NATO ASI Series, Series F: Computer and Systems Sciences, Vol. 192. 1998 128-156.
287. O.M. Saad, Stability on multiobjective linear programming problems with fuzzy parameters, *Fuzzy Sets and Systems*, 74(1995) 207-215.
288. M. Sakawa and K. Kato, Interactive decision making for large-scale multiobjective linear programs with fuzzy numbers, *Fuzzy Sets and Systems*, 88(1997) 161-172
289. B. Schweizer and A.Sklar, Associative functions and abstract semigroups, *Publ. Math. Debrecen*, 10(1963) 69-81.
290. S.C. Schneider and A.D.Meyer, Interpreting and Responding to Strategic Issues: The Impact of National Culture, *Strategic Management Journal*, 12(1991) 307-322.
291. W. Slany, Scheduling as a fuzzy multiple criteria optimization problem, *Fuzzy Sets and Systems*, 78(1996) 197-222.

292. R. Słowiński and J. Teghem Jr. *Stochastic versus Fuzzy Approaches to Multiobjective Mathematical Programming under Uncertainty*, Kluwer Academic Publishers, Dordrecht 1990.
293. T.Takagi and M.Sugeno, Fuzzy identification of systems and its applications to modeling and control, *IEEE Trans. Syst. Man Cybernet.*, 1985, 116-132.
294. H. Tanaka and K. Asai, Fuzzy solution in fuzzy linear programming problems, *IEEE Transactions on Systems, Man, and Cybernetics*, Vol. SMC-14, 1984 325-328.
295. H. Tanaka, H. Ichihashi and K. Asai, A value of information in FLP problems via sensitivity analysis, *Fuzzy Sets and Systems* 18(1986) 119-129.
296. J. Tang and D. Wang, An interactive approach based on a genetic algorithm for a type of quadratic programming problems with fuzzy objectives and resources, *Computers & Operations Research* 24(1997) 413-422.
297. E. Triesch, Characterisation of Archimedean t-norms and a law of large numbers, *Fuzzy Sets and Systems*, 58(1993) 339–342.
298. E. Triesch, On the convergence of product-sum series of L-R fuzzy numbers, *Fuzzy Sets and Systems*, 53(1993) 189-192.
299. Y. Tsukamoto, An approach to fuzzy reasoning method, in: M.M. Gupta, R.K. Ragade and R.R. Yager eds., *Advances in Fuzzy Set Theory and Applications* (North-Holland, New-York, 1979).
300. E. Turban and J. Aronson, *Decision Support Systems and Intelligent Systems*, (Prentice Hall, 1998).
301. A.Tversky, Intransitivity of Preferences, *Psychological Review*, 76(1969) 31-45.
302. J. L. Verdegay, Fuzzy mathematical programming, in: M. M. Gupta and E. Sanchez eds., *Fuzzy Information and Decision Processes*, North-Holland, 1982.
303. J.L.Verdegay, Applications of fuzzy optimization in operational research, *Control and Cybernetics*, 13(1984) 230-239.
304. P. Walden and C. Carlsson, Enhancing strategic market management with knowledge-based systems, *HICSS-26 Proceedings*, IEEE Computer Society Press, Los Alamitos, 1993 240-248.
305. P. Walden and C. Carlsson, Strategic management with a hyperknowledge Support System, *HICSS-27 Proceedings*, IEEE Computer Society Press, Los Alamitos, 1994 241-250.
306. P. Walden and C. Carlsson, Hyperknowledge and expert systems: A case study of knowledge formation processes, *HICSS-28 Proceedings*, IEEE Computer Society Press, Los Alamitos 1995.
307. L.-X. Wang and J.M. Mendel, Fuzzy basis functions, universal approximation, and orthogonal least-squares learning, *IEEE Transactions on Neural Networks*, 3(1992) 807-814.
308. L.-X. Wang, Fuzzy systems are universal approximators, in: *Proc. IEEE 1992 Int. Conference Fuzzy Systems*, San Diego, 1992 1163-1170.
309. H.-F. Wang and Miao-Ling Wang, A fuzzy multiobjective linear programming, *Fuzzy Sets and Systems*, 86(1997) 61-72
310. J. Watada, Fuzzy portfolio selection and its applications to decision making, *Tatra Mountains Mathematical Publications*, 13(1997) 219-248.
311. B.Werners, Interaktive Entscheidungsunterstützung durch ein flexibles mathematisches Programmierungssystem, Minerva, Publikation, München, 1984.
312. B. Werners, Interactive Multiple Objective Programming Subject to Flexible Constraints, *European Journal of Operational Research*, 31(1987) 324-349.
313. M.J. Wooldridge and N. R. Jennings, Intelligent Agents: Theory and Practice, *The Knowledge Engineering Review*, 10(1995) 115-152.

314. Y. Xia, B. Liu, S. Wang and K.K. Lai, A model for portfolio selection with order of expected returns, *Computers & Operations Research*, **27**(2000) 409-422.
315. R.R. Yager, Fuzzy decision making using unequal objectives, *Fuzzy Sets and Systems*,1(1978) 87-95.
316. R.R. Yager, Sergei Ovchinnikov, Richard M. Tong and H.T. Nguen eds., *Fuzzy Sets and Applications: Selected Papers by L.A.Zadeh*, (John Wiley & Sons, New York 1987).
317. R.R. Yager, Ordered weighted averaging aggregation operators in multi-criteria decision making, *IEEE Trans. on Systems, Man and Cybernetics*, 18(1988) 183-190.
318. R.R. Yager, Families of OWA operators, *Fuzzy Sets and Systems*, 59(1993) 125-148.
319. R.R. Yager, Fuzzy Screening Systems, in: R.Lowen and M.Roubens eds., *Fuzzy Logic: State of the Art* (Kluwer, Dordrecht, 1993) 251-261.
320. R.R. Yager, Aggregation operators and fuzzy systems modeling, *Fuzzy Sets and Systems*, 67(1994) 129-145.
321. R.R.Yager, On weighted median aggregation, *International Journal of Uncertainty, Fuzziness and Knowledge-based Systems*, 1(1994) 101-113.
322. R.R.Yager, Quantifier guided aggregation using OWA operators, Technical Report, #MII-1504, Mashine Intelligence Institute, Iona College, New York, 1994.
323. R.R. Yager and D.Filev, *Essentials of Fuzzy Modeling and Control* (Wiley, New York, 1994).
324. R.R. Yager, Constrained OWA aggregation, *Fuzzy Sets and Systems*, 81(1996) 89-101.
325. R.R.Yager, Including importances in OWA aggregations using fuzzy systems modeling, Technical Report, #MII-1625, Mashine Intelligence Institute, Iona College, New York, 1996.
326. R.R.Yager, On the inclusion of importances in OWA aggregations, in: R.R.Yager and J.Kacprzyk eds., *The ordered weighted averaging operators: Theory, Methodology, and Applications*, Kluwer Academic Publishers, Boston, 1997 41-59.
327. R. R.Yager and D. Filev, Induced ordered weighted averaging operators, *IEEE Trans. on Systems, Man and Cybernetics – Part B: Cybernetics*, 29(1999) 141-150.
328. M.-S. Yang and M.-C. Liu, On possibility analysis of fuzzy data, *Fuzzy Sets and Systems* 94(1998) 171-183.
329. A.V. Yazenin, Fuzzy and Stochastic Programming, *Fuzzy Sets and Systems*, 22(1987) 171-180.
330. A.V. Yazenin, On the problem of possibilistic optimization, *Fuzzy Sets and Systems*, 81(1996) 133-140.
331. Po-Long Yu, To be a Great Operations Researcher from a MCDM Scholar, *Computers & Operations Research*, (19)1992 559-561
332. L. A. Zadeh, Fuzzy Sets, *Information and Control*, 8(1965) 338-353.
333. L. A. Zadeh, Outline of a new approach to the analysis of complex systems and decision processes, *IEEE Transanctins on Systems, Man and Cybernetics*, 3(1973) 28-44.
334. L. A. Zadeh, Concept of a linguistic variable and its application to approximate reasoning, **I, II, III**, *Information Sciences*, 8(1975) 199-249, 301-357; 9(1975) 43-80.
335. L. A. Zadeh, Fuzzy sets as a basis for theory of possibility, Memo UCB/ERL M77/12, Univ. of California, Berkeley, 1977.

336. L. A.Zadeh, Fuzzy sets as a basis for a theory of possibility, *Fuzzy Sets and Systems*, 1(1978) 3-28.
337. L. A. Zadeh, A theory of approximate reasoning, In: J.Hayes, D.Michie and L.I.Mikulich eds., *Machine Intelligence, Vol.9* (Halstead Press, New York, 1979) 149-194
338. L. A. Zadeh, The role of fuzzy logic in the management of uncertainty in expert systems, *Fuzzy Sets and Systems*, 11(1983), 199-227.
339. L. A. Zadeh, A computational theory of dispositions, *Int. Journal of Intelligent Systems*, 2(1987) 39-63.
340. L. A. Zadeh, Fuzzy logic, *IEEE Computer*, April, 1988, 83-93.
341. L. A. Zadeh, Knowledge representation in fuzzy logic, In: R.R.Yager and L.A. Zadeh eds., *An introduction to fuzzy logic applications in intelligent systems* (Kluwer Academic Publisher, Boston, 1992) 2-25.
342. M. Zeleny, *Multiple Criteria Decision Making*, (McGraw-Hill, New-York, 1982).
343. M. Zeleny, An Essay into a Philosophy of MCDM: A Way of Thinking or Another Algorithm? *Computers & Operations Research*, (19)1992 563-566
344. H.-J. Zimmermann, Description and optimization of fuzzy systems, *International Journal of General Systems*, 2(1975) 209-215.
345. H.-J. Zimmermann, Fuzzy programming and linear programming with several objective functions, *Fuzzy Sets and Systems*, 1(1978) 45-55.
346. H.-J. Zimmermann and P. Zysno, Latent connectives in human decision making, *Fuzzy Sets and Systems*, 4(1980) 37-51.
347. H.-J. Zimmermann, Applications of fuzzy set theory to mathematical programming, *Information Sciences*, 36(1985) 29-58.
348. H.-J. Zimmermann, *Fuzzy Set Theory and Its Applications*, Dordrecht, Boston 1985.
349. H.J.Zimmermann, Fuzzy set theory and mathematical programming, in: A.Jones et al. eds., Fuzzy Sets Theory and Applications, 1986, D.Reidel Publishing Company, Dordrecht, 99-114.
350. H.-J. Zimmermann, *Fuzzy Sets, decision-making and Expert Systems*, Kluwer Academic Publisher, Boston 1987.
351. H.-J. Zimmermann, decision-making in ill-structured environments and with multiple criteria, in: Bana e Costa ed., *Readings in Multiple Criteria Decision Aid* Springer Verlag, 1990 119-151.
352. H.-J. Zimmermann, Cognitive sciences, decision technology, and fuzzy sets, *Information Sciences*, 57-58(1991) 287-295.
353. H.-J. Zimmermann, Fuzzy Mathematical Programming, in: Stuart C. Shapiro ed., *Encyclopedia of Artificial Intelligence*, John Wiley & Sons, Inc., Vol. 1, 1992 521-528.
354. H.-J. Zimmermann, Fuzzy Decisions: Approaches, Problems and Applications, in: *Publications Series of the Japanese-German Center*, Berlin, Series 3, Vol. 8, 1994 115-136.
355. H.-J. Zimmermann, Fuzzy Mathematical Programming, in: Tomas Gal and Harvey J. Greenberg eds., *Advances in Sensitivity Analysis and Parametric Programming*, Kluwer Academic Publishers, 1997 1-40.

# Index